DATE DUE

DE 19 01			
FE 2 05			

DEMCO 38-296

THE CHANGING FACE OF U.S. POLITICS

THE CHANGING FACE OF U.S. POLITICS

Working-Class Politics and the Trade Unions

PATHFINDER

NEW YORK • LONDON • MONTREAL • SYDNEY

Edited by Steve Clark

Copyright © 1981, 1994 by Pathfinder Press

ISBN 0-87348-785-0 paper; ISBN 0-87348-791-5 cloth
Library of Congress Catalog Card Number 94-66880

Manufactured in the United States of America

First edition, 1981
Second, expanded edition, 1994
Second printing, 1996

Cover design: Toni Gorton
Cover painting: Hans Hofmann, *Abstract Euphony,* 1958, oil on canvas, 50" x 40"/
127 x 101.6 cm. Private collection, courtesy of the André Emmerich Gallery, New York.

Pathfinder
410 West Street, New York, NY 10014, U.S.A.
Fax: (212) 727-0150 ● CompuServe 73321,414 ● Internet: pathfinder@igc.apc.org

PATHFINDER DISTRIBUTORS AROUND THE WORLD:
Australia (and Asia and the Pacific):
    Pathfinder, 19 Terry St., Surry Hills, Sydney, N.S.W. 2010
    Postal address: P.O. Box K879, Haymarket, N.S.W. 2000
Canada:
    Pathfinder, 4581 rue St-Denis, Montreal, Quebec, H2J 2L4
Iceland:
    Pathfinder, Klapparstíg 26, 2d floor, 101 Reykjavík
    Postal address: P. Box 233, 121 Reykjavík
New Zealand:
    Pathfinder, La Gonda Arcade, 203 Karangahape Road, Auckland
    Postal address: P.O. Box 8730, Auckland
Sweden:
    Pathfinder, Vikingagatan 10, S-113 42, Stockholm
United Kingdom (and Europe, Africa except South Africa, and Middle East):
    Pathfinder, 47 The Cut, London, SE1 8LL
United States (and Caribbean, Latin America, and South Africa):
    Pathfinder, 410 West Street, New York, NY 10014

CONTENTS

ABOUT THE AUTHORS

JACK BARNES has been national secretary of the Socialist Workers Party since 1972. Active in defense of the Cuban revolution and the struggle for Black rights, Barnes joined the socialist movement in 1960. In the mid-1960s he served as national chairperson of the Young Socialist Alliance and as a member of the editorial board of the *Young Socialist* magazine. Barnes has been a member of the National Committee of the Socialist Workers Party since 1963 and has carried leadership responsibilities in the world communist movement since that time.

Barnes is a contributing editor of *New International,* a magazine of Marxist politics and theory, and has written many articles for it, including "Their Trotsky and Ours: Communist Continuity Today," "The Fight for a Workers and Farmers Government in the United States," "The Politics of Economics: Che Guevara and Marxist Continuity," "The Coming Revolution in South Africa," and "The Opening Guns of World War III: Washington's Assault on Iraq."

Articles, speeches, interviews, and introductions by him appear in numerous books and pamphlets, including *Malcolm X Talks to Young People, Revolutionary Strategy in the Fight against the Vietnam War, The Eastern Airlines Strike, Letters from Prison,* and *FBI on Trial: The Victory in the Socialist Workers Party Suit against Government Spying.*

MARY-ALICE WATERS, who wrote the article "Forging the Leadership of a Revolutionary Party" in these pages, is the editor of *New International* magazine. Waters joined the Young Socialist Alliance in 1962 under the impact of the Cuban and Algerian revolutions and the civil rights movement. Since 1967 she has been a member of the National Committee of the Socialist Workers Party and has traveled widely as a leader of the world communist movement.

Waters was editor of the *Young Socialist* magazine and later of the *Militant* newsweekly and the socialist magazine *Intercontinental Press.* She is the author of *Feminism and the Marxist Movement* and editor of *Cosmetics, Fashions, and the Exploitation of Women.* Waters is the author of numerous articles on the Cuban revolution, including *Che Guevara and the Fight for Socialism Today: Cuba Confronts the World Crisis of the '90s.*

Introduction

The Changing Face of U.S. Politics: Working-Class Politics and the Trade Unions is above all a handbook for the generations of workers coming into the factories, mines, and mills in the last half of the 1990s, workers who will react to the increasingly uncertain life, ceaseless turmoil, and brutality that will accompany the arrival of the twenty-first century. It is a handbook for the millions of workers whose class consciousness will grow as resistance to these worsening conditions mounts, and who—before they are through—will revolutionize themselves, their unions, and all of society.

This new edition is also an important guide for all young people who, in growing numbers, are repelled by the racism, women's inequality, and other increasingly intolerable social relations of oppression and exploitation reproduced daily by capitalism on a world scale. It is a book for all fighters who, regardless of their starting point, sense that this worldwide social system, if not replaced, will lead humanity to economic devastation, fascist tyranny, and world war.

This book grows out of the experience of the working class over the last twenty years. It reflects hard-earned lessons drawn from the activity of the organized class-conscious and revolutionary-minded section of that class. Much in these pages was discussed and adopted by conventions and elected leadership meetings of the Socialist Workers Party in the United States. Workers and youth from around the world participated in these gatherings, contributed their experiences, and put a decisive mark on the decisions taken.

The book attempts above all to show why only the working class—who own no property in large-scale means of production—can inspire their allies and lead humanity out of the social crisis endemic to capitalism in its decline. The pages that follow try to show why the industrial workers and their primary defensive organizations, the trade unions, have the potential to be the most powerful battalions of the working class, and why this is true around the globe.

These perspectives are rooted in some 150 years of communist experience and tradition in working-class politics and the trade unions. The earliest systematic presentation of these conclusions, and in some ways still the best, is entitled "Trade Unions: Their Past, Present, and Future," drafted in 1866 by Karl Marx.[1] Based on these historic lessons, *The Changing Face of U.S. Politics* presents a strategy to fight to transform the unions from the weak, bureaucratically dominated institutions of bourgeois society they became after World War II—institutions less and less capable of defending even the day-to-day interests of union members—into a weighty component of a revolutionary social movement of workers and farmers and their allies.

It is through daily involvement and political work on the job, in the unions, and in movements of social protest that the members of what are as yet relatively small communist leagues such as the Socialist Workers Party in the United States earn the ability to participate effectively in politics—from shop-floor skirmishes, strikes, and street demonstrations today, to the much wider class battles and explosive proletarian-led struggles of tomorrow. Out of these battles, as part of growing international class conflicts, strong communist parties can and will be forged whose aim, as stated in the constitution of the Socialist Workers Party, is "to educate and organize the working class in order to establish a workers and farmers government, which will abolish capitalism . . . and join in the worldwide struggle for socialism."

Worldwide depression and social crisis

These pages describe the changing face of U.S. and world politics since the curve of capitalist development turned downward in the early 1970s after the long post–World War II economic expansion. An acceleration of that slide was signaled by the crash of the New York stock markets on October 19, 1987, the steepest one-day plunge this century. Literally overnight it became worldwide. By the opening years of the 1990s the capitalist system entered a worldwide depression. So long as capitalism exists, and despite ceaseless ups and downs of the business cycle, these depression conditions with their wearing deflationary bias will not be reversed unless the most powerful ruling classes in North America, Europe, and Asia and the Pacific are able to deal major defeats to the working class and labor movement and, through sharpening cutthroat competition and trade battles, destroy masses of commodities and capital. The inevitable companion of such an outcome would be devastating financial collapse, growing fascist movements, and world war.

Declining profit rates worldwide are intensifying capitalist competition for markets, sources of raw materials, and domination of low-wage "export platforms" in the semicolonial world. Many capitalists have slashed prices to the point of near-bankruptcy to push their rivals to the wall. In the United States beginning in the late 1980s, "downsizing" and "re-engineering" have become the code words under which the superrich owners of industry and the banks are waging a ruthless cost-cutting drive. They have been laying off middle managers, technicians, and office employees, as well as industrial workers; simplifying production and administrative routines through computerization; and shutting down obsolete plants and equipment and dumping less profitable divisions. They are restructuring production lines and imposing "just in time" inventory balances and delivery schedules of parts and raw materials—in the process making factories much more vulnerable to stoppages.

The capitalists are carrying out unremitting warfare—sometimes open, sometimes disguised—against the health and safety, the unionization, and the very humanity of the working class. The employers keep pushing to cut back wages and benefits. They are expanding overtime work, as well as part-time and "temporary" jobs with low income and no benefits. They are intensifying speedup, increasing differentiation among employees hired for the same jobs, and raising the eligibility age for pensions. The ruling families throughout the imperialist world are conducting a fierce assault on the social wage—the elementary, government-funded social security programs the working class has fought for and won in order to safeguard the class as a whole by protecting its most vulnerable members.

The capitalist rulers seek to free their hands to deepen this anti-working-class offensive by chipping away at the rights working people have conquered on and off the job. Management seeks to restrict workers' right to act as unionists and political people in the workplace and uses "drug testing" and other ploys to victimize militants. The employers and their government, seeking to weaken the unity and striking power of the working class and labor movement, try to roll back affirmative action gains won by Blacks, women, and the unions. To curb the rebelliousness of young workers and press them to conform to capitalist discipline and values, the bosses target young people with "anticrime" campaigns and more draconian punishments. The cops, courts, and Congress crack down on the most fundamental rights of both the accused and convicted.

Working farmers, capital's rural debt slaves, continue to face attacks on their right to a living income and on the viability of their efforts to till the soil to produce food and fiber. The rulers' drive to maintain profit rates multiplies their disregard for measures to protect the environment.

In the closing years of the twentieth century, the evolution of the capitalist crisis is giving new force to the conclusion of Karl Marx some 130 years ago that this exploitative system of production "simultaneously undermin[es] the original sources of all wealth—the soil and the worker."[2]

Capitalism's march toward war and depression

By the mid-1990s it has become clear that for the moment the U.S. rulers have come out on top in the initial bouts with their main rivals, including the most powerful, Germany and Japan. Moreover, U.S. capital is increasing its edge. "Concern about the economy's sluggish pace obscures a welcome development of transcendent importance: a remarkable improvement in America's ability to compete in world markets," crowed the *Wall Street Journal* in a front-page column in September 1993. While this "may seem cold comfort for Americans whose jobs have recently disappeared or whose paychecks buy less than a few years ago," the *Journal* said, it is the only way to beat out U.S. capitalism's rivals "in an increasingly interconnected, competitive world."

Cold comfort indeed. But then the column was addressed to the wealthy minority who live off the labor of others, not to the producing majority whose labor creates social wealth and the material possibility of all culture.

The cost-cutting and capacity-reducing onslaught of the U.S. rulers in recent years has allowed them to take back substantial "market share" around the world in automobiles and trucks, electronics, semiconductors, telecommunications, steel, agricultural and construction equipment, and other products. This ground conquered by the U.S. capitalists vis-à-vis their chief rivals, combined with an upturn in the business cycle, has led the employers to begin hiring workers in order to increase output and boost profits. In fact, as this new edition is being prepared for press in April 1994, large numbers of young workers are getting jobs—many for the first time—in auto factories, steel mills, mining construction, railroads, and other industries. Being among these new hires is the biggest opportunity and challenge facing workers who are communists since they stood in the forefront of those in their workplaces and unions who came to oppose the imperialist military buildup that culminated in Washington's murderous assault against Iraq.

The opening section of this book, "Capitalism's March toward War and Depression," was written during that war drive in late 1990. It describes the blows dealt to the living standards, job conditions, and social welfare of the working class in the United States in the 1980s as a result of the bosses' antilabor offensive and the bipartisan rightward direction of government domestic policies. These trends have continued throughout the 1990s. The employers are taking advantage of a weakened labor movement to hire younger workers, playing fast and loose with seniority lists, hiring panels, job assignments, and other contract provisions. Management not only wants young bone and muscle, more capable of holding up under brutally intensified production lines and gutted work rules. The employers also hope these younger workers will be less union conscious and, glad to have some money in their pockets, will be more willing to go along to get along.

The report adopted by the 1979 convention of the Socialist Workers Party that appears in this book points to a time earlier this century when the bosses and others made similar assumptions about young workers—and were soon sadly disappointed. In Minneapolis in the early 1930s, many cadres of the communist movement came to carry central responsibilities in the strikes and labor battles that made that city a union town. Socialist workers helped build the Teamsters into a powerful union throughout the upper Midwest and took initial steps toward forging a class-struggle leadership of the labor movement from North Dakota to Texas, from Seattle to Cincinnati. These experiences, which young communist workers study and restudy, are recounted in the four-volume Teamsters series by Farrell Dobbs, a Teamsters organizer during the rise of the industrial union movement in the 1930s and longtime central leader of the SWP.[3]

"The Minneapolis socialists," the report explains, "understood and valued aspects of . . . situations that were seen by many others as obstacles—for example, the inexperience and rawness of the young workers. As Farrell [Dobbs] points out, this meant the ranks didn't have to unlearn so many things. They hadn't been brainwashed to believe that a layer of labor bureaucrats was to their left. Once these young workers went into action, they learned fast. True, it took a series of blows from the employers before they looked to their union, and some further blows before they looked beyond their initial union leaders." But look—and act—they soon did.

The capitalists and their spokespeople project onto the working class their own class-based, self-serving, and self-deceiving notions about workers, who they in fact consider trash. To the employers, workers are simply objects—tools of a special kind to be used, used up, and then tossed as others are hired on. The bosses count on the corroding effects of the competition for jobs and divisions among working people bred by the market system and its dog-eat-dog values. They assume that the employed will never take up as their own the cause of the unemployed. The rulers believe that racism, discrimination against women, chauvinism against immigrants and workers in other countries, and generational conflicts will, in the final analysis, keep the working class and labor movement weak and divided. The capitalists are surprised when human solidarity—of which the working class is the bearer for the future of all humanity—comes together in explosive and unexpected resistance to assaults on the living standards, job conditions, and democratic and social rights of working people.

Young people who are coming into the factories and other workplaces today find themselves alongside workers from several previous generations. New hires can and do learn from these experienced workers about the blows that have been dealt to wages, working conditions, and the unions over the past two decades. These attacks are also detailed throughout this book.

But these setbacks and their consequences do not bear down on the young generation of workers as they do on those who waged a strike battle some years ago and lost. The impact is different on those who fought a strike to a frustrating stalemate or who—as happened for nearly half a decade following the devastating 1981-82 recession—made deep-going concessions to the bosses with virtually no fightback at all, only to find themselves bounced from plant to plant anyway as the owners shut down productive capacity. The factories and the unions as they exist today are the only thing that younger workers have ever known; that is their starting point. Setbacks and standoffs from the past do not loom very large in how they judge when to say "no" to the employers' takeback demands, or in how they weigh the timing or the terrain for a fight. Neither aging nor the trade union bureaucracy have taught young workers what they "can't do." Nor have they been taught who they can't listen to or what they shouldn't bother reading.

For these very reasons, the new generation is more likely to spot important shifts, to recognize new weaknesses in the employers' position, and to seize the opportunity to initiate a fight that can strengthen the union. Free from demoralization born of past setbacks and standoffs, and not yet "socialized" by more privileged layers in the plants, younger workers can explode into resistance regardless of moral lectures from preachers and pundits, rationalizations for givebacks by the labor officialdom, or promises by the capitalists and their government of what "we" can accomplish if "you" sacrifice just a little bit longer. In the process, many older workers will reach into their reserves and discover they too are different people than they thought they had become.

The key to new advances by the working class and labor movement will be the combination of hard-won experience from years of struggle and the combative freshness and initiative of young fighters.

Evils of capitalism generate moral revulsion among youth

These characteristics of young people are not limited to those currently working a job. The history of the modern class struggle confirms that before deepening social crises erupt into mass movements in the streets, into large-scale labor struggles and the growth of revolutionary organizations, millions of young workers and students begin questioning the social and political consequences of the capitalist order. Stirrings of a radicalization among youth signal broader social conflicts that are welling up below.

When young people look at the capitalist world today, they find they are also staring their own futures in the face. They see the kind of human beings they are being educated and groomed to become. More and more they find the image grotesque and intolerable. They are repelled by the greed, hypocrisy, cynical smarminess, brutality, and inhumanity they see all around them—especially among the "caring" layers of ruling-class apologists. They question the credibility of the government, its military and police, and other capitalist institutions. They foresee an even more horrifying future emerging from an already horrifying present. More and more of them want to take the moral high ground by speaking the simple truth about the results of exploitation and oppression the world over and by unconditionally opposing these horrors, regardless of the consequences. Growing numbers, as individuals and in small groups, start challenging the legitimacy of capitalism itself and are attracted to socialism, to the communist movement, to the traditions of the working class. They are attracted to a life whose practical implications are in harmony with their deeply felt political opinions, where there is not a gulf between words and deeds.

Since the 1987 stock market crash, the world has become one in which, for the first time in more than half a century, millions of working people in the imperialist countries themselves sense that we are in the early stages of a catastrophic social, economic, and political crisis. It is a world in which the Stalinist apparatuses in the former Soviet Union and Eastern Europe, the greatest obstacle for more than sixty years to the historic line of march of the world working class, have come crashing down one after another. It is a world in which political polarization has already reached the point in economically advanced capitalist democracies that ultrarightist, Bonapartist, and outright fascist demagogues and movements are carving out growing space for themselves from a base within bourgeois politics. Patrick Buchanan and Ross Perot in the United States; the heirs of Mussolini in the rightist electoral blocs in Italy; nationalist, ultrarightist currents in Russia; fascist street gangs in Germany, France, the United Kingdom, and elsewhere across Europe—all these point in the same direction so long as bourgeois power and politics dominate the world. The prospect that such a Bonapartist force could once again seize the reins of government in an intolerably crises-ridden industrialized capitalist country also focuses attention on the possibility of a future war between imperialist powers in North America, Europe, and Asia—something virtually ruled out for nearly half a century following World War II.[4]

To readers of this book who are in their late twenties or older, these developments register major shifts in politics that necessitate substantial adjustments in their assumptions about the world. But this world is the one that young workers and students take for granted. It is the only reality in which they have ever practiced politics—even if it is also a world whose evils and injustices are more and more unbearable to them. There is much less to unlearn, once they have begun serious education in class politics and socialism.

Young people who radicalize and become active in politics do so in reaction to what they are *against;* what they are concretely *for,* and how to achieve it, usually remains vague for a while longer. Students and young workers were among the first to organize protest actions against the U.S. government's slaughter in Iraq in 1991. They are in the front ranks of those defending abortion clinics against physical assaults, and of those looking for a piece of the ultrarightists who organize such attacks. They hate the injustice and indignities of racism and will use whatever means necessary to eradicate them, if offered clear and effective leadership. They take to the streets spontaneously to demand an end to cop brutality like the beating of Rodney King in Los Angeles in 1991. They despise the rulers' arrogant contempt for immigrants and for their languages, culture, and capacities. Youth are repelled by the U.S. rulers' unceasing hostility toward the Cuban revolution and by the devastating economic and social consequences of decades of apartheid oppression in South Africa. They are outraged by the poisonous destruction of the environment as a result of a social system that puts profits above all other priorities.

But young people also rapidly begin trying to figure out what is causing the evil they are against, and what can be done about it. They begin searching for a force in society with the power to bring about change. They become interested in radical ideas and in newspapers, magazines, pamphlets, and books that they hope will present clear answers to the questions they are grappling with. A number of them start checking out socialist organizations, hoping to find one serious enough to join.

The intensifying exploitation of workers on the job and the employers' increasing antilabor assaults are often among the evils of capitalism that young people—especially those not currently working in industry, or not union members—have the most difficulty initially recognizing and reacting against. Strikes and other union battles are seldom among the first struggles that many radicalizing youth look to as being related in a decisive way to opposing the ills of capitalism that are causing them to become socialists. Once they are introduced to workers resisting worsening conditions of life under capitalism in decline, however, young fighters soon broaden their scope and concretize the political foundations on which they act.

Over time, a growing fightback in the union ranks will converge with mounting social protests. Both represent resistance to the brutality of capitalism, a brutality that is the biggest barrier to human solidarity and social progress. Young people and other fighters will come to understand that all the ills of the modern world are a product of its most fundamental evil—the way in which capitalism reproduces its exploitative social relations to enrich a handful of wealthy ruling families, and in the process grinds human beings into the dust, destroys the natural environment, and reinforces every aspect of oppression and degradation inherited from millennia of class-divided society.

Building parties of socialist workers

This book explains the kind of party the working class needs in order to prepare for the coming class battles that will decide whether humanity's future will be marked by fascist tyranny and war, or by revolutionary victories by working people over the horrors of a moribund capitalism and the reconstruction of the world on new, socialist foundations. If proletarian communist parties are not being built long before the decisive battles are joined, it will be too late; workers and their allies among the toiling majority of humanity will go down to defeat.

From its origins in the mid-nineteenth century, the modern communist movement has put at the center of its efforts something new in human history: building parties whose leaders as well as members are, in their big majority, workers. With the worldwide expansion of capitalist industry in the twentieth century, communist parties—from the Bolsheviks under the leadership of V.I. Lenin, to the Socialist Workers Party of the United States and its cothinkers in communist organizations in other countries today—have worked to anchor their activity in the most strategically central and powerfully organized bastion of the working class, the industrial workers and their unions.

For reasons explained in these pages, the SWP was forced from the mid-1950s through the early 1970s to retreat from carrying out political work on a broad scale through organized groups of worker-bolsheviks in the industrial unions. The political conditions that necessitated this retreat shifted in the aftermath of the

1974-75 recession, which was the deepest since 1937-38 and the first downturn since then that was worldwide in scope. It dealt a blow to workers' illusions in the capacity of capitalism to deliver some semblance of ongoing security to them and their families. This changing consciousness came on top of deep-going shifts in attitudes as a result of the civil rights and Black Power movements, the anti–Vietnam War protests, and the new wave of women's rights fights in the 1960s and 1970s. In the mid- and late seventies a round of struggles for school desegregation in Boston and several other cities, resistance by members of the United Mine Workers and United Steelworkers unions, and a rise in protests by working farmers were manifestations of these changes among working people and of the resulting expansion of space for political work by class-conscious workers in the labor movement.

Given this new situation, the Socialist Workers Party decided in 1978 to initiate a turn to the industrial unions. The goal was to organize the big majority of its members and leaders to get jobs in industry and to be active members of industrial unions. "Our turn has to do with what is changing in the American working class," states the report adopted by the party's 1979 convention. "When our kind of party has the opportunity to go to the weightiest and most powerfully organized sections of our class and do political work, we have to do it. That's ABC for a proletarian Marxist party that strives to lead the workers to a socialist revolution."

"Doing so *strengthens* everything we do," the report says. "It strengthens the party. It strengthens every member of the party. It strengthens our participation in every struggle of the oppressed."

Many of those who carried out this turn had been won to the socialist movement in the 1960s and 1970s, having come into political activity as young people through defending the socialist revolution in Cuba and involvement in the social protest movements of those years. In the process they came to admire communist leaders such as Fidel Castro and Ernesto Che Guevara and revolutionary figures such as Malcolm X.

SWP members were getting into industry in early 1979 when a

revolution triumphed in Iran and the toilers changed forever the position of U.S. imperialism in that part of the world. Victorious revolutions later that same year in Nicaragua and the Caribbean island of Grenada brought two new workers and farmers governments to power in the Americas. These two victories renewed prospects for an extension of the socialist revolution in the Americas and made it possible for Cuban workers and their communist leadership to take new steps forward in building socialism and advancing their proletarian internationalist course. From among those in the United States and other countries who rallied to these revolutions, more young fighters were won to the communist movement and helped build the organized fractions of SWP members in the industrial unions.

Many of these young people had first joined the Young Socialist Alliance, an independent youth organization in political solidarity with the SWP, and subsequently became convinced of the need to build a communist workers party. "It was our movement's ability to recruit from the new generation of radicalizing youth—from the early sixties on—that today poses the possibility of making this turn" to the industrial unions, points out a report to an international gathering of communists in 1979 included in this book. "And this *possibility* now coincides with a pressing political *necessity*," the report continues, not only for the SWP but for communist organizations around the world.

SWP's proletarian political continuity
The closing section of this book describes how the communist movement in the United States carried out a turn to the industrial unions in the late 1930s. Opportunities for communist political work in the labor movement had expanded with the battles that built the industrial unions into a powerful social movement. Among hundreds of thousands of the most class-conscious workers, there was growing openness to the need to break from political subordination to the capitalist Democratic and Republican parties and to begin building an independent la-

bor party based on the unions.

At the same time, the sharpening crisis of the world capitalist system was bringing down growing pressures on working people in the United States and worldwide. Workers in Europe had sustained the biggest defeats in the history of the working class in the 1920s and 1930s with the victory of fascism in Italy, Germany, Spain, and elsewhere. By the end of the 1920s a privileged bureaucratic social layer, which came to be headed by Joseph Stalin, had pushed the working class out of politics in the Soviet Union and defeated those in the leadership of the Communist Party and Communist International who had fought to continue carrying out the revolutionary internationalist course of V.I. Lenin, who died in early 1924.

Coming out of World War I (1914-18), the underlying conflicts among the rival imperialist bourgeoisies in the United States, Europe, and Japan—not one of which had been decisively resolved by the outcome of the war—rapidly reemerged at the center of world politics. As international capitalism plunged into a deep social crisis during the Great Depression of the 1930s, the combined defeats dealt to the working class by fascism and Stalinism cleared the way for the imperialist rulers to drag humanity toward a second world slaughter. This time, moreover, the various imperialist ruling families sought not only to redivide the world to their own benefit at the expense of their rivals, but also to destroy the Soviet workers state and reconquer its land and labor for capitalist superexploitation.

In the United States, the preparations for war by the Democratic administration of Franklin Roosevelt and the devastating effects of the sharp 1937-38 downturn in the business cycle shifted the relationship of class forces to the disadvantage of the working class. A class-collaborationist officialdom began to consolidate its political hold on parts of the young industrial union movement. The U.S. rulers took advantage of Moscow's counterrevolutionary crimes and political betrayals to whip up bourgeois public opinion against the Soviet workers state and communism, in whose

name the Stalinist regime falsely claimed to speak. The union bureaucracy did its best to reverse the momentum toward independent working-class political action and hitch the labor movement to the employers' parties and their bipartisan drive toward
war. Rightist demagogues like Father Charles Coughlin and fascist
outfits like the Silver Shirts became more active in response to the
labor upsurge that had recently peaked.

Faced with this political situation, communists in the United
States recognized the pressing need to center their party-building
activity even more in the working class and industrial unions. The
importance of this challenge was discussed in an exchange of letters in 1937 between U.S. communist leader James P. Cannon, a
founder of the SWP, and Leon Trotsky, a central Bolshevik leader
who had been driven into exile by Stalin in the late 1920s because
of his leadership of the worldwide fight to maintain Lenin's revolutionary course. Trotsky, who closely followed the class struggle
in the United States and efforts to build a communist party there,
wrote to Cannon in October 1937:

> The party has only a minority of genuine factory workers. This is an
> inevitable beginning for every revolutionary workers' party every-
> where, and especially in the United States. . . . [But the party leader-
> ship must now] orient in practice the whole organization toward the
> factories, the strikes, the unions. It seems that this should be one of
> the most important tasks of the new convention. . . .

This political course ran into growing resistance from a petty-
bourgeois layer in the leadership and ranks of the party and in the
socialist youth movement of that time. Under the pressures of
Washington's war drive, as the threat of imperialist aggression
mounted, this political current began to beat a panicky retreat
from defense of the Soviet workers state. The resulting fight for
the soul of the communist movement in the United States is recounted in the books *In Defense of Marxism* by Leon Trotsky and
The Struggle for a Proletarian Party by James P. Cannon, both published by Pathfinder.[5]

This political fight unfolded throughout the closing years of the 1930s and culminated in a split by the petty-bourgeois opposition from the Socialist Workers Party as the U.S. rulers' entry into World War II drew inexorably closer. Shortly before the split, on the eve of the party's 1940 convention, Cannon summed up the fight in the following words:

> The convention will meet and conduct its work under the sign of *the proletarian orientation.* That is the way to meet the coming war. Preparation for war means, for us, not some esoteric special task. It means turning the face of the party to the workers, penetrating deeper into the trade unions [and proletarianizing] the composition of the party membership.[6]

That remains the banner under which the Socialist Workers Party and young socialists today conduct their work, in face of the growing crisis of world capitalism and the renewed march toward fascism and war.

Meeting the challenges of the 1990s and beyond

During the 1980s and early 1990s, the Socialist Workers Party in the United States and communist leagues in a number of other countries successfully carried out the course outlined in this book. These parties and their elected leadership committees are composed in their substantial majority of workers in industrial union jobs. In a rapidly shifting world situation—one heading at a pace no one can predict toward violent class battles of a kind not seen since the long buildup toward World War II—the communist movement in the United States today is not faced with organizing a radical turn to proletarianize its composition on the scale confronting its forerunner half a century earlier.

At the same time, the SWP and communist organizations elsewhere in the world have felt the effects of the blows that have been dealt to the working class and labor movement over the last fifteen years. Despite important strikes and resistance by workers, struggles were not generalized and the working class and unions remained in retreat. By the close of the 1980s, the revolutionary workers and farmers governments in Grenada and Nicaragua had both gone down to defeat.[7] The mass worker and peasant struggles that toppled the shah of Iran in 1979 had been deflected by a new bourgeois regime that used nationalist and religious demagogy to justify its class rule.

Neither in the United States nor in any other industrially advanced capitalist country, however, have the capitalists taken on the working class and labor movement in major class battles and defeated them, as happened with the spreading triumph of Bonapartist and fascist reaction across Europe and in Japan during the 1920s and 1930s.

Moreover, the working class internationally is much stronger than it was fifty years ago. What Karl Marx and Frederick Engels called the hereditary proletariat—wageworkers and their families, with no prospect of any return to the land or other forms of successful petty commodity production—comprise the big majority of the population of every imperialist country today. There are fewer and fewer countries even among the oppressed nations of Latin America, Asia, the Middle East, or Africa in which there is not a growing working class, including industrial workers. Capitalist forms of land tenure, agricultural production, and the exploitation of peasants and farm labor continue to expand as well.

Intensified exploitation and imperialist oppression throughout the so-called Third World are accelerating class polarization and differentiation; working people are being driven off the land into swollen urban slums and across borders and seas in search of jobs and a living income. The earth is more and more a single world, as toilers from every continent become part of the working class in cities and towns across the United States, Canada, Europe, Australia, New Zealand, and to a smaller but growing degree even Japan. Throughout the capitalist world, women have been drawn into the workforce—and into the industrial unions and social and political life—more than ever before in history.

Of particular significance in the United States is the growing weight in the working class of Blacks, Chicanos, and other oppressed nationalities and national minorities. As SWP leader Mary-Alice Waters explains in a May 1979 report on "Forging the Leadership of a Proletarian Party," which appears in these pages, "In the 1930s the Black population and the Chicano population were much more rural and engaged in agriculture. They were more an ally of the working class than a layer of the working class. This has changed dramatically over the past forty years. . . . That is why it is both more necessary and more possible today to construct a proletarian party that is multinational in composition and leadership."

Finally, among the most important factors improving the prospects of the working class today is the weakening of world Stalinism. For more than sixty years the privileged parasitic caste used its state power and its siphoned wealth to portray its self-interested actions and policies as the continuity of the Bolshevik revolution and Marxism. It presented a counterfeit of communism as the real thing. Trading on the power of the October revolution, the Stalinists won to their ranks the vast majority of revolutionary-minded workers and youth around the world who, generation after generation, became convinced of the need to join the socialist movement. Inside the Stalinist parties, these fighters—many of them the best of their generation—were either politically broken and corrupted as revolutionists or eventually demoralized and driven out of politics. With the collapse of the Stalinist apparatuses throughout Eastern Europe and in the Soviet Union since 1989, that brake on the development of genuine communist parties and youth organizations has been largely released.

The fracturing of the international Stalinist murder machine decreases the weight in world politics of petty-bourgeois alternatives to proletarian leaderships that will emerge from struggles by the toilers. It opens the road to further political progress by the new generation of leaders in Cuba who are seeking to emulate and build on the communist course exemplified by Che Guevara and Fidel Castro. It lowers barriers to the revolutionary advance of leaders of the African National Congress such as Nelson Mandela and others as they march toward a democratic, nonracial South Africa and open political space for the oppressed and exploited to organize to press for their class interests. It increases the capacity of thinking workers and youth everywhere to absorb the revolutionary political legacy of Malcolm X; of Thomas Sankara, leader of the revolutionary government in the African country of Burkina Faso from 1983 to 1987; of the Grenada revolution's Maurice Bishop; of Carlos Fonseca, the founder of Nicaragua's Sandinista National Liberation Front who in the early 1960s, inspired by the example of the Cuban revolution, brought genuine Marxism to Central America for the first time.

Pathfinder, the publisher of *The Changing Face of U.S. Politics,* is today also the major source in English of the writings and speeches of these late twentieth-century revolutionary and communist leaders. They take their place alongside Pathfinder's political arsenal of communist works by Karl Marx, Frederick Engels, V.I. Lenin, Leon Trotsky, Rosa Luxemburg, and leaders of the Socialist Workers Party in the United States such as James P. Cannon, Farrell Dobbs, Joseph Hansen, and George Novack.

With the discrediting of Stalinism, these books and pamphlets can now win a much wider and more serious readership around the world. It remains true today—as the 1979 SWP report on "Educating the Leadership of a Proletarian Party" explains—that "the role of ideas is increasingly important in the class struggle."

Despite increasing class tensions and political polarization since that time, it is still the case, as that 1979 report points out, that "we are at a stage in which the radicalization of the working class does not express itself through any mass organized forms. There is no class-struggle left wing, not even the nucleus of one in any meaningful sense. There is no large political party that is part of the workers movement. There are no radicalized mass organizations of the oppressed with a proletarian line. The working class has no voice, no mass vehicle either for expressing its historical political interests or for representing thinking workers who begin to develop class-conscious ideas."

"But we know that this situation cannot stop the large-scale increase in thinking and debate that is going on in the working class," the report says. "The depth of this process has been confirmed over the past several years since we began the turn." And this interest in ideas will grow as resistance increases among workers and youth.

Narrowing the gap

The 1985 Socialist Workers Party resolution that closes this book explains that "a growing number of class battles, combined over time with a deepening social crisis, uprisings in the colonial and semicolonial countries, and imperialist wars, will transform politics and the labor movement in this country. We have entered the initial stages of a preparatory period, which will lead in coming decades to a prerevolutionary upheaval marked by revolutionary struggles of a kind that workers and farmers in the United States have not waged in more than a century."

The resolution goes on to say, however, that today there is "a gap between the current experiences and consciousness of the working class, and the radically transformed conditions and methods of struggle that will emerge as social, economic, and war crises tear apart the current framework of relative social stability and bourgeois democracy."

The 1985 resolution points out that given this gap between today's conditions and the class battles that lie ahead, "a worker who understands that the course of the current labor officialdom is gutting union power and leading to a dead end still must make an individual leap in consciousness in order to see the strategic line of march of the proletariat toward power. But even under the impact of today's initial experiences, these leaps can and are being made. Opportunities are being created for the Socialist Workers Party to influence a still small but important layer of the working class and the labor movement, and to recruit to the party the most politically conscious workers. This deepening proletarianization and political education of the party is decisive not only in rising to today's challenges and meeting its pressures, but in preparing for what is coming."

Nearly a decade later, that gap is still very much a political fact of life. But something else needs to be said that is new and more important: The world that has emerged since the 1987 stock market crash has narrowed that gap substantially in the political imagination of millions of working people and youth. It has been closed still more by U.S. imperialism's 1991 war against the people of Iraq. Amid the wartime din of Washington's murderous bombing campaign and ground invasion, and of its patriotic political bombast, the most politically conscious workers and revolutionary-minded youth could hear the opening guns of other wars to come, including wars between nuclear-armed imperialist powers.[8]

As this book goes to press, the war in Bosnia, the first European war in half a century, continues to spread. The rival imperialist powers are being drawn into this carnage more deeply to protect their interests, threatening wider war and providing a truer picture of the Europe of coming decades than most would like to believe.

These economic, social, and political conditions put new challenges before the communist movement. By the opening years of the 1990s, under the impact of the continued retreat of the unions and defeats of workers and farmers governments in Nicaragua and Grenada, the Socialist Workers Party was attracting fewer young people and its average age had risen. Upswings of the capitalist business cycle had been marked by very slow job growth, limiting opportunities for communist workers to get into new industrial union jobs and revitalize their trade union work.

But today as this edition of *The Changing Face of U.S. Politics* begins circulating, young workers and students in the United States are tapping new political opportunities to form a nationwide young socialists organization once again. Young people come into revolutionary politics with the energy and the will to fight and with a visceral hatred for the brutality, destructiveness, social injustice, and inhumanity produced by the capitalist system. What they need above all is to become part of a disciplined working-class organization whose cadres, spanning several generations of experience in the class struggle, embody a political tradition—a revolutionary political continuity going back to the founding of the modern communist movement nearly 150 years ago. In a revolutionary workers party they will receive the education, and the political respect as equals, that is denied them everywhere else in bourgeois society.

At the same time that young socialists are launching a new organization in the United States, communist workers are taking advantage of the first significant hiring during an upturn in the business cycle in more than half a decade. A new levy of workers, many of them in their late teens or twenties, are getting jobs in large unionized factories that have not taken on new workers for a long time, and the Socialist Workers Party has the seemingly sudden opportunity to revitalize and reorganize its industrial union fractions. The extent of such a revitalization of the SWP's turn to the industrial unions—the numbers of experienced party cadres involved—will be the single most decisive factor in making it possible for the new layers of youth being attracted to socialism to become integrated in advancing a revolutionary proletarian party.

The convergence of these two opportunities to strengthen the communist movement—each with its own concrete political dynamics, but with the same social roots in the long curve of capitalist development—will be uneven, but the outcome will truly be greater than the sum of its parts. As indicated in the 1979 report on the international character of the turn to industry, worker-bolsheviks always have their eyes on "the *young rebels* in the working class. They will be decisive for us and for our class in the coming period. That's who we're after."

This new edition of *The Changing Face of U.S. Politics* is among the richest lodes to mine for the Marxist continuity these young fighters need and that they have begun to seek.[9] The book comes at this communist tradition from the particular strategic standpoint summarized in its subtitle: "Working-Class Politics and the Trade Unions." As emphasized in the 1979 SWP convention report published here: "Our goal is quite simple: to do everything possible to transform the American unions, as Trotsky explained, into 'instruments of the revolutionary movement of the proletariat.' What we do is aimed at advancing toward revolutionary unions as combat organizations of the American working class. In the process of doing this, we'll build the irreplaceable political instrument of our class—a revolutionary party of industrial workers."

Jack Barnes
April 15, 1994

NOTES

1. Contained in Karl Marx, Leon Trotsky *Trade Unions in the Epoch of Imperialist Decay/Trade Unions: Their Past, Present, and Future* (New York: Pathfinder, 1990), pp. 33-35.

2. Karl Marx, *Capital*, vol. 1 (New York: Random House, 1977), p. 638.

3. The four volumes are *Teamster Rebellion, Teamster Power, Teamster Politics,* and *Teamster Bureaucracy,* all published by Pathfinder.

4. See issues 10 and 11 of *New International*, a magazine of Marxist politics and theory, as well as "The Opening Guns of World War III" in *New International* issue no. 7.

5. Readers can also refer to the Education for Socialists publication *Background to "The Struggle for a Proletarian Party"* by James P. Cannon, Leon Trotsky, and others, also published by Pathfinder. The October 1937 letter from Trotsky to Cannon cited above appears in full in this publication.

6. James P. Cannon, *The Struggle for a Proletarian Party* (New York: Pathfinder, 1972), p. 82

7. See "The Rise and Fall of the Nicaraguan Revolution" in *New International* no. 9 and "The Second Assassination of Maurice Bishop" in *New International* no. 6, both available from Pathfinder.

8. See "The Opening Guns of World War III" by Jack Barnes in issue no. 7 of *New International.*

9. Others include the issues of New International magazine and its sister publications in French, Spanish, and Swedish, *Nouvelle Internationale, Nueva Internacional,* and *Ny International,* as well as the range of communist books and pamphlets published by Pathfinder Press.

LIST OF INITIALS

ACTWU	Amalgamated Clothing and Textile Workers Union
AFL-CIO	American Federation of Labor–Congress of Industrial Organizations
AFT	American Federation of Teachers
AFSCME	American Federation of State, County and Municipal Employees
CLUW	Coalition of Labor Union Women
Cointelpro	Counterintelligence Program
ERA	Equal Rights Amendment
IAM	International Association of Machinists
ILGWU	International Ladies' Garment Workers' Union
NAACP	National Association for the Advancement of Colored People
NATO	North Atlantic Treaty Organization
NEA	National Education Association
NLRB	National Labor Relations Board
NOW	National Organization for Women
OPEIU	Office and Professional Employees International Union
SWP	Socialist Workers Party
UAW	United Auto Workers
UFW	United Farm Workers
UMWA	United Mine Workers of America
USWA	United Steelworkers of America
YSA	Young Socialist Alliance

I. CAPITALISM'S MARCH TOWARD WAR AND DEPRESSION

INTRODUCTORY NOTE

"Capitalism's March toward War and Depression" is based on several talks given by Jack Barnes, national secretary of the Socialist Workers Party, at the close of 1990, as Washington prepared for the bloody culmination of its several-month-long naval blockade of Iraq and massive military buildup in the Arab-Persian Gulf. The six-week bombardment of the people of Iraq that began in mid-January 1991, and the one-hundred-hour invasion launched by Washington and its allies on February 24, were among the most horrendous massacres in modern warfare. The U.S.-led assault left large areas of Iraq in ruins. As many as 150,000 human beings were killed, millions were made homeless, and countless others suddenly faced hunger and life-threatening diseases.

For most working people in the United States today, the war in the Gulf was the first time they had faced a large-scale armed assault launched by Washington in a world of slowly grinding depression conditions and polarizing social crises. The Vietnam War and the fight against it, in contrast, had unfolded during the culminating years of a long period of world capitalist boom. But the 1987 crash of the world's stock markets confirmed that stagnating growth rates from the mid-1970s on, rising jobless levels, and growing social dislocation were not aberrations.

"Washington's war against the Iraqi people signaled the opening guns of broadening class, national, and interimperialist conflicts. These are inevitable," wrote Barnes in an article entitled "The Opening Guns of World War III," which appears in issue no. 7 of *New International*, a magazine of Marxist politics and theory. "What is far from inevitable is that these battles will culminate in a third world war that would set back the progress of humanity beyond our capacity to imagine. That will depend on the outcome of class battles in the years ahead, in the course of which workers and farmers will have our chance—the opportunity to win revolutionary victories and take the power to make war out of the hands of the imperialist ruling classes."

"Capitalism's March toward War and Depression" describes the working-class campaign against imperialism and war carried out by hundreds of communist workers in mines, factories, and mills throughout the United States leading up to and during the Gulf conflict. It explains how they worked as part of the labor movement to get out the truth about the coming imperialist slaughter and engage in discussions and debates about it from the factory floor to the campuses, as they helped lead broad antiwar protests.

Capitalism's march toward war and depression

The same week in November 1990 that the United Nations Security Council adopted a U.S.-sponsored resolution authorizing war against Iraq, top U.S. government officials were finally forced to admit that the recession already unfolding in Canada had also begun in the United States.

It was also the same week that the federal government announced that for the fourth year in a row the average life expectancy of Black people in the United States had *declined*—declined in absolute terms. That decline was large enough to result in a drop of the overall average life expectancy in the United States. Moreover, this decline has been very class-divided. It results from rapidly deteriorating health conditions among the worst-off layers of the working class, not limited to those who are Black.

The very fact that average life expectancy can drop in the last decade of the twentieth century in the world's wealthiest imperialist

This is a section from "The Working-Class Campaign against Imperialism and War," published in *New International* no. 7. It is based on talks originally presented in late November and early December 1990. *SEE PAGE 437 FOR NOTES* power—and that it can decline for four years in a row for working people from an oppressed nationality—is a sign of the depth of the underlying capitalist economic crisis. Driven to reproduce the social relations of production necessary for its own existence, capitalism is regenerating and extending the institutions of racist oppression. This process intensifies the exploitation of working people as a whole and deepens class polarization.

Behind this statistic lie many others; all of them point to the truth about what is coming, about the character of the international social crisis we are heading into and the stakes for working people in the battles that lie ahead. We can't predict the exact timing or how events will unfold, but we can say with certainty that the imperialist ruling classes today are marching workers and farmers toward war and depression.

As the working class in the United States goes into the current recession, it has already been the victim of a more than decade-long offensive by the employing class against our living and working conditions. Workers' real wages dropped by 8 percent in the 1980s. In fact our buying power has dropped so sharply that it is now at the same level as in 1961. Since 1980 our pensions, health benefits, and insurance protection have dropped about 15 percent on average in real money terms. As a result of the pressures from this assault on workers' incomes, the debt burden on working-class families has skyrocketed as they desperately seek to somehow buffer the blows to their living standards.

With unemployment already rising sharply, only one-third of those out of work in this country are currently receiving jobless benefits, largely because of major government slashes in the form of stiffer eligibility requirements. This contrasts to more than three-quarters of jobless workers during the 1974-75 recession and about half during the deep capitalist downturn in 1981-82.

Working farmers are in for another round of accelerating indebtedness, bankruptcies, and foreclosures. The capitalist farm crisis that drove tens of thousands of exploited producers off the land in the early and mid-1980s—the worst times since the 1920s and '30s—is far from resolved.

The capitalists are weighed down under an enormous debt structure that reached historic heights during the 1980s. Investment in new, capacity-expanding plant and equipment stagnated throughout the decade. Meanwhile, there was an explosion of real estate speculation, debt-financed buyouts and mergers, and junk bonds, plus growing instability on the stock and commodities markets. The Third World debt continued to climb to staggering levels, devastating the workers and peasants in those countries and putting new strains on the imperialist banking structure. The banks, savings and loan institutions, and giant insurance companies in the United States—as well as the funds today available to government agencies that supposedly protect depositors and beneficiaries—are in their weakest condition in many decades.

Sudden breakdowns or partial crises on any one or more of these fronts—all of which are more vulnerable given today's capitalist downturn—threaten to turn a recession into a collapse of the international banking system that can plunge the world into a major depression and social crisis.

Antilabor offensive

The employers, their government, and the Democratic and Republican party politicians continue to press their anti-working-class, union-busting offensive. The ultimate solution to all the country's economic problems, they insist, is to guarantee workers the "right" to work in a "union-free environment." More and more they act as if the only good worker is a "permanent replacement" worker.

The bosses continue to demand takeback contracts that deepen divisions in the working class by agreeing to trade off wages, conditions, and job opportunities for younger workers and new hires in return for the will-o'-the-wisp of "job security" for a declining number of higher-seniority union members. The employers continually push to gut health and pension benefits, speed up production with less union control over safety on the job, and ravage the environment.

City and state governments around the country—as in the mid-1970s—are complaining of "declining tax revenues" and "tightening budgets," and "reluctantly" point to the need to sharply cut the rolls of public employees and impose takeback contracts. Governors and mayors are slashing expenditures on basic health services, education, child care, and other social programs that millions of working people depend on. Bridges and roads continue to deteriorate dangerously.

So workers and farmers in this country face a double march today: a march toward a horrible war; and a march not only into a recession but toward a seemingly inexorable worldwide depression and social crisis.

This reality is sensed by growing numbers of working people. And it poses big challenges and responsibilities for every thinking worker, every rank-and-file union militant, every communist.

Labor movement not pushed out of politics

The U.S. working class and labor movement have suffered blows; our unions have been further weakened by the class-collaborationist and proimperialist course of the labor officialdom; and we have been put on the defensive by the accelerated onslaught of the employers in the 1980s.

But we have not been defeated. The labor movement has not been shoved out of the center of politics in this country. Our capacity to resist has not been broken.

Since the middle of the 1980s, as resistance by the working class and unions in the United States has evolved, a pattern has emerged. Despite the difficulties, despite the blows, workers and unionists in the United States pushed to the wall by the employers' assaults have found ways to fight. Layer after layer of workers have managed to avoid simply being handcuffed, chained, and prevented from organizing to defend themselves. They have done so even when the bosses and labor bureaucrats have combined to block them from using standard union tactics that have brought victories throughout the history of the labor movement—that is, even when they are blocked from organizing union power and solidarity to shut down production.

As workers have moved into action in the face of these odds, other working people have expressed solidarity with their battles. Important experiences with rich lessons on how to forge unity, overcome divisions, and wage an effective struggle have begun to be accumulated by a small vanguard of fighters in the labor movement. These defensive efforts are waged from a position of weakness. The ranks are not in a strong enough position to push aside the current labor officialdom and replace it with another leadership that has an alternative, class-struggle strategy. Their efforts have to take place largely within the limits of the strategy imposed by this ossified bureaucracy. But this fact makes these experiences no less important as the arena where rank-and-file fighters find each other and test each other.

All this is being experienced right now as the *Daily News* strike unfolds in the greater New York City area.

This is a strike that began in October 1990 as one of the most cold-blooded, brutal, militarily organized lockouts by management in years. The union officialdom hoped against hope that this fight would not happen. As a result, the ranks of the drivers, press operators, and other unionized employees were forced into a fight without any preparation. The ranks have no democratic union structures through which to organize, make decisions, argue out tactics, strive for greater unity among themselves, and reach out for broader solidarity from the rest of the labor movement—in order to bring their real potential power to bear.

Management, on the other hand, was well prepared. Production never stopped. The *Daily News* didn't miss a single edition. It had scabs lined up months in advance to do everything from writing copy, to typesetting and printing the papers, to transporting them throughout the metropolitan area. The scabs were at their posts within a matter of minutes—together with armed thugs to go after the unions. The rest of New York's big-business media joined in the company's violence-baiting of the unions.

But then something happened that management had not anticipated. They could write the paper, print the paper, and truck the paper with "permanent replacements." But they couldn't get working people to buy it! The working class in the New York area pulled together to keep the *Daily News* off the newsstands. They put pressure on the owners of the newsstands they patronize not to carry the scab paper; they argue with them, try to convince them. Some of these small shopkeepers have put up solidarity signs announcing, "We don't carry the *Daily News*."

Workers argue with co-workers on the job and with friends and family members not to buy the paper. They've made buying the *Daily News* an immoral, rotten, unconscionable act for any working person with an ounce of decency, human feeling, and solidarity. Unionists have volunteered to go out and ring doorbells to urge people to cancel their subscriptions.

There are thousands of retail outlets that carry daily newspapers in greater New York. Prior to the strike, the *Daily News* was the second-largest-selling metropolitan daily in the country. Yet, today it's difficult to find a newsstand that carries it. This was not accomplished by centralized organization. It took the actions of tens of thousands of workers and unionists. Newsstand owners found that carrying the *Daily News* was considered an insult by regular customers—people they've gotten to know, made friends with, depend on for steady business. These kinds of factors play a role in labor and other social struggles, and they are having a big impact on the *Daily News* strike.

The point here is not to try to predict what the outcome of this strike will be, given the character of the officialdom in these unions and the overall state of the labor movement. To keep moving forward against the *News* management, space must continue to be opened by the printing trades officialdom for the ranks to operate, and the ranks must have time to find ways of organizing and structuring themselves, as we saw happen in the Eastern Airlines strike.

The entire working class feels a growing hatred for the antiunion assault, and this enables strikers like those at the *News* to gain increased solidarity from other unionists and workers. As a result, even if the strike does not have the ability to shut down production, some unexpected space is opened up for it. But other expressions of struggle and solidarity are not a substitute for the strike; they are a supplement to it. They become a way for the ranks to assert themselves and prove that union busting is not a sure winner for the bosses. All this is very important right now and deserves the active support of all workers, regardless of the duration or expected outcome of the effort.

The *Daily News* strike is just the most recent example of the pattern that has emerged from the labor struggles in this country in recent years. It is an uneven pattern, one with gaps and breaks. But the pattern is nonetheless clearer today than when it began to take shape back in August 1985 with the strike of the packinghouse workers against the Hormel Company and other battles in meat-packing over the following eighteen months to two years.[1]

Since then there have been other fights: by paperworkers, by cannery workers, by coal miners in both the eastern and western fields, by telephone workers, by hospital employees. All have been defensive in character, waged by workers pushed deeper and deeper into a corner by the employers. They've had various outcomes: some substantial setbacks or defeats, some standoffs, a few victories. The most weighty victory in the recent period has been that won by members of the United Mine Workers of America and their supporters against the union busting of the Pittston coal company.[2]

But through all these fights you can watch not just the cumulative impact of the assaults, but also the cumulative effect of workers finding ways to resist for slightly longer, or surprising the employers a bit more with what they are able to accomplish, and thus giving greater confidence to other layers of the working class who will find themselves in struggle.

The strike by members of the International Association of Machinists against Eastern Airlines that began back in March 1989 has been a little different from the rest. There, through the initial months of the battle, a rank-and-file leadership of the strike came forward and had enough time to structure itself. It kept reaching out to maintain maximum unity while drawing in broader solidarity from elsewhere in the labor movement. These strikers demonstrated the capacity to take the blows and withstand the shocks that came their way and to outlast and outfight the employers. And it was not your run-of-the-mill boss they were up against. Frank Lorenzo was the man the employing class considered the union buster of the decade, a model for them all.

The Eastern strikers blocked Lorenzo from imposing on them the kind of nonunion operation he had rammed down the throats of workers at Continental Airlines in 1983. In fact, the IAM strikers drove Lorenzo out of the airline industry, and their nearly two-year-long fight has brought both parts of Lorenzo's former Texas Air empire—Eastern and Continental—to bankruptcy. They have made the government step in and openly take direct responsibility for Eastern's future—to the horror of its individual stockholders and creditors. This has made other employers, suppliers, and bankers—inside and outside the airline industry—less confident that blatant union busting, "Lorenzoism," is the high road to high profits that it seemed to be in the mid-1980s.[3]

The labor movement is not on the offensive against the employers. There are no developments anywhere in the unions that represent the organized beginnings of an alternative, class-struggle strategy. The labor movement is still being weakened by the class-collaborationist course of the officialdom in the face of the rulers' continuing offensive. All that is correct.

But that is not the entire story. The pattern of resistance by workers and unionists over the past half-decade, the search for ways to bring class solidarity to bear, the openness to reaching beyond themselves, beyond the union movement, beyond the country to seek and extend solidarity—these facts, too, have to be brought into the picture. And they are among the decisive facts on the basis of which communist workers, who are part of this working-class vanguard, must chart our strategy and tactics—including in campaigning against the imperialist war drive.

Independent working-class political action

These struggles bring a vanguard layer of workers additional experience that makes them more open to seeing themselves as part of a class with interests different from and opposed to the employers, the employers' political parties, and the employers' government. The unity workers have needed to forge in order to advance their own fights, and the solidarity they have reached for, helps clear away some of the divisions and reactionary prejudices promoted by the employers. This increases the capacity to recognize common interests with other working people both in this country and around the world.

These shifts are important for communist workers because they provide new opportunities—grounded in common experiences of rank-and-file union militants—to win broader understanding of the need for a labor movement that operates on the basis of democracy, class solidarity, and independent working-class political action. A labor movement is needed that rejects the narrowness of unionism as conceived by a timid officialdom. A fight is needed for a labor movement that thinks socially and acts politically—in the interests of its own class, not that of the bosses. This becomes more necessary than ever in the face of increasing imperialist war moves.

The tactical divisions in the ruling class are real, and we haven't found it difficult to explain the reasons for them. They enable us to see the dangerous character of the con being promoted by the bourgeois press—namely, that the debate in Congress pushes us further away from war. The truth is the opposite. The imperialist assumptions and goals shared by both Democratic and Republican Party politicians and the bipartisan policies they have already set in motion—these are the very ingredients propelling forward the probability that the siege war [against Iraq] will become a massive ground war (perhaps with a devastating air war as a prelude).

Workers and farmers, as well as any authentic opponent of Washington's course toward war, have no voice, no representatives in Congress of any kind. There have been tactical divisions and squabbles among bourgeois politicians in Congress, and between Congress and the White House, prior to every imperialist war in this century. There has also been a growing concentration of governmental power in the executive branch. But without exception, whenever the president has asked Congress for support in a war—whether in the form of a declaration of war such as in 1917 and 1941, or the Gulf of Tonkin resolution in 1964, or simply military funding—there has been overwhelming bipartisan support. This time around will be no different.

What the working-class movement needs is space to organize a broad public discussion of the connection between the rulers' war policies at home and abroad—a discussion with all those willing to debate the issues in a civil manner; space to organize active opposition to those policies in the factories, through our unions; space to take our protest to the streets; space to engage in politics in the class interests of workers, farmers, and our allies here and around the world. This debate should be organized above all among the almost half-million citizen-soldiers sent to the Arabian desert by Frank Lorenzo's friends in Washington.

Those who are going to have to fight and die in any war waged by the bipartisan rulers of this country should have the direct say over whether or not such a war is declared. On the face of it, that simply seems decent and just. But there's a lot more to it than that. For the question of war poses the biggest single problem facing the working class: we have no independent political organization, no political voice of our own, no policies that advance our class interests against those who are responsible for exploitation, oppression, and war.

The working class has no foreign policy. The labor movement has no foreign policy. The labor *officialdom* faithfully pushes the foreign policy of the employers and does what the bosses tell them to do. But the labor *movement*—the workers, the ranks, who are the unions—has no foreign policy. The classes who die in the wars waged by the bosses' parties and government—and who are pitted in those wars against working people like ourselves in other countries—have no foreign policy.

Many workers agree that it's unacceptable for the bosses to have a monopoly over setting all sorts of other policies: the policies that govern our unions; health and safety policies and conditions in the mines and factories; work rules on the job; the right to slash our wages or throw us out of work; the right to bust our unions and keep up production with scab labor.

But when it comes to foreign policy, the monopoly by the bosses is still largely accepted as almost a fact of life. The spectrum of valid choices is set by their two political parties. What's more, their foreign policy is viewed as "ours," the foreign policy of "our" country. But countries don't have policies. Countries are divided into social classes, and classes have foreign policies. And the foreign policy of the capitalist class in this country—and in every other capitalist country, everywhere in the world—is not "ours," it's "theirs." As Malcolm X taught us, working people in this country are not "Americans," we're the *victims* of this kind of Americanism.

Workers have no military policy, either. The labor movement has no military policy. Only the ruling class has a military policy. It begins with the hired thugs and the cops they use to bust up our strikes, to ride in scab trucks in West Virginia or in Bayside, Queens. And it goes right on through the organization of massive imperialist armed forces.

But the working class needs our own military policy as well as our own foreign policy. And there are layers of workers in recent years who have learned why, even if they haven't yet drawn this conclusion or thought of it this way. The *Daily News* strikers who have been victims of the goon squads brought in by management are learning about the military policy of the bosses; so are the coal miners, paperworkers, meat-packers, and others whose picket lines have been attacked by cops, whether "private" or "public." Also learning about it today are the workers and farmers in uniform—the cannon fodder (a term that has horrible concrete meaning in face of today's march toward a desert war of heavily armored armies) who make up the armed forces used by the imperialists to fight *their* wars to advance *their* class interests.

As long as capitalism and imperialism exist, there will be no peace. As long as the working class has no political party of our own—no labor party based on the unions and independent of the imperialist Democratic and Republican parties—we will have no effective mass political organization to resist the war policies of the employing class by counterposing and fighting for our own foreign policy and military policy. And we will have no political party of our own to organize a fight against the bosses' war on our rights, our living standards, and our unions here at home, either. Instead, we will always be facing the framework of political choices set by *their* parties.

Let the people vote on war

For the same reasons, communists are raising as part of our working-class campaign against the imperialist war that the people in this country should have the right to vote on war.

The point here is not to divert the energies of workers, farmers, and other opponents of the war into electoral channels—there will be plenty of referenda to do that. The point is just the opposite. Our demand is that the question of war and peace be taken out of the hands of the Democratic and Republican politicians, out of the hands of Congress and the White House, and be taken into the factories and into the streets.

We know that the imperialists always seek to tighten and restrict the space to organize and practice politics when they go to war. That's what happened during the first and second world wars, during the Korean War, and during the Vietnam War. And it will happen again. Many of us remember the so-called Cointelpro spying, disruption, and harassment operations organized by the FBI, CIA, local police "red squads," and other government cop agencies during the period of the Vietnam War. The Socialist Workers Party was a direct victim of those assaults, along with others involved in the fight against the war, in the struggle for Black liberation, and in other social and political struggles. Recognizing this reality puts a special premium on vanguard workers treasuring and fighting for every inch of space we can.[4]

That's why thinking workers pay special attention to any group of individuals and organizations who want to reach out and use democratic rights to publicly oppose the war drive—to discuss, to debate, to march; to initiate public protests, rallies, teach-ins, demonstrations. Those activities help create greater space for discussion and action around the war, greater space for the working class to get involved in politics.

This is the opposite of the terrain to which the capitalist rulers always seek to restrict the discussions and decisions on war. We are told that a great debate is taking place on Capitol Hill today on launching the war against Iraq. But it's a debate that involves at tops 535 people—536 if you include the vice president—most of them millionaires, and all of them (Democrats, Republicans, and their "socialist" subspecies alike) opponents of independent political action by the working-class movement. These are the same people who have led workers and farmers into every bloody war in this century.

The fight against the war and the fight to defend democratic rights necessitates the broadest forum for public debate and exchange of views, as well. The bourgeois politicians will try to block such discussion. And as in the past, the union bureaucrats, petty-bourgeois pacifists, Stalinists, and social democrats will often join them in this reactionary effort—usually in the name of supporting this or that proposal or election campaign by a capitalist politician.

The working class, on the other hand, has every interest in promoting such discussion. Political clarity becomes more important than ever, and such clarity can be advanced only through *political differentiation*. That's why we advocate the norms of civil discussion—the right to express your point of view, to argue for it without fear of verbal abuse or physical recriminations—inside the workers movement. This also means having the courage to clarify differences—which often reflect conflicting class outlooks and interests—rather than paper them over.

At the same time, proponents of a wide range of different views can and will join together to act, to organize, and to participate in antiwar demonstrations and other public protest actions. Communist workers are the most energetic advocates of such united action for common goals, and the staunchest opponents of efforts to exclude individuals or organizations from such efforts because of their political views.

We seek to draw more workers, more soldiers, more farmers into these activities, so that those who have been struggling against the employers' offensive in this country can become part of the debate and a growing component of the fight against the war drive.

II. LEADING THE PARTY INTO INDUSTRY

INTRODUCTORY NOTE

As Washington pressed its bipartisan war preparations in the closing years of the 1930s, the officialdom of the newly formed industrial unions blocked the working class from moving forward to organize a labor party independent of the two bourgeois parties that dominate politics in the United States. The affairs of the unions were reduced by the emerging bureaucracy to wages and other economic matters. In both words and deeds, top union officials made it clear that politically confronting the capitalist system—which not only exploits labor on a daily basis but also breeds war, racism, unemployment, and other social and political ills—is not a "union issue." Despite turf wars among themselves, the business unionists, Stalinists, social democrats, and liberals in the officialdom closed ranks around this class-collaborationist course.

With U.S. imperialism's entry into World War II in the final weeks of 1941, labor officials cooperated with the capitalist rulers to police the unions with government boards, compulsory wage controls, and a no-strike pledge. In the process the petty-bourgeois officialdom began consolidating its stranglehold on the unions, despite a surge of labor resistance that began in the closing years of the war and swelled into a strike wave in 1945-46; that consolidation was completed by 1950.

During the world capitalist economic expansion from the late 1940s through the early 1970s, the U.S. labor movement steadily retreated. Unionized workers declined as a percentage of the labor force—from a high of 25.5 percent in 1953 to 20 percent twenty-five years later (and less than 16 percent today). The fighting potential of the unions was blunted. Good times made it possible for workers to win modest but real wage increases and "fringe benefits" without increasing conflicts with the employers. In exchange for not directly challenging the officialdom's relatively stable dues base, the capitalists demanded—and got—faithful service from these bureaucrats. Over time, the unions became the flabby institutions they are today.

Functioning along these class-collaborationist lines, the labor misleaders ignored the needs of unorganized workers, except where deals with particular employers or bourgeois politicians made it possible to fatten the dues base with little or no struggle. The demands of Blacks, Chicanos, immigrant workers, and women, as well as the political fight for health care and other social programs for the entire working class, were exchanged by the bureaucrats for so-called fringe benefits restricted to those already unionized. Labor's political perspectives were confined to the limits set by the government and the twin political parties of big business. The top union officialdom became among the most zealous boosters of the anti-working-class foreign policy of U.S. imperialism, including the drafting of young workers to die in wars against the Korean and Vietnamese peoples.

Mass struggles did begin breaking out in the late 1950s and

1960s, beginning with the civil rights movement for Black equality and then opposition to the Vietnam War. But their character as part of the class struggle in the United States was difficult to see, since the labor bureaucracy fought against active involvement of the unions in these struggles. Nonetheless, these social protest movements deeply affected the political consciousness of millions of workers, many of whom participated as individuals even if blocked in most cases from doing so through their unions.

A sudden explosion of oil prices in 1973 and the 1974-75 worldwide economic recession—the first downturn since the 1930s to hit all the major industrialized capitalist countries simultaneously—began to undermine the illusion among many workers in the United States that the post–World War II prosperity would last forever. This shock, combined with shifts in attitudes coming out of the anti–Vietnam War movement and struggles by Blacks and women, changed politics in the United States. This change is at the heart of the resolution "Prospects for Socialism in America," adopted by the Socialist Workers Party in 1975, which opens this section of the book.

The blows to the rights and living conditions of working people in the aftermath of the 1974-75 recession met resistance in sections of the union movement. In late 1975 a movement called Steelworkers Fight Back was launched in the United Steelworkers union to topple the bankrupt I.W. Abel regime and establish the right of USWA members to vote on contracts. USWA District 31 director Ed Sadlowski challenged Abel for the union presidency. Although this bid fell short, the Steelworkers Fight Back against "country club unionism" struck a chord among many rank-and-file USWA members and was a sign of new developments in U.S. politics.

In 1977 the coal bosses' association provoked a showdown battle with the United Mine Workers, counting on "the desperately weak position" of the UMWA, as one Wall Street magazine put it at the time. But what the coal operators got was a 110-day strike—one of the most important labor battles in decades. Thousands of rank-and-file miners placed their stamp on the fight and won solidarity from millions of working people throughout the country. President James Carter came to the aid of the coal bosses, declaring a "national emergency" and ordering the miners back to work. But the miners defied the government and the bosses, and in the process blocked a concerted union-busting assault and strengthened the union.

These fights and the changes in U.S. politics they registered convinced the leadership of the Socialist Workers Party that the opportunities now existed to bring the party's social composition and structure into greater harmony with its working-class program. Out of the Black rights battles, anti–Vietnam War protests, and women's rights fights of the 1960s and early 1970s, the SWP had won hundreds of radicalizing students and youth to the communist movement, primarily through recruitment to the Young Socialist Alliance, an independent youth group in political solidarity with the SWP. Many of these young socialists later joined the party.

In response to the new stage in politics, SWP members threw themselves into activity in solidarity with the embattled coal miners, steelworkers, and other unionists. Party members began to take jobs in factories organized by several industrial unions and to carry out organized political and trade union work in the labor movement.

On the basis of this experience, as explained by Jack Barnes in the February 1978 report in this section, the party decided to "subordinate everything else to immediately organizing to get a large majority of the membership of the Socialist Workers Party into industry and the industrial trade unions." The May 1979 report by Mary-Alice Waters that closes this section centers on the new opportunities and new challenges to advance working-class leadership in the party opened by the turn to the industrial unions.

Prospects for socialism
in America

RESOLUTION OF SOCIALIST WORKERS PARTY

The effects of the combined social and economic shocks of the last half-decade, coming on top of the changes in attitudes wrought by the movements of social protest and the radicalization of the 1960s and 1970s, have brought us to the threshold of a new period in the transformation of the political consciousness of the American working class.

A different stage in the process of radicalization is opening; new types of struggles are coming onto the agenda.

This resolution examines on a world scale the roots and the various components of the crisis of American capitalism. These are compared and contrasted both to the post–World War II period of capitalist economic boom and political reaction, and to the depression and labor radicalization of the 1930s. The goal is to explain the dilemma faced by the ruling class, the structural and ideological changes taking place in the American working class and among its

This is the main political resolution adopted by the Twenty-seventh National Convention of the Socialist Workers Party, held August 17-21, 1975.

SEE PAGE 437 FOR NOTES

53

allies, and the revolutionary perspective inherent in the radicalization of the working class that is just beginning to unfold.

I. Growing contradictions of world imperialism

In the three decades since World War II, recessions have occurred in each of the major capitalist powers. Each of these separate slumps, however, was cushioned by the fact that industrialization, productivity, employment, and trade continued to run their expansionary course in at least several other capitalist countries. The current American depression is not only the longest and deepest of the six U.S. postwar slumps; more important, it is a component part of the first *world* recession since 1937-38, simultaneously affecting all the major capitalist economies.

This recession on a world scale is a product of the increasing exhaustion of many of the motor forces that fed the quarter-century world capitalist boom—for instance, the reconstruction of European and Japanese industry, the massive growth of the automobile and related industries in the 1950s and 1960s, the mechanization, automation, and computerization of whole new branches of industry.

The expansionary stimulants of deficit financing and massive credit growth, used to help bring capitalist economies out of slumps in the last quarter of a century, have turned into perilous measures. Government-engineered inflation is less effective and more dangerous than ever before as a means of bringing capitalist economies out of a recession. It can threaten to soar out of control even in the midst of a depression.

The war in Indochina brought clearly into the open the shift in the world relationship of class forces against imperialism. It demonstrated the new limits imposed on the *use* of American imperialism's massive military machine. The imperialist giant today finds itself increasingly hobbled not only by the nuclear power of the Soviet Union, but by the absence of semicolonial allies and clients with solid popular support in their own countries, by the drain on U.S. capital that propping up dictatorial regimes entails, and by political opposition from the American people. The defeat in Southeast Asia was a setback of historic proportions for U.S. capitalism.

Meanwhile, in Europe, the powerful working-class offensives registered in the May 1968 prerevolutionary upsurge in France and the "creeping May" in Italy in the autumn of 1969 demonstrated the growing trend toward broad *social* crises in the heart of the imperialist powers of Europe. This trend has been reconfirmed by the revolutionary ferment that exploded in Portugal in the spring of 1974.

From being an allied reserve, offering military, political, and economic support for embattled American imperialism vis-à-vis the colonial revolution and the workers states, sectors of European capital are becoming an additional source of weakness.

As the oil crisis, the prelude to the 1974-75 depression, demonstrated anew, American imperialism remains by far the single most powerful force in the world capitalist arena. Its economic output alone is as great as all the other major capitalist powers put together.

Furthermore, the competitive pressures of the unfolding social and economic crisis eliminated all pretense that the European Common Market countries would establish a single currency and state structure as a counterweight to U.S. imperialism and an effective challenge to its hegemony.

However, all these events of the end of the 1960s and beginning of the 1970s coincided not only with the end of the long wave of the post–World War II capitalist economic expansion; they also reflected a major decline in the productivity edge American capitalism had over its most powerful competitors.

The edge in labor productivity had enabled the dollar to play its role as the world currency, exporting inflation and allowing modest but real wage increases for American labor. It had also enabled U.S. imperialism to make massive investments and military expenditures abroad simultaneously. The peaking of the postwar international capitalist boom in the 1968-71 period thus signaled the opening of a period of increasing interimperialist competition and conflict, of further shifts in the relationships among the imperialist powers, and of a new long wave of economic stagnation and explosive inflation.

Before the nuclear arms age, such shifts in the relationship of forces would have precipitated an interimperialist war for the redivision of the shrinking world market, as in 1914 and 1939. But the qualitative military superiority of American capitalism within the imperialist camp and the deterrent presence of the Soviet nuclear arsenal have radically altered the framework in which these classical interimperialist contradictions have to be resolved.

The policy of détente, too, is based on a mutual recognition of these new economic and military relationships of forces. While Moscow counts on economic aid from the capitalists to boost Soviet industrial and technological capacities, American imperialism, through a tacit political understanding, is assured of assistance from the Soviet bureaucracy in the form of counterrevolutionary intervention against the independent actions of the world working class. The Stalinist parties around the world are called upon to collaborate in this task. This *quid pro quo* constitutes the essence of the policy of détente and is brought to bear in every new revolutionary upsurge of the oppressed.

The convergence of these factors has precipitated a major crisis of world capitalist leadership.

II. Crisis of perspective of the American ruling class

The American ruling class that was so confident and arrogant from 1945 on is now floundering in search of a new world strategy. This is reflected in the pessimism expressed by the bourgeois statesmen and commentators as they seek to assess the prospects of American imperialism from a broader historical perspective. To them the collapse of the "American century"—which they were so sure of thirty years ago—evokes visions of declining empires and a coming "dark age." They see the world as careening toward a new "era of scarcity," or suggest decades of zero economic growth as the only alternative to the destruction of the life-supporting capacity of the earth's environment. They "philosophically" weigh the probability that "democracy" cannot be maintained much longer if inflation and social unrest continue.

Such pessimism stems from a recognition of the shift in the world relationship of class forces to the disadvantage of capitalism, the shift in relative weight among the imperialist rivals themselves, and the scope of the problems generated today by a decaying world capitalist order.

This crisis of leadership and orientation is not confined to the American bourgeoisie. Despite the relative decline of the American dollar and Washington's power, there is no other capitalist power, not even the strongest, Germany or Japan, capable of stepping in and replacing Wall Street's hegemony.

However much the lesser capitalist powers may chafe under U.S. domination, they cannot free themselves from dependence upon Washington. Singly or collectively, they cannot afford, nor are they able, to police the world. Yet they cannot afford not to have it policed.

These are the sources of the disarray in the American and world bourgeois leaderships and the increasing divisions among them. As these divisions become intensified, they lead to further loss of confidence among the ruling classes in their own ability to rule. These conflicts, and the crisis of capitalist leadership, deepen the general malaise in the population.

Under these circumstances the *real* perspectives that continued capitalist rule present to the American workers are cuts in the standard of living, new military adventures, and curtailment of democracy.

1. The ruling class will seek to boost profit rates by squeezing even more out of the American workers. This means holding

down real wages, whittling away working conditions, lowering the standard of living, and slashing social welfare programs. It means seeking to increase divisions among the workers through the use of racism and sexism especially, and trying to prevent the development of international working-class solidarity.

It also means cutting down on the social legacy to be bequeathed to future generations—the natural environment, schools, hospitals, housing, organization of the cities, and the entire productive system. And it means increasing social dislocation—crime, alcoholism, drug addiction, mounting social and psychological pressures, and deepening alienation. This is the quality of life capitalism has in store for the great majority.

In its struggle against the relative advance of German and Japanese capital, the American bourgeoisie calls on the masses to be "realistic" and accept the doleful fact that American capitalism cannot sustain the relatively high and growing standard of living the working class has come to *expect* as a *right*. The capitalists call upon the workers to sacrifice to make up for "excessive" wage increases and consumption of social services, and to lower their expectations in order to "keep America strong."

2. The threat of military adventures, and along with them the possibility of nuclear annihilation, will continue. Rivalries among the imperialist powers will sharpen as they compete for markets and raw materials. There will be increased efforts to impose American imperialist needs and perspectives on the masses of the colonial and semicolonial world with the inevitable resistance this will generate.

Washington will continue to come up against the limits of the Stalinists' capacity to control the outbursts of class struggle on a world scale. Since détente was proclaimed, events in Greece, Cyprus, Portugal, the Arab East, and Indochina have amply shown how impossible it is for Moscow and Peking to prevent the masses from disrupting the status quo.

At every opportunity, the ruling class will push as far as it can, testing the limits on the use of its massive military power and nuclear blackmail, trying to see how much of an edge it can get through threat of military action. The danger of miscalculation is always inherent in this bellicose probing.

3. The ruling class will seek to curtail the democratic rights of the American workers, to undercut their ability to learn the truth about the actions and activities of the big corporations and the government, to hamper them from entering the political arena in an independent manner. They will strive to drive back both the social gains and the new rights won by the oppressed minorities and women in recent years.

Driving down the living standard of the masses of American workers, maintaining American economic positions abroad by deploying U.S. military might, curtailing the rights and liberties won by the American people on the job and in society as a whole—these are the realities America's imperialist rulers hold out for the coming period.

III. Changing consciousness of the working class

Black struggle

A mounting skepticism toward what was vaguely seen as "the American system" began in the 1960s. It took the form of a *moral* questioning by young people as they came to see "the system's" refusal or incapacity to meet the just demands being made by Black people. Little Rock, the sit-ins, Mississippi and Selma, then Watts, Detroit, and Newark became symbols of the social injustice and inequality pervading America. Bourgeois democracy was not based on liberty and equality for all as the schools taught.

From the Black struggle and all it revealed about the racist inequalities of American democracy, this questioning spread to other benighted outlooks and institutions upholding capitalism and upheld by it—religion, the "work ethic," unequal education, anticommunism, the "organization man" and hierarchical authority, marriage, and the family.

A new stage was opened by the Vietnam War as outrage over the aims and methods of American imperialism became a mass phenomenon reaching beyond the campus and the youth. The resulting radicalization extended to new arenas of struggle and challenged more of class society's sacred cows. Other oppressed nationalities, soldiers, women, gays, prisoners, the elderly, began to vocally and actively demand their full human rights.

Legacy of Vietnam

The experience of the Vietnam War produced a profound change in the attitude of masses of American workers.

The strength of what the bourgeois pundits call the "new isolationism" constitutes the heritage of the overwhelming opposition of the American people to the government's intervention in Indochina, and their skepticism toward Washington's military adventures.

The American people have been sensitized to threats to use American military power. The credibility gap makes it more difficult to stage provocations like the Tonkin Gulf incident.[1]

"Revisionist" reassessments of Washington's role and designs in the origins of the Cold War, the Korean War, and even World War II are gaining a wider audience.

There is more awareness that increasing escalation of the military budget brings something besides jobs for those employed in the war industries—it brings death, destruction, senseless maiming and killing, and misery to the world, to American GIs, and to workers' families here at home.

Among the radicalizing effects of the Vietnam War and the antiwar movement was the dawning realization that war, war preparations, and the accumulated burden of the costs for past wars are central parts of the rulers' "answer" to world capitalist competition and its periodic crises.

Impact of Watergate

In the last half decade an alteration has also occurred in the American workers' understanding of the reality of American democracy.

The working of American "democracy" abroad has been revealed in Vietnam and Chile, in Cuba and the former Belgian Congo, as a part of the real story has been unearthed from the records of the Pentagon, the CIA, the State Department, the White House, and Congress. But even more than the foreign operations, it was the extensive violations of democratic rights at home that were profoundly shocking to so many Americans as Watergate unraveled and the domestic crimes of the CIA, the FBI, and the Internal Revenue Service were exposed.

As the Watergate scandal unfolded, American workers began to see this spectacle not as an isolated case of crooked politicians being caught, but as proof of a general mode of operation that constituted a threat to fundamental democratic rights.[2] These methods were initiated, carried on, and covered up by a ruling class determined to halt and eventually roll back the social and economic gains made in recent years by the working class and its allies. The real targets of the Watergate methods—as revealed by the Huston plan, Cointelpro documents, the Ellsberg case, the murder of the Chicago Black Panther leaders—were the Blacks, the Chicanos, the women, the youth, the prisoners, the antiwar GIs, the undocumented immigrant workers. The Watergate methods were part of the "law and order" response by the ruling class to the spread of the very idea that working people have a right to a say over war, a right to basic human necessities, and a right to fight for these things.

More Americans came to suspect that references to "national security" were intended to hide the real actions and motivations of the rulers. The "credibility gap" that began with Vietnam and escalated to unprecedented proportions with Watergate represents in reality a crisis of political confidence in the government, the beginning of a crisis of legitimacy. For the first time since the 1930s tens of millions of American working people not only disbelieve what the rulers tell them but question the goals and values of the ruling class.

Changing social values

Significant and progressive shifts in cultural patterns and values have already taken place in broad layers of the population, even though some of these have been expressed in escapist and subjective responses.

These shifts are reflected in such developments as the rise of the gay liberation movement, the independence displayed by juries in political cases, the politicalization and mood of rebellion in the prisons, the readiness to reveal secrets that led to exposures of such scandals as the Pentagon Papers, and the Cointelpro revelations.

Social norms and relationships are being newly examined from the standpoint of the historically oppressed or exploited. The critical reappraisals testify to a loosening of the bonds of bourgeois ideology and its conservative assumptions.

Modern means of communication, especially television, have played an unprecedented role in the rapid spread of news, ideas, and action, making more vivid the realities of wars and crises, and spreading innovative trends.

The actions connected with the radicalization of the 1960s took place by and large outside the framework of organized labor. This absence of the organized power of the working class was the strongest limitation upon the development of the radicalization.

But by the beginning of the 1970s the young workers especially were beginning to be significantly affected. They responded not so much as producers or unionists but as young people sensitive to the injustices of society.

Between the wage-freeze offensive of August 1971 and the economic depression of 1974-75, the workers began to discover that, in addition to being morally questionable, the system as a whole was just not giving them what they expected and needed. They reacted against the strong doses of wage controls, speedup, food shortages, the energy crisis, cutbacks in social welfare, double-digit inflation, double-digit unemployment in some sectors of industry and layers of the population, and large-scale layoffs.

Today growing numbers of American workers sense that they are faced not with just a temporary economic depression, as serious as that may be, but with a more enduring *social* crisis that is worldwide. It is not simply that they hear such admissions from prominent figures on television; the working class can see the evidence all around. They can see it in the decline in education, public facilities, health care, and housing, and in the growing pollution of the environment.

They are beginning to sense that the economic problems they face are much greater than before, that the prolonged period of relative prosperity has definitely come to an end; and while the period now opening may have its ups, the ups won't be high or lasting and the downs will be really deep and long.

The forebodings of the workers are accurate. We face a period in which stagnation will predominate over boom and in which the employers will seek to tighten their control over job conditions, speed of the line, health and safety conditions, the organization of the work.

Combinations of breakdowns and shortages, slumps and inflation, speedup and degradation of labor, new wars—that is what American capitalism promises for the future.

Fed by unrest over the current depression, the greatest collapse in public confidence since the Hoover administration has accelerated the crisis in leadership faced by America's rulers.

The only program capable of blocking eventual radicalization of the unions would be massive social reform—that is, large-scale concessions in the form of job-creating public works programs, unemployment benefits, housing, medical care, education, protection against inflation, and similar reforms.

While the ruling class is capable of making concessions and may even at some point initiate a number of highly publicized projects as part of a new "New Deal," social reforms of the scope that could meet today's expectations are beyond their reach. That course would necessitate the stabilization of the world capitalist economy, renewal of its expansionary course, and a vast strengthening of America's dominant position.

Three major obstacles block a perspective of reform so far-reaching as to assure an extended period of social and political stability.

First, the international evolution of the class struggle itself will touch off new explosive convulsions throughout the world. An imperialist foreign policy able to block further advances of social revolution is beyond Washington's reach. It was the transformation of the "New Deal" into the "War Deal" that rescued the capitalist economy from the crisis of the 1930s and defused the radicalization of those years. Any attempt to emulate that course today would spark massive political opposition.

Second, the state of the international capitalist economy following the end of the long boom precludes social and economic concessions to the working class on a scale sufficient to close their minds to radical ideas. The more likely perspective is continued convulsive developments in the world capitalist economy, sharp fluctuations, unexpected breakdowns, renewed inflation and shortages, with some of the satellite regimes skirting bankruptcy. A new massive increase in the already bloated war budget of the Pentagon, far from helping to resolve the crisis as it did at the end of the 1930s, would rapidly set off another round of rampant inflation, triggering new social struggles by the American people.

Third, American capitalism's real economic perspectives will make it increasingly difficult for the ruling class even to maintain concessions and advances already won, let alone meet the heightened expectations of the oppressed and exploited.

There will be no willing patriotic sacrifices for some supposedly higher "national interest." While appeals to racist and sexist attitudes to offset the radicalization will evoke a response in some sectors of the working class, they will be qualitatively less effective than before and will stiffen the resistance of their victims.

The United States is not heading back to the prolonged prosperity, reaction, and quiescence of the 1950s and early 1960s. The road ahead is one of increasing class consciousness, class struggle, and class polarization, leading from radicalization toward a revolutionary situation, regardless of the oscillations along the way.

The world crisis of capitalism does not favor extensive and effective long-term capitalist *reform* in the United States but development of the prerequisites for a *revolution*.

IV. Changing character and composition of the working class

Contrary to the widely trumpeted myth of bourgeois sociology, class differences did not vanish during the postwar boom nor was the American proletariat dissolved into a generally comfortable new petty bourgeoisie. In fact, the opposite occurred.

Wealth and economic control have become concentrated in the hands of a smaller and smaller percentage of the population. At the same time, the extensive industrialization, automation, and monopolization of factory, farm, and office in the 1950s and 1960s led to a massive increase in the size of the American working class, both in absolute terms and in relation to other classes.

Spurred on by the needs of monopoly capital in a period of accelerated expansion, these changes of the last three decades have produced major alterations in the composition and placement of the class:

• Agricultural industrialization and mechanization drove millions of farm families off the land while simultaneously increasing the key role played by the agricultural proletariat on the farms.

• Industrialization of the South brought about the proletarianization of the majority of the southern population.

• These two processes, together with the large-scale northern migration of the Black population, produced a rapid proletarianization of Afro-Americans.

• Chicano and Puerto Rican labor entered the urban workforce, as well as the agricultural proletariat, in large numbers. Like Blacks, the Chicano and Puerto Rican people have become more urbanized than the white population.

• The expansionary boom brought millions of women into the labor market.

• The growing utilization of "part-time" workers absorbed additional large numbers of women as well as youth into the workforce. Alongside this extensive proletarianization of the population, there have been important changes produced by the automation and monopolization of American industry in the placement, disposition, and character of American labor.

• The percentage of workers employed as craftsmen, operatives, and laborers, what government statistics call "blue collar workers," has fallen.

• As in all advanced capitalist countries, there have been sharp increases in the service sector of the economy, the percentage of clerical workers, and the number of public employees working for the various departments of the federal, state, county, and municipal governments (none of whom the ruling class statisticians call "blue collar workers").

• The mechanization of many trades has eroded the skill levels and standing of a growing number of crafts. For example, in the building trades, the skills of masons, carpenters, and painters are less needed as prefabricated construction increases.

• The "industrialization" and automation of a large amount of white collar office and sales work, and even what is referred to as "intellectual labor," has created a new reservoir of proletarianized and alienated labor.

This monopolization and industrialization, extending up and down the line from farms and mines, processing and transportation, to storage and distribution, has sharply reduced the classical petty-bourgeois dreams and illusions of even skilled sectors of the American workers. Proletarianization has altered the workers' concepts of themselves in comparison with earlier generations. American workers think of themselves nowadays more as permanent workers than as potential independent producers. Fewer believe they will one day be able to have a shop, farm, or small business of their own, assuring them an independent livelihood. They are more interested in wresting some degree of control over the machinery, work decisions, and health and safety environment they are subjected to, than in aspiring to own a small business or escaping back to the land.

At the same time, while they do not expect to be able to rise above their own social class, they believe their children are *entitled* to a better education and a better life than they had. With fewer traditional petty-bourgeois illusions than any previous generation of American workers, they nonetheless feel they have a *right* to what are considered "middle class" standards of living. These encompass a guaranteed income, rising as productivity increases; expanding medical and retirement guarantees; adequate transportation; a decent and continuing education; peace; and a healthy environment for their children. They believe that the American economy, if run correctly, can produce this standard of living for all. These convictions are a revolutionizing—not a conservatizing—factor.

The changes in the composition of the working class and in the mass organizations of the workers, the unions, deserve a closer look.

Blacks

The Black population is today more proletarianized and more urbanized than the white. A significantly higher percentage of Black women are in the labor force than white women.

A higher percentage of Blacks than ever before are engaged in basic industry, especially auto, steel, and transportation. Through affirmative action suits and quotas they have made gains in jobs, upgrading, pay, and job security.

Blacks comprise about 22 percent of all workers employed in manufacturing and in construction. At the same time Blacks make up a disproportionately large percentage of the lower-paid service jobs and lower rungs of public employment. About 27 percent of all employed Blacks are service workers.

The unionization of Black workers reflects this employment

pattern. In the United Automobile Workers; the Steelworkers; American Federation of State, County, and Municipal Employees; Letter Carriers; and Postal Clerks, Blacks comprise about 20 percent of the union membership. In many locals it is significantly higher. In the Longshoremen the percentage rises to nearly half.

The unions today are the organizations having the largest Black membership in the country. In auto the percentage of Black union-local officials is higher than the percentage of Blacks in the industry, and many locals are run largely by Blacks. The Coalition of Black Trade Unionists is an initial reflection of this development.

The rapid expansion of the service and public employee sectors of the economy; the proletarianization of Black and female labor; the significant concentration of Blacks and women in these sectors; and the fact that these are also the most rapidly growing sectors of union organization are all interrelated phenomena.

Women

The increase in the percentage of women in the workforce has been one of the biggest changes brought about by American capital in the postwar period.

In 1930 women constituted only 20 percent of the workforce, and less than 25 percent of all women of working age were employed. By 1945, largely because of the needs of the war industry, women constituted 30 percent of the workforce, and more than a third of all women of working age were employed. But by 1972 women constituted 37 percent of the workforce, and 44 percent of all women were employed.

While the decade following World War II saw a small decline in the number of women in industry and employment, reversing some of the gains established during the war years, by 1955 the curve of employment began to climb again. The last twenty years have seen a steady rise in female employment. During the boom of the 1960s two-thirds of all new jobs created were taken by women. This rate of increase in female employment occurred because of the rapid rate of expansion of the economy as a whole.

The highest percentage of working women, while classified by the government as "white collar," went into the fastest growing sectors of the working class—office workers, service employees, sales, public workers, and teachers.

Toward the end of the postwar boom, through the enforcement of quotas and affirmative action suits, women even began to win a slightly larger percentage of jobs in basic industry.

Forty percent of all working women are either the sole or major wage earners in their households. At the same time, working wives are the single largest source of the "affluence" of many American working-class families.

The growing integration of women into the workforce has brought with it a heightening of class consciousness among women. As they increasingly see themselves as long-term and permanent members of the workforce and are recognized as such by others, the need to protect their jobs and working conditions by joining unions and bringing their militancy to bear in the labor movement becomes more obvious and urgent. This is part of the process that has given rise to formations such as women's committees in the unions and the Coalition of Labor Union Women.

Youth

The American working class in the 1970s is younger than at any time since the 1930s. In 1960 only 16 percent of the workforce was under twenty-five years of age. Today it is more than 23 percent.

The rise in the formal educational level of the working class as a whole is especially marked in this generation of young workers, male and female, who spent more time in school before permanently entering the labor market. Today more than 27 percent of the labor force has completed one or more years of college education, up from only 16 percent twenty years ago.

This means that more of the American workers coming into industry are subjected to the social, cultural, and ideological influences affecting their generation as a whole for a longer period before their assimilation into the workforce.

The young workers of the present generation are different in another sense. They are a completely fresh and undefeated layer that does not bear the scars or the memory of the Great Depression, the witch-hunt, and the Cold War. They are imbued with the more militant attitudes of the developing radicalization. Since they came into the labor force when there was close to steady work for all adult members of the household who wished to be employed, they expect more as their rightful due.

It is the young workers who have reacted most militantly to the speedup and deterioration of working conditions in the last half-decade. And they look least to the ossified union bureaucracies to protect their interests. They have been the initiators of several waves of wildcat strikes and local actions. Their deep alienation is often expressed through sabotage on the line, high turnover rates, and absenteeism.

In the decade of the late 1960s and early 1970s the young workers often tended to be hostile to the unions or indifferent to them, not identifying with them as *their* organizations. But, as the struggles with the employing class intensify, the problem of either transforming the unions into instruments of struggle against the bosses or facing massive defeats is beginning to appear in a new light.

Trade unions

At the beginning of the radicalization of the 1930s barely 5 percent of the working class was unionized. Those who were organized were trapped in the antiquated structures of craft unions led by a conservative bureaucracy that stood in the way of building fighting organizations of the working class.

Labor's giant step in the 1930s and 1940s—the organization of basic industry and the establishment of industrial union shops in auto, steel, rubber, and elsewhere—transformed the character of the American labor movement. In a few short years it became one of the most powerfully organized working classes in the world.

By the end of the 1930s close to 16 percent of the labor force was unionized. By the end of the war it had risen to more than 23 percent, and the percentage continued to rise until 1953 when it peaked at 25.5 percent.

The ossification of the union leaderships over the last two decades, their failure to fight to maintain working conditions, to organize the unorganized, to combat antilabor legislation, and to mobilize the unions in behalf of progressive social struggles, and their political subordination to the needs of the employers' two-party system, have led to a stagnation and decline in union membership since then. Today roughly 23 percent of the labor force is unionized.

Among the more striking defaults of the union bureaucrats has been the absence of any sizable advances in unionizing the South, parallel to the growing industrialization and urbanization of that region.

Similarly, they have shown brutal indifference to—and in the case of the Teamster bureaucracy even helped lead the attack against—the fight to unionize farm labor.

Big inroads have been made by the construction bosses against the craft unions. Mechanization and prefabrication in the construction industry, coupled with the reactionary white-job-trust mentality of the bureaucracies of the skilled trades, led to stagnation and a decline in membership among the skilled craft unions and the undermining of union-shop conditions. The weakening of such unions is now being registered in the mechanization of the building trades like painting and carpentry, and automation of the printing trades. Industrial conditions are tearing down the craft-union structure along with its accompanying business-unionism mentality and customs.

But expecting the big boom to last forever, the union bureaucracies set themselves up, not as the leadership of a class with a historic mission in society, but as representatives and defenders of the benefits enjoyed by a small layer of the most privileged white male workers.

V. Radicalization and mobilization of the allies of the proletariat

The failure of the union bureaucracies to fight for the elementary needs of the masses of workers they represent has already led to the first revolts against some of their most corrupt sectors. The overturn of the Boyle machine in the United Mine Workers, the establishment of the right of the miners to vote on their contracts, and the growing social consciousness of the miners have given a glimpse of the initiatives to be expected from the powerful industrial proletariat.

The large-scale, rapid unionization of public employees in the last decade, including the unionization of millions of teachers and others who formerly considered themselves "middle-class professionals," has brought significant new forces into the labor movement.

For public employees, every struggle comes up against a series of obstacles. Antistrike and antilabor laws are used against them. They are weakened by the lack of broad labor unity mobilized in their support. They are crippled by the past failures of their leaderships to support the struggles of the oppressed communities. And they must confront not only the government as boss, but the Democratic and Republican parties to whom the unions have been subordinated by the misleadership of American labor.

Public employees are today the main target of the ruling-class offensive to drive down wages, working conditions, social welfare, and social services, and to weaken and demoralize American labor. They are more vulnerable to attack than the powerfully organized industrial workers, who create the profits for America's rulers. Successful efforts by the public workers to fight back and overcome these obstacles could provide an example and constitute a turning point for the entire American working class.

But this will require a new kind of leadership, new consciousness, and new methods of struggle. The transformation of American labor into a class-conscious social and political force will be heralded both by massive social struggles outside the unions and by the rise of a class-struggle left wing in the union movement. Such a formation will strive to provide leadership for all types of social struggles by the oppressed. It will chart a political course of class independence for the unions, breaking millions of workers and their allies away from the two-party system of the bourgeoisie and its agents.

Even in a country like the United States where the workers comprise the vast majority of the population, the working class cannot succeed in wresting power from the capitalist rulers and beginning the socialist reconstruction of society without strong support from its allies. At the same time, these allies—the oppressed minorities, women, small farmers, craftsmen, proprietors, the GIs, and the student youth—all have a life-and-death stake in the socialist revolution.

The traditional allies of the workers have been primarily the small independent producers, craftsmen, and proprietors, both urban and rural. This still held true during the radicalization of the 1930s when the farm population was about 30 percent of the total. However, the large-scale changes wrought since then in the structure of industry, agriculture, and the labor force through the growth and further monopolization of American capital have radically reduced the size and altered the configuration of these classical petty-bourgeois strata.

The composition and character of the allies of the proletariat have undergone significant changes as the structure and composition of the proletariat itself have altered dramatically. But these changes in no way lessen the importance of understanding the independent needs and struggles of these allies or of winning them to the side of the socialist revolution. To the contrary, clear and concrete answers must be given to their demands if the revolutionary workers are to mobilize full striking power against the forces of capital. In so doing, they will eliminate the central obstacle before the coming American revolution—that is, the divisions within the working class.

The oppressed nationalities and national minorities

The oppressed nationalities and national minorities have a dual character. They constitute a growing percentage of the working class itself and at the same time they are the most important allies of the working class. In this respect they differ from the oppressed layers of the petty bourgeoisie, and all other allies except the women. To see only one side of this duality, and to ignore the other, would be a fatal error for a revolutionary party.

Oppressed nationalities and national minorities are exploited as proletarians. This exploitation is intensified by their pariah status since they are at the same time oppressed as distinct peoples. The struggle against this twofold oppression is one of the central driving forces of the coming American revolution. It is closely intertwined with all the problems and issues facing the American working class.

Their importance as allies of the proletariat stems from several factors:

National oppression and the racism used to justify it are rooted in the historical development of American capitalism, in the uncompleted tasks of the second American revolution (the Civil War, which emancipated Afro-Americans from slavery but failed to lead to full equality), and in the rise of imperialism with its self-justifying racist ideology.

National oppression is used by the ruling class to divide the working class, to buy off leaders and privileged strata, thus weakening both the class consciousness and political independence of the workers, and bolstering capitalist rule. With or without legal sanction, a major component of the industrial reserve army has been kept in a pariah status.

The overwhelmingly proletarian composition and superexploitation of the oppressed nationalities and national minorities mean that they will be the most consistent and cohesive of all allies of the working class in its struggles. More and more they will furnish leadership in the fight to transform the labor movement into a fighting social movement, using labor's power to back the struggles of all the oppressed.

Blacks

The most important changes in the Black population have already been noted:

- The postwar mechanization of southern agriculture.
- The urbanization and proletarianization of the Black population in the South.
- The massive northern migration of the Black population.
- The big influx into basic industry during and after World War II.
- The increase in the number of years Black youth spend in school and the percentage that receive high school diplomas and some post–high school education.

The period since 1945 has also seen a historic advance in the struggle for Black liberation.

'Jim Crow must go'

In the postwar years American imperialism drove to expand its domination in Asia, Africa, and Latin America. To do so it needed a new, less racist image. In addition, the changes taking place in the economic structure of southern society created the need for new forms of social control. The more alert representatives of the American ruling class began to recognize that Jim Crow, the southern system of legal segregation maintained through legal and extralegal terror, had ceased to be the most effective means of perpetuating the second-class status of the Black proletariat.

Under pressure from growing mass resentment, the U.S. armed forces were formally desegregated during the Korean War, and then in 1954 the Supreme Court declared school segregation unconstitutional.

But it was only the decade-long direct-action struggles, mobilizing millions of Blacks and their supporters, that downed Jim Crow. Their power and determination played a decisive role in altering Black consciousness and self-confidence. This was reflected in the rise of Black power and Black nationalist sentiments; in the popularity of Malcolm X; in the upsurges of other oppressed minorities and social groupings; in the moral questioning that has so deeply motivated the youth radicalization; and in the modification of the opinions of masses of white workers.

The effects of the mass struggle to end segregation, followed by the powerful rise of Black nationalist sentiment, were subsequently seen in the vanguard role played by Black GIs in opposition to the Vietnam War.

The high point in the "civil rights period" of the new rise of the Black struggle came with the battle of Birmingham and the march on Washington in 1963, the passage of the 1964 Civil Rights Act and the 1965 Voting Rights Act, and the Selma, Alabama, confrontation. The impact of the masses in action was even grotesquely echoed in Lyndon Johnson's "We shall overcome" speech before the Congress.

The ghettos explode

Rebellions in the Black communities, beginning in New York in 1964, spreading to Watts in 1965, and Newark and Detroit in 1967, and culminating in the 1968 nationwide outbreaks after the death of Martin Luther King, ushered in a new stage of struggle in which Black nationalist ideas spread rapidly. These spontaneous upsurges, along with intensified struggles by Black students and other sectors of the Black community, forced more concessions from the ruling class and brought forward new leaders who became targets of stepped-up government repression.

Riding the crest of the postwar boom, the ruling class co-opted a layer of the leaders or potential leaders of the rising Black radicalization by granting them economic, political, and social concessions.

The percentage of Black enrollment in the country's colleges and universities tripled in a five-year period at the end of the 1960s and beginning of the 1970s. "Great Society" dollars were poured into poverty program funds, a good part of which went into salaries of "aspiring leaders," Black and white.

The face of the Democratic Party also underwent a significant change. The threat posed by the unconditional opposition of Malcolm X to the Democratic Party and the first halting steps toward independent Black political action, such as the Michigan Freedom Now Party and the Lowndes County Freedom Organization, was adroitly countered. From the Mississippi Freedom Democratic Party to the election of Black mayors in a half-dozen major industrial cities, to the emergence of the Congressional Black Caucus, and the election of more than 1,100 Black officials in the deep South—where less than a decade ago the masses of Blacks were barred even from voting—the lure of "working within the (two-party) system" attracted the overwhelming majority of a generation of potential Black leaders.

The following features should be added to the picture of the crisis of leadership of the Black movement:

1. The total default of the organized labor movement, whose class-collaborationist leadership was unable to rise above its own narrow concern of maintaining its privileged position and refused to mobilize the power of the labor movement in support of the Black struggle.

2. The calculated policy of the powers that be of eliminating any potential individual leaders—such as Martin Luther King, who inspired the Black masses to struggle, or Malcolm X, who was beginning to urge Black people toward independent political action against capitalist oppression.

3. The failure to effectively meet government harassment and murder of a layer of leaders in the generation of the 1960s. Groups like the Black Panthers, whose ultraleftism turned them away from any mass perspective, were left defenseless before the government's cold-blooded use of agents provocateurs and terror.

4. The numerical weakness of the revolutionary Marxists, which prevented them from providing a revolutionary leadership except in the realm of program and socialist perspectives.

But despite this crisis, the rise of Black nationalism and the massive ghetto explosions brought about a historic advance in the self-confidence of Blacks and their image of themselves as a people. The upsurges also changed the way white Americans viewed Afro-Americans. Despite the lack of adequate leadership of the Black movement, its power won numerous concessions and registered advances throughout the decade of the 1960s. This has been symbolized in the at least token participation of Blacks at every level of society and culture, from TV commercials to sports, from elected union posts to the Supreme Court. In the late 1960s even the income differential between Black and white workers narrowed by a tiny, though perceptible, amount. Blacks began fighting for preferential quotas, training, and upgrading in industry and the educational system, as necessary and irreplaceable steps along the road to real equality.

THE COUNTEROFFENSIVE

But the costs of the Vietnam War and the increasing economic crunch brought an end to the Johnson period of concessions and buy-offs as a tactical expedient in coping with rising Black militancy. The Nixon-Connally 1971 wage controls and economic offensive followed recognition that the new economic realities and world relationship of forces not only precluded continuing increases in real wages and social services, but meant that many concessions already won would have to be reversed. Further progress toward equality became more and more incompatible with maintaining competitive superiority in the world market.

The Black population did not share in the brief economic upturn of 1971-72. From the high point of Black median incomes equaling 61 percent of white median incomes in 1969, the ratio fell to 58 percent in 1973. Black unemployment rose steadily from 6.4 percent in 1969 to 10 percent in 1972.

The 1972-73 Nixon policy of rollback in virtually every area of social expenditures—housing, education, transportation, child care, welfare, etc.—was part of the drive to take back the gains won by the radicalization of the 1960s. These cutbacks, aimed at the working class as a whole, hit Blacks and other oppressed nationalities and minorities the hardest. But instead of reversing the radicalization, the cutbacks helped, along with the antiwar movement, to create the opposition that spurred forward the Watergate crisis and the downfall of Nixon.

These are the present battle lines in relation to Black liberation and the labor movement. While the ruling class is forced to try to reverse the drive toward real equality, the Black movement must press forward with demands for immediate government enforcement of concessions already won and for preferential treatment. Especially in a period of economic stagnation, the racist counteroffensive in education, housing, jobs, and other areas puts the Black leadership and the labor movement to a decisive test.

Chicanos

The late 1960s and early 1970s saw an upsurge of Chicano nationalism. As with Afro-Americans, the new militancy was rooted in the major economic and social changes within the Chicano population that took place during and after World War II—a significant urbanization and proletarianization of the Chicano population and a large influx of Mexican workers to provide inexpensive labor for the expanding agribusiness in the Southwest.

The ascending Chicano movement in the 1960s was influenced by the advances of the Black civil rights movement and the rise of Black nationalism, the colonial revolution, and the student radicalization.

Later the growing opposition to the Vietnam War plus the disproportionately high Chicano casualty rates helped fuel the militancy. The Chicano movement, led by a layer of radical Chicano leaders who were less affected by ultraleftism than those in the Black movement, organized sizable actions against the war.

Starting in the mid-1960s, the focal point of the Chicano movement became the broad campaign developed in support of attempts to organize the Southwest and West Coast migrant farm labor employed by the most advanced monopoly agribusiness in the world. Radical students were rapidly drawn into support activities.

From the beginning *la causa* was conceived not only as a union organizing drive, but as a broad social movement in the interests of all Chicano people. As such, it was—and remains—in marked contrast to the prevailing character of the rest of the labor movement.

While Chicano nationalism partly took its inspiration from the Black movement, several important differences should be noted:

1. While statistics vary, as much as half of the Chicano population may consider Spanish to be their first language. The right to use their own language in school, at work, on the ballot, and in all aspects of life is one of the central demands of the Chicano struggle.

This is closely tied to the struggles of Chicano students who face, in addition to inferior educational facilities, a denial of the right to study and learn in their own language, resulting in an even higher rate of functional illiteracy than among Blacks. Language and related cultural oppression were major factors in precipitating the massive Chicano high school student rebellions in Los Angeles, Denver, and several Texas cities in the 1960s.

2. Eighty percent of the Chicano population is located in a well-defined geographical area of the country, and is linked by history, culture, and language to both Mexico and the United States.

3. A racist and xenophobic offensive against foreign labor and particularly "illegals," who are easiest to victimize, is one of the central campaigns of the ruling exploiters in every economic crisis. International labor solidarity is fundamental to unifying and defending the working class, its gains, and its organizations. The right to move freely back and forth across the border, the right to work in the United States when and where a worker chooses, without fear of harassment because of lack of work papers or immigration documents, is one of the demands at the very heart of the Chicano strug-

gle. This claim puts the labor movement to a severe test, one that the AFL-CIO officialdom has flunked miserably up to now.

Because the bulk of Chicano workers are concentrated in basic industry, and comprise a significant proportion of the members of the trade unions in the Southwest, they can play a major role in fighting to reverse the reactionary prodeportation policy of the AFL-CIO leadership.

THE FARMWORKERS

The farmworker organizing drives in California, Texas, and elsewhere face tremendous obstacles. A factory in the fields is more difficult to organize than a factory within four walls. The increasingly seasonal and migrant character of the labor force compounds the difficulties. Farmworkers also face some of the most powerful monopolies in the world, whose interests are protected by the federal, state, and local governments. The strikebreaking role of the Teamster bureaucracy and the foot-dragging indifference of the AFL-CIO bureaucracy have created additional problems.

Yet despite these enormous difficulties, the United Farm Workers union organizing drive in California has scored some significant victories. In the elections that followed the August 1975 passage of the California Agricultural Labor Relations Act, the UFW came out ahead despite coercion, intimidation, and widespread rigging. This testifies to the viability of *la causa* and its deep roots among the field workers.

The UFW has also been strengthened by the position it now takes on the undocumented Mexican workers. Recognizing that its earlier demand for deportation of so-called illegal aliens was hurting the farmworkers' struggle, the UFW leadership has been working to win the votes of the undocumented workers and fighting grower-Teamster efforts to victimize them.

Although a minority of the Chicano labor force is employed as agricultural workers, the fierce exploitation and brutal oppression they suffer will continue to generate renewed struggles. Efforts to mobilize the Chicano community and other allies in support of *la causa* will continue to be a focal point for the entire Chicano movement.

Experience is showing that it will take a determined, independent mass movement to force the growers to terms—even after union elections are won—and to extend the organizing drive to other sections of agriculture. The question of political orientation and the need for independence from the liberal Democrats, or any other capitalist politicians, is sharply posed.

In recent years the Democratic Party has increased its efforts to hold onto the Chicano vote. This has resulted in the election of Chicanos to two state governorships for the first time. While most influential figures in the Chicano community have remained tied to the Democratic Party, the response to various attempts by Raza Unida Party formations to move in the direction of mass independent political action has confirmed that when presented with a viable alternative, significant numbers of Chicanos can be broken from the Democratic machine.

LA RAZA UNIDA

The Chicano movement has stepped ahead of the Black movement on this important front. The various attempts to construct Raza Unida parties—with their strengths and weaknesses—are some of the most advanced initiatives yet made in the direction of political action independent of the two capitalist parties.

A key test for the Raza Unida parties came in the 1972 presidential elections. At the first "National Convention of Raza Unida Parties" in El Paso, Texas, in September 1972 it was clear that a big majority of party activists favored maintaining independence from both the Democrats and Republicans.

The real test came in the actual campaign. The Texas party ran its most ambitious statewide election campaign and, despite programmatic limitations, it was clearly independent of and in opposition to the Democratic Party. In Colorado the Raza Unida Party also ran a clearly independent campaign, although on a smaller scale than the Texas party.

Although there are excellent opportunities for developing a powerful mass Raza Unida Party movement, the growth of the parties remains limited and uneven.

The clearest indication of this unevenness is the smallness of the Raza Unida groupings in Southern California, where there is a Chicano population of more than one million in Los Angeles County alone. Moreover, the Los Angeles Chicanos have repeatedly displayed their combativity, and several independent election campaigns have demonstrated significant support for independent political action. Yet, no leadership has emerged capable of organizing that support and consolidating even the nucleus of an independent party.

The Texas Raza Unida Party is the strongest, having enjoyed a growth in organizational and political influence over a period of several years. While even the Texas Raza Unida Party has achieved only a small part of its potential, its survival and progress offer testimony to the viability of the concept of an independent Chicano party.

The challenge that confronts these independent Chicano political formations is to win the Chicano masses away from the Democratic Party and to the banner of the Raza Unida parties. This can only be done by combining electoral actions with a program of immediate, democratic, and transitional demands around which the Chicano masses can be brought into struggle for their needs and aspirations. In the process of fighting around such a program, Chicanos will gain confidence in their own power and inspire other victims of capitalist injustice, winning them over as allies of the Chicano movement. Such an accomplishment would be a powerful example for emulation by Black organizations and trade unions.

Puerto Ricans in the United States

Some of the biggest changes in any of the oppressed national minorities since the radicalization of the 1930s have been among the Puerto Ricans. Because of the massive emigration from the island since World War II, 40 percent of all Puerto Ricans now live in the United States, with the largest number in New York City.

The superexploitation of the Puerto Rican colony by U.S. imperialism imposes conditions much worse than those on the mainland even in prosperous times. Prices are higher than in the United States, wages are one-third to one-half those on the mainland, and unemployment is three to four times higher. During a depression, this superexploitation has a catastrophic impact on the Puerto Rican working masses.

The Puerto Rican minority in the United States is concentrated in the hardest, lowest paid, and least organized jobs in industry. However, in some public employee unions such as the hospital employees and service workers, Puerto Ricans make up a considerable part of the membership, and they are a significant and growing percentage of the garment workers on the East Coast. There are also between 50,000 and 100,000 Puerto Rican seasonal farmworkers, most of whom are employed on the truck farms and in the tobacco fields of the East Coast.

The struggles of Puerto Ricans living in the United States are primarily directed against the racist discrimination they suffer and toward bettering their living and working conditions. In this sense they are distinct from the struggles in Puerto Rico. But the connections between Puerto Ricans living in the United States and in Puerto Rico also serve to link them with the struggle for independence in Puerto Rico and to the colonial revolution in general.

The Puerto Rican minority has been deeply affected by the Black struggle and has close contact with it because of the proximity of the Black and Puerto Rican populations in the ghettos and because there is a significant percentage of Black Puerto Ricans. However, the ruling class has tried to find ways, especially through the use of poverty funds, to pit Puerto Ricans and Blacks against each other and prevent them from uniting in struggle.

In a few cities in the Midwest, particularly Chicago, Puerto Rican and Chicano communities exist side by side. Struggles of mutual interest include those against discrimination on the basis of language and against the general racist abuses directed at people of Latino heritage, and the organization and mobilization of migrant farm laborers.

The right to bilingual education, bilingual civil service exams, bilingual ballots; the right to Spanish-speaking personnel in public facilities like hospitals and libraries; and the right to be able to conduct legal proceedings in Spanish are fundamental democratic rights around which significant battles are being fought. The struggle for Puerto Rican, Black, and Chinese community control over the schools in District One in New York City stands as one of the most advanced struggles of this type.

As with the Black and Chicano movements, the ruling class has sought to draw the Puerto Rican radicalization into the two-party system to prevent it from taking an independent route. Herman Badillo's election as the first Puerto Rican in Congress, representing the Bronx, is a case in point.

Native Americans

Their size, location, and place in industry do not give Native Americans the same social weight as Blacks, Chicanos, or Puerto Ricans. But their moral weight is immense. They stand as a living reminder of the real 400-year history of American capitalist expansion and its attendant degradation. They testify to the fact that class society could advance only on the basis of extermination of collectivist, egalitarian forms of social organization, and subsequent misery and crushing oppression of Native Americans.

The nationalist cultural awakening of the Native Americans and the growing militancy of their struggles against the abysmal conditions into which they have been driven has added another important element to the upsurge of the oppressed national minorities.

The coldly calculated victimization of the leadership of the American Indian Movement as part of a government plan to destroy it as an organization shows that the ruling class ascribes a political importance to Native American struggles beyond their social weight. Their demands for political and cultural autonomy, for respect of treaty rights, and for restoration of lands stolen from them are a component part of the coming American socialist revolution; the granting of these demands will be one of the responsibilities of the coming workers government.

Other oppressed national minorities

Chinese-Americans, Filipinos, Japanese-Americans, Dominicans, Haitians, Arabs, and other oppressed national minorities each have their own particular history of emigration, oppression, and superexploitation. American imperialism's white racist ideology has provided justification for discrimination against them as pariah sections of the industrial reserve army.

Lacking a social and political weight comparable to the Afro-Americans, Chicanos, or Puerto Ricans, these national minorities are neither as large in size nor as extensively employed in basic industry. Nevertheless, the radicalization and accompanying nationalist awakening have already increased the militancy of these groups against their oppression as racial minorities.

The emergence of Asian-Americans against the Vietnam War; the role of Chinese parents in the District One struggle for community control in New York; Asian-American student struggles in California; Chinese struggles against discriminatory hiring policies in the construction industry and against police brutality; the role of Filipinos in the California farmworkers' organizing drive; the actions of Dominicans and Haitians against the deportation of undocumented workers and political exiles; and the demonstrations of Arab auto workers are all signs of this development.

Even national or racial groupings that are not oppressed national minorities or nationalities in the United States suffer from the pervasive racism and xenophobia intensified by the ruling class in periods of social crisis. Anti-Semitism aimed at Jews is the clearest example.

Women

Women constitute both a growing percentage of the working class and an increasingly important ally of the working class. Women are not a minority. They constitute more than one-half the population and are not restricted to any geographical area, social stratum, or occupation. Like the American population as a whole, they are increasingly proletarian in composition.

Sexism is also one of the main ideological tools by which the ruling class keeps the working class divided, weakening class consciousness and unity, and reinforcing reactionary religious and obscurantist ideology.

Widespread acceptance of the idea that "woman's place is in the home" is used to promote the myth that women do not seek employment out of necessity but out of choice. The consignment of women to the home keeps a reservoir of extra labor available, and reduces the social costs and consequences of large numbers of periodically unemployed women.

The oppression of all women as a sex, like national oppression, creates a pariah section of the industrial reserve army, a labor pool whose superexploitation generates high rates of surplus value, helps drive down the wage level of all workers, and weakens the labor movement.

The oppression of women as a sex does not stem from the particular needs of capitalism alone. Its historic origins go back to the dawn of class society. Sexism is the necessary ideological underpinning of the maintenance of the family as an institution of class rule. The family is a primary mechanism for inculcating authoritarian, hierarchical attitudes into each new generation. It is the institution to which the rulers abdicate social responsibility and care for the young, the old, the sick, and the unemployed, and to which they shift the burden of economic crisis and breakdown—a burden felt especially keenly by the working class.

The struggle for women's liberation poses the problem of the total reorganization of society from its smallest repressive unit (the family) to its largest (the state). The liberation of women demands a thoroughgoing reorganization of society's productive and reproductive institutions in order to maximize social welfare and bring about a truly human existence for all.

The search for solutions to the issues raised by women's liberation is one of the driving forces of the coming American revolution. The ability of the workers vanguard to provide clear and concrete answers to the questions posed by capitalism's oppression of women and to fight for their realization will be decisive in mobilizing the forces necessary to overturn capitalism.

WOMEN'S LIBERATION MOVEMENT

A women's liberation movement emerged in the late 1960s with a political character and social depth vastly different from the forms through which women participated in the last working-class radicalization, in the 1930s. Three processes—developing over the postwar decades—led to this resurgence.

• The large-scale integration of women into the labor force and the significant rise in the general educational level that accompanied this process.

• The growing realization among millions of people that the development of the productive and technical capacities of industry and science has now made possible unlimited abundance and the socialization of "women's work" if society is rationally organized and planned.

• The challenge to bourgeois social and moral norms, a consequence of the broad radicalization, made it possible for significant numbers of women to develop as organizers and political leaders.

All of these conditions converged at the end of the 1960s when the antiwar movement and student radicalization were at their height. Many of the initial organizers of the women's groups came out of these movements. The rapid spread of the movement, its deep reverberations through all layers of society, penetrating into the organized labor movement, attested to the ripeness of the conditions that bred it.

Because of women's distribution throughout society, and the radical character of the questions posed, the rise of the women's liberation movement has already deeply affected mass consciousness and every aspect of culture in the broadest sense of the term. Literature, TV, movies, and other avenues have felt its impact. There is a tendency to challenge all values and mores and to review all aspects of existence, every facet of society by looking at them through women's eyes.

The most basic assumptions of class society about women are being carefully scrutinized and rejected by millions of women and men. The ferment over the woman question today recalls the radicalization of the Debsian pre–World War I period, or even the pre–Civil War radicalization, where the specific question of women's role in society was also a distinct component of the general social ferment—although on a much more restricted practical and theoretical basis. The vanguard role of women in other social movements is also parallel.

Struggles by women directed toward their emancipation are among the clearest indicators of the depth of the current *social* crisis and radicalization. The fact that these struggles began to emerge *before* the effects of a major economic crisis were felt confirms this all the more emphatically.

PROGRESS AND REACTION

The large increase in the percentage of employed women, in the number of women who are heads of households, and in the unionization of working women, combined with the rise of the women's liberation movement, has created a difficult problem for the ruling class. The acceptability of the use of women as reserve labor—the vast majority of women who drop out of the labor market in hard times are not even counted as unemployed—has been diminished.

As with the oppressed nationalities, the road toward true equality and equal opportunity for women lies through preferential treatment—quotas and affirmative action in industry, education, politics, and society—to correct the inequality of opportunity established by centuries of discrimination.

Thus, the attempt by the ruling class to wipe out the gains that oppressed national minorities and women made through preferential hiring and upgrading victories is an important part of the political and economic counteroffensive mounted by the Democrats and Republicans. And the resistance of women to being shoved out of work on the basis of last hired, first fired is growing. There has been rising opposition among women to having seniority rights broken by maternity leave, being denied access to apprenticeship programs for skilled or "heavy" jobs, receiving unequal pay, or being denied the right to participate in bargaining units because of "part-time" classifications.

The radicalization of women and the examples of direct action by others in the last decade have made housewives react with anger and frustration to the economic squeeze on their budgets and have led them to be more inclined to try to do something about it themselves. The 1973 meat boycott and the popularity of consumer investigations like those of Ralph Nader are harbingers of the protests to come.

The challenge to the bourgeois social order represented by the rise of the women's liberation movement means that the gains won by women have become a major target of reaction, second only to the Black movement. In Boston the antibusing drive, the attempt to reverse the right to abortion, and the anti-ERA demonstrations have provided an instructive example of the combination of targets selected in the country as a whole by the most rabid reactionary forces.

The right to abortion and constitutional and legislative guarantees of equal rights for women, as obvious as they may seem to some, represent a challenge to class society and its entire ideological superstructure. The protectors of the bourgeois order know this. They will continue to try to chip away at all such gains.

Many of the initial participants in the women's liberation movement rapidly faced a crisis of perspectives. Some were won to revolutionary Marxism. Others went in the direction of ultraleftism or forms of personal escapism. Still more were drawn into the two-party game of capitalist politics, where the ruling class was again quick to create openings for leaders of the movement.

Like the withdrawal of troops from Vietnam and abolition of the draft, the Supreme Court decision to legalize early abortions was part of the ruling class's general attempt to defuse the radicalization and eliminate some of the issues that had become focal points for mass mobilizations.

But the abortion victory, as with other democratic concessions to women, cannot eliminate the roots of the oppression of women or defuse their struggle for long. On the contrary, while such gains may lead to temporary lulls or downturns in mass action, over time they only serve to generate new demands and to create more favorable conditions for building an independent mass feminist movement capable of mobilizing women in struggle against their oppression.

Small farmers
The mobilization of the traditional petty-bourgeois allies of the working class in the United States poses problems far different from those in countries where the working class is a minority and surrounded by large numbers of independent producers, including a massive peasantry.

The extensive monopolization and mechanization of American agriculture in the decades since World War II; the vertical growth of many of these monopolies, giving them control of everything from the land, seeds, fertilizer, and farm machinery to harvesting, processing, packaging, distribution, and giant retail outlets; the generation of a sizable agricultural proletariat that has a significant "nonwhite" composition and is overwhelmingly seasonal and migrant; the transformation of many farmers' cooperative associations into big businesses or subsidiaries of the largest commercial banks; the internationalization of the agricultural monopolies, which play an important role in American imperialism's foreign policy—all this has been one of the biggest economic "revolutions" of the last quarter-century.

The elimination of the less productive small farmers who cannot compete with finance capital's collectivization, mechanization, and monopolization of food production continues. At the end of World War II, 17.5 percent of the population lived on the land. By 1960 this had fallen to 8.7 percent. Today it stands at 4.5 percent and continues to drop. During the same period farm output per hour of labor increased 600 percent. Agribusiness is now the sector of American imperialism with the greatest relative productivity edge over all foreign competitors.

The results of this gigantic explosion in agricultural productivity help highlight the disproportion between the productive capacity of American labor and the limitations and distortions of production and distribution brought about by the capitalist market and national boundaries. The glaring contrast of vast personal wealth for some while millions go hungry or die of famine has become one of the generators of the coming upheavals in both the United States and other countries.

While farm dwellers today constitute a small percentage of the total population, their importance is greater than their numbers would indicate. Disruption of the relationship between agriculture and industry directly affects the quantity, quality, and cost of the food, fibers, and other farm products the working class must buy. Soaring food prices, threatened shortages, as well as militant actions taken by small farmers to dramatize *their* plight, have brought this home to American workers in the last few years.

The Democratic and Republican politicians do their utmost to exacerbate conflicts between the farmer and worker, to set each against the other in order to maintain the dominance of capital over both. If the workers vanguard proves capable of pointing to and fighting for solutions to the problems faced by the small farmers, it will be able to win them to labor's side. Thus, the real antagonism—that between the small working farmer, the agricultural worker, and the urban proletariat on one side, and the interests of monopoly capitalism, including the giant agribusinesses on the other—will be understood and will emerge as one of the important elements in the coming American revolution.

The 'middle class'

While the monopolization of American capital has diminished the relative importance of the petty bourgeoisie, it has not eliminated it. In fact, monopolization continually breeds a petty bourgeoisie that occupies the cracks and crevices of production, distribution, and services, where they play an essential role. Some sectors of the petty bourgeoisie—those offering specialized services and technical skills—even increase in significance relative to the population as a whole and relative to their own past weight.

The exact configuration of the middle classes must always be examined concretely since it varies greatly from one country to another and often from one area to another inside a country.

For example, in the United States the independent owner-operator truckers—whose job action in early 1974 attracted national attention to the way they were being squeezed by soaring oil prices —play an important role in distribution. But, unlike France, the small independent baker is a marginal phenomenon.

It is also necessary to examine the spectrum of professionals, technicians, and others situated between wage labor and the bourgeoisie.

At one end, sizable numbers of teachers, technicians, service employees, government employees, etc., are really for the most part skilled or semiskilled, usually salaried, workers. They have no perspective of ever being able to make their living other than by selling their labor power to industry or the government. Their goal, in good times or bad, is not to open their own little school or laboratory somewhere. Growing numbers are willing to consider the idea that the solution to the social and economic squeeze they feel is to organize as part of the union movement and fight collectively—using labor's methods of struggle—to better their condition. The ruling class does its utmost to perpetuate the illusion that they are really "professionals" who belong to the "middle class," not the working class. In reality, however, the distinction between a teacher, or a lower salaried technician, or a municipal employee, and a woman or man on the assembly line at Chrysler is a distinction within the working class itself between skilled, semiskilled, and unskilled, between wage and salaried workers.

To an intermediate category belong the modern small masters, the independent truckers being one example. The small masters are a broad and variegated category, hybrids between capitalist and laborer. Included are those who have accumulated enough capital to begin to hire others to work along with them, those who are on the verge of becoming capitalists. Also included are those who simply own their own tools, even if they are expensive tools, hire no labor, and with each turn of the business cycle find themselves much closer to joining the unemployment lines as "fellow workers."

At the other end of the spectrum of professionals and technicians are the well-heeled doctors, engineers, and lawyers, many of whom are self-employed and whose skills are remunerated by the ruling class at a rate enabling them to live at a standard qualitatively above even the most skilled workers. They are able to make sizable investments, assuring them security in old age. This layer as a whole consciously identifies with the employing class, its political command, and its ideology.

However, even these professionals, especially the younger ones, are not immune to the changes in social values and mores, as actions like resident doctors' strikes in New York and New Orleans indicate. Beginning to react against capitalism's archaic and inhuman organization of medicine as a priestcraft, utilizing labor's methods of struggle, the young doctors are advancing demands that are quite comprehensible to the masses of workers (eighty-hour week; no more than forty-eight hours on duty at a stretch, etc.). The more radical young members of such professions can move sharply to the left under the hammer blows of a growing social crisis.

ALLIES AND FOES

Leaders of the working class also have to distinguish between occupations required to maintain the present *relations of production*, and those needed to maintain and expand the *forces of production*.

Among the former are those whose function is to increase the rate of exploitation (time-and-motion experts, foremen), those whose role is related to the state's repressive apparatus (cops, parole officers, certain social workers), and other social parasites (lawyers, advertising specialists, insurance agents).

Among the latter are many skilled individuals such as technicians, engineers, and statisticians.

History shows that while the vast majority of the former remain enemies of the movements of the workers and their allies, many of the latter can be attracted to a revitalized class-struggle workers movement and are needed in the tasks of establishing workers control of industry and planned production of the economy.

It is also important to examine carefully the character of protest actions often dubbed "middle class" by the media, that are taken under the pressures of capitalist crisis. Many are not petty-bourgeois actions as such, that is, actions aimed at winning demands that concern and interest the petty bourgeoisie as a specific social class (like the silver standard crusade among the small farmers of the 1880s and 1890s or the fight backed by small merchants to maintain "fair pricing" laws).

While large numbers of middle-class women were involved in and helped spark the meat boycott, for example, this was an action including and appealing to masses of workers as *consumers,* and certainly was not a petty-bourgeois movement.

Interest in and support to consumer protest and environmental protection movements, and muckraking exposés like those initiated by Ralph Nader and his associates are not the concern solely of the petty bourgeoisie and a thin layer of the most privileged workers. The availability and cost of credit for housing, cars, and durable consumer goods; the quality, operating costs, and safety of these goods; and the profiteering in utility rates, medical expenses, transportation costs, pension funds, the oil shortage, and similar items directly affect the great majority of the American working people.

The impact of protests around such problems is limited at present by the absence of a class-struggle labor leadership capable of linking up with them, associating the power of labor with them, and generalizing and leading them in a class-struggle direction. Nevertheless, these protests are bound to increase as the social crisis deepens, and the labor movement will find it more and more difficult to abstain from playing an active role in them. It will be increasingly obliged to participate not as part of the Democratic Party machine or through government agencies but as the independent and unifying organizer of the working people as a whole.

Students

Under the impact of a virtual technological revolution, the changes in the needs of American industry since World War II have meant vast alterations in the size and character of the student population since the 1930s. As potential allies of the proletariat, college students occupy a place different from the one they held earlier in the century, when they were predominantly bourgeois and petty-bourgeois careerists attending college to better prepare themselves to take on their responsibilities within the bourgeois world.

Today more than 75 percent of teen-age youth in the United States graduate from high school, and of those well over 50 percent go on to some college institution. The average number of years spent in school is one of the biggest differences between today's youth and the generation of their parents. In 1940 the average youth leaving school had not completed the ninth grade. Today the figure is 12.3 grades.

Another trend toward increasing education is illustrated in New York City, where open enrollment victories, won in the big student struggles at the end of the 1960s, more than tripled the number of Black and Puerto Rican college students.

Each student is, of course, deeply marked by his or her class origins. The family unit in which they are raised gives a child his or her first class identity, outlook, and expectations. Students are affected by the attitudes of the social class to which they belong, or to which they believe their education will lead them. But students as a social grouping *per se* have no direct specific relationship to production. In terms of their role in the economic structure, students do not function as workers, capitalists, or petty bourgeoisie. They are preparing to assume one of these economic roles. The majority of students today are on their way to becoming wage or salaried workers of some kind; and they anticipate a future in which they will be able to live only by offering their labor power for sale.

Thanks to the vast increase in the number of students, the percentage of workers with some college education is up; the percentage of college students who will become wage and salaried workers is up; the percentage who are working on jobs while going to college is up. The relative homogenization of social and ideological values of youth is increased by the length of time they spend together in high schools and college institutions.

While there can be a decline in the percentage of students as a proportion of the population because of conjunctural factors—especially economic downturns—there will be no fundamental reversal of the trend or the changes that have already taken place. The overall requirements of capitalist production and accumulation preclude this.

STUDENTS AND POLITICAL ACTION
Given the large concentrations of students, their social composition, intellectual stimuli, the antiauthoritarian attitude of many youth, and the relative freedom of student life, the majority of students can be highly sensitive to social and political issues. In large numbers they can be radicalized by and respond to major developments in the class struggle on a national and international scale. The concerns of the majority of students are part of this larger picture, and almost invariably related to it. The tendency of the majority of them today is to ally themselves with progressive social struggles taking place at home and abroad whose goals and values they can understand and appreciate.

The new political importance and potential of students, resulting from the massive post–World War II expansion of the educational system, was admirably demonstrated by the key role the student movement played in developing and maintaining a mass opposition to the imperialist war in Vietnam. This experience drove home the permanent importance of systematic political work among students, organized through a revolutionary socialist youth organization.

The "red university" strategy, on which the Trotskyist youth organization, the Young Socialist Alliance, has been built, is not a narrow "student power" orientation, but an overall strategy intended to help turn the universities into organizing centers at the service of the working class and its allies—including the students—in their struggles. They are bases from which to win large numbers of campus youth to Trotskyism and to the revolutionary workers movement.

In the period since the signing of the Paris peace accords and the withdrawal of U.S. combat personnel from Vietnam there has been a downturn in the intensity of student political activities. But it would be a mistake to confuse a period of relative quiescence with either a basic turn to the right or a long phase of political apathy on the campuses.

The campuses have become permanent centers of dissatisfaction and protest. Many students are losing confidence in the capitalist system and the institutions and future of American bourgeois democracy. But as throughout the rest of society, the coming crises will have a *polarizing* effect on the campuses. This polarization will turn the campuses into an important battleground of competition for political cadres between the reactionary right and radical left, as well as among the various working-class tendencies. There will be no return to the long political quiescence of the late 1940s and 1950s.

The GIs

The ranks of the armed forces must also be counted as one of the most important allies of the working class. Young, overwhelmingly working class in composition, and with a high percentage drawn from the oppressed nationalities, the soldiers today are deeply affected by all the changes taking place in their generation and their class. Because of their assigned role as cannon fodder for the interests of private property and imperialist oppression and aggrandizement at home and around the world, their attitudes are of great importance.

Unlike World War II when there was general—if at bottom reluctant—support for the "war against fascism," the Vietnam War from the very beginning generated profound suspicion concerning the motives and goals of the rulers, and growing opposition among GIs to being used in Washington's schemes to police the world.

The antiwar radicalization and deepening disaffection within the army itself—reflecting the attitudes prevalent in the rest of American society—was one of the important factors that blocked U.S. imperialism from pursuing the war of aggression in Vietnam. The emergence of the antiwar GI as a conspicuous and widely popular figure marked a change in thinking of historic import.

The American army, owing to its composition and to today's political climate, is less and less suited to play its assigned role as a world police force. The American imperialists know full well that they must have such an instrument because planes, bombs, and the dragooned troops of a puppet regime are often not sufficient, as Vietnam has again demonstrated. But Washington does not have too many options. The legacy of the Vietnam War and the accompanying radicalization outside and inside the army is one of the new minus factors the ruling class must include in its calculations.

Every social protest movement—women's liberation, the radicalization of the national minorities, gay liberation, etc.—was reflected inside the armed forces.

The radicalization within the army itself inevitably focuses on the struggle to defend and extend the democratic rights of the soldiers. The concept of the citizen-soldier as one who gives up none of his elementary freedoms and rights upon entering the armed forces is deeply embedded in American history from the time of the militia forces of the Revolutionary War to the present. Such concepts, which originated 200 years ago in the popular support for the political goals of the militia forces, are anathema to a military caste formed in the Prussian pattern. But they are so closely associated with the fundamental rights the American people believe to be theirs that the ruling class has not dared to risk a head-on confrontation on this matter during a period of rising mass antiwar sentiment.

The ruling class's decision to eliminate the draft in hopes of creating a more reliable instrument for implementing its imperialist aims creates two new problems for them. First, the rising percentage of Black troops in the combat divisions leads to a composition of this repressive force that makes it less reliable for use against the colonial revolution or in the suppression of ghetto uprisings and labor battles at home. Second, modern wars cannot be fought without conscription; and attempts to reintroduce the draft in the future, as the ruling class will be obliged to do in new imperialist aggressions, will inevitably call forth a quicker and greater antidraft sentiment than appeared during the Vietnam War.

VI. The real course of American bourgeois democracy

Bourgeois democracy in America has had an uninterrupted 200-year history. During that time, extensions of democratic rights—beginning with white male property owners—have been gradually won despite reactionary attempts to reverse the process. The gains were made at great cost. To win even elementary rights for non-property owners, nonwhites, workers, Blacks, women, and youth, a second revolution and civil war and immense efforts in the class struggle over a prolonged period were required.

But these gains in rights are only one aspect of bourgeois democracy in America. As a form of class rule that only rich capitalist ruling classes can afford, American democracy has always rested on brutal force and crushing exploitation. First and foremost was slavery. There were also other forms of forced servitude, the expropriation and virtual extermination of the Native American population, the conquest and incorporation of half of Mexico, the superexploitation of immigrant labor, spoliation of vast natural resources, and the advance into the Caribbean, Latin America, and the Philippines.

As American imperialism emerged in the late nineteenth century, the continuation of bourgeois democracy in America increasingly required the massive superexploitation of other countries, the vast international "slave holdings" of American capitalism.

The economic crisis of the world capitalist system in the 1930s ended the prosperity and ate into the reserves on which dollar democracy rested. Democracy in the weaker imperialist countries (Italy, Germany, Spain, Portugal) went under first. If the capitalists instead of the workers were to have the last say, the political future of the United States was foreshadowed in the march of reaction and fascism in Europe.

Cold War to Vietnam

Post–World War II democracy in America was based on the uncontested domination of U.S. imperialism, which had vanquished its rivals (both "Axis" and "Allies") and brought whole new sections of the world under its yoke. Much of the former empires of the British, Dutch, French, Italian, German, Belgian, and Japanese ruling classes fell. U.S. imperialism took over the colonial slaves of its competitors. To keep them in bondage, financial, political, and military support—American foreign "aid"—were extended to the most brutally repressive and totalitarian "independent" regimes throughout the former colonial world.

The advances of the socialist revolution following World War II were countered with the institutionalization of the Cold War at home. The reactionary domestic political climate was intended to support a world anticommunist "rollback" strategy.

The first phase of the Cold War involved utilizing the monopoly of the atomic bomb to put heavy pressure on the Soviet Union. In preparation for war, careful attention was paid to the home front. Efforts were intensified to whip the liberals into line behind the Cold War and to strike at the militancy and independence of the CIO. By the end of the 1940s the witch-hunt had largely succeeded in housebreaking the CIO bureaucracy and intimidating the ranks of labor. With the "loss of China," the Cold War was deepened in the United States. A protracted period of conservatism and labor quiescence set in.

McCarthyism, which was the extension of the Cold War antilabor policies and loyalty purges initiated by Truman, had an incipient fascist logic of its own that eventually proved counterproductive to the ruling class. The reactionary Wisconsin demagogue had his wings clipped. But it was only the world capitalist boom of the 1950s and 1960s that provided the economic base for eliminating, for the time being, any serious threat of a fascist advance within the United States. In the post–Korean War period the "normal" methods of bourgeois-democratic rule proved adequate.

The qualitative disparity between the economic, financial, and military power of the United States and that of its competitors insured American imperialism's dominance. There seemed to be no limits—military, economic, or political—to Washington's arrogant actions as world cop, although the military stalemate in Korea, and the less than fervent patriotic sacrifices of labor in that intervention on the mainland of Asia, gave warning signals of what was to come.

The rulers were convinced they could provide sufficient quantities of both guns and butter. They believed they could both militarily crush resistance to imperialism abroad and make wage concessions at home ample enough to assure social peace. The capitalist economy, touted to be free of depressions, brought a feeling of relative security to broad layers of the working class to whom the Great Depression was still a vivid personal memory. It also fashioned a "silent generation" of youth in the 1950s. For that entire decade the only significant social struggle was that of Black people, who fought largely on their own, unsupported by the labor movement or other powerful forces.

The decisive turning point came in the second half of the 1960s, following Johnson's decision in 1965 to escalate armed intervention in Vietnam. Primed earlier by the small "ban the bomb" movement and the Cuban revolution, and spurred on by the Black struggle and the student radicalization, Johnson's escalation gave rise to an unprecedented antiwar movement and radicalization. For the first time in American history an imperialist war became the catalyst for mass political opposition to the policies of the regime.

The Vietnam radicalization originated in a growing appreciation of the hypocrisy of the claim that the White House was establishing democracy abroad. The forced evacuation of villages and the My Lais of the Kennedy-Johnson years, the napalming of children, the Nixon-Kissinger carpet bombings, the Tiger Cages, the invasion of Cambodia—these crimes stirred mounting revulsion from 1965 through Nixon's second inaugural in 1973.

DEMOCRACY'S TRUE FACE

This sentiment was accompanied by the growing conviction that there must be some connection between the actions of American imperialism abroad and the methods applied against domestic critics. The police assaults on the Black civil rights fighters in the South, the habitual police brutality against the inhabitants of the Black ghettos in the North and South, the murderous suppression of the ghetto rebellions, the police rampage against the demonstrators at the 1968 Democratic Party convention in Chicago, capped by the Kent State and Jackson State massacres during the May 1970 Cambodian invasion, drove home the point that the real face of American democracy was something quite different from the pleasant countenance millions of Americans had been taught to revere.

Underneath the formal liberties and democratic guarantees, the real decisions were made in secret by a tiny minority with brutal disregard for the needs, interests, or rights of the majority.

President after president from Truman to Nixon pretended to speak in candid terms to the American people, only to be exposed as liars and self-serving hypocrites. The demagogic double-talk of capitalist politics became clearer.

All this developed before there was widespread knowledge, or even suspicion, of the degree of secret government infiltration, surveillance, provocation, and disruption of the Black, antiwar, and radical movements. It was unthinkable to the majority of the American people that such practices were applied not only to the "radical" or "minority" social protest movements but to the labor movement and even the "loyal opposition" within the two-party system.

When such things began to come to light in the Watergate affair, a chain reaction was set off that has not ended. The Watergate experience marked the opening of a stage in which people are more perceptive and critical in judging the nature of the institutions of bourgeois democracy, the nature of the executive powers, the system of checks and balances, the role of Congress, secret diplomacy, etc.

The Watergate revelations about the application of imperialist policies abroad were new and shocking to millions. But most significant was their deeper impact in altering public consciousness: the feeling became widespread that foreign and domestic policy may be but two sides of the same coin.

Imperial arrogance, contempt for human values, unspeakable brutality, disregard for the fundamental democratic rights the American masses believe in, police-state methods of political spying, provocation, and assassination—these are not only the policies of American capitalism abroad; they are the practices of American capitalism at home.

The single most important ideological gain of the initial radicalization was a loss of confidence in the veracity of the capitalist leaders of the United States. This has been reinforced by the Watergate crisis and the attempted cover-ups, along with the offshoot exposés concerning the FBI, CIA, IRS, and secret diplomacy. They have deepened popular doubt about the rulers' intention to administer a government or to decide domestic and foreign policy in the *interests* of the broad majority.

The confidence of the American working people in their own ability to see things as they are, and their feeling that there is no remedy but to take action in *their own interests* have grown as their trust in the "elected officials" has diminished.

The radicalization of the last decade can be measured in the escalation of the struggle for fundamental freedoms. This includes legal and democratic rights, but goes beyond them. Motivating the struggle is a basic stand in favor of what Malcolm X called *human rights*.

This concept of inalienable human rights has motivated all the social movements of the 1960s and early 1970s—struggles by Blacks, women, prisoners, soldiers, veterans, farmworkers, mine workers, "illegal" residents, gays, and the aged.

Concurrent with the growing determination to extend and redefine basic freedoms and to prevent acquired rights from being eroded, millions of Americans sense that American capitalism is heading in an antidemocratic direction.

Such forebodings are well founded. The four classical conditions for the maintenance of imperialist democracy—sustained economic prosperity, a satisfied or docile working class, contentment among major sectors of the petty bourgeoisie and other potential allies of the working class, and a successful foreign policy—all are being eroded.

VII. Labor's strategic line of march

The Marxist model for constructing a revolutionary program in the imperialist epoch is the founding document of the Fourth International, the world party of socialist revolution, founded by Leon Trotsky in 1938. The program is entitled *The Death Agony of Capitalism and the Tasks of the Fourth International.*[3]

This "Transitional Program," as it has come to be known, was adopted by the Socialist Workers Party and presented for discussion and approval to the founding congress of the Fourth International at a time when world capitalism had been undergoing a deep economic and social crisis for nearly a decade. The new economic downturn of 1937 had further deepened political polarization in America. Both fascist currents and labor party sentiments were on the rise in this country. The New Deal was becoming the "War Deal" as the clouds of World War II gathered rapidly, threatening unheard-of slaughter and destruction.

Neither the Stalinized Communist Party nor the social democrats, nor the assorted ultraleft, sectarian, and centrist groupings were capable of presenting a program adequate to the needs of the masses searching for a way out of the crisis. In Trotsky's estimation, solidly planting the Fourth International on a correct programmatic foundation was a key requirement.

Today's situation offers some important parallels, both in the objective situation and in the tasks facing revolutionists. After almost a quarter-century of expansionary development, world capitalism has entered a period of economic stagnation—with the threat of debilitating inflation, shortages, famine, unemployment, bank failures, business crashes, world depression, sudden political shifts, and severe crises. Cyclical economic crises in each country tend to be deeper and more synchronized internationally.

This will inevitably lead to a sharpening of the American class struggle in all its forms and to deepening class polarization. While the tempo of this polarization cannot be predicted, its general features are clear. Millions of workers will search for the road to independent political action and will more and more turn to class-struggle methods. On the other hand, rightist demagogues and fascist movements pretending to offer "radical" solutions to the capitalist crises will come forward as candidates for power.

The sharpening of interimperialist competition and conflict, the pressure for a redivision of markets on a world scale, the persistent tendency toward wars directed at halting the colonial revolution—with China and the Soviet Union as the ultimate targets—are all on the agenda. And any military adventure by the White House carries with it the threat of escalating into a nuclear showdown.

The confusion and disorientation generated by the Stalinists, social democrats, and the new assortment of ultralefts, centrists, and opportunists demonstrate that the need for clarity on program and perspectives remains decisive.

As in 1938, we can see unfolding on a world scale a prerevolutionary period of education, organization, and agitation. After a long period of relative quiescence, the workers in the advanced capitalist countries, beginning with the weaker of the European imperialist powers, are once again beginning to move. Sections of the masses more and more tend to enter into action, and are open to revolutionary alternatives, as they seek a way out of the impasse.

Method of the revolutionary program

In the United States, as elsewhere, the revolutionists constitute a relatively small nucleus grappling with two central problems:

• How to help the masses, through their own experiences of struggle, to cross the bridge from general dissatisfaction and demands that stem from their immediate problems, to revolutionary socialist solutions.

• How, in this process, to gather fresh forces and train the cadres who, in the course of their experiences in the class struggle, can build a mass revolutionary party capable of leading millions of working people to victory.

The key to the solution of these problems is the correct and flexible utilization of the method of the Transitional Program, giving clear and timely answers to the problems faced by the working class and its allies in their struggles.

The conversion of the current radicalization into a revolutionary situation will be determined by mass forces beyond our control.

In this situation we must strive to use whatever time we have to win members and gain experience in the class struggle. We must strive to reduce whatever relative advantage the Stalinists or social democratic currents have over us in size and position in sectors of the labor movement, organizations of the oppressed nationalities, and other sectors of the mass movement.

Several points must be borne in mind in relation to the method of our program, the transitional method:

• We begin from the *objective* contradictions of the capitalist system and the direction in which these are moving. On that basis we derive our demands, and we formulate them in terms that are, as much as possible, understandable to the masses at their given level of consciousness and readiness for action.

• We do not begin by demanding that the masses understand what "the system" is or that they reject any particular aspects of it. Instead we chart a course, raise demands, and propose actions aimed at shifting the burden of all the inequities and breakdowns of capitalism from the shoulders of the working people onto the employers and their government, where it properly belongs.

• We champion the progressive demands and support the struggles of all sectors of the oppressed, regardless of the origin and level of these actions.

• We recognize the pervasiveness of the deep divisions within the American working class bred by imperialism and class society, and we press for revolutionary unity based on support for the demands of the most oppressed. We press the working class to give clear and concrete answers to the problems faced by its allies. And we unconditionally reject any concept that the oppressed should "wait" for the labor movement to support them before entering into their own struggles.

• We raise demands that challenge the "rights" of capitalist property and prerogatives claimed by the government to control the lives of the working masses and the wealth they create. We do not stop with the necessary struggle to defend and extend all democratic rights. We carry the fight for democracy into the organization of the economy and the process of making decisions over the standard of living of the working class. This is the dynamic leading to control by the workers over the institutions and policies that determine the character of their work and life, the dynamic of direct democracy through councils or committees of action, and the dynamic leading to a workers government.

• Our method is one of class-struggle action leading to deeper and clearer class consciousness. We promote the utilization of proletarian methods of struggle where the workers can make their weight count advantageously in direct mass actions in the streets and in the workplaces. In this perspective united-front-type tactics are central. Our goal of mass independent political action by the working class precludes any subordination to the needs of bourgeois parties, figures, or institutions. It necessitates the workers building their own political instrument, a mass party of the working class capable of leading their struggles to their revolutionary conclusion, the establishment of a workers government.

Think socially; act politically

To meet this revolutionary perspective the American workers will have to learn to think socially and act politically. They must see the big social and political questions facing *all* the exploited and oppressed of the United States as issues of direct concern to them. They must stop placing their hopes in "individual solutions" to capitalism's blows and begin moving toward collective political action independent of the employers and their Democratic and Republican hirelings.

Defensive struggles against the bosses and their government will generate the nuclei for a class-struggle left wing in the unions. Striving to defend themselves against the squeeze on jobs, real income, social welfare, and on-the-job conditions, the workers will come into direct confrontation with the entrenched labor bureaucracy and its class-collaborationist perspective. A class-struggle left wing will begin along these lines—a wing that stands for the transformation of the unions into instruments of revolutionary struggle whose independent power will be used on every level in the interests of the whole working class, organized and unorganized, and its allies.

Labor's next giant step will be to break the stranglehold of the bourgeois two-party system to which it is tied and through which it vainly tries to find solutions to capitalism's breakdowns. With a labor party based on the organized power of the unions, all the interrelated social, political, and economic interests of labor and its allies can be encompassed and fought for. This will reinforce the independent mobilizations of all sectors of the oppressed and help aim their force at the common enemy. And the workers can effectively counter the efforts of the rulers to diffuse and co-opt independent struggles of the masses by using their two-party monopoly.

The precise slogans and demands that will be raised, and the order in which they will appear, will depend on the development of the crises faced by American imperialism and the intensity of the pressures generated by the spontaneous struggles of the oppressed and exploited. But it is along this line of march that the politicalization of American labor will take place. The role of independent political action will begin to become clear to millions, placing on the agenda the decisive question of which class shall govern—the workers or the employers.

Against the imperialist war machine

The task of hobbling and disarming the American imperialist world cops with their vast arsenal of nuclear weapons is a special responsibility of the American workers. No other force can do the job. The survival of humanity rests on their ability to accomplish this task in time. We demand immediate, unilateral, unconditional nuclear disarmament of U.S. imperialism.

The enormous size of Wall Street's war budget is difficult to grasp. The billions in resources consumed by the war budget must be reallocated to help meet the basic needs of the workers and their allies. The first step in that direction should be a 100 percent tax on all profits made from armaments production. Take the profits out of war.

We reject the insidious lie that the workers have no choice but to rely on massive "defense" industry contracts or else suffer large-scale unemployment. The war industry plants must be national-ized and put under the control of workers committees charged with retooling for the production of useful goods.

The U.S. military machine is the key piece in all the imperialist alliances. Our call is: out now—an end to NATO, an end to all the imperialist pacts. Support and link up with the struggles by work-ers and youth in other countries against NATO. End all the mili-tary and diplomatic alliances that are directed against the colonial masses and the workers states. Hands off the workers struggles unfolding in the imperialist countries.

Labor should insist on the dissolution of all special paramilitary or "advisory" bodies set up to police situations where the use of U.S. troops would be embarrassing to Washington but which of-ten serve as a preliminary step for open aggression. Get out of the Mideast. End the military and CIA police training programs around the world.

No support to reactionary butcher regimes, the puppets of im-perialism. End all the fake "food for peace" programs and other so-called humanitarian props to these regimes around the globe.

INTERNATIONAL SOLIDARITY

The American workers have a special responsibility toward the co-lonial revolution because of U.S. imperialism's role as the fore-most slave master in the world. The slogan expressing our funda-mental line is: HANDS OFF! No intervention anywhere. The half-million GIs stationed abroad must be brought home now.

We pay special attention to the fight against racism, xenophobia, and all forms of chauvinism, which are a powerful ideological prop of imperialist foreign policy and supply implicit justification for colonial aggression. In this respect the fight against racism at home is closely linked with the fight against imperialist aggression abroad.

In the spirit of international class solidarity we champion the rights of foreign students and workers in the United States and uphold their freedom to travel, immigrate, study, work, live, and engage in political activity wherever they wish.

It is the youth, especially its most oppressed and exploited sections, who are called upon to fight imperialism's wars. In the long run the Pentagon cannot raise an army large enough to meet Wall Street's needs without conscription. Opposition to counterrevolutionary wars is at the heart of our opposition to the capitalist draft.

We take the offensive in regard to democracy within the armed forces. Soldiers have the right to know and to discuss the true aims of the government, to form political associations, to publish their own leaflets and papers.

We fight for the right of the citizen-soldier to exercise every democratic right guaranteed to other Americans, including the right to run for office.

Old enough to be squeezed into the "volunteer" army—old enough to vote and hold office.

End secret diplomacy and backstage deals. Publish all secret international correspondence. The people have a right to know all commitments made by the government.

Take the war-making powers out of the hands of Congress. Let the people vote directly on war.

In defense of the working class
The starting point of workers struggles is the defense of their standard of living and conditions of work.

In a society based on exploitation, a decent job is the most fundamental right of every worker.

In a depression, the first requisite in addition to unemployment insurance is a massive program of public works. Another called-for emergency measure is reduction of the workweek, with no reduction in take-home pay, in order to spread the work among those who need jobs.

The trade unions and other mass organizations of the workers and oppressed must take responsibility for organizing workers with jobs, those without jobs, and those with only "part-time" jobs. They should prevent the employers from creating a pariah category of unemployed whom the employed do not regard as fellow workers. Those out of work must be viewed as part of "us," not as "them."

To protect themselves against inflation, which is a permanent scourge today, the working class needs a sliding scale of wages—an escalator clause—with prompt and full compensation for every rise in the cost of living. A consumer price index drawn up under the supervision of the workers and consumers—not the bosses—is required. Escalator clauses must cover all social welfare payments, such as unemployment benefits and Social Security.

The workers and their families will have to fight to keep social welfare programs from being eliminated and to bring them up to adequate standards. During periods of unemployment, health insurance coverage should be maintained by the government. Mortgages and installment payments on homes, cars, appliances, and furnishings should likewise be underwritten by the government. Child-care facilities must be kept open and expanded.

Unemployment compensation should be at full union scale, and with no time limit.

The threat of being laid off and denied an income because of the bosses' control over hiring and firing is the source of all pernicious "job discipline." The bosses must be prevented from using rising unemployment to reverse gains the working class has won and to divide the working class.

The seniority system won through previous battles by the workers movement is one tool in limiting the bosses from picking and choosing whom they will fire at will, starting with the most militant workers. It, like the hiring hall and closed shop, established a degree of workers control over hiring and firing. In a similar way the workers will have to prevent the bosses' use of "last hired, first fired" to reverse the gains recently made through preferential hiring and affirmative action quotas. Layoffs cannot be allowed to reduce the proportions of minority and women workers.

The trade union movement should also firmly reject all attempts by the monopolists to solve their own profit problems at the expense of workers abroad. Protectionist measures professedly aimed at "keeping jobs in the United States" have the central object of permitting U.S. corporations to charge higher prices and reap greater profits in the face of foreign competition. They are no less inflationary than the devaluation of the dollar, which deprives workers of the possibility of purchasing less expensive foreign-made goods. Protectionism, tariffs, devaluations, are all aimed at workers in the last analysis, whether here or abroad.

WORKERS CONTROL ON THE JOB

On the job the workers must protect themselves from the attempts of the bosses to extract a higher rate of surplus value through speedup, automation, chipping away at health and safety standards, and all the other ways of making the workers pay for the capitalists' growing problems.

Struggles will grow for protection against speedup and layoffs, for safety and health conditions, regulation of and veto power over work rules, and health codes to protect workers against industrial hazards—asbestos fibers, coal dust, and chemical or radiation poisoning.

The workers must have veto power on questions of safety. They should insist that production be shut down at once on demand of the workers and at no loss in pay whenever safety of personnel is at stake. All safety controls and the speed of the production line must be set by the workers themselves. Acceptable levels of chemical pollution, control over purification of waste products, and similar standards must be established by the workers after full access to technical information and consultation with experts of their own choice.

Workers committees must be empowered to decide directly, in consultation with citizens committees responsible to the community, on projects to establish plants or use industrial processes that may adversely affect the environment of cities and regions. Such decisions have to be made on the basis of full and accurate information about the ecological and health effects involved, and with no concern for profits such as motivates the lobbyists and government representatives of big business. Only labor can fight to put science to work as the liberator of humanity, not its destroyer.

Just as they must reject the false dilemma of having to choose between unemployment or making instruments of mass murder, workers must reject the lies of the bosses that they cannot afford to stay in business unless pollution controls are lifted and safety standards lowered. The workers and the community cannot afford pollution, shutdowns, or bosses who put profits above all other considerations. Any plant closed down by such bosses must be nationalized and reopened under the control of workers committees with complete access to all the financial and technical information required for retooling or meeting the requisite standards on pollution and safety.

OPEN THE BOOKS

"Open the books for inspection by the workers" is a necessary provision to protect the public against the shortages, sudden breakdowns, and rampant inflation endemic in the decline of capitalism and to counter any claims of the bosses that they cannot satisfy the needs of the workers, either as employees or consumers.

The claimed "right to business secrecy" is used by the employers' bankers and their politicians in a drive to cut back on wages, working conditions, and public services in every city, county, state, and federal jurisdiction they control through their two-party system. When monopolies like the utilities, the postal service, the agribusinesses, the railroads, and the aerospace industries cry "bankruptcy," charge exorbitant rates or prices, or refuse services to those who cannot pay, they should be nationalized and run under control of the workers and worker-consumer committees.

In order to make their decisions on a sound basis, the workers committees will have to proceed in cooperation with similar committees throughout their industry on a national scale, and other industries in their region. The facts must be shared nationally and internationally, and the public kept fully informed.

To acquire the needed information and resources of credit and planning, the entire banking system—now the accounting and credit system of the capitalist class—will have to be expropriated and opened up to the committees of workers and placed under their control as well. Only by winning that struggle can the workers begin planning and organizing the economy so as to prevent breakdowns, chaos, and the lowering of the standard of living of the entire working class and its allies. And along this line of march, beginning with individual industry and sectors, the expropriation of the bourgeoisie will be posed.

Even partial steps along this course, imposed by a rising mass movement that is rapidly gaining in social and political consciousness and led by a growing class-struggle wing of organized labor, will meet with stiff resistance from the bosses. To them it is a sacrosanct prerogative to run their business as they see fit—to keep the details of their operations secret from those they exploit, to throw thousands onto the unemployment lines, to charge extortionate prices, to move "their" factories to where the workers are less organized and less experienced in fighting for their rights, to slash the educational system and social services the workers have fought for, to destroy the earth's ecosystem if this will assure high profits today, to use legislatures and "public" agencies to advance their schemes to make a fast buck.

An increase in class polarization will go hand in hand with deepening class struggle. Fascism, along with war, was the ultimate "solution" imposed by the ruling class to the last world capitalist crisis.

To protect their struggles and gains against murderous attacks by goons, cops, and fascist bands, the workers will have to organize and train their own forces and use them in the most effective way. Starting with defense of picket lines and the right to strike, the protection of their demonstrations or those of their allies, and proceeding to workers defense guards, workers militias, and the requisite arming of the working class, the working masses will learn from their own experiences what measures to take. The lessons of history, incorporated into the general strategy of the workers movement, will prove invaluable on this life-and-death question.

Human rights, not property rights

The strong belief of the American people that they are entitled to basic democratic rights has a progressive dynamic. As the capitalist system declines, bourgeois democracy does not gain in vigor but grows progressively weaker. This will lead to struggles that tend to go beyond the limitations of bourgeois democracy and strengthen the radicalization and politicalization of the American working class. Thus a fundamental responsibility of socialist workers and a feature of their program is to defend and strive to extend democratic rights against every attempt by reaction to encroach upon them or to roll them back.

The workers must fight to protect themselves against the bosses' attacks upon the right to organize; the right to strike, including the right to strike against the government; the right to vote on contracts; the right to settle all issues in a dispute without any government interference or government meddling in union affairs. Above all the workers must fight against wage controls proposed or imposed by the government under whatever name or guise.

The workers have everything to gain from taking the offensive whenever possible in behalf of those social and economic rights that they more and more consider their due—decent housing, decent jobs, education, transportation, health, social security, freedom from government harassment, etc. In the course of struggle they will learn the necessity of fighting to extend human rights for all the allies of the proletariat. Every such gain reinforces the strength and unity of the working class as a whole.

The struggle to maintain rights already won and to extend them to new areas—economic rights, social rights, rights on the job, rights to a direct say on issues of war and peace—has marked every aspect of the radicalization. This is exemplified in the struggles for abortion rights and the Equal Rights Amendment; the eighteen-year-old vote; civil rights for less than "legal" age high school students; human rights for soldiers, veterans, gays, the elderly, and children; full human rights for all prisoners; language rights; rights of noncitizens.

Still other rights have been redefined in the course of struggle—attempts to impose prior-restraint laws on publications have been fought with some success, literary and artistic censorship restricted, and capital punishment curtailed.

There is growing recognition of the right to preferential treatment—quotas, affirmative action in industry, education, politics, and society—to correct the inequality of opportunity established by centuries of discrimination because of race, nationality, or sex. Millions of working people see that without this there can be no true equality or equal opportunity for those historically oppressed and discriminated against by class society.

None of these advances have been won without hard struggle, and each gain has to be defended against attempts to dilute or reverse it.

The vision of the social and economic rights people should have is being considerably widened. They include the idea that every human being has a right to enough food, to decent housing, medical care, education, and well-made products; that tenants and urban residents have rights; and even that future generations have rights—the right to an environment capable of healthfully sustaining human life.

The fight to extend democratic rights into industry means establishing various forms of direct democracy. It necessitates finding ways and means for the workers and their allies themselves to make the fundamental decisions that affect their lives instead of letting the bosses and their political representatives do that for them. It means establishing broad united action committees through which the workers and their allies can fight to impose their solutions to economic and social problems, both at the workplace and in society as a whole.

THE RIGHT TO KNOW

As demands for *personal* privacy have increased, so have demands to *limit government and industry's* "rights" to secrecy. Not only is there a feeling that our lives are our own business but that "their" business is our business, too.

The exposures of government lies and duplicity in domestic and foreign policy have led to greater acceptance of the idea that the people have a right to *know* what the government is up to, what deals have been made behind closed doors, what commitments contrary to the interests of average working Americans have been made. Such mechanisms of direct democracy as referendums on major policy issues like the war, child care, and environmental questions have become increasingly popular, as the assumed prerogatives of the bourgeoisie to rule through institutions elected under their rules are challenged.

We persistently struggle to extend the frontiers of what the workers consider to be their inalienable economic, social, and political rights that no government has the right to take away from them.

And in all these efforts we advocate proletarian methods of struggle based on the mobilization of the collective strength of the workers and their allies independent of the needs or desires of the rulers and their institutions.

VIII. The revolutionary party

The breakdowns and cyclical fluctuations of the American economy are rooted in the contradictions of world capitalist production and trade. The very ascent of American capitalism to world supremacy has paved the way for a cataclysmic explosion on its home grounds.

In America, a country that has never been carpet-bombed, invaded, occupied, or made to pay war indemnities, capitalism for all its achievements has not been able to assure liberty, justice, and a decent standard of living for all of its people. As the mightiest and wealthiest capitalist power celebrates the 200th birthday of its revolutionary origin, growing numbers of Americans are beginning to ask, "If not here, then where?" If capitalism can't make good in the United States, maybe something is decidedly wrong.

The end of the long postwar boom, and the rise of unrest and social struggles in the United States, once again call attention to the fact that the victory of the European socialist revolution is not a necessary prerequisite for the development of a revolutionary situation in the United States.

Just as the first workers and peasants revolution could succeed in Russia, where the operation of the law of uneven and combined development thrust the most backward of the major capitalist countries in Europe to the forefront of the world revolution, so those same laws can produce severe shocks in the coming period within the heartland of the most advanced imperialist power.

But even the most devastating breakdowns of American capitalism cannot automatically produce a victory for the socialist revolution. As Lenin pointed out, there is no absolutely hopeless situation for capitalism. However deep the crisis, if enough commodities can be destroyed or devalued through war, depression, and bankruptcy, and the standard of living of the working class can be driven low enough, capitalism can recover for the moment.

While powerful *world* forces are laying powder kegs under American imperialism, only forces *inside* the United States can take power away from the American capitalists and disarm them. In the nuclear age this is more decisive for humanity's salvation than ever before; the alternatives are the eclipse of civilization or a worldwide scientifically planned economy.

Various developments in the United States can leap ahead of those in other parts of the world in a rather brief period. In the last decades this happened with the rise of the struggles of oppressed nationalities, the antiwar movement, the youth radicalization, the women's liberation movement, and similar struggles for human rights. At the same time the advanced decay of American capitalism poses problems to these movements that cannot be solved short of a socialist revolution. And at a certain point revolutionary trends within the American working class can develop at a truly American speed and tempo.

Questions of perspective, program, and party building cannot be postponed with the expectation that they will be resolved by the colossal objective forces of a revolutionary upsurge. On the contrary, even a small propaganda nucleus that intends to become a mass party must be armed with a clear revolutionary perspective that puts the construction of the revolutionary party in first place.

The social democrats and Stalinists
There has been a striking change since the 1930s in the relationship of forces between the revolutionary party—the Socialist Workers Party—and its reformist socialist opponents on the left.

The American social democracy retains a base in the labor bureaucracy, where its influence is stronger than its small and fragmented organizations would indicate. The role of the social democracy is circumscribed by its perspective of trying to improve capitalism through petty reforms and its political orientation of participating in the Democratic Party in the prayerful hope of its "realignment." But we can anticipate that social democratic formations will play a more active and open role in the coming period.

Within the social democratic framework differences exist between the reactionary, racist, anticommunist, diehard conservatives of the Meany-Shanker-Rustin wing and the anticommunist, liberal reformers of the Harrington-Gotbaum-Reuther wing. The two wings differ over the tactical course to be followed inside the

Democratic Party machine. The differences involve such questions as how to manipulate the weight of the labor movement in order to win some concessions and how to teach the labor bureaucrats to adapt more adroitly to radically changing expectations and attitudes.

Deepening social crises and rising class struggles will lead to further differentiations and splits within the social democratic circles, with some moving further to the right and some important forces moving to the left as centrist currents.

DECLINE OF AMERICAN STALINISM

The shift in the relation of forces on the left is most strikingly registered in respect to the Stalinists. In 1945 the Communist Party claimed 100,000 members. They dominated several major industrial unions and had a periphery of hundreds of thousands of fellow travelers, intellectuals, Black sympathizers, and so on.

American Stalinism began losing its leading position in the American left from that point on. Their wartime line of speedup and a no-strike pledge, their postwar line of support for the perspective of American-Soviet maintenance of the status quo and of class peace, yielded its first fruits when the ruling class turned against their wartime servitors in the Cold War witch-hunt. The Stalinists looked around for popular support and found they had none. The only permanent factor in their policies—subordination of the class struggle in the United States to the diplomatic needs of Moscow—won a bitter reward from the workers they had misled.

The crushing of the Hungarian revolution and Khrushchev's admission of some of Stalin's crimes further weakened the CP. The inability of the Stalinists to launch a viable youth organization and to recruit broadly out of the radicalization of the 1960s while the Trotskyist movement was making steady gains further altered the relationship of forces in our favor.

Unlike the situation in the 1930s the relative strength of the Socialist Workers Party puts us in position to challenge them for leadership in the struggles of the working class and its allies. But it is important to underline that the pro-Moscow Communist Party remains our single most important and strongest opponent on the left.

The pro-Peking Stalinists have neither the cadres, periphery, nor material base of the pro-Moscow party. They are divided into numerous groupings with deep differences, especially on domestic politics. But the Chinese revolution, which they claim to represent, gives them an international banner that attracts a following, often among youth inclined to ultraleftism. In the climate of deepening radicalization they are growing. For some time to come, our party will be competing with the various Maoist currents for cadres and influence among the radical youth and oppressed nationalities. It is important to note that the ultraleft mood that arose in the late 1960s was worldwide. It has not yet run its course.

The Socialist Workers Party

The two-party system of American capitalism remains the greatest shock absorber of social protest. The single biggest anomaly in the American political scene is the absence of a political party of the working class and the lack of a tradition of independent working-class political organizations in the American labor movement. To transcend this political backwardness remains the single greatest leap to be taken in the politicalization of the American working class.

There is, of course, an advantageous side to the political inexperience of the American working class. The class-struggle minded socialist workers confront no powerful traditional reformist party to which the working class remains stubbornly loyal. The workers are not weighed down with the conservatizing force of the class-collaborationist political routinism ingrained in the European proletariat by the mass social democratic and Stalinist parties. Although the American union bureaucracy is far stronger than in the 1930s and acts as a formidable surrogate for a mass reformist party, it is less of an obstacle to socialist revolution than the reformist workers parties in the advanced capitalist countries of Europe.

The political education of the American working class does not necessarily have to pass through a reformist labor party or come under the domination of Stalinist or social democratic misleadership. Explosive developments, propelling events at extraordinary speed, could bring about a rapid transition to revolutionary class consciousness. A mass revolutionary socialist party could emerge during such a revolutionary upsurge—but only if its cadres are prepared beforehand with a clear perspective and program and only if they are conscious that *a revolutionary party is the historical key to victory.*

As Trotsky explained in the Transitional Program, "The building of national revolutionary parties as sections of the Fourth International is the central task of the transitional epoch."

CENTRAL TASK OF OUR EPOCH

The Socialist Workers Party is internationalist to its core. Not only are world developments shaping the coming struggles at home, but the American workers' enemies are the exploiters on a world scale. The perspective of the Communist Manifesto—"Workers of the world, unite"—remains our fundamental goal. While reactionary legislation precludes formal affiliation to the Fourth International, the Socialist Workers Party, since its founding, has been an integral political component of the world party of socialist revolution.

At the heart of the Socialist Workers Party's revolutionary program and internationalist perspective is its proletarian orientation. Only a party that has deep roots in the working class, that is composed primarily of workers, and enjoys the respect and confidence of the workers, can lead the American working class and its allies to power.

The proletarian orientation means concerted, systematic work to root the party in all sectors of the mass movement and to recruit the most capable fighters to the party. It means participation in labor organizations, in industry and among the unemployed, in the organizations of the oppressed minorities, in the struggles for women's liberation, and in the student movement. Over the last eighteen years the Young Socialist Alliance, the Trotskyist youth organization, has established itself as *the* revolutionary socialist organization in the student movement.

Our proletarian orientation means functioning as a homogeneous campaign party capable of choosing realistic objectives and concentrating our striking power and resources with maximum effectiveness. It means professionalizing our work and adjusting ourselves to the demands and direction of the mass movement in order to help lead that movement forward.

The need to integrate the party into all aspects of the mass movement shapes every activity we undertake. The deepening crises of the American capitalist system and its reactionary interventions abroad do not imply any esoteric new "tactics" for building the party. They only reinforce the need to deepen our proletarian orientation and to take advantage of the new opportunities opening on all sides.

The perspective of increasing class struggle and class polarization indicates more than ever the need for a disciplined combat party of the working class.

The revolutionary party that seeks to lead the socialist revolution is a voluntary organization. Without a common bond of mutual confidence, experience, and loyalty to the program and goals on which it is founded, it will never accomplish the immense tasks before it. Thus, for us the concept of loyalty to the party we are building, pride and confidence in our collective efforts—what Trotsky referred to as party patriotism—is simply the proletarian orientation and internationalist perspective applied to the construction of the revolutionary instrument necessary to realize our program.

THE CONDITIONS FOR VICTORY

The "Manifesto of the Fourth International on the Imperialist War and the Proletarian World Revolution," drafted by Trotsky in

May 1940, outlines the following basic conditions for the victory
of the proletarian revolution:

> (1) the bourgeois impasse and the resulting confusion of the ruling
> class; (2) the sharp dissatisfaction and the striving towards decisive
> changes in the ranks of the petty bourgeoisie, without whose sup-
> port the big bourgeoisie cannot maintain itself; (3) the conscious-
> ness of the intolerable situation and readiness for revolutionary ac-
> tions in the ranks of the proletariat; (4) a clear program and a firm
> leadership of the proletarian vanguard.[4]

The manifesto points out that the main reason for the defeat of
so many revolutions is that these four conditions rarely attain the
necessary degree of maturity at one and the same time.

In the period now opening, we can clearly see the forces building on a world scale that will bring these conditions to maturity in
the United States. But the central question, the one over which we
will have a decisive say, is that of gathering together the forces that
are committed to forging a revolutionary party in time.

Leading the party into industry

The Political Committee believes that this plenum must have one overriding goal: we must subordinate everything else to immediately organizing to get a large majority of the membership of the Socialist Workers Party into industry and the industrial trade unions and to do this in such a way that the majority of the branch executive committees, the majority of the local executive committees, the majority of the party leadership, will soon be made up of comrades in industrial unions.

This party effort must be a universal one. That is, it is the goal of *every* single branch and local. There are no exceptional cities in this country where we have branches located but no surplus value is produced by industrial workers. It is universal also in the sense that it relates to *every* single individual in the party. Every comrade without exception—employed and unemployed, new and experienced—should now sit down with the leadership and collectively review their situation—their job, their assignment, the city they

The general line of this report was approved by the National Committee of the Socialist Workers Party, February 24, 1978.   *SEE PAGE 438 FOR NOTES* live in, their various contributions—and decide how they fit into this decision.

This is not simply another "area of work." This is not simply another "campaign" of the party. This is not "one of the important tasks" or "one of the main axes of work" of the party. This is not something to be counterposed to some other things we're doing in the party. This is the entire framework of the party's activity in the immediate future—beginning *now*.

It is to workers in industry that we want to speak with all of our campaigns. This is where we intend to take our election campaigns, our newspaper, all our activities. This is who we want to influence and recruit to the party. This is the power we fight to mobilize on behalf of all the exploited and oppressed. This is where we think the majority of the future leaders of the women's movement and of the struggles of the oppressed nationalities will come from. And this will become the central arena for the development, training, and testing of our cadres.

It is the workers in industry who are our milieu, our central audience. Their potentially powerful unions are our base.

What we propose is a *political* move, not a hygienic or therapeutic move for the party. We are not doing this to cleanse the party of petty-bourgeois elements or any such nonsense.

Our judgment that this political move is necessary and timely flows from the big changes in the situation facing the capitalist class on a world scale, the need of the American ruling class to drive forward their offensive, to more and more make the industrial workers and their unions the target. Our judgment flows from the changes in the attitudes of the working class in response to this offensive.

We are still in a preparatory period—not a period when we are leading mass class-struggle actions. We must make no mistake about that. But it is a preparatory period in which the *center of American politics has shifted to the industrial working class.* That's the central political judgment we put before the plenum.

But one can't end there. Although we are not proposing this

move for therapeutic or hygienic reasons, the question of the composition of the party poses a challenge. We will not become a party whose big majority are industrial workers, automatically. It must be consciously *led* and it must be organized.

If we did not bring about a significant and rapid change in the composition of the party, we would place ourselves, *now unnecessarily,* outside of the arena in which the decisive changes and developments are happening in the class struggle. We would not have our hand on the pulse of the working class, feel the real rhythm of its developments and changes. By not making this move quickly, now, we would unnecessarily cut ourselves off from the center of American politics.

By making this move, we will get rid of the disorientation in priorities and perspectives that comes from not having the party *living* in the center of the most important political developments that are occurring. And when new comrades join the party, or Young Socialist Alliance members on campus graduate, it will be automatic for them to consult the party leadership to help make a decision as to which city they should live in and what industry they should work in.

The only way to accomplish this is by consciously acting—by consciously acting *now.*

Driving through this decision to become a party in which the great majority of our members are worker-bolsheviks is the central task of the leadership of the party—at every level—from the branch executive committees to the Political Committee.

To accelerate the proletarianization of the party by changing the jobs of the majority of the SWP members is, of course, a *tactical* question. It's not the same thing as the historic proletarian orientation of the Socialist Workers Party, which has always existed and always will exist. But adopting this tactic of sending the majority of comrades into industry, and doing it today, is a historic decision in many ways. It affects everything we do. If we fail to do this, the party will regress, it will slide back on its accomplishments, and it will miss opportunities. It will become disoriented and will begin making political errors. And this will also mean a default in our responsibility to set an example for the entire Fourth International.

Trade union work, properly understood, now becomes the center of responsibility of every single leading committee. Trade union work, properly understood, means finding ways to advance the concept of the working class thinking socially and acting politically, and providing the class-conscious leadership for the struggles of the oppressed, carving out a class-struggle left wing, and advancing the fight for independent working-class political action. This is where worker-bolsheviks are going to lead in struggles. This is where we have to be.

This also means we're at a new stage in the party, a new stage in the development of its leadership. This is a test, but it's also a historic opportunity. The party is waiting for the leadership to lead on this question, and there's every reason in the world to think that the party will respond in its totality.

We're not primarily seeking large immediate conjunctural gains. We're not doing this because of the coal miners strike, or because we are excited over some contacts we've made somewhere.[1] We are doing this because it's the only concrete way right now to implement and carry forward the basic proletarian orientation the party has had for decades, and the turn toward new opportunities in the working class we began in 1975. It's the only tactic now available to us that advances and does not cut across our general strategy.

The purpose of this report is to lay out the basic orientation we have and the leadership conclusions we draw if we adopt this proposal from the Political Committee.

Six basic questions

The best way to do this is to pose a series of basic questions.

First: Why this decision now? Why not earlier?

Second: Why industry, with special attention to basic industry? Why concentrate on industrial unions rather than on the American Federation of State, County, and Municipal Employees (AFSCME), the Office and Professional Employees International

Union (OPEIU), the American Federation of Teachers (AFT), the National Education Association (NEA), or some other unions?

Third: What is the concrete character of the ruling-class offensive against workers in industry? What political line best counters this offensive? And how does this affect the movements and needs of the allies of labor?

Fourth: What is trade union work in industry? What does the party miss by not having the overwhelming majority of its members there?

Fifth: What is a worker-bolshevik? What is a party whose big majority are worker-bolsheviks? What are the structural and organizational implications of becoming a party of worker-bolsheviks?

Sixth: What must be the character of the leadership of this kind of party? What new light can we shed on this in view of the progress we have made the last year on what James P. Cannon called the question of questions—the conscious development of the leadership of the revolutionary party?[2]

Why now?

Why now, and why not earlier?

Part of this is relatively easy to answer. We did not make this move before the turning point of the 1974-75 depression because the economic realities prior to the 1974-75 depression were such that, although we knew in a general way what was going to happen, we did not know *when* it would happen. And we couldn't base our tactics on conjunctural economic guesses. To make the move we're now deciding prior to this fundamental change would have been a blunder. It would have been a gimmick. It would have disoriented the party. It would have been built on guesses, not tied to the real developments in the working class and the political life of the country. Prior to 1974 much of the political activity took a course around and not through either the industrial unions or the workers in industry. But following Nixon's 1971 wage-price freeze, that changed. As we got closer to the 1974-75 depression it changed more and more. Prior to this, though, the best arena for recruitment to our working-class program was not in these unions.

That was our basic framework for an entire period, which definitively changed in 1974-75. We came to agreement on the character of this change in our resolution "Prospects for Socialism in America."[3] We have no Armageddon point of view based on conjunctural economic estimates. But we know that by 1974-75 we had entered a period of crisis for capitalism—one we will not come out of without gigantic battles for power. That's what we are convinced of.

That's the first part of the answer to the question: Why not earlier? But there's another part.

Why not in 1974-75 instead of 1978? Why not simultaneously with the turn in 1975? There are several things we should say about this. First, we had to absorb not only the character of the worldwide recession of 1974-75, but the character of the conjunctural recovery that would inevitably follow. In this country the initial years of so-called recovery have seen more jobs but also high levels of both inflation and joblessness, and an escalation in the ruling-class offensive against the workers on all fronts. We've had to absorb the meaning of this, its effects on the working class and the unions, and its concrete effect on the most oppressed sectors of the working class—the oppressed nationalities, youth, women.

Second, we had to go through some experiences in the American labor movement. We had to go through the rise of Steelworkers Fight Back[4] and see the real political and organizational possibilities, as well as the limits, of this stage of the changes among industrial workers. We had to go through the strike on the Iron Range in Minnesota, where we saw every one of our assessments concerning the meaning of Steelworkers Fight Back verified. We had to go through the beginning of the carriers' offensive in rail, and the local experiences on the railroad in Chicago, Philadelphia, and elsewhere. We had to go through a variety of local experiences in the Bay Area, Houston, Pittsburgh, and other places where we could probe, test, feel the changes and possibilities. Then we had to see the development of the current showdown between the mine workers and the employers and their government.

All these experiences were necessary to know concretely what was changing and how much it was changing. The Political Committee became convinced that there are more workers developing anticapitalist sentiment or greater openness to anticapitalist conclusions and solutions today than at any other time in American history.

We had to go through the experience of seeing what it means to have more Blacks, more Chicanos, more Puerto Ricans, more females, and more young workers in industry and the unions. We had to see in real life how the attitudes and reactions, the combativity—which we talked about and correctly anticipated—began to manifest themselves.

We were able to confirm that we are not going to see the development of some sort of nonwhite or nonmale vanguard. We saw literally hundreds of thousands of young workers come forward and get involved in this or that struggle. Probably the majority of them were young, white, male workers. We saw many of them become open in a new way to anticapitalist ideas. We saw the importance of generational divisions in the working class and we saw young workers, including young, white, male workers in the hundreds of thousands, begin to express the kinds of changes and new attitudes that we knew were coming, too. We understood better not only the differential effect of the rulers' offensive along nationality, sex, and skill lines, but also along generational lines.

We began seeing the dynamic between "bread-and-butter" issues and the broad social and political questions labor must face up to. The ideas we projected in our 1971 Political Resolution[5] got more concrete in our 1975 "Prospects" resolution. We began to see a response—uneven, but general—to political and social questions and campaigns brought into the labor movement, brought to the working class. And we saw the links between this new response and the upswing in class combativity.

So the first thing was the reality of the post–1974-75 recovery and the second was the evolution of the subjective changes in the industrial working class.

But there is a third thing we had to go through before the decision we're making today. Maybe it is the most important. The party had to go through its *own* experiences and accomplishments in the labor movement before we could make this move. The branches and locals, the fractions, had to get their feet wet in industry. We had to gain experience with our industrial fractions. For the first time in almost thirty years we had functioning and growing national industrial fractions, and we had to learn how to lead this work at every level.

We had to learn to assess the possibilities as well as the frustrations and difficulties with events we participated in such as Steelworkers Fight Back and the post–Steelworkers Fight Back period. We had to learn how to use the *Militant,* our other institutions, and our political campaigns.

In other words we had to enter a whole new stage in leadership understanding, experience, and political breadth. We had to start by having the leaders of the party on every level go into industry themselves to lead this. We had to see with our own eyes, in branch after branch, how this process had a positive impact on the individual comrades who took the lead by going into industry. It raised their spirits and gave them a new political outlook, a new focus.

Then we were ready to responsibly generalize. So that's why now, not earlier.

Why concentrate on industry?

Why concentrate on industry? Maybe this is sort of an embarrassing or unnecessary question to raise for Marxists since this is the traditional Marxist view. But it's worth reviewing.

Let's look at two sides of the question, the economics and the politics. The economics are simple. Raw materials like coal and ores and oil, and products like machine tools, steel, major electrical components, have tremendous leverage in the whole economy. These are the things that must enter into production in the earliest stages to make every single part of the economy run. Industries producing raw materials, semifinished products, transportation, construction, agriculture, have leverage because without them the entire economy stops. It can't function. Capital goods—electrical equipment, automotive equipment, heavy manufacturing of all sorts—are simply different stages in the use of labor power to produce the gigantic wealth the American workers create. In each stage as you get farther from the "final" product, there's more strength, more power—from simply an economic point of view.

There's another economic side to this too. The labor power in these industries is the main source of surplus value. It is the major source of all those revenues that are used to keep the government, service, and "professional" sectors of the economy going. By looking at it this way we begin to see something that's not often talked about: the increasing, not decreasing, vulnerability of the modern capitalist economy. The more complicated and highly organized the economy gets, the more vulnerable it becomes to stoppages, disorganization in basic industry. This would come through even more clearly in the miners strike right now if the United Mine Workers had the entire coal industry organized.

The political side is even more important. First, let's look at the political side from the point of view of the ruling class itself, the enemy. It doesn't take much to understand politically that coal is more important to the rulers than social work. Their system can operate much easier and for longer periods without social workers than without coal. The capitalists don't even need social workers personally because they get their welfare checks straight from the trust departments of banks.

This point becomes clearer if you look at it from the standpoint of the competitive needs of U.S. imperialism on a world scale. This labor power is the source of the international power of the American capitalist economy, the source of their exports of goods and capital.

These are the fundamental reasons that the industrial workers, who are a minority of the American working class, have such fundamental strength, such potential power. This also demonstrates the fakery of the academic theories about the "new working class," and the "postindustrial society."

But we must also look at the political side of this question from the point of view of our class, the working class.

First, much of industry is organized. This sounds obvious but it has only been true for the past few decades in American history. Before the mid-1930s (in many ways before World War II) this was not true, basic industry was not organized. It was primarily a relatively thin aristocracy of labor that was organized. But now, to a significant degree, industry is organized.

Secondly, one has to consider the character of the industrial workplace and what the factory does socially and psychologically to workers. The social character of the work, the large concentration of workers, the extremely high division of labor—these factors give workers an awareness of their collective power. The fact that collective bargaining—rather than personal relations with the bosses—governs so much of what is done, leads to greater self-confidence, to "no contract–no work" consciousness even in periods of ruling-class offensive. It is a reflection of self-confidence in their collective power. As one miner recently explained on television, when you're a tiny baby, before you learn to say "mama" or "dada," you learn to say "no contract–no work."

It's important, third, to remember the changing age of the workforce in industry. There are many more younger workers, the so-called post-Vietnam generation that the bosses keep complaining about in relation to the miners strike. And we've detailed the racial composition of selected industries many times the last few years.

Fourth, we should note the tradition of radicalization among the industrial working class. It shouldn't be exaggerated, but it's real. The industrial unions were built in the massive struggles of the CIO. It took bloody battles to build the Auto Workers, to build whole sections of the Teamsters, to build the Steelworkers, etc. That tradition, even if much of the continuity is lost, is still part of the reality.

The fifth point is the degree to which many of these industrial unions affect much more than the workforce. They affect entire areas of the country. Take the miners strike once again, for example. When you talk about the real stakes in the UMWA strike, you're talking about the health and welfare and future of all of Appalachia, an entire region of this country. When you talk about the UAW, you're talking about the future of entire cities, the city of Detroit for example. These industries and unions affect much more than just the industry, the factory itself. We have no reason to challenge Leon Trotsky's view that in certain circumstances industrial unions could play the role of soviets in some parts of this country. We have no way of knowing, but we don't preclude it beforehand.[6]

Finally, and most importantly, this is where the brunt of the real attack of the ruling class is coming down more and more. They can beat down AFSCME in different places, they can impose cutbacks on teachers, they can do all kinds of things like that, but it just begins the process. They must "tame" the industrial working class. They must "tame" the most strategically located producers. This is the target of the ruling-class offensive. This is the reason that we put our priorities here.

We must maintain our central priority in steel and add rail and auto to our *national* priorities. In addition, we've got to take a look at local situations. In some places we'll put priority on the Machinists union, which has organized whole sectors of industry in some areas; or the Oil, Chemical and Atomic Workers; or electrical; or the shipyards; mining; transport—whatever fits into our general needs and makes sense in local areas.

As Jim Cannon said thirty-seven years ago, "We are a small party and we can't go colonizing all over the lot. We must colonize in those places which offer the best opportunity at the time, and when this opportunity which we seize at one occasion proves later on to be not so fruitful, we have got to shift our people."[7] It's a lot better to have a couple of viable and functioning *fractions* in a local or branch than to have a lot of "fractions" of one or two individual comrades each. That's a standard guide.

It is necessary that we now set these priorities and consciously say that we're de-AFSCMEizing the party. We are de-AFSCMEizing the party not from the point of view of downgrading the work we do in unions like AFSCME or recruiting to the party excellent contacts we may have there; but from the point of view of where we are going to put people. We are not neutral or indifferent whether a comrade becomes a teacher, a social worker, gets into the OPEIU—or goes into industry. We want to help our comrades to get into industry.

This doesn't mean we won't do work in, or pay careful attention to, AFSCME or the teachers union. This decision will strengthen our work in unions like AFSCME and the teachers. In fact, as we grow, we will recruit bigger fractions in the AFT, NEA, AFSCME, and so on. This does not detract from the importance of the work of our comrades there either. Or the political struggles coming among teachers for instance. Or the recruitability of many AFSCME members. But we must make a decision about what unions we are going to send comrades into. This must be a conscious, explicit orientation of the party, with no ambiguities or exceptions.

The offensive against industrial workers

The next question we want to discuss is: What is the concrete character of this offensive against the industrial working class and what political response is needed? I won't repeat the general things we've said before—the character of the attacks on the public employees and social services; the impact of the offensive on oppressed nationalities, women, and the youth; the rightward shift in bourgeois politics, which gives encouragement to the right in the midst of an increasing class polarization. I want to focus on the particular character of the attacks on the industrial workers, on the industrial trade unions.

When we talk about the social and political responsibilities of labor we explain the need to combat the ruling-class policy of imposing on the individual family the responsibility for social services that should be taken care of by society—the care of the young, the elderly, the sick and disabled. But that's not the only way capitalism works. The employers also try to impose upon the individual workers responsibilities that should be met by society. And more and more they try to establish that these responsibilities will be met only according to the profitability of each worker's own boss. I leave aside the most grotesque single examples such as the public-employee unions' officials sinking massive amounts of pension funds into city bonds in New York City. But more and more so-called general fringe benefits—pensions, health-care plans, supplemental unemployment benefits—all become contingent on the continuing profits of the boss you work for. We see this growing in industries like coal, steel, and auto.

These benefits are not won for the class as a whole, or even a section of the class. It's almost like a march back toward feudalism, not a march forward toward socialism. These fringes are good in good times—for workers who have them—because they're a substantial addition to everything else industrial workers can count on. But when the squeeze comes on, this all begins to fall apart. Your pension funds are threatened. Your health-care plans are dismantled. The supplemental unemployment benefits run out. And the squeeze is on.

This is the payoff when the debt of business unionism comes due. This is the price paid for the class-collaborationist policy of refusing to fight for the real needs of the class—the social security of the class, national health care, for national unemployment insurance that's real and high enough, for a shorter workweek at no cut in pay, for protection against inflation, and for independent working-class political action. This is the price paid for a bureaucracy that says independent social and political struggles are secondary, and says the employers' promises in the contract are decisive.

This is the payoff for the refusal of the labor bureaucracy to fight for the broad social needs of the working class and to build a political instrument to fight for them. And this is what raises the labor party question in a new way. This concretizes it in a new and more understandable way, because now these problems are immediately facing the section of the working class that thought they were the least vulnerable and had the best deal.

Another thing that is happening in this offensive is a conscious attack on trade union democracy. The *right to strike* becomes a special target of the employers. Other restrictions are institutionalized, such as lengthy probationary periods that give the bosses a chance to weed out union militants, "troublemakers" of all kinds. Speedup and the erosion of safety and health protection on the job, are more and more a factor. Incentive pay and piecework plans are introduced in one form or another. Schemes like the Experimental Negotiating Agreement in steel with its no-strike pledge are generalized as much as possible.[8] And arbitration procedures are put into every nook and cranny of every contract, tying the workers' hands and leaving them without the right to use their strength to fight back. In this way class collaboration becomes institutionalized.

Class collaboration isn't simply a program or an attitude of bureaucrats. Class collaboration takes the form of institutions that tie the individual worker hand and foot, that make a worker dependent on someone other than the power of his or her co-workers and class. Trade union democracy of any kind, union control of conditions and pace of work, individual workers' rights on the job, are more and more opposed by the employer. The right to know, the right to vote on contracts, the right to elect your stewards and officers—these things can less and less be afforded by the employers. And they can less and less be tolerated by the union bureaucracy as well.

Finally, of course, class collaboration is the total dependence on the political parties and social programs of the employers.

A third thing that happens as a result of the offensive is the growing need for *solidarity*. That's become clearer in the struggles of the last couple years. Solidarity becomes crucial to success in the struggles that are breaking out. Each of these struggles, like the one on the Iron Range, like the coal miners today, turns into a political fight for the minds of the working class. Not only of the workers who are on strike but of the entire class. The strikers must appeal for support, and the employers, the government, must try to prevent that support, must whip up opposition. This is not only the source of the need for solidarity, it's also the source of the need for internationalism. Because ultimately class solidarity has to be worldwide. It has to take up and oppose ruling-class policies such as protectionism, deportation of undocumented workers, chauvinistic "Buy American" campaigns, and so on.

There's another side of solidarity: to have real solidarity you must have solidarity inside the union itself, inside the working class itself. The elementary and immediate need for class solidarity—with the striking miners, with any strike—puts the spotlight on the importance of having the correct stand on big social issues like Black rights, women's rights, and affirmative action. Without a correct position on these issues, without fighting for these rights, solidarity is crippled right within the union, right within the workforce itself. And so is democracy. Without programs like child care, without the needs of women being met and fought for, the union is made less democratic. Sections of the workforce are prevented from participating on an equal footing. The total workforce cannot be mobilized to make and carry out the decisions needed to struggle.

The employers' offensive has different effects on different layers of the working class. It hits hardest those who are least prepared to defend themselves. This fact poses directly and immediately the need for the labor movement to lead the fight for broad social needs not only of the workers, but also of the unemployed, women, the oppressed nationalities, the youth, the working farmers. If the unions don't lead, they will reap a whirlwind of deepening suspicion and hatred by those who should be allies and even members! And that will ultimately be decisive.

This means it pays to look at *Militant* articles in a broader context. *Militant* articles must be seen as not aimed just at the people who would be most immediately interested in them, but aimed at the entire working class. Because every one of them ties into the needs of the class. It becomes more possible, and more necessary, to explain the *class* side of all questions.

To fight for these social needs, to fight the political battles, the workers need a *labor party,* a political instrument that will fight for the needs of the entire working class. This goes hand in hand with the need for solidarity and trade union democracy.

We should argue the labor party question on all levels. Why do the capitalist politicians have to act as they do? We have to explain what the politicians do, what the capitalist parties are and what their connections are to the employers, the cops, the government, the state. We have to explain in each case the concrete cost to the whole working class of having no labor party, the price that is paid for being unarmed in the political arena. All this becomes easier, not harder, to explain effectively.

Parallel to all this is the fact that the union bureaucracy has less and less breathing space, less room to maneuver. They have to negotiate the right kind of contract to satisfy the boss. But if they don't negotiate a contract that's good enough for the ranks, at a certain stage the workers just won't have anything to do with them anymore. They don't want to become like Arnold Miller, president of the Mine Workers union, and find themselves between a rock and a hard place. But that's just what's happening.

And finally, something else becomes clear. That is the fact that the state of the bureaucracy is not identical to the state of the unions. That's a big lesson from the strike on the Iron Range and from the coal miners strike. The union and the bureaucracy are different things. The union is weakened and crippled by the bureaucracy. And while the bureaucracy is more and more in a bind, under pressure, the rank and file of the unions is becoming more ready to fight, and more ready to think about new methods of struggle, new perspectives and programs.

What is trade union work?

What is trade union work in industry? Properly understood, it's work that should be central to everything we do. The simplest way to describe it is talking socialism to workers. That's what trade union work is: talking socialism to workers. And we do this collectively, not simply individually. We do it through organized fractions, not anarchistically, with each comrade on their own. This work is led by the party. And we use the party's institutions to do most of it.

There is no handbook that will make any comrade an overnight expert. Only class-struggle experience can mold that. But there is something that every comrade should read or reread when they go into industry. It should be a kind of party law. That's Farrell Dobbs's four books on the Teamsters—*Teamster Rebellion, Teamster Power, Teamster Politics, Teamster Bureaucracy.* It is unlikely that a better "handbook" explaining all sides of bolshevik trade union work will ever be written.[9]

There are no prescriptions we can distribute on how to do trade union work. But there are some things to keep in mind. One is the variation that sometimes exists between the kind of work you can do on the job and the kind of work you can do in the union. Sometimes you can do one and not the other, and then this can change rapidly and you can do both.

Second, we should take every opportunity to concretely talk about trade union democracy, independent political action, solidarity. Raise these questions, talk about them, whenever we get an opportunity. There are a lot of variations here, too. For instance, in Baltimore comrades report all kinds of discussions about the coal miners going on among steelworkers; how to support the miners strike, the importance of it. But comrades in the Brooklyn shipyards, where union consciousness is low, find they have to start by explaining to workers that they should be interested in the miners, that the miners struggle is important to them. Especially a lot of Black, Puerto Rican, Latino workers say, "If they're making seven to eight dollars an hour with all those benefits why should we be interested in giving them support?" In other places it is the Black and Latino workers who are taking the lead in understanding and explaining solidarity. It varies tremendously.

A third thing is to learn the industry, learn the skills, learn the unions, and help others to do so.

The fourth thing is to always see everything as a *team* effort. Everything is a team effort. We should never put a comrade in industry in a situation where that comrade feels that he or she is *individually* responsible for trade union work, or ask them to give you a list of individual accomplishments. We don't do anything else that way. We don't individually credit one person for the results of an election campaign. We don't individually praise Fred Halstead because half a million people marched on Washington against the war.[10]

We don't regard comrades as individually responsible for what we accomplish or don't accomplish in trade union work. What we look for is what we accomplish in fractions, led by the party as a whole. That is how trade union work has to be understood. We can't look at a day-to-day balance sheet of the individual ups and downs of this work. We don't judge by the dry periods, in which little can be done. We've got to go by the long-run, team effort of the party and the fractions as a whole, on a nationwide scale. That is the only possible way to measure the accomplishments of trade union work. What individual comrades can do will vary greatly—from time to time in the same job and from job to job in the same industry.

Trade union work must not be seen as separate from party campaigns. It's not "another campaign" somewhere in the list of priorities. No, it determines our basic axis, it aims at our milieu, and our arena of work. And it strengthens all our campaigns as it strengthens the work of the YSA.

We can also talk about a few lessons we've learned from our work in steel and other industries so far. One lesson is we don't have to sit around waiting for the big struggles to occur before we can do something. The struggles have already begun. They're just not always happening in every single place at all times, for all comrades. We don't have to wait. On the other hand, we can't begin with the idea we're going to stir up the big struggles if they are not occurring. Our size precludes that. As long as we avoid these two errors, we can do an immense amount of work.

We have to ask ourselves another question about trade union work. What would the party miss if it were not to get into industry in its big majority, *today?* Not after our next national gathering, not after the next plenum, but *today.* One of the main things the party would miss would be learning the life of the working class in a rich way. By not being in industry the party would miss having its fingers on the pulse of the real changes that are beginning to take place in the politics of the United States. We would miss learning the real life of the factories, the mills, and the mines. We would miss learning the life of the unions, and life in bureaucratically degenerated, declining unions. We would miss learning the life of the workers, the rhythms, the problems, the experiences, the difficulties. All this can really be known only one way—by being there. Once we're there, we don't need these fake Gallup polls to try to figure out what the workers are thinking.

Farrell Dobbs reminded me of a story about Lenin during the July Days in Russia in 1917, when Lenin had gone underground. A worker says, "They're afraid of us, Comrade Lenin." Lenin asks, "What have you heard, comrade?" The worker replies, "The bread is better."

Lenin didn't need a poll, he didn't have to wait for the Petrograd Gallup to come out, which may be fake and wrong. A party of worker-bolsheviks is the best poll.

The key thing for us is the fruitful party-building work to be done right now in the center of political life in the United States— the industrial working class. By center, of course, we're not saying this is the only place. There are not big political street actions taking place there. But more and more what happens in the unions and to the unions deeply affects the entire relationship of class forces. And it's here that the leadership, the future class-struggle leadership of all the movements of the oppressed and exploited, is being forged and has to be forged if they are to be led to victory. Thus changing the composition of the party, while not a hygienic or therapeutic need, becomes the source of a great strengthening of the party as a whole. We'll not only have our fingers directly on the pulse of the key sections of the American working class, but we'll get to know workers who are being tested and trained, including ourselves, to become leaders in the coming battles. This is the single most important arena of training for the proletarian leaders—including women and the oppressed nationalities—of the struggles to come.

A party of worker-bolsheviks

What is a worker-bolshevik? What is a party whose big majority are worker-bolsheviks? Let's look at it first from the point of view of the individual worker-bolshevik. The individual worker-bolshevik is somebody who is in a revolutionary party of workers, a party known by the workers, a party that knows the workers. A party trusted by and trusting in the workers. A party made up, in its ranks and leadership, of workers. Very simple. But there is much more.

A worker-bolshevik is a worker for whom the party comes first, not the union. The party comes first. A worker for whom the party is everything. We're in industry, in the unions, for one reason: to build the party. This will be the arena of battle where the party will either win the leadership and lead the oppressed and exploited in the battle for power, or lose leadership to one of the petty-bourgeois currents and see the counterrevolution triumph. That is why we're in the unions and why we are going to be in deeper and deeper.

Worker-bolsheviks are professional revolutionists in the best sense of the term. As we know, professional revolutionists are not the same thing as the full-timers. A professional revolutionist is the revolutionist whose real profession—regardless of how he or she makes their money—is being a political worker-bolshevik. A worker-bolshevik is someone who at all times takes on major responsibility as part of a party team, in whatever way it is necessary. A worker-bolshevik is a comrade who is ready at any time to be full-time at the request of the party, who sustains financially and supports politically the professional full-time staff of the apparatus, the press, the machinery the party needs to function.

A worker-bolshevik is ready to move—into a new industry or a new city—when the need arises. Ready to aid the expansion of the party, making it possible to become stronger nationwide, making it possible to respond to a particular opening such as in Morgantown, West Virginia, or on the Iron Range. Ready to pitch in and build the branches we've begun in important political centers—centers that affect whole regions and states—such as Albany, Raleigh, Salt Lake City, Miami, San Antonio, and Toledo. Worker-bolsheviks are those who will respond to the party's needs, who will pack up and move wherever, whenever, the party needs. Those who will join the comrades in new cities who are making progress in building branches, but need reinforcements if they are going to be able to take advantage of the openings.

To stress this, the leadership is obligated to praise pyromania.

One of my favorite quotes from Jim Cannon is from his summary speech to the party plenum-conference in 1941. He was talking about colonizing industry, as we are today, and he said, "I am only sorry that we have encountered a little difficulty in doing this [colonizing] because some of the comrades have apparently settled down. . . . I don't know of anything more disgraceful for a young revolutionist than to get settled down and get so encumbered in a place that he cannot move. . . . It would be a damn good thing for him if he had a fire . . . to blow away some property encumbrance and make him footloose and revolutionary again."[11]

That should be put up on the wall of every worker-bolshevik. It's the truth.

When a worker joins the party he or she sees their co-workers serving on branch and local executive committees, on forum committees, as financial and education directors, as campaign heads, as candidates, etc. If this were not normal in a party of worker-bolsheviks—the whole concept would be a utopia.

A worker-bolshevik is a comrade who doesn't believe that you do political work only after you get off the job. They don't wait to get away from their job, or find a job that makes them "available" for other things but minimizes the opportunities for political work on the job.

The worker-bolsheviks see themselves as socialist propagandists on the job and off. They sell the *Militant*. They raise ideas about leading the class struggle, opposed to the class-collaborationist policies of the current leadership. They are talking continually to workers about politics, about our campaigns, about our paper, about meeting other revolutionists, about supporting social struggles that must have the support of labor. Last, but most important, they talk about joining the party.

A party structure
What about a party of worker-bolsheviks from the point of view of party norms and structure? There are some general things worth noting.

The key thing, once again, is that the party must lead. The party can never leave a fraction on its own. An industrial fraction is not a fraction of Steelworkers Fight Back, or some caucus of Mine Workers, or of the Oil, Chemical and Atomic Workers. It is a fraction of the Socialist Workers Party. And above all else, this fraction of the Socialist Workers Party must be led in harmony with the rhythm of the class struggle and the character and pace of the party campaigns we have to take into the unions. This points to a series of adjustments that will become norms in the party.

The relationship of the industrial fractions to the branches and the locals must be developed. The specific forms will vary. In some places we have trade union directors, for example in Houston, working in collaboration with all the fractions as part of the city leadership. In other places, such as in the Bay Area, we use ad hoc forms. We have a Bay Area–wide steel fraction, which a National Committee member helps lead. We will find the best forms and use them.

This affects everything we do, every aspect of our structure and functioning. Branch meeting times have to change so that comrades working in industry can attend. Branch sizes have to be reevaluated.

We will more and more need full-time branch organizers. We have to look at sales of the *Militant* and *Perspectiva Mundial* in this framework. Sales at plant gates on a regular, consistent basis are going to be essential as part of providing outside help for the fractions in industry.

The party has to lead by putting comrades in industry. This must be a conscious, organized campaign. We have to review the situation of every single comrade in the party. And the leadership has to go into industry. It has to be the norm that the majority of the executive committees are in industry. We have to release comrades who are branch and city organizers to do this—and bring forward a new layer of comrades to get the experience of being organizers. We are releasing members of the National Committee from other assignments, members of the trade union steering committee, and some members of the Political Committee to go into industry now.

We must also put greater stress now on education. Like the class itself, worker-bolsheviks have a great need and a great thirst for education. We have to read, talk, think. We have to think about how to explain things, and learn things to keep up with the people we're talking to. It means we have to pay attention to local and branch educational programs. It means we have to think through how best to use our national educational conference this year. It means we have to seriously consider restarting something like the old Trotsky School,[12] to provide a systematic way to take elected party leaders, members of the NC and the PC to start with, take them out of the day-to-day responsibilities and help them to educate and reeducate themselves through a program of concentrated study for four or five months.

The key thing is to act *now* to get the majority of the party and the majority of the leadership into industry. That's the great opportunity, that's the responsibility of leadership. All these structural and organizational questions are only problems if industrial workers are a minority of a branch. Then they seem to be out of step with the normal life and functioning of the branch. But once industrial workers are a big majority of a branch, the rhythms and the needs of the majority of the comrades naturally become the norm. And life teaches that the average comrade doesn't become a less active trade unionist but a more active bolshevik.

These changes we must make in our structure are changes that will come naturally and will be seen not as problems but as a normal part of party life, of taking advantage of opportunities as we succeed in transforming the party. As this happens, a new norm is established. You forget what was normal yesterday. What becomes normal is what is normal today.

Leadership lessons

What is the leadership of this kind of party like? We have a new, large (the largest in the history of the party), relatively young National Committee. But it has one of the biggest responsibilities and maybe the biggest opportunity of any national leadership in the history of the party. So we wanted to take a little time on this part of the report to discuss this question of questions—the question of leadership.

We have to begin by looking at what our leadership concepts are derived from. Forms, structure, and norms of leadership are derived basically from three things:

• One, the character of the revolution we are out to lead. Different kinds of leadership are necessary to lead different kinds of revolutions.

• Two, the character of the party we need once we decide the character of the revolution we are determined to lead.

• Three, the concrete stage we are at in building that party.

Our leadership needs and norms will be different at different stages in the development of the party. Let's step back and look at each of these.

The character of the revolution is no mystery to us. Its rich concreteness is, but not its essential character. We have come to agreement on this and have codified it in our resolutions. We believe that the coming American socialist revolution will have a combined character. It will be a revolution to free the working class from exploitation, to free the toiling masses from oppression. The revolution will also be a struggle for the right of self-determination of the oppressed nationalities. The Black struggle and the struggles of the other oppressed nationalities have great weight and importance. As Trotsky reminded us, the class-conscious workers of these nationalities will play a role as the vanguard of the proletariat.

The coming American revolution will be a combined revolution in another sense, too. The drive to achieve equality for women, to solve the problems the women's liberation movement is posing, will be one of the central motor forces of the revolution. The revolutionary mobilization of women will be decisive in defeating capitalism. The revolution will have to combine the solutions to this question with all its other tasks.

What does the revolutionary party fight for to bring this combined socialist revolution to fruition? The establishment of a workers government. A workers government must replace the current capitalist government. That workers government must get rid of the capitalist state and establish a workers state. *Not* a combined state but a workers state. That's the only way that these combined tasks can be accomplished successfully. The bourgeoisie cannot do it. Only the proletariat can do it. Thus the combined revolution must be a workers revolution, if it is to establish a workers government. It is important not to confuse these two things—the *combined tasks* of the socialist revolution, and the *proletarian character* of the revolution that makes it possible to accomplish these tasks.

Character of the party
What can we conclude from this about the character of the party? If the party is going to lead a proletarian revolution to establish a workers state, it has to be a proletarian party. It has to be a proletarian party in program, in composition, and in its experience. And it must understand and consciously relate to the epoch it is in: its task is not one of reforming capitalism, its realistic perspective is the elimination of capitalist rule.

It has a single program, not a bunch of different programs. It has what we call the Transitional Program. We reject any concept of sectoralism or polyvanguardism. We are opposed to any idea of a combined state, or a combined party. The way forward is that of a proletarian revolution and the vanguard has to be the organized, conscious vanguard of the proletariat.

The most powerful, centralized ruling class in history has to be displaced. But that doesn't end the matter. There's an additional important problem: the proletariat is not homogeneous. If the proletariat—who are the big majority—were totally homogeneous, if every worker went through the same experiences and came to the same conclusions at the same time, a conscious, politically homogeneous combat party wouldn't be so needed. You could try to slip by through utilizing the broadest class institutions—the industrial unions, councils, soviets, whatever. These are the institutions that by definition encompass the great active majority of the whole class. But in reality, just when that stage is reached—the stage of the transformation of the gigantic industrial unions into revolutionary instruments of struggle, the establishment of workers councils, the establishment of soviets—it's just at that point that the heterogeneous character of the class, based on historic differences along lines of craft, race, sex, age, and political experience—makes the need for the party so acute.

At that point a party is needed that will speak for the most conscious elements of the proletariat, and lead the fight to oppose and win the least conscious and the most backward elements, those most affected by bourgeois and petty-bourgeois ideology. It will lead the most conscious elements to take power for the class. Thus, it is not a matter of indifference whether the party is rooted in, and a significant part of its leadership as well as its membership is composed of, sectors of the working class that are doubly oppressed in capitalist society. These are the workers who will be among the best fighters and the most courageous and conscious leaders of the party and of the class.

The rise of the Black struggle and the explosion of nationalist consciousness, and the rise of the women's struggle, have had a great impact, a historical impact we've often discussed. But they have one meaning above all others for the revolutionary party: the human material, the potential leaders of the proletarian party, have been increased many times. And that may be the most important meaning for us.

If this is true it says something else about the leaders of the party. They *all* lead the party, not a sector of the party or a grouping in the party. Naturally, leaders are looked to in a special way by sections of the party. Leaders who are women are looked to by younger women in the party as examples, as people to learn from. The same with Black comrades. We all go through this experience. When you find someone like yourself, with whom you can identify, it helps you have the confidence to take strides forward.

But what we are after is not Black leaders of the party, or Chicano leaders of the party, or women leaders of the party, or worker leaders of the party. What we are after is leaders of the party—rounded leaders of the party, looked to by the entire party, who are Black, Chicano, Puerto Rican, female, and workers in industry. Not Black leaders of the party, but party leaders who are Black. Not leaders who take responsibility for only one section of the party, or one area of work, but leaders who take overall responsibility, who lead the work of the entire party, and who are looked to by the entire party.

The stage we're at in building the party and the decision we're making at this plenum also has an important bearing on the leadership question. Industry is where the proletarian leadership will develop. Industry will not be the only place, because there are struggles of the oppressed occurring in other arenas also. But industry will be the major place, and these struggles of the oppressed will be led by workers. It will be primarily in industry where our leaders will gain experience and confidence and come forward. This is universal, for the party as a whole.

No different roads

We do not have different roads to leadership. We cannot have different roads, for white and Black, male and female, more and less experienced cadres. We cannot have different roads or it simply won't work. Our work in industry, and getting into industry, is the central responsibility of the party. It is the central leadership responsibility of all cadres. This is where the next leadership of the proletarian party historically, and the leaders of the next stage of the mass movement, will be found. It is true not only for the future class-struggle left wing in the unions, but for the Black movement, the Chicano movement, the Puerto Rican movement, the women's movement. It's from here and not from the ranks of lawyers, preachers, professors, labor fakers, petty-bourgeois politicians, and ex–government officials that the leaders of the Black movement, the women's movement, will come. They are going to be found among the American working class and that is where we have to go and get them.

There is another side to this, too. In thinking about this report I went back and read *The Struggle for a Proletarian Party*.[13] I was struck by something that I hadn't remembered so much from earlier readings: the stress that Jim Cannon put on *attitudes* toward leadership and organization. He listed a lot of the characteristics of proletarian leaders. Seriousness toward the organization of the leadership. Objectivity. Subordinating personal considerations in putting the party first. Having a professional attitude toward it. Being deadly opposed to gossip, cynicism, bureaucratism, super-sensitivity to criticism. Jim stressed that all of these traits, and more, were proletarian attitudes toward the party.

And it wasn't only Cannon's view. Trotsky's praise of *Struggle for a Proletarian Party* and his writings on organization and leadership in *In Defense of Marxism* made the same point, based on the decades of experience of the Bolsheviks.[14] We incorporated this view as part of the fundamental program of the party.[15]

Above all, *objectivity is the key to this*. To lead and set an example on the organization question, on the leadership question, above all we have to be objective and not subjective. The vantage point has to be not "me and mine" but "us and ours." The starting point has to be the needs of the party, the needs of the class.

National Committee

These considerations bear directly on the evolution of the party's National Committee—on the question of leadership, where we are right now in the turn, and what kind of leadership we are going to have to have.

We all know how the working class is divided along race and sex lines, how society is divided. The revolutionary unity of the class, within the class and with the allies of the class, must be based on championing the needs of the oppressed, not defending the privileges a thin layer gets from the oppressors. This is the only basis on which the working class can be led to victory.

A revolutionary party must reflect this fact not only in its program but in the composition of its leadership. This isn't something that can be left to nature or left to chance. It will not happen "naturally"—that is, without conscious leadership. Why not? Because part of the division of this society is what the oppressed are taught about themselves from the day they are born. Blacks, Chicanos, females, are taught in a hundred different ways that they are not leaders, they are not self-confident, they are not clear thinkers, cold-blooded, decisive, Leninist types. That's the idea. The schools, churches, and mass media try to structure society's consciousness that way. A party that won't pay special attention and affirmatively act in such a way that will move forward leaders and potential leaders from the oppressed is simply avoiding its responsibility.

An objective necessity

That's why the term *affirmative action* applies well to what we must do.

I don't know of any better term to use. I think we should take affirmative action to advance into the leadership of the party, in every possible way, comrades from the oppressed nationalities, female comrades, young workers who come into the party. We must say that explicitly and we must do it if what we say is true about the character of the U.S. working class, the character of the coming revolution, and the character of the party that derives from this.

Of course, we cannot lead the proletarian revolution without hundreds of thousands of white males in the party, and this will be reflected also in its leadership. It's safe to assume there's agreement on this.

At the same time, we must act affirmatively to advance in every way possible the development of women, Black, Chicano, and Puerto Rican comrades, and comrades recruited out of working-class struggles. We must set a framework in which this responsibility and this opportunity can be advanced. This has nothing to do with guilt or moralism or similar hypocritical mouthings that mark so many "socialist" sects. It is an objective question of whether we will be able to do what we have to do. The coming American revolution cannot be led by a party that has a sexual and racial composition—in its ranks and in its leadership—like other revolutionary parties in the past, including even the Bolsheviks. This need is dictated by the nature of the American working class, and the history of the class struggle. Anything short of the goal we have set isn't going to be good enough for us in this country in this period.

We cannot confuse affirmative action with quotas. We are for affirmative action but we are ironclad in our rejection of quotas in the construction of the Leninist party. We are the world's experts on quotas. I don't have to explain to this plenum why we say affirmative action is a fake in industry, in education, without quotas. Quotas are the only possible way we can check the rulers, can force them to retreat. It's the only way that we can raise people's consciousness about this.

Quotas are necessary in another arena too. Quotas are needed in the workers movement. For instance, in various situations in the unions today. Why must we have affirmative-action quotas in the unions? Why do we fight for the establishment of women's committees, for the right of all-Black caucuses and all-women's caucuses to function in the unions? We do it because of the program of the union bureaucracy. It is not a program in the interest of the class. And the leadership of the unions is not democratically elected to carry out a program in the interests of the class. One of the ways we can bust this down and change this is by fighting for quotas.

This is not just a question of the unions today. We will be for quotas under a workers government in the United States. We will be for quotas because the workers government will represent all the workers, not just the most conscious workers. It will be a government that will have more than one party. These different parties will represent different strata in the working class. These parties will have different programs. They will contend with each other. The coming to power of a workers government, and the establishment of a workers state, will not totally erase differentiations within the working class. Not at all. The most conscious section of the working class will still need to fight for the unity of the class through support to the interests of the most oppressed. It will still have to fight to bust through the effects of decades of misleaders of the working class and the legacy of centuries of oppression.

Program and Leninist norms

But we do not use the same criteria within the Leninist party. We must remember the differences. The party's program is a revolutionary program. The party's leadership is democratically elected. The only way the party can function is to base every decision on *political* criteria. And the only way to keep the real leadership (in the eyes of the party) and the elected leadership the same is to function in this way. The party is the *conscious* vanguard of the class. These are the decisive elements that make the party different from the unions today, from the other mass organizations of the class, from the future soviets. Remember, we don't advocate all our Leninist organizational norms for any other organization.

So we are against quotas, against caucuses in the Leninist party. But we are for affirmative action in leadership development and advancement. We are for finding ways and means on all levels to advance party leadership experience of comrades of oppressed nationalities, women comrades, young workers. We are for maximizing the pace of that experience, and maximizing the formal decisions that reflect and encourage that experience.

But that is *not* the same as saying that we *won't* advance that leadership experience for white males (or Jews or older comrades or any other "category"). It is not the same at all. Even the way we elect leaderships proves this point. And this is important.

When we elect the National Committee, the delegates vote *for* the nominees they would like to see on the NC. They are not asked to choose whom they *don't* want on it. The mathematics of it has an important political meaning. What happens is a group of delegates, all with equal weight, democratically elected, write down on a piece of paper 83 names of people they would like to see on the National Committee. They don't write down the 10 or 50 or 1,600 names of those they don't think should be on it. This is true no matter how many nominations there are. There may be 2,000 nominations or there may be 83 nominations. The delegates write down those names, then their votes are added up, and the 83 highest vote getters are the National Committee of the party for a year or two.

It is not the party's job to pick people *not* to be leaders or *not* to have responsibilities. It's not our job to put obstacles in anyone's way to shouldering more responsibility. To the contrary. It is true that when we elect someone to a certain responsibility we are excluding other people from having that formal responsibility at that time. But that exclusion is never our starting point.

What is the National Committee?
There is a second aspect of this question. What is the National Committee? The first thing to say is that it is a *committee*. Being an individual "NCer" doesn't really mean much—at least in the way of privileges. The only one I know of is listed in article V, section 3, paragraph 4 of the Constitution, which says if an NCer

is caught being disloyal to the party he or she can be suspended only by a two-thirds vote of the NC, losing all rights and twisting in the wind until the next convention chucks them out. Some privilege!

"The Organizational Character of the Socialist Workers Party" lists some unambiguous *responsibilities* however:

> Membership in the leading staff of the party, the National Committee, must be made contingent on a complete subordination of the life of the candidate to the party. All members of the National Committee must be prepared to devote full-time activities to party work at the demand of the National Committee. . . .
>
> The leadership of the party must be under the control of the membership, its policies must always be open to criticism, discussion and rectification by the rank and file within properly established forms and limits, and the leading bodies themselves subject to formal recall or alteration. The membership of the party has the right to demand and expect the greatest responsibility from the leaders precisely because of the position they occupy in the movement. The selection of comrades to the positions of leadership means the conferring of an extraordinary responsibility. The warrant for this position must be proved, not once, but continuously by the leadership itself. It is under obligation to set the highest example of responsibility, devotion, sacrifice, and complete identification with the party itself and its daily life and action. It must display the ability to defend its policies before the membership of the party, and to defend the line of the party and the party as a whole before the working class in general.[16]

But the National Committee *as a committee* means a great deal. When the committee meets as a committee and makes decisions as a committee, it acts as the national leadership of the party, as if the party is in the room. That's what's important.

Secondly, it's important to remind ourselves that the National Committee is not the totality of the leadership of the party. The leadership of the party is much bigger and broader than the National Committee, the Political Committee, local executive committees, or any other committees. The leadership of the party is those who lead. It's good to keep that in mind.

Leadership development

What can be accomplished in the actual election to the National Committee? The National Committee election simply reflects something that has *already taken place*. The National Committee *election* is not important as it sometimes seems. It's not a historic event in the class struggle. The National Committee election is a way of democratically formalizing a rounded committee of eighty-three, or whatever the number is, of comrades who have already taken leadership. To be *elected* to the National Committee doesn't *make* you a national leader. Being elected to the National Committee has nothing to do per se with being a leader. Either you are a leader or are not. If the national convention recognizes it, good. If it doesn't, wait until next year.

However, if it doesn't recognize enough of the leadership over time, then we have a real problem. Then a disparity develops between the real leadership and the formal leadership. The purpose of the election of the National Committee is to recognize and formalize the reality of the party leadership.

If it did not do this, we would be in trouble. Everyone knows who the leadership of the party is. The real leadership of the party is those you go to when you have political problems, those whose opinions you listen to when important decisions are being made. Those you look to for leadership. The National Committee had damn well better be those same people, basically, or it won't have the authority and the respect of the party. That's where we should begin. Thus, there are narrow limits on what the election of the National Committee itself accomplished in terms of affirmative action. Of course, certain things can be done. If the nominations commission and delegates are conscious of what we are trying to do—as they are—this process can be nudged forward somewhat. But that's about all.

But the heart of the process of leadership development, including affirmative action, does not occur during the election of the National Committee. Broadening and training the leadership of the party must occur in the branches, the locals, the fractions. That's where our affirmative action takes place, where the conscious leadership development takes place. That's where it happens. There we can use some guidelines. We have to be conscious of what we're doing. For one thing, we have to fight against *stereotyping* of assignments.

Another thing that we want to keep in mind is that every responsibility is a collective one. You never stick a comrade in a job and then say that comrade is over his or her head and then criticize them for it. The comrades who have given the assignment or have given the responsibility, the executive committee or the branch, are responsible for the comrade who takes it. Every assignment is collective. Every assignment must be worked on in a collective way.

Next, leadership more than anything else means taking *general* responsibility. Leaders are not those who just exert themselves in their particular assignment. Leaders are those who, in addition to their responsibility within whatever division of labor we have, are always shouldering other responsibility. They are thinking about the party as a whole, the branch as a whole, and helping.

There are obvious things the leadership can do, some affirmative action we can take, to advance the process of leadership development. One, we can explicitly encourage it and we can aid the party to do this, in every structure—from the national field organizers to the branch executive committees.

'Sandstone University'
The second thing we can do is start what Jim Cannon described as The National Full-Time Training School, popularly called the Trotsky School. (We could call it the Cannon School or Sandstone University or some other appropriate name. I like Sandstone University since the idea was developed collectively in discussions by the com-

rades serving the Smith Act sentences at Sandstone, Minnesota.) The original proposal is reprinted in *Letters from Prison.*[17] It's worth rereading. It also serves to remind us that we'll all probably get a chance sometime to do graduate work under similar conditions.

We are not ready to make this decision now. For one thing, we've got to find ways to finance it without disrupting other things. Maybe we can start a campaign to raise the money to do it. Maybe some comrades will come forward to help us finance it. But it would be irresponsible not to begin it soon.

There's a very simple law to the development of leadership, one that we have to watch. Comrades who shoulder all sorts of responsibility, who move forward and take more and more responsibility, will not automatically take the time—if they are active workers and active comrades—to step back, think, read, and periodically rearm themselves politically. This is especially true for comrades who develop in the party along certain roads. I think this can be true, for example, among many women comrades. Some comrades become extremely efficient and experienced organizers. They organize branches and fractions and all kinds of things. But along the way they don't have the time, the inclination, the encouragement, or the training to thoroughly and consistently arm themselves politically.

We have got to get rid of any implicit idea that this is okay. That it's just going to be that way. That's baloney. We are not a party in which some *do* extremely well and some *think* extremely well and it all works out. That would be a fatal weakness of a party. The Sandstone University relates to our affirmative action. But that's not all it is. It is aimed at advancing all the cadres of the party.

Developing every comrade

As important as our special responsibility is to advance women and comrades of the oppressed nationalities, this is subordinate to and must be placed within the framework of our main job. That job is to maximize, in all ways possible, the conditions for the development of *every single member* of this party as cadres of the SWP and leaders of the proletariat, in whatever fields are open to them. That is our overriding responsibility.

There are different ways we can do this. One of the most fundamental is very simple. The leadership has to give every single comrade a fair shot. We must work with each comrade in the same way, have no favoritism, regardless of nationality, sex, age, background, or experiences. Every leader is a leader of the party. They must see themselves as a leader of the whole party. Every member of the party must have confidence in every single leader—that they will get an objective hearing, a fair shot, and working relations with them on the same footing as anyone else. This is our strength.

We don't want any comrades thinking that they lead certain comrades but not others. We don't want a leadership that doesn't have the confidence of the entire membership. The party's elected leadership body is responsible for the work of the party as a whole and the development of all comrades. This is what we seek, and we have made important strides forward in this in the last couple of years.

Within this framework, there are all kinds of organizational norms that help. One is that committees are more important than individuals. We should think of ourselves less as directors of work and more as a fraction head or a committee chair, because this approach is more efficient and you get better ideas. Anyone who sits alone in a room can come up with ideas—often weird ideas. When you just talk to people who think exactly like you, you can get off on a tangent. When you hang around people not all like you, you get more rounded ideas. If you think your closest friends are the people you work together with best as a political team, you are going off the track.

It is useful to review the role of the executive committees and the organizer. The organizer is not the organizer of the branch or the local. The executive committee is the organizer of the branch or the local. The organizer is simply the executive officer of the executive committee. It's more important that the committee itself function well and take more and more responsibility than to have a superefficient high-powered organizer. We don't care if we don't accomplish some task perfectly because the most experienced comrade is not assigned to it. We care about the experiences and development of the cadre as a whole.

What a good organizer can accomplish is measured in terms of how well the executive committee develops how many cadres for the next stage of leadership. Of course, this is true not just for organizers, but for work directors and fraction heads. Anyone leading anything at all is always preparing their own future replacement. What you do and what you accomplish in the short run is less important than how the party machine works after you have left for another assignment. Measure what you've accomplished by how many comrades you have made more self-confident and knowledgeable. How many you have taught by example that leaders are those who lead, and that every single comrade who does so is a leader of the party.

The second norm we should keep in mind is that leadership is how, and not what. People lead by *how* they do things, and not by *what* particular thing they do. Think of all our tasks as being accomplished by bolshevik labor power. It's not *what* concrete form it takes that determines its value to the party. It's *how* well we all work that counts. And that's what we value.

Leaders never accept or reject a responsibility because of a post involved. They never reject responsibility because they are not on a committee. They accept general responsibility, for the success of their assignment and for everyone else's, as much as humanly possible.

Professional revolutionists

There is another aspect to this: leadership has nothing to do with being full-time. Leaders have to be ready to take full-time assignments. But all leaders have to consider themselves professional revolutionists, whether they work full-time for the party or not.

No one ever got paid in the revolutionary party for leading. It has never happened. You lead, and whether you are full-time or not is irrelevant to *that* fact.

Finally, we should get rid of any mechanical conception of leadership development up a ladder. Our party is not the kind of party where leadership begins by being a member of a branch committee. Then you become head of another committee. Then you become head of the sales committee. Then you become a candidate. Then you become an assistant organizer. Then you become branch organizer. Then you become city organizer. Then you become bishop of the archdiocese. Of course, there is a problem. That's the way the whole world works. But that's not the way this party works.

This is where the conjuncture comes in, where the colonization of industry comes in. There is no ladder like that in developing the leadership of the party. The leadership question is connected directly with making this turn. Leadership right now means, above all, leading this party into industry and shouldering the responsibility this implies on every level. We want the majority of the local and branch executive committees in industry. We want a bunch of our current organizers in industry as soon as we can replace them. We want to continue the process that we began with comrades on the National Committee, the trade union steering committee, and the Political Committee—releasing leaders to get jobs in industry, to recognize and take advantage of the openings, to go to where the future leaders of the mass movements are, and to go where our cadres are going to come forward nationally, be trained, and be tested. This is where the conjuncture and our immediate tasks come together with the more general character of the party, the character of the revolution, and the development of the leadership.

* * *

We have stressed that this is a preparatory period. We say that we are not going into industry because we are expecting immediate conjunctural gains. We should also stress something else. If we carry this out, and get the big majority of the party into industrial unions, if the leadership leads, if the majority of the branch and local leadership lead this work, we are going to recruit. We are beginning to recruit in industry, not fast, but it will step up.

The party is going to be transformed. We will have a different milieu for our campaigns and we will recruit. This will strengthen every part of the party's work. It will strengthen us in community struggles, in NOW, in the Chicano movement, in the NAACP, in the anti-*Bakke* work,[18] in every single campaign that we are involved in.

We should be grateful we have a preparatory period so we can use it. But we don't want to dawdle. What Trotsky said about the American workers moving with American speed wasn't just to enthuse us. It is the truth. We have no mass Stalinist party, no mass Socialist Party, no reformist labor party. We do not have a defeated working class, or a discouraged working class, no enraged petty bourgeoisie. These obstacles do not exist. We know historically, we know as sure as we are sitting here, that the kind of crisis that we are now in—the economic crisis and the offensive of the ruling class—has always produced in this country an explosive radicalizing motion in the American working class. It is going to happen again.

This is a unique opportunity for the party in another way. We have never before decided on a shift like this, responded to an opening like this, when we didn't have to have a faction fight inside the party. We don't have an opposition in the party today. We have a party that is waiting to be led. The comrades are waiting to have presented to them what we are going to do. In the opinion of the Political Committee, that is the challenge of this plenum. It is the opportunity—and the real test—for this leadership.

Forging the leadership of a proletarian party

MARY-ALICE WATERS

The election of the National Committee at the upcoming convention of the party will be one of the most important items of business before the delegates.

Our starting point is the character of the coming American revolution and the strategic goals of our class that flow from it. The kind of leadership we must develop is determined by the kind of party it will take to lead that revolution. It will be a proletarian revolution to establish a workers government. Thus the party that leads that revolution must be a proletarian party. It cannot be a "combined party." It cannot be a coalition of sectors. There are not multiple vanguards. Our party must be the vanguard of the working class in program, composition, and collective experience. It must include in its ranks the most conscious vanguard fighters of the proletariat. Its composition must reflect the vanguard role of Black workers and the growing number of women workers, especially those who are fighting their way into

This report was adopted by the SWP National Committee in May 1979.

SEE PAGE 440 FOR NOTES

sections of industry previously closed to women.

Once we have defined the character of the coming American revolution, and clarified the class character and composition of the party needed to lead that revolution, we must ask ourselves: What stage are we at right now in the construction of that party? What are the challenges and the tasks we face today? How do we go about transforming a cadre party of some 1,500 members— very few of whom are from working-class backgrounds, most of whom were recruited as students around the various social protest actions of the 1960s and early 1970s—into a party of industrial workers? Where are we in relation to our goal of transforming the membership and the leadership? Transforming the milieu in which we live and work? Transforming the axis of our work and making it revolve around our industrial fractions? Beginning to recruit young workers who will develop as leaders of our party?

What is leadership?

What is leadership in a bolshevik party?

Our answer must start not with party leadership but with the party itself. In other words, we start with the leadership of the working class.

What is a member of a bolshevik party? It's hard to come up with a better initial definition than the one Marx and Engels set forth in the Communist Manifesto. Communists "have no interests separate and apart from those of the working class as a whole."

That's what members of our party are. Individuals who subordinate everything to centralized collaboration with others who share and are totally committed to our revolutionary goals and perspectives. Individuals who strive in a disciplined way to help the party lead the working class to realize its historic tasks, which are the interests of all humanity.

In the party we're building, each and every member is a leader, a leader of the working class, part of the conscious vanguard of our class. We strive to maximize the political capacities and develop the leadership abilities of every single member. That's what we mean by a cadre party: a party in which all members are trained as leaders and are prepared to train others as leaders of their class. In other words, for us leadership is not an individual question, it is the question of the party itself.

This is a fundamental point. It's worth stopping to think about. It is the opposite of everything we are taught by class society. The party is made up of individuals, of course. But our strength is in our collectivity, not our individuality. Our strength is in our ability to function together as a team, as a machine. John G. Wright called it a thinking machine.[1] It's a thinking machine, it's an acting machine, but it's a machine.

In this sense, too, we are like our class, because the strength of our class also lies in its collective power. Every worker knows that individually he or she has very little power. But together we can change the world. Solidarity, cooperation, and collaboration are the essence of strength.

This is the opposite of the consciousness created by bourgeois and petty-bourgeois conditions of life. For the bourgeoisie and petty bourgeoisie, success *does* depend on individual action. You come out on top only by pitting yourself against and defeating everybody else. Competition, not collective effort, is the precondition for survival. And for the bourgeoisie, the rewards all come from the exploitation of another class.

In the proletarian party, our concern about developing individuals as leaders is not to promote egocentric "self-fulfillment," but to increase our collective strength and advance the party and our class. That is what gives each of us as individuals a great deal of satisfaction.

This is why a bolshevik party ultimately cannot be forged outside the conditions of life and the day-to-day living struggles of our class. This is why it must be proletarian in composition as well as in program.

Thus we arrive at the first criterion of leadership in a bolshevik party: the ability to see ourselves in relationship to the party, not the party in relationship to ourselves. We derive our personal satisfaction from helping make the machine run, not from seeing our names up in neon lights.

Our pride is in what the party does well, maximizing the results of that collective effort. Our reward is in advancing the party, not advancing ourselves as individuals; competing for greater recognition from others.

We discussed this at our plenum a year ago in reference to the development of strong industrial fractions. Our aim, we said, is not to somehow try to ensure that every party member will become an outstanding individual leader of big working-class battles. That's an impossible goal, and an unnecessary one. Those natural leaders of the class are important, of course, and the SWP is training some of them today and will recruit more.

But that's not what's decisive for the party or for the class. That's not why we're so determined to get the overwhelming majority of party members and leaders into industry.

What is decisive, we've explained, is never what an individual comrade can accomplish on the job, whatever his or her strengths and weaknesses, but what the fraction accomplishes. More than that, it is what the national fraction accomplishes. And every single comrade in those fractions makes a contribution to that joint effort.

The effectiveness of the party depends on what we can do as a team through the branches, locals, fractions, committees, and leadership bodies. That is the kind of party our class needs to take it forward.

The National Committee

The fact that the party is a machine made up of cadres who function as a collective unit is one of the reasons why we stress that leadership of the party is much broader than the members of the National Committee.

The National Committee is the leading *committee* of the party.

It is selected by the membership on the basis of both the general political capacities and the proven abilities of the individual members to lead the struggles through which the party is being built at any given stage. But it is put together as a committee, as a team. The core of the committee are the most tested and experienced leaders of the party over an extended period of time, but the team is and must constantly be renewed and changed. It is a living organism that grows and develops as the party and our class change and go through new experiences.

The National Committee is a team that incorporates comrades who are politically experienced in and lead diverse aspects of party activity—comrades carrying administrative responsibility, writers, speakers, organizers, mass workers, and so on. It includes different generations, different layers and experiences of the working class. In putting together the committee, we try to look ahead to where we're going, as well as to take account of where we've come from.

Above all, the National Committee is not a list of individuals. It is a committee in which the membership has political confidence as the leadership of the party.

In the course of the discussion here at this plenum, a number of comrades have referred to the new Education for Socialists bulletin entitled *Background to 'The Struggle for a Proletarian Party.'* This valuable bulletin contains, along with other items, a selection of letters Trotsky wrote to American comrades in 1937. Most of the letters dealt with the leadership question. We were starting to make a turn to the industrial working class then, and Trotsky was hammering away at us to speed it up. I'm sure those of you who have had a chance to read the bulletin have been struck by how timely and relevant it is.

In his letters, as later in *In Defense of Marxism*, Trotsky refers over and over again to the tendency toward "individualism" on the part of the petty-bourgeois members of the American party and of the old Russian Bolshevik Party. He points out that these are often very good comrades, but their attitudes are conditioned by their class experiences. He notes their tendency to criticize for the sake of criticism, to oppose for the sake of opposition, to doubt for the sake of covering their own deep skepticism concerning the revolutionary capacities of the working class. He contrasts these attitudes toward the party, and toward themselves, to the attitudes of working-class members.

Trotsky explained that seeing yourself in relation to the party—not the other way around—is a proletarian attitude.

To develop new leaders

Trotsky points to a second aspect of leadership in those letters as well.

Leaders are those who help others become leaders.

The party leadership has the responsibility to carefully prepare and thoroughly explain every decision, every policy, every shift, so that the membership is comfortable not only with what we are doing, but why. We try to work with and develop the self-confidence of every member as a thinking, experienced cadre who understands not just the tactics of the moment but the fundamental strategic concepts that determine our always-changing tactics.

This concern to develop the capacities of every single member of the party and the leadership's political responsibilities toward the membership is summed up quite well when Trotsky said full-timers "of a revolutionary party should have in the first place a good ear, and only in the second place a good tongue."

Our need to help every single comrade develop her or his understanding and abilities is one of the reasons that we organize our work through committees and fractions. Of course, a committee or fraction functions better than an individual, since we all have our weaknesses. Working collectively, we try to balance each other and compensate for our weaknesses. That's obvious.

But working through fractions and committees is also how to develop comrades. We never put comrades all alone in an assignment and then say, "Well, that was over their head. They just couldn't handle it." Every assignment is a collective responsibility. Ultimately, the decisive test of how well we lead is how well we prepare our replacement, how well we pass on what we know and train somebody else to take over from us.

Affirmative action

Third, Trotsky explains that both proletarianizing the party and what we would today call affirmative action are indispensable to developing a proletarian leadership. He argues that conscious measures must be taken to increase the proletarian composition of the leading bodies of the party and to advance the self-confidence of young worker cadres as leaders. The key points he makes are along the lines that we've been discussing over the last few years in relationship to the development of leaders of the party who are Black and Latino and female.

Trotsky explains that if you just let nature take its course, given the composition and arenas of activity of many members, workers who aren't glib with "general formulas and fluent pens"—just rich in their "acquaintance with the life of workers and practical capacities"—are likely to be overlooked as part of the leadership. He proposed that a whole layer of such working-class cadres with proven abilities and capacities should be consciously placed on the National Committee and other leading bodies to strengthen the leadership politically and, at the same time, allow these comrades to develop. He points out that participation in the leading committees of the party is important in and of itself at a certain stage of a leader's education. Trotsky urged the party to cut through all the "secondary, factional, and personal conditions [that] play too great a role in the composition of the list of candidates" for the leading bodies of the party, and consciously renew the leadership through these kinds of affirmative action measures.

Leadership and party democracy

Fourth, Trotsky explains that these concepts of leadership are inextricably interconnected with the question of party democracy.

He asks, What is party democracy? And he lists three elements.

1. "The strictest observance of the party statutes by the leading

bodies"—regular conventions, full discussion periods, right of minorities to express their opinions, right to form tendencies, and so forth. All the things that are codified in our constitution and organizational principles. But, Trotsky writes, that is only the very beginning.

2. "A patient, friendly, to a certain point pedagogical attitude on the part of the central committee and its members toward the rank and file, including the objectors and the discontented, because it is not a great merit to be satisfied 'with anybody who is satisfied with me.' "

He goes on: "Methods of psychological 'terrorism,' including a haughty or sarcastic manner of answering or treating every objection, criticism, or doubt—it is, namely, this journalistic or 'intellectualistic' manner which is insufferable to workers and condemns them to silence." Eradicating this kind of conduct by "leaders" is also at the heart of party democracy.

But, Trotsky insists, these two elements still aren't enough. It is not sufficient merely to abide by formal rules of party democracy and outlaw terroristic methods or ridicule of comrades who raise questions and new ideas.

3. The leadership must also maintain "permanent, active, and informal contact with the rank and file, especially when a new slogan or a new campaign is in preparation or when it is necessary to verify the results of an accomplished campaign." The leading bodies, Trotsky says, must be "closely connected with the rank and file, organically representative of them."

Trotsky insisted that only that kind of party, with those kinds of conscious leadership attitudes, could make the turn to industrial workers that was necessary in 1937. And this holds for us in 1979.

Finally, we should add what we have stressed before. Leaders are those who willingly shoulder broad general political responsibility—beyond whatever specific assignments they have regardless of what "posts," if any, they have. To put it most simply, leadership is not what assignment you take but how you carry out whatever's necessary. Leaders are those who lead.

These are some of the basic concepts about the party and about party leadership that the SWP had learned from Trotsky and from our own experiences by the end of the 1930s. The basic cadre of our party absorbed these attitudes and was able to pass them on without a break in continuity. That has been decisive in enabling us to go as far as we have in assembling—in a qualitatively different way than most of the other parties of the Fourth International—a homogeneous leadership team, composed of comrades of different generations, men and women, and comrades of oppressed nationalities. The success we have had in this is based on these most fundamental proletarian attitudes toward the party and leadership. It has allowed us, among other things, to carry through an unprecedented transition in leadership.

Some proletarian attitudes

Many of these lessons—and a few others, too—were touched on by Farrell Dobbs in his tribute to Joe Hansen. We published Farrell's remarks to the San Francisco memorial meeting in the April 16, 1979, issue of *Intercontinental Press.*

Farrell pointed to Joe's understanding that leadership is not what you do but how you do it. He capsulized this in the story of how Joe took the assignment of *Militant* business manager after the Cochranites bellyached about having a leader of their faction asked to take such a politically unimportant "technical" assignment.[2] Joe carried out that assignment in a serious and professional way. He loved it. And he loved demonstrating to the whole party that every single assignment is important.

Farrell was paying Joe one of his highest tributes when he called him a "disciplined soldier." Someone who knew that everything we do—whether organizing a branch, serving as the SWP observer on the United Secretariat of the Fourth International, promoting the circulation of our press, getting a job in steel—is all just working as part of the team. We are all thinking, acting, disciplined pieces in a much bigger thinking and acting machine. As Joe used to say, "It's all labor power." Everything we do is part of building the party. That's what counts.

Secondly, Farrell emphasized Joe's self-control and self-discipline. Especially under pressure, sometimes enormous pressure, whether in Mexico in Trotsky's household, or working to hold the party together throughout the period of McCarthyism in this country. Joe never "lost his cool," Farrell said.

Third, Joe was supremely conscious that leaders have a general responsibility for maintaining the equilibrium of the party. They take the party seriously. If you have an idea or a proposal or something that you think is wrong, you don't just pop off with it, no matter what the time of day. As Farrell put it, you don't "start making a racket like a mule in a tin barn" when you have a difference.

You raise your ideas, criticism, proposals, in a balanced way, at the correct time and place, and with a sense of proportion about the needs of the entire party. The more leadership responsibility you carry, the more your actions and opinions can have an impact on the stability and the equilibrium of the party and its ability to function.

In one of the letters I mentioned earlier, Trotsky recalled Lenin's view on this matter. When Lenin called for Ordzhonikidze to be expelled from the party in 1923, Trotsky wrote, "he said very correctly that the discontented party member has the right to be turbulent, but not a member of the central committee." Farrell noted that Joe always acted like a leader in this respect and understood that leaders have less right, not greater leeway, to indulge their "individualism," their personal whims and foibles.

Fourth, Farrell stressed that Joe wasn't one of those people who try to show how brilliant they are by trying to make others seem stupid. Joe didn't try to prove he was an "independent thinker" by refusing to learn from Trotsky. The result was that he was able to learn. He learned how to think through whatever problem was before him, to approach questions systematically, to see all the different angles, and to solve those problems.

The leadership qualities Farrell pointed to in Joe are not inherent qualities in anyone. They are things that everyone can learn. They are acquired proletarian attributes of leadership that we all can develop.

Leaders who are Black, Latino, and female

I want to turn now to a specific aspect of the leadership question that we have been discussing since the last convention: the challenge we face in developing Black and Latino and women comrades as rounded leaders of the party.

We should add that in the 1980s, we will face a similar challenge in developing young workers we recruit out of the plants. Many of them will be Black, Latino, and women as well.

The special challenges we face in developing this kind of leadership are real. But 99 percent of the answers are to be found in the general approach we have to all leadership questions.

We should begin by separating the questions of developing leaders from the oppressed nationalities and developing leaders who are women. Some aspects are similar, but there are differences as well.

Let's start with the challenge facing us in the development of Blacks, Chicanos, Puerto Ricans, and other comrades of oppressed national minorities. Beginning with the report and discussion at the February 1978 plenum, we have come to a much clearer understanding of why a party that is genuinely multinational in its ranks and its leadership cannot be built unless it is proletarian in composition and milieu. A proletarian program alone is not sufficient.

We can, of course, assemble a vanguard around our program, as we have done in the last decade and a half. The scope of this recruitment and development of Black and Latino comrades is an accomplishment new in the history of American Trotskyism. As we turn to the new political openings in the industrial working class, this accomplishment will enable us to better recruit and integrate young Black and Latino workers.

But the next step forward in the construction of a multinational leadership can only be taken by a party whose members are part of the industrial working class. Why do we say this?

So long as the party was composed primarily of students and white-collar, semiprofessional workers, and the radicalization took the form of social protest actions in which the mass organizations of the working class played little role, it was more difficult to overcome the deep suspicions of Blacks and Latinos attracted to us. It was more difficult to recruit comrades of oppressed nationalities than to recruit whites. This was true because in addition to all the other obstacles—which still make the recruitment of every individual exceptional—the class milieu in which we functioned, the petty-bourgeois conditions of life, maximized conflicts of interests.

There is no way around the fact that for white students—especially those from petty-bourgeois backgrounds, but from working-class families as well—there are invariably choices and options not open to Blacks and Latinos. This is true for comrades as well.

Most white comrades have had the experience of working to recruit a Black or Latino contact and being asked—sometimes openly, sometimes implicitly—"You *say* you stand on this program, but how do I know you mean it? Will you really be around when the going gets tough? What's in it for you?"

The issues around which the radicalization was deepening, and the conditions of struggle, didn't always provide a lot of opportunities to prove that we weren't just idealistic supporters of good causes. So we recruited only those Blacks and Latinos who were able to overcome tremendous objective barriers. They had to be exceptionally clearsighted and tough.

Those kinds of obstacles are diminished, though, as the party becomes proletarian not only in program but in composition and milieu. The relations between Black and white workers on the picket line in Newport News are different from the relations between Black and white radicals on the campus.[3] The relationship between Black and white comrades on the line in an auto plant are different than in an antiwar coalition.

Solidarity is the precondition of survival in the working class. Your common class interests are obviously great, despite the national oppression that one worker suffers and another doesn't. You have the same material interests as members of the same class. And that is what comes to the fore, especially in periods of struggle.

Moreover, as the class polarization deepens, it becomes clearer that the road forward for both the Black liberation struggle and the labor movement are inseparably intertwined. Both the forces necessary to win Black rights, and the Black leadership whose class understanding and political courage will make possible the next stage of struggle, will be found in the mills, the factories, the shipyards, etc. You don't have to choose between fighting for the needs of Black people or transforming the labor movement. The forging of a class-struggle left wing in the unions and the revitalization of an uncompromising movement for Black rights are intertwined.

Attitudes begin to change in struggle. Mutual confidence is forged among the best fighters, among those who lead. You're not supporting a good program. You're fighting for your own common needs. The answer to "What's in this for you or me?" is obvious. It becomes not a choice, but a necessity.

It's only under these conditions that a broad multinational composition and leadership—not just a thin layer, but a broad-based cadre—can be built. The leaders and members of the SWP must have unshakeable confidence in each other. We have to be prepared to put our lives in each others' hands. And that kind of party can be forged only in real proletarian class combat. It becomes obvious why the party must be politically homogeneous and steeled through common leadership experience in the class struggle.

We should also keep in mind an important objective change that makes our perspective of building this kind of party realistic. The kind of *multinational* party and leadership that must be built today could not have been built several decades ago because the composition of the proletariat itself was not the same. During

World War II, and in the postwar years, massive urbanization and proletarianization of the oppressed nationalities took place.

In the 1930s the Black population and the Chicano population were much more rural and engaged in agriculture. They were more an ally of the working class than a layer of the working class. This has changed dramatically over the past forty years.

Of course, you had to have a multinational party in the 1930s, too. You had to have the correct line on Black self-determination. You had to have a correct understanding of the vanguard role that the Black proletariat would play. And we did.

But the degree and the extent to which the forging of a broad multinational cadre is both possible and a life-or-death question to the American revolution is different today than it was fifty years ago. And it becomes more crucial each passing year, as the proletarianization of the oppressed nationalities continues.

That is why it is both more necessary and more possible today to construct a proletarian party that is multinational in composition and leadership. It's important to keep this in mind as we look back and evaluate the history of our own party.

But the fact that it is more possible to build a multinational party today, as well as more vital to the future of humanity, does not mean it will happen automatically.

It doesn't eliminate the extra barriers created by this society— barriers that must be overcome in the development of leaders of the party who are Black, or who are Chicano, or Puerto Rican, or any oppressed national minority. It doesn't mean that we no longer have to take special measures to encourage the development of Black and Latino comrades as party leaders.

That's why we have and will continue to have a policy of affirmative action, that is, of consciously encouraging and giving special attention to the leadership development of comrades of the oppressed nationalities.

But these special steps now take place within the framework of our turn into industry, of our progress toward building a more proletarian party. As Blacks and Latinos gain confidence as leaders of the working class, they will also become more self-confident as leaders of the vanguard party of our class.

Blacks and Latinos will be in the forefront of those workers who push toward a class-struggle left wing in the unions. They will fight to unify the class around a program that champions the demands of all the oppressed and exploited. They will provide the proletarian leadership necessary to revitalize massive social protests for Black and Latino rights.

Through these experiences, and as part of a revolutionary combat party, they will participate in leading the mass proletarian actions that will culminate in the conquest of power and the establishment of a workers government.

This is the perspective that the SWP can and does offer the Black and Latino workers we are talking to and working with as we get into industry. This is the road to the development of a multinational proletarian party.

Party leaders who are women

What about developing leaders of the party who are women?

Most of what we've said so far applies to women. But we also have to say more.

We face the challenge of building a party and leadership unlike anything that has ever existed before. That's a historical fact. And the explanation is simple. The sex composition of the American working class today is unlike anything that has existed before. The changes on this level are similar to what we were just saying about the race question.

A party with the sex composition of the Bolshevik Party of 1917 could not lead the American revolution today. There was not a single woman in the central political leadership of the Bolshevik Party. Krupskaya may have been one of the strongest women, but she was never a member of the central committee. Kollantai played an important role, but she was not a rounded political leader, never carried any general central leadership responsibility.

I think that if you look back cold-bloodedly on the history of the Marxist movement, you would have to say that there is really only one woman who stands out as that kind of central political leader—Rosa Luxemburg. Perhaps it would be correct to include Eleanor Marx, too.

But if Luxemburg was unique in the history of the Marxist movement, that is not something we need to be defensive or apologetic about. It is no fault of Marxism or Leninism or the leaderships of genuine Marxist and Leninist parties.

Rather, it is a result of two historical factors: first, the stage of development of capitalism itself and the sex composition of the workforce; and second, the depth of women's oppression, institutionalized through the family, and the profound affect this has on the character structure of every female raised in class society.

If we who live in the economically strongest capitalist countries, in the last part of the twentieth century, can be relatively optimistic about our ability to build a party and leadership that is different in leadership composition from anything that has existed so far, it is because of the changes produced by the development of capitalism itself.

The post–World War II economic expansion, with its great acceleration in the 1960s, brought about a qualitative increase in the percentage of women in the labor market: in the United States it is now more than 60 percent of women between the ages of 18 and 55. It brought about a qualitative increase in the percentage of the labor force who are women: it is now more than 40 percent. These changes, more than any other *single* factor, underlie the "second wave" of feminist struggle.

Moreover—and most important for us—women have begun over the past decade to bust down the barriers to entering the sectors of industry from which they were previously excluded. This is new. It has happened since the late 1960s. And when the next bad recession hits, the working class will have a real battle to prevent these women from being driven out of industry.

These changes are decisive for the development of women who are leaders of the working class, and the creation of a proletarian party of the kind our tasks require. And our turn gives us a new framework to advance the political self-confidence of women comrades. Many comrades who have gotten industrial jobs in the last months have already experienced this.

When you go from working as a personal secretary and servant for some man in an office, to an auto assembly line, the change affects your own consciousness. It affects your attitudes toward yourself and what you're capable of doing.

Getting out of the isolation and dependency of the home and into the workforce is a gigantic step for women that changes consciousness. But taking the next step into sectors of industry previously closed to women is now even more crucial to the development of the kind of leadership we need.

As women bust down the barriers to industry, you also see changes—often rapid changes—in the attitudes of men on the assembly lines or in the steel plants. They see the women they are working with in a different light. Sexist prejudices begin to break down.

A party with a significant component of women in its central leadership cannot be built except as a working-class party—in composition as well as program. We can say this definitively. It is not a question of individuals. We're not saying that only women who are workers can overcome the barriers and develop as leaders. But a revolutionary party with a broad cadre of leaders who are women can only be forged in the real battles of our class, and this will be totally intertwined with the changing composition of the industrial labor force.

Women have a deep fear of leadership. We are conditioned from the day we're born to fear the consequences of attempting to lead—to lead men, especially. We are taught that such a course will inevitably mean loneliness and personal rejection by men. That no man can tolerate a challenge to his "masculinity" by an independent, self-confident woman who acts as a leader. And few men can.

This is the biggest obstacle to the development of women leaders. It is rooted in the character structure, the psychology, of the oppressed sex. It is something that every woman faces and has to deal with.

This is why the development of women as leaders is even more of a challenge than developing Black and Latino leaders of the party. Of course, for Latinas and Black women, these factors are compounded. The challenge for them is even greater.

The changes in women's consciousness and self-confidence will go hand in hand with changing attitudes among men. Men will lose their fear of being challenged by women as women gain the economic independence and psychological self-confidence to become leaders of men. And that's one of the reasons why the changes in our class, the affirmative-action battles we are winning, are so important. It is a question of the future of humanity—male and female.

The SWP leadership today

How is all this reflected in the leadership of the party today? The progress we have made as well as the obstacles we have yet to overcome, are indicated by the composition of the National Committee elected at the last convention.

The membership of the SWP is roughly 42 percent female, but 33 percent of the National Committee is women. On the other hand, 6 or 7 percent of party members are Black but 26 percent of our National Committee is Black. The Latino members make up about 5 percent of the party, and about 7 percent of the National Committee.

As of this plenum, about 39 percent of the membership, and 30 percent of the National Committee are industrial workers.

My own opinion is that the composition of our National Committee is not out of harmony with the real leadership of the party. Give or take a few percentage points—and that is not important— those figures fairly accurately register what we have accomplished. In that sense, the National Committee elected at the last convention is good. Because, as we pointed out at the time, our elected leadership and our real leadership had better coincide, or else our leading committees would lose their authority. We would be as phony as a three-dollar bill if our real leadership and our elected leadership got out of mesh.

But I want to talk about something else. What is behind those statistics? What do they tell us about the party? We should take a look at this in relation to the need for the party to take special steps to aid and to challenge women comrades to develop leadership capacities.

This is one of the questions that came up during the discussion on the election of the National Committee at our August 1977 convention.

But it was posed in the wrong framework. Election to the NC was seen as a solution to leadership questions, rather than as a register of where we are. We all sensed there was something wrong with that discussion. We were uncomfortable with it. But why did it happen?

In part, we in the leadership fostered it. At the convention we called attention to the fact that there was a significant discrepancy between the percentage of the party that is female and the percentage of women on the National Committee. And we indicated that we thought that the new NC would register the continuing progress we had made in the development of leaders who are women. But we didn't say anything more. We didn't discuss, "Why is there a discrepancy of this kind? Where does it come from? Does it mean women aren't getting adequate consideration in nominations for the NC? What step do we need to take?"

As a result, there was a tendency to give the easy answers, to look for the easy solutions. That's natural. But when the problems are hard, easy answers don't get you very far. And they often point in the wrong direction.

One easy answer is to approach the leadership as a sum total of categories and percentages, rather than thinking about the real leadership of the party. That is, to start with trying to make the statistics look the way we'd like them to, not with the election of a committee to politically lead the party. Many comrades hoped the nominating commission would rectify the *percentages.* When there was still a discrepancy (though a smaller one), comrades were disappointed. They felt that a mistake had been made. That was how we got into the situation where, by a closely divided vote, the delegates decided on the spot to enlarge the NC by five. Of course, that's in order and not necessarily a mistake. There are always many comrades qualified to serve on the NC beyond those put forward by the nominating commission to open the nominations.

But the discussion took place within a false framework that assumed the election of the NC is itself a way of developing leadership. It isn't. It can't be. All it can do is *register,* as accurately and objectively as the human beings who are the convention delegates are capable of doing, the progress we have made *before* we get to the convention. Of course, the convention can push things a little bit in the right direction—but only a little bit. If it tries to push too far, it can come up with a list of nominations that does not accurately reflect the real leadership of the party.

The task of developing leadership is not the job of the nominating commission, or the delegates to the convention. It is a job that begins on the branch level, in every single party committee and fraction.

Misconceptions about what can be accomplished in the election of the NC are closely related to another easy answer. Does the fact that women are a smaller percentage of the National Committee than of the membership indicate that women are not being given due consideration for the NC? Put more broadly, does the *party* place obstacles or barriers in the way of the development of women as leaders? Does the party restrict women comrades to certain kinds of assignments, certain roles? If that were true, then the solution would be simple. Just remove the barriers in the party.

But this is false. The record of the nominating commissions at the last conventions unambiguously indicates that women are given preferential consideration for election to the NC. And I think that is generally true at all levels, and for most assignments in the party. I would say, moreover, that in relationship to other organizations of our class, our leadership is excellent on this score. And everyone knows it is *real*.

If, even with preferential consideration given to leaders who are women, the percentage of women on the NC is lower than the percentage of women in the party, this tells us we have a bigger challenge to overcome, a bigger problem to face up to in developing women as rounded political leaders. There is no reason for us to be defensive about this. We are dealing with the way *society* perpetuates the oppression of women. What women are taught and conditioned to believe about themselves from the day they are born. Women don't overcome that just by joining the SWP, or understanding our program.

There are many women who are leaders in our party. We all know that. Moreover, there has been a marked expansion of the leadership responsibilities of women in recent years. The women's liberation movement had a deep impact on all of us, female and male. For example, the number of women who are organizers and candidates, write for our press, and carry out other important assignments is qualitatively greater today than twenty years ago.

But we also know something else. There is a tendency for women to develop as leaders of a certain kind, as organizers who do a good job of organizing the campaigns of the party, working with comrades, pulling things together. But often women tend to reach a plateau at some stage that they can't go beyond because they're not politically equipped. It is not enough to understand tactics, or to be able to explain our position on this or that, or to be good at working with people.

All party leaders—men and women—have to become thorough Marxists. Have to be politically grounded with an understanding of our broad strategic perspectives and challenges we face today. Have to develop that kind of political self-confidence and learn to think politically in clear class terms.

If there is a tendency for women comrades to develop as leaders of a certain type, it is not because the party fosters it. The problem lies much deeper. All the social pressure and the psychological conditioning of women push us in that direction. The institutions of class society work to produce in us a deeply ingrained lack of self-confidence. After all, society doesn't take us seriously; why should we consider ourselves important?

So we often shy away from the broadest, general leadership responsibilities. Consciously or not we often hide in a narrower, more comfortable niche, where we feel less pressure. We become very good, become real leaders, in some aspect of party functioning. And we derive satisfaction from knowing we are doing something well, that it's important, that we are leading.

But, at the same time, we can't fool ourselves. We know what we're doing.

Feminist laments

We all know the signs of this that bother us. We feel uncomfortable when few delegates who are women take the floor at conventions whenever the discussion is on broad general, political questions. We often go to each other and say, "Hey, why don't you speak on this?"

We're dissatisfied with the number of women who write for our press. But it's the same challenge as the convention debates. Women comrades more often than men lack the general political self-confidence that comes from the combination of experience and systematically making time to read, to absorb in the light of new events things we may or may not have read before by Marx and Engels and Lenin and Trotsky. In order to write clearly, you have to understand clearly, to be able to explain what you understand to others.

And we're unhappy that despite preferential consideration, there are not significantly more women on the National Committee.

But sometimes we hide the central problem, our own tendency

to pull back from shouldering general political leadership responsibility, by what I call feminist laments. Why isn't a woman doing
this or that? Why aren't we being recognized?

In the Fourth International you sometimes hear it in extreme
forms. Some comrades express the idea that Leninism itself is a
"male" concept of leadership that inherently oppresses women;
that women are by nature leaders of a different kind than men.

We can't allow our feminist consciousness to become an excuse
to hide behind, rather than an aid to us in thinking out how to
meet the challenge we face. In order to survive in capitalist society,
women have learned to act in certain ways. That is, you know you
never get a fair shake; that whatever abilities you may have will
never be the reason you do or don't "get ahead"; that you have to
shoot every angle, fake it, sell yourself, and that if you do it right,
you can go a long way. If we act like that toward the party, it can
only lead to a self-defeating disaster and a self-perpetuating
"woman problem."

Each and every one of us was born and raised in capitalist society, and we have all the problems and hang-ups that come with
that. But the party *is* different from capitalist society in general.
Our conscious goal, as we discussed earlier, is to work together
collectively to maximize the political development of every comrade. The real pressure on women in the SWP is not that we are
held back but that we are constantly pressed to take on greater and
greater responsibility.

At the same time, no one in the party can fake it politically, not
in the long run. Either we become self-confident and rounded
Marxists, or we reach a limit before too long. The party is too serious, and women and men in the SWP are too serious, to tolerate
anything that is phony.

A personal challenge

The most important question is: "What are we going to do to
move forward on this front?"

The first thing is to frankly discuss the real challenge before us and not try to hide behind false explanations and fake solutions. It should give us a great deal of confidence that we *can* squarely confront this and apply the same materialist analysis and class perspective that we apply to every other question before our party and our class. There are no phony solutions. There are no organizational cure-alls.

We are not going to change the character structure of the oppressed sex—or of men either—between now and the revolution. But that is no excuse for not moving decisively to affect the conditions we can. Just the opposite. Being clear about the nature of the obstacles we face is the first step.

Second, there is a personal challenge before every single woman in the party. Whatever the party does collectively to help educate and maximize the political development of every individual, at a certain point there is one and only one thing that makes a difference: our own individual determination to educate ourselves. We all have to begin by recognizing that we have to combine our day-to-day activities and experiences in the class struggle with reading, studying, learning to think every political question through for ourselves. No one else can do it for us.

Education in our movement doesn't come from ivory tower study. We don't decide: Okay, I'm going to learn how to think like a Marxist, so I'll go off somewhere by myself and read the classics for a year or two. We can educate ourselves only in the course of the living experiences we go through in the class struggle, and how we respond to them.

When the revolution in Iran comes along, or the events in Southeast Asia, or the Newport News strike, we get excited. We try to think through, "What does this mean about the class struggle nationally, internationally? What does this change? What are the class forces at work? How should revolutionists respond?" The answers are not always obvious. So we go to our bookshelf and pick up a few books, to read or reread, to think about what is happening. If we don't do that, if we aren't politically inspired by what is happening and what we're doing, if we don't want to read and study—then no one else can do it for us. No one else can pick up that book. No one else can force us to make time. No one else can read it for us, think about it for us, study it for us.

Is this a *personal* challenge? Yes.

Is it harder for women to do this? Yes, it's harder. That is a historical fact, a fact of life in class society.

Are many problems that we used to think were personal shortcomings, really not our own fault? Yes.

But then, we have to add, *so what?*

Because it is harder for us, do we think it is less necessary? Do we think the standards of leadership for us should be lower than for men? Do we think there can be some definition of leadership for women that is different than for men? Of course not. We know that nothing would be more patronizing, degrading, or insulting to women in the party.

At a certain point, each one of us has to face up to the challenge, and decide to work to overcome it. It is that simple. We can all be very supportive and understanding of each other's problems and difficulties. We can recognize they are largely created by the society in which we live. But that is not going to help lead the American revolution—unless we also challenge each other to overcome the obstacles, to face up to the real needs of our sex and our class, and to see our responsibilities in that light.

A collective challenge

Of course this doesn't mean women must meet this challenge only as individuals. The party as a whole has responsibilities, too. We think that one of the most important things we can and must do in the near future is establish the full-time cadre school, the leadership school that we have talked about before—Sandstone University, or whatever we decide to call it. We need to systematically take leaders of the party, in small groups, relieve them of other responsibilities, and give them several months for organized, intensive study.

There are always many reasons why we "can't" do this right

now: we don't have the money, we're too tight on personnel, there are too many other responsibilities, and so on. But the Political Committee is proposing that we now cut through all those problems—which, of course, are real—and decide that we can't afford *not* to do this. Now.

We thought that the Evelyn Reed Scholarship Fund was a good way to start collecting the money necessary to finance this project.[4] We will have to raise a significant amount to carry it through, and we have to find the resources outside our normal operating budget. If comrades agree, we will make this the center of the expansion fund presentation at the convention, and we will plan to hold the opening session of this school before our 1980 Oberlin conference. If we are serious about this, we think we will find the extra money needed to do it.

Second, the party as a whole has the responsibility to continue a policy of affirmative action to encourage women and comrades of the oppressed nationalities to overcome the additional obstacles they face. As with every member, our aim is to stretch comrades' capacities to the fullest, to encourage them to take assignments that challenge them to grow, and then to work collectively to maximize what we accomplish and learn in the process.

Third, we need to continue to do everything we can to maximize the number of women comrades who are in industry. Women in the party must help lead the turn into industry, where we can gain experience as leaders of our class. After getting off to a slow start, we've done well on this in recent months. Last summer, for example, there was only one woman on the National Committee in industry. There are now nine, and one more looking for a job. And I should add that four of these nine comrades are Black women.

We should be absolutely clear that this general approach is the exact opposite of the course toward the establishment of women's caucuses in the party, and toward the "development" of leaders by setting aside quotas on the leading bodies for women, etc. The challenge before us—especially for the women—is not to organize and lead the women in the party, but to lead the whole party, the branches, the fractions, the committees, the men and the women. Any other kind of leadership is counterfeit. Exclusive caucuses, based on sex, race, or any similar nonpolitical criteria, are both undemocratic and counterproductive. Far from encouraging women to become leaders of the party, they reinforce the idea that there is a separate kind of leadership role for women comrades.

Preparing the convention

Now, what does all this say about preparations for the election of the National Committee at the next convention?

First, we think we should recommend to the Nominating Commission and to the convention delegates that there be no further increase in the size of the National Committee. We now have a National Committee of eighty-three members. It is the largest National Committee the party has ever had, and one of the youngest.

At the 1975 convention we made a major transition in leadership. We eliminated the category of advisory members on the National Committee. Since none of those who had been advisory members ran for the committee, and since we increased the number of full and alternate members, we in effect enlarged the National Committee by ten in 1975.

Then, we enlarged the National Committee by sixteen at the last convention: eleven regular members and five alternates. There was a particular reason for recommending that increase in the size of the NC at the 1977 convention that doesn't apply this year.

We had held three successive yearly conventions of the party in 1975, '76, and '77. We pointed out that a time period of only one year is often not sufficient for the party to judge the performance of new members of the NC. It's an error to replace people on the National Committee prematurely, without their having a chance to go through a number of experiences, and without the party really being able to gauge their leadership functioning. But it has been two years since the last convention, so this is less of a factor this year.

Enlarging the National Committee further will not help resolve the leadership question that we're trying to deal with.

Secondly, the delegates and the Nominating Commission will have before them the thinking on the leadership question contained in this report, and the report on the turn from the February 1978 plenum.

These establish a political framework for the Nominating Commission and the branch delegations in considering their NC nominations before the convention.

Most important, we should remember that the National Committee is a committee. Like the party, it is a living, changing, growing, and developing organism. It is constantly adjusting and being renewed. One thing you can be sure of is that no National Committee will be perfect. Every delegate will have some idea of how it could have been a better committee. But we should all have a sense of proportion and perspective. Over time, any mistakes that are made get corrected. The goal is to make sure that we elect a committee in which the party has political confidence.

I think we can be confident, more confident than ever before, in our ability to rise to the challenges before us. We have made progress that we can now build on. We have a clear and balanced approach to the leadership question, to leadership functioning, to revolutionary centralism and proletarianization, to aiding and accelerating the development of every single comrade as a leader. We start with the things we learned from Trotsky and Lenin, the things that have become part of the consciousness and practice of our party.

This gives us a tremendous advantage in moving forward the process of forging a multinational leadership. A leadership with a significant component of women. A leadership that reflects a party whose great majority are becoming industrial workers. A leadership with continuity, stability, and political authority. A leadership that is constantly growing and adjusting. We can be proud of what we've done, and confident we can do more. I am not talking about patting ourselves on the back, but taking advantage of what we have accomplished to lead the whole party forward in meeting the leadership challenge.

Summary

A number of comrades discussed the question: What does it mean to develop rounded political leaders of the party. This is posed not only for women or for comrades from oppressed nationalities. It's *the* supreme challenge for every single member of the party, for every single leadership body, in everything we do. That's our reason for being, to develop every individual we recruit as a rounded Marxist politician and part of the leadership of our class.

We are all being pushed, collectively and individually, by the objective situation today, pushed to deepen our political understanding, to think through the questions being posed in a new way by the development of the class struggle.

The leadership is challenged to make every branch meeting a political meeting. To make every fraction meeting a political meeting.

We know there are additional obstacles and difficulties for women comrades and comrades from oppressed nationalities. This will be true for many comrades we recruit on the job in industry. We have to give special leadership attention to helping overcome these barriers, reinforcing comrades' self-confidence, and deepening their political understanding.

One comrade began to discuss the question, "What do we mean when we say 'political'?" That branch meetings have to be "political." Or comrades have to be more "political." This is important. Of course, no one joins the Socialist Workers Party unless they are a political being. There is no other reason to join a revolutionary Marxist party in the United States today.

Being political doesn't mean becoming a "theoretician." It doesn't mean trying to be an "intellectual" or an "educator." These are all false definitions.

What we're trying to get at is the fact that everything we do, every task we have—from the sale of our press, to the branch finances, to antinuclear work, to attending a trade-union meeting, to organizing the printshop of the party—every single thing we do has to be related to the broadest strategic goals of our class. That's the only reason we do anything. Only when we understand how our tasks today, what we are doing right now, this hour, are related to our ultimate goals, will we feel confident about where we're going, why it's all important. We always have to be forcing ourselves to think in broad class terms—because it's easy sometimes to sink into routinism, to give organizational, not political motivations for our tasks today. That's the heart of what we're trying to get at when we say our branch meetings and fraction meetings have to be "political."

We try to find ways to explain not *that* we need to sell the paper this week, but *why*. Ways to politically inspire comrades. Not inspire in the false sense—rah, rah, get everyone hepped up. That never works anyway, because there is really only one thing that motivates any of us. We get inspired by understanding where our class is going and how we are all going to help get there.

Marxist theoreticians don't come from universities. Theory doesn't develop in a vacuum. It grows out of the class struggle itself, as the working class confronts new problems, as a proletarian party responds to the living class struggle.

That's why we don't urge comrades to go lock themselves up in a room alone to read the classics. You will *never* become a Marxist if you do that. Perhaps you will become very "well educated" in the bourgeois sense, but you will understand nothing about Marxism. You can only learn that by combining your reading and thinking with being a part of our class and its struggles, with being a member of a Marxist party. Some comrades aren't "organizers" while others are "educators." "Activists" aren't counterposed to "theoreticians." You can't be an organizer unless you understand this and lead a branch or a fraction politically.

What is happening now is that we're being challenged to organize in a new way, to think through everything we do in relation to a new situation. That's what we mean when we say we have to be more political today. It's exciting to relate everything we're doing in a new way to the broadest strategic questions. We're all learning.

Another term we sometimes misuse is the word "intellectual." It comes from a time in the history of the Marxist movement when the majority of the working class couldn't read or write. Those who were educated, who could read or write, often played a very valuable role. It was important to win a section of the educated middle classes, the "intelligentsia," to the side of the working class and the workers movement.

But this distinction between intellectuals and nonintellectuals more and more disappears as the level of education in the working class rises. Someone who went to college, or can write an article on philosophy, or knows several languages is no longer an intellectual. Individuals make particular contributions to our collective efforts to develop our theoretical understanding or political position on one or another question. But the whole party is a thinking machine. It's out of the collective process that theory and our political positions develop.

Women in industry

Several comrades discussed the impact that working an industrial job has on the consciousness and self-confidence of women, including our own comrades.

Of course, all the comrades who get into industry find that we have to go back to the basics to rethink things. We have to explain our ideas to people in a new way. We have to deepen our understanding in order to be able to explain our positions in a popular way, to be understandable to the people we're meeting and talking to on the job today.

But getting into industry has an even greater impact on women comrades—not only those who are already in, but on the whole party. Our self-confidence as leaders, the realization that we have power as part of our class, the sense of solidarity, the clarity about how we can build a powerful, fighting women's liberation movement that brings the power of the unions behind it—our consciousness is being transformed on many levels.

Women in our party are used to being leaders. They already think and act like leaders. When our women comrades go into industry, they're not so likely to be cowed by things that might be more intimidating to other women. That growing self-confidence feeds back into the party as well.

There is a general point about our leadership needs that we have to begin to assess. We have been pressing hard to get the maximum number of comrades into industry. This has put a tremendous leadership strain on us. We have bent the stick toward getting as many leaders in as possible. But we're starting to reach the point where we will have to take comrades out—to meet some leadership responsibilities and to give another layer of comrades the chance to go in.

We can't keep putting more comrades in and taking no one out; it won't work that way. The experience of being in industry is extremely valuable. If you then take some time away from work to become organizer of a branch or take a national assignment, you understand a lot better what we're doing, what we're trying to accomplish.

A historic opportunity

The leadership challenges we're talking about are not basically conjunctural questions. They're real historical challenges. They're not things you resolve overnight or that you leap over in an ahistorical act of will. It's not being pessimistic to say that. That doesn't mean there is nothing we can do to effect changes. We *can* move forward in a fundamental way, if we are honest about the real challenge.

But we shouldn't think that if we get everybody into industry, we're going to solve all leadership questions overnight.

What is new, what is different, is that the kind of transformation the entire party is going through gives us a new and positive framework in which to address ourselves to these questions. That will maximize our ability to deal objectively with the challenges we face and move forward in the political development of the entire leadership of the party.

That is a very optimistic perspective.

III. BUILDING A PARTY OF SOCIALIST WORKERS

By the close of the 1970s the industrial working class had moved to center stage in U.S. politics. This class is the most powerful force the capitalists must defeat in the long-term, worldwide battle to reverse the effects of their declining profit rates. In order to carry out an elementary defense of their wages and conditions, the industrial workers and their unions found themselves drawn to the center of resistance to the bosses' offensive against the living and job conditions of working people and against their political and social rights.

This section of *The Changing Face of U.S. Politics* takes a look at the opening two years of the SWP's turn to industry. Over that time the majority of the party's members had begun working industrial jobs and become active members of their unions. On the basis of their initial experiences, these communist workers were

201

grappling with important practical questions about what it means to be a worker-bolshevik and how to function politically on the job and in the union movement—questions taken up in the reports in this section.

Why is Marxism not a doctrine, but instead the generalization of the strategic line of march of the working class? What are the goals of communist work in the trade unions? Is it adventurism to talk socialism on the job and in the unions? How should socialists in the trade unions organize to carry out their work in an effective manner? What are the implications of the turn to industry for the character of weekly public political meetings that party members support and participate in, sales of the socialist press, bookstores that feature Marxist literature, and socialist election campaigns and other propaganda activity? Should socialist workers begin accepting nomination for posts in their union locals? How do socialists function to bring the power of the unions, as well as their co-workers, into civil rights struggles, the fight for women's rights, battles of debt-burdened farmers, campaigns to stop nuclear power, protests against U.S. military intervention abroad, and fights around other social and political questions that seem far removed from the factory floor?

Above all, how do communist workers seek to influence other workers, recruit the most far-sighted of them, and build a stronger communist party?

The objective political changes that made the turn to industry a necessity if a revolutionary workers party was to be built in the United States also pointed to the need for such an orientation by communist organizations in other parts of the world. That is the topic of the report "The Turn and Building a World Communist Movement," presented by Jack Barnes at a world congress of the Fourth International in November 1979.

At the time, the Socialist Workers Party had fraternal ties with the Fourth International, an international communist organization the SWP had helped found and lead since 1938. The Fourth International was forged by communists around the world who refused, from the late 1920s on, to capitulate to the counterrevolutionary politics and police-state terrorism imposed by the rising privileged caste governing the USSR and who fought to continue the communist policies of V.I. Lenin. The political perspective presented by Barnes on the turn to industry was adopted by the November 1979 world congress of the Fourth International. It soon became evident, however, that contrary to the course followed by the SWP, the leadership in country after country was unwilling to translate the adopted words of that report into deeds. Political divergences also widened as the SWP leadership, along with others, continued to insist on the historical importance and weight of the communist leadership in Cuba, as well as the necessity for communists to orient toward the revolutionary victories in Nicaragua and Grenada in 1979 and learn from the experience of the workers and farmers governments that rose to power in those countries. By the end of the 1980s, the SWP and other communist leagues in Australia, Britain, Canada, France, Iceland, New Zealand, and Sweden, while maintaining the revolutionary political continuity out of which the Fourth International had been formed, each decided to terminate affiliation to this international organization as it had evolved.

This section concludes with the report "Educating the Leadership of a Proletarian Party," which explains why the turn to industry and the changes in world politics and the class struggle that underlie it expanded the possibility to learn Marxism and advance systematic education in the communist movement.

Building a revolutionary party
of socialist workers

RESOLUTION OF SOCIALIST WORKERS PARTY

I. Perspectives for the Socialist Workers Party in the 1980s

1. During the years of Cold War and political reaction following World War II, the American labor movement went into a political retreat as a petty-bourgeois bureaucracy consolidated its hold on the unions. Modest but real wage increases and "fringe benefits" were negotiated as the postwar economic expansion unfolded. In exchange, the bureaucracy collaborated with the employers and the government to gut the unions as fighting instruments. The workers were bound in red tape. Union democracy was strangled. Control over job conditions was rolled back. The needs of the unorganized workers and labor's allies among the other exploited and oppressed sections of the population were ignored. Their demands and the fight to win broad social programs for the working

This is excerpted from the main political resolution adopted by the Thirtieth National Convention of the Socialist Workers Party, held August 5-11, 1979.

class were subordinated to the needs of the bosses' two-party system. The anti-working-class foreign policy of U.S. imperialism, including the drafting of young American workers to die in the wars against the Korean and Vietnamese peoples, was supported by the top union officialdom.

For almost a third of a century, this conservative bureaucracy blocked the unions from participating in, much less leading, important social and political battles. Growing numbers of organized workers accepted the argument of the labor bureaucracy that class collaboration was the road to prosperity and security and that the sole function of the unions was to bargain for periodic wage hikes and "fringes" for their members. These workers saw little connection between their desire for better living standards and job conditions, and most progressive social and political protests.

The class struggle grew sharper in the 1960s and early 1970s. This was initiated by and expressed through the Black civil rights struggles, and the rise of nationalist consciousness, followed by waves of ghetto rebellions; and then the anti–Vietnam War movement, Chicano struggles, and the women's liberation movement. But fighters in these battles were forced to detour around the union movement because of the roadblock thrown up by the labor bureaucracy. They had to organize against the opposition of the labor officialdom, which not only defended the domestic and foreign policies of the imperialists but denounced and slandered uncompromising leaders of struggles against their policies.

To millions of radicalized young activists, including industrial workers, the class-struggle strategy of transforming the labor movement into a fighting instrument mobilizing the working class in battle against exploitation and oppression seemed utopian. The fundamental class conflict underlying all politics was successfully camouflaged.

The working class did not participate through its basic class institutions—the unions—in the social protest movements of the 1960s and early 1970s. However, these struggles had a profound impact on the attitudes of millions of workers and changed the entire political framework and relationship of class forces in this country.

Today, this changing social consciousness among American workers and their growing desire to fight back against the rulers' austerity offensive make it possible to begin tearing down the bureaucracy's roadblock and drawing the ranks of the labor movement into political action. The workers' growing need to take hold of their unions and use them to resist the attacks on their living standards and job conditions, combined with the radicalizing influence of movements of social protest originating outside the union movement, will mark the class struggle in the 1980s. This combination of economic and social struggles will be at the center of the battle to transform the unions into organizations of mass political combat.

2. Through their austerity and antiunion drive of the past half decade, the rulers still hold the offensive in the class struggle. The employers, their government, and their two political parties have shifted the axis of capitalist politics rightward.

But the underlying reality is that a class polarization is sharpening. An upswing in the combativity of American workers followed the initial shock of the 1974-75 depression. The industrial working class and its unions are being forced to the center of the fightback and radicalization process today.

As the employers press their antilabor drive, the union officialdom's capacity to prevent the resistance of the workers is declining. It is less able to isolate workers from each other, from their allies among the oppressed, and from the influence of social protest movements. Despite the buffer of the bureaucracy, the employing class is beginning to come up against the power and determination of the ranks.

3. In the increasingly frequent skirmishes against the bosses, stalemates and setbacks still outnumber victories. The workers are discovering how seriously their unions have been weakened by decades of "labor-management cooperation" and isolation from the

struggles of their allies and much of their class.

As a result, more and more workers are beginning to learn the necessity of solidarity within the labor movement and with its allies. They are beginning to learn that union democracy is necessary to organize and unleash union power. They are beginning to learn that even the shrewdest tactics on the picket line or at the bargaining table are undercut by political obstacles, including the direct intervention of the capitalist government. They are beginning to discover that the labor movement needs an entirely new strategy.

Workers are beginning to look for a program and a leadership that can point the way out of the class-collaborationist straitjacket the bureaucracy has strapped on the unions.

4. The blows to the rights and living conditions of the oppressed, especially since the 1974-75 depression, have spotlighted the growing inadequacies of the petty-bourgeois leaderships that dominate the major organizations of oppressed national minorities and women. Unable to chart an effective course of action to fight for the needs of Blacks, Latinos, and women, the current misleaders have brought these struggles to an impasse. As a result of the tightening competitive squeeze on American capitalism and its resulting austerity offensive, greater social power is needed to defend past gains or conquer new ones as we enter the 1980s.

In search of a road out of this impasse, many fighters are being forced to turn to the labor movement and demand that it use union power in the fight against discrimination and its effects. At the same time, growing numbers of unionists are beginning to understand that they *need* allies outside the unions; that action by oppressed national minorities and women in defense of their needs weakens the employers and advances the unity and interests of the working class.

This growing interaction will be one of the distinctive features of the American class struggle. It creates new opportunities to bring the power of the unions into the struggles of Blacks, Latinos, and women. It creates new possibilities to involve workers in these struggles and develop the proletarian leadership needed to take them forward. It creates a more favorable political atmosphere for the fight to defend and extend democratic rights, shut down nuclear reactors, prevent imperialist wars, and achieve other progressive social goals.

New leaders of these struggles and organizations of the oppressed must and will come from the working class and industrial unions. These Black, Latino, and women leaders will also play a crucial role in the struggle to replace the current misleaders of labor and transform the unions into instruments of class struggle—into a powerful movement of workers who think socially and act politically.

The fight to transform the labor movement will both inspire and take inspiration from the massive social protest movements and mobilizations that will mark the 1980s.

5. Although no significant wing of the labor movement is yet crystallizing around a class-struggle program, the forces and the understanding necessary for such a left wing are being forged in the ranks of the unions today, especially the industrial unions. The breadth of the social and political tasks confronting the working class has grown with the historic delay of the proletarian revolution. Thus a class-struggle left wing in the unions today must be built around a program that is more sweeping in the issues it addresses than could have been envisioned during previous upsurges of the American labor movement.

The workers who adopt this class-struggle perspective will have to chart a course breaking from subordination to the capitalist two-party system and build a labor party based on the unions.

Black and Latino workers will play a vanguard role in forging this class-struggle left wing. This is because of the increased weight of Blacks and Latinos in the industrial working class; the reinforcement of their class consciousness by nationalist self-confidence; and their direct stake in the elimination of all forms of discrimination.

While women still comprise a much smaller percentage of the

industrial working class than Blacks or Latinos, their numbers are growing. The combativity and self-confidence of women workers are heightened by the battles they have fought to break into jobs previously closed to them; the vast changes in social consciousness of both men and women; and the direct stake that women, too, have in eliminating discrimination. Thus women workers will also play a vanguard role in forging a class-struggle leadership in the unions.

For these reasons, the revolutionary party in this country must be multinational, not only in membership but at all levels of leadership. It must also have a strong component of leaders who are women. Without a composition that reflects the young vanguard fighters of the working class, no party can unify the American workers around a revolutionary program and lead them to political power. Without a proletarian orientation, a party with such a composition cannot be built.

6. In February 1978, the Socialist Workers Party National Committee voted unanimously to "subordinate everything else to immediately organizing to get a large majority of the membership of the Socialist Workers Party into industry and the industrial trade unions. . . . This is the entire framework of the party's activity in the immediate future—beginning *now*."

In the brief period since that decision, the party has made significant progress in carrying out this turn. Our branches are building industrial fractions and organizing more and more political work through them. The SWP is becoming a workers party in composition and day-to-day activity.

The experiences of our industrial fractions and events in the class struggle here and abroad confirm the timeliness of the party's turn and the political assessment on which it is based.

The SWP is subordinating everything else to deepening and completing the turn. As we get more of our members and leaders into industrial fractions the party is beginning to draw together a Marxist tendency in the American labor movement: workers who read the socialist press and increasingly understand and agree with the basic Marxist premises of the SWP. These workers want to join with SWP co-workers to democratize and strengthen their unions to better defend the workers' interests, to involve the labor movement in progressive social struggles, and to advance the process of transforming the unions into instruments of class struggle that fight on behalf of all the oppressed and exploited. Out of our tendency in the labor movement, we will contribute decisive cadres to the development of a class-struggle left wing, and we will win thousands of co-workers to the SWP as the vital political instrument to combat the catastrophe American capitalism has in store for them.

All the party's perspectives, tactical judgments, and priorities flow from and are subordinate to this overall *strategic* orientation. We judge the social weight and political centrality of all struggles and issues from the standpoint of advancing the working class along its strategic line of march. We act as the most politically conscious and organized section of our class.

In this way, the SWP will participate in and increasingly provide political direction to the battles in which the new class-struggle leadership of the unions will be forged. We will advance the development of proletarian leaders who fight uncompromisingly for the needs of their class and for demands of Blacks, Latinos, and women. We will help provide leadership for increasingly revitalized movements of mass social protest.

With this Leninist strategy of party building, the SWP is constructing the revolutionary proletarian leadership needed by the American workers in their fight for a workers government and the socialist transformation of society.

The turn and building a world communist movement

One central, practical consecuence flowing from the political resolution submitted to this congress by the United Secretariat majority overshadows all others—that is, that the sections of the Fourth International must make a radical *turn* to immediately organize to get a large majority of our members and leaders into industry and into industrial unions.[1]

This task links the four line resolutions we are going to vote on. It flows from the analysis of the world situation developed in the political resolution that we discussed. So I'm not going to review in detail the structural, demographic, and economic changes behind this decision.

The resolution points to the growing weight of the proletariat in all three sectors of the world revolution. It points to the urban explosions and proletarian forms of organization that have been, and will continue to be, the focus of revolutionary upsurges in the years ahead.

The general line of this report for the United Secretariat, given in November 1979, was approved by the world congress of the Fourth International.

SEE PAGE 440 FOR NOTES

Combined with these structural factors behind the turn are, on the one hand, the long-run stagnation that the world capitalist system faces and the antilabor offensive it engenders; and, on the other, the undefeated working class that the bourgeoisie faces going into the crisis. To this *capitalist* crisis must be added the growing *crisis* of world *imperialism*.

All this makes the world situation more, not less, explosive. It means that uncontrolled forces—spurred either by the actions of the oppressors or those of the oppressed—can be set into motion. We've seen this in Iran and Nicaragua. And this explosive potential is not limited to the semicolonial world.

Superimposed on these factors is another very important conjunctural factor, the world recession of 1974-75. This downturn, the first generalized recession on a world scale since the 1930s, came on top of the events that had transpired since 1968.[2] What this definitively set in motion throughout the world is an intensifying austerity drive by the ruling class against the working class, against all the oppressed, and against the political rights the masses need to organize and fight back. This is not just a tactical or short-run policy of the rulers. It is a fundamental policy that economic realities *force* them to carry out.

The ultimate target of the rulers' austerity drive is the industrial workers, for the very same reason that the industrial workers have been at the center of our strategy since the founding of Marxism—their economic strength; their social weight; the example they set for the whole class; the power of their unions to affect the wages, conditions, and thus the entire social framework of the class struggle; their resulting potential political power vis-à-vis the enemy class; the obstacle they pose to rightist solutions by the bourgeoisie. The industrial workers are both the source of most of the rulers' surplus value and the ultimate enemy that the rulers must defeat if the entire economic and social crisis of their system is to be turned around.

The ruling class cannot afford, and will not allow, these industrial workers to organize *solidarity* with fellow workers, with the oppressed, and with their allies throughout the world. It cannot afford, and will not allow, the industrial workers to develop *trade union democracy* so that the power of the working class can be organized and used.

In other words, the rulers will not allow without a mighty battle *the evolution of a class-struggle left wing in the labor movement.*

This ruling-class offensive brings down increasing pressure on the entire working class, on national minorities, on women, on every exploited and oppressed person fighting for their rights. It intensifies pressures on small vanguards seeking to chart a course forward toward the victory of the working class. Everyone who is seeking the revolutionary road, a class-struggle perspective, everyone who is seeking progressive alliances, feels this pressure. It is a fundamental aspect of the austerity drive, of the offensive of the rulers—and one that will be magnified as the offensive deepens.

As we discussed yesterday, the only possible reversal of the capitalist crisis, in the judgment of the political resolution, is through a large and decisive enough defeat of the industrial working class to rationalize and restructure capital, to attack with force every upsurge of the colonial peoples, and thus open a new period of expansion.

What conclusions must we draw from this?

That a political radicalization of the working class—uneven and at different tempos from country to country—is on the agenda.

That the rulers' offensive will force big changes in the industrial unions.

And that the key for revolutionists is to be there, in and part of the decisive sector of the working class, prior to these showdowns.

It is *there* that we will meet the forces to build the Fourth International, to build workers parties. It is *there* that we will meet the young workers, the growing number of women workers, the workers of oppressed nationalities, and the immigrant workers. It is inside the industrial working class that revolutionary parties will get a response to our program and recruits to our movement.

In light of all these factors it's also important to step back and look at the turn from a broader historical point of view. Our movement's current social composition is totally abnormal. This is a historical fact, not a criticism. In fact, far from being a criticism, it was our movement's ability to recruit from the new generation of radicalizing youth—from the early sixties on—that today poses the possibility of making this turn. And this *possibility* now coincides with a pressing political *necessity*.

Only parties not only proletarian in program, but in composition and experience, can lead the workers and their allies in the struggles that are on the agenda.

Only parties of industrial workers will be able to withstand the pressures, including the ideological pressures, of the ruling class. And these pressures will increase.

Only such parties will have their hand on the pulse of the working class, and thereby not misread their own attitudes, ignorance, and moods as those of the workers. In other words, only parties of industrial workers can move forward and outward.

Only parties of workers that have been tested *in action* by the workers themselves, long before the decisive showdowns, can decisively grow and chart a way forward. Only that kind of party can attract and link up with the militant class-struggle currents that will break loose as the crisis of the reformist leaderships and centrist organizations deepens.

Marxism's proletarian heritage

We are not blazing a new trail in this regard. In the history of the Marxist movement, the most proletarian parties have been the best parties—the most revolutionary, the least economist, the most political. Go back to the Bolsheviks. Go back to Rosa Luxemburg. Go back to the goals the Fourth International set for itself, with the advice and leadership of Trotsky, at the end of the 1930s.

In fact, it is the proletarian tradition and orientation of the Fourth International that enabled us to arrive where we are today as a unified revolutionary organization on a world scale—an organization that has cadres to make this turn. And it's the turn—universally organized and carried out—that is the only way to preserve and enrich our proletarian orientation.

At the same time, it is crucial to recognize and state clearly that the turn is *not* a continuation of what we've been doing. It is the way we can continue our proletarian orientation, but to carry out this turn on a world scale we must make a break with what we've previously been doing. That's why we call it a *turn.*

This turn will dictate no tactics. Our tactics and campaigns in each country are dictated by the class struggle, by the conflict of class forces. But the turn affects every single one of our tactics, all of our political work, all of our institutions, and every single mode of party functioning. The turn is not a *sufficient* condition to take advantage of the opportunities before us and to meet the crises facing our class. But it is a *necessary precondition* for the next steps forward. Failing that, we can make no progress.

This is what the world political resolution lays out as the central task for the entire Fourth International: to organize and *lead* the overwhelming majority of our cadres into industry and the industrial unions "without further delay."

"The goal," according to the resolution, "is parties of experienced worker-bolsheviks who act as political leaders of their class and its allies."

It goes without saying that we will not carry out the turn in exactly the same way in every country or part of the world, whether we have ten members or a thousand. But for the political and organizational reasons we've discussed, the turn is a *universal* one for our international movement, in all three sectors of the world revolution. That needs to be understood, so that we can carry out this task as a disciplined world party.

There comes a time when a political problem, a sociological fact, and a leadership decision coincide. This is one of those times. To put our movement in a position to move forward politically, we must simultaneously take our cadres and our program into the decisive sections of our class. Otherwise, we'll become *part* of the growing crisis of leadership in the world labor movement, rather than part of its solution.

Experiences and lessons

The resolution was drafted a little more than a year and a half ago. Since that time, our movement has had a great deal more experience with the turn. We've already had the chance to test our conclusions and develop a richer knowledge of the facts than we possibly could have had when we first adopted this resolution. This report and discussion will help us take cognizance of these experiences and changes and, if adopted, report them in printed form to our entire movement.

Of course, there is unevenness from one country to the next in the current stage of implementing the turn. There are differing stages in the development of the political situation in various countries. Some important experiences have been unique to a single section or a single industry. We can put those aside for today's discussion.

But there is also an entire set of experiences that are common everywhere that we have seriously begun the turn—from Iran to Canada, from Sweden to New Zealand. These common lessons are decisive everywhere that we have significant forces in the Fourth International. They are lessons for the *practical leadership* of the next step forward in carrying out this common task.

What are these lessons of the last few years?

First. There is no possible way to make the turn unless the leaders of the party lead. This means that the leadership must analyze and effectively intervene in the unfolding of the class struggle, so that both the political basis of the turn and its practical application are always presented clearly to our cadres.

Comrades cannot be ordered or shamed to make the turn. They have to be politically convinced, inspired, and organized by the leadership. The membership is *waiting* to be led on this turn. That's our universal experience.

But this can only be accomplished if the leadership itself goes into industry. Our goal is not just to get a majority of the membership into industry, but a majority of our elected leadership bodies as well, on a local and national level. Only such a leadership can carry through the turn.

Second. The turn has to be approached collectively, not individually. The party must lead comrades into industry. They're not doing it on their own. They're not sent in someplace and then left to fend for themselves. Every time we've done that, we've reaped the whirlwind. We've lost comrades to demoralization, to opponents, to the Stalinists. The turn is a conscious *party* task, not a routine task of a small group of comrades individually.

Connected with this, we've found everywhere that what is decisive in making the turn and practicing politics in industry is not what comrades accomplish as individuals, but what they accomplish as fractions and as part of the party. Comrades with different strengths and weaknesses work together as a disciplined unit of the party, learning from their joint successes and errors.

Third. Experience has taught us that there is no gradual way of accomplishing the turn. Of course, the turn takes place over a period of time. Comrades go into industry in successive waves, not all at once.

But the turn cannot be presented or implemented as a gradual, routine, or partial campaign. It must be organized and led as a decisive act by the entire organization. Whenever it has been tried any other way, the turn stalls to a halt and recoils, rather than going forward in waves. If we don't recognize this and act on that basis, we will fail; we will not carry out the turn.

When we gather the statistics from each national leadership for the next meeting of the International Executive Committee, we will get a feel for how much progress we're making—country by country—in leading a big majority of comrades into industry.

Fourth. In every single country where we've made progress with the turn, we've learned—sometimes from false starts—that there can be no such things as exempted jobs, or categories of jobs, or exempted layers in the party. Such exemptions always end up as excuses not to carry out the turn, not to participate in the turn. Trade unionists who are now working jobs *outside* of industry have a particularly important role to play in personally leading party cadres into industry and bringing their experiences to bear in building our fractions. They can provide essential political and practical leadership.

I think we've now bypassed a false debate—the debate over the public versus private sectors. What's important is not whether comrades are paid by the government or a private employer. What's important is whether or not we are in factories, mines, mills, transport centers, communication centers—whether in the private or public sector. *Our goal is to get into industry, to become part of the industrial working class.*

We don't begin by looking for where most women currently are working or where the bureaucracy is weak, although these factors can play a role in targeting particular industrial sectors. We look for where our class is concentrated and where class battles will, by necessity, open up in the coming period. That's where decisive class-struggle leadership will be needed and where we must go. That's the line of the resolution.

We are looking for the natural leaders of the working class—those who are looked to for leadership by other workers. Some of them have already been elected to union posts, but our eyes are not on official leaders at any level. We'll win the best of them by going after the *young rebels* in the working class. They will be decisive for us and for our class in the coming period. That's who we're after.

Fifth. This recognition of the centrality of young workers drives home the importance of launching, rebuilding, or helping to strengthen revolutionary youth organizations. Having a youth organization—and one that is fully geared into the industrial turn—becomes *more* important, not less important, as we concentrate our cadres in industry and the industrial unions.

The world Marxist movement has traditionally recognized the need for proletarian youth organizations as a central party-building instrument. As growing numbers of young industrial workers are repelled by capitalism and attracted to radical ideas and alternatives, this need becomes more pressing. There will be a separate report on the youth work of the International later in the congress, so I won't attempt to develop this point. But we're learning that we must consciously recognize this as an indispensable part of the turn in order to tap the opportunities before us and make the maximum gains for our parties among radicalizing workers.

What not to expect
Our initial experiences with the turn have also taught us what we should *not* tell comrades to expect.

We can't promise rapid recruitment. That depends on a whole series of other factors—the unfolding of the class struggle, the stage of class politicization, and the capacities of the party.

While we make no promises that the turn will solve other problems facing the party, we can guarantee that the turn puts us in the best position to solve those problems and take advantage of opportunities. And without the turn, we can guarantee disaster.

Finally, we can't promise that the turn will be painless or easy. It's not, because it's unlike any other thing we normally do and have become accustomed to. It's not a change in political line or a correction of a political error. It's not a shift in tactics. It's not the launching of a new campaign.

The turn means a change in the life of thousands and thousands of comrades. That's different. And that takes leadership.

Everywhere that we've begun to carry out the turn in a systematic and thorough way, there have been some losses of individual comrades. There are comrades for whom the turn sharply poses the question of what they are doing with their lives, what their personal commitments and priorities are. Then, the party also inevitably makes some errors and false starts. And some other comrades drop away.

But the more important lesson that we've learned is that the turn *saves* comrades. It prevents demoralization and turns around the malaise that sets in when our parties don't have the necessary political and organizational moorings in the heart of our class. It provides a perspective, and a realistic base from which to move our work forward. Unsuspected capacities in comrades have come to the fore when they get into industry as part of a strong fraction.

That's one of the most crucial aspects of the turn, and another reason why it must be carried out quickly and led decisively.

Some organizational conclusions

From our initial experiences, we have also drawn some conclusions on important organizational questions connected with the turn. And all the organizational forms of our parties have to be subordinated to carrying out the turn.

One. Comrades who go into industry have to function as fractions, as a unit, as a collective team—whatever the particular term may be in different sections. They have to have formal, structured ways to make decisions democratically, to be tied together politically, to work out problems, and to integrate and develop new comrades that go into industry or are recruited there.

If this does not happen, we can isolate, demoralize, and finally lose comrades. They begin to feel personally responsible for making party gains and personally to blame for any failures or setbacks. We carry out work in every other arena collectively, and that's how we must carry out the turn. It is crucial to organize and lead comrades through fractions. And the party leadership must pay close attention to their work.

Two. As we get more and more comrades into industry, it is crucial to pay close attention to maintaining the basic units of the party—branches, or whatever a section may call them—as *rounded political bodies.* They must be of sufficient size and organized politically so that the comrades in them obtain something there that they cannot get through the industrial fractions or in other ways. That is, these basic party units must provide the rounded political experience, leadership, Marxist education, and political discussion that comrades can only get from the party as a whole.

Failure to do this can even exacerbate the problem of how to combine what is often called trade union or factory work with more general socialist political activity.

Of course, this doesn't solve any of our tactical problems of how to link factory work, trade union work, with other party tasks and campaigns. Those will be solved concretely in each section and specific situation.

But the lesson that comrades in industry must also be active members of rounded political units of the party—in which they have regular and systematic political decision-making power and responsibilities—is a key one for avoiding unnecessary pitfalls.

Three. The turn both necessitates and helps accomplish further professionalization of the party. The turn makes more immediate and real our concept that every comrade, every worker-bolshevik, is a professional revolutionist. The need to have a professional apparatus, the willingness of comrades to be full-time, the need for professionalism at every level of the organization—all this becomes more necessary as we become parties of industrial workers.

At the same time, it is important to avoid any concept that there are two categories of party members—those in industry and those not in industry. All party members have equal rights and equal responsibilities. The turn in no way establishes a category of second-class membership for comrades who for whatever reason are not currently working an industrial job.

Four. The turn also brings into sharper focus the question of leadership norms and general party norms, which must be reviewed to make sure they are in step with our advance along the historical line of march of our class.

Trotsky wrote a series of letters about these matters to the American Trotskyists in the years leading up to the fight with the petty-bourgeois opposition in the late 1930s, when the party was carrying out an industrial turn. Most of these letters dealt with the leadership question. He listed some key characteristics of proletarian leaders and proletarian attitudes: Seriousness toward your organization and its leadership. Subordinating personal considerations in putting the party first. Having a professional attitude toward it. Being deadly opposed to cynicism, gossip, bureaucratism, supersensitivity to criticism, and other such things common in petty-bourgeois circles. And above all, looking at things not as *me* and *mine*, but as *us* and *ours*.

These were not just moral lectures. Trotsky considered changes along these lines—and the open recognition of the need for such changes—to be a precondition to building proletarian parties and a revolutionary international.

In one 1937 letter, Trotsky wrote: "I have remarked hundreds of times that the worker who remains unnoticed in the 'normal' conditions of party life reveals remarkable qualities in a change of the situation when general formulas and fluent pens are not sufficient, where acquaintance with the life of workers and practical capacities are necessary."

In a letter several days later, Trotsky spoke of the need to educate the party in a spirit that "rejects unhealthy criticism, opposition for the sake of opposition." The key to this, he said, is "to change the social composition of the organization—make it a workers organization. . . . [Workers] are more patient, more realistic. When you have a meeting of 100 people and between them 60-70-80 are workers, then the 20 intellectuals, petty bourgeois, become ten times more cautious on the question of criticism. It's a more serious, more firm audience."[3]

The petty-bourgeois intellectuals' tendency to criticize for the sake of criticism, says Trotsky, is a way to "muffle their inner skepticism."

"The young workers," he says, "will call the gentlemen-skeptics, grievance mongers, and pessimists to order."

Full-timers in a revolutionary organization, Trotsky stressed, "should have in the first place a good ear, and only in the second place a good tongue." And as the party begins to recruit industrial workers, Trotsky warned, it must "avoid a great danger: namely that the intellectuals and white-collar workers might suppress the worker minority, condemn it to silence, transform the party into a very intelligent discussion club but absolutely not habitable for workers."

Awareness of these questions of attitudes is not only a necessity if we are to carry out the turn to the end; but by driving through the turn, we will have the greatest chance to alter the orientation, combat alien attitudes, and improve the atmosphere and functioning of our parties. We will begin acting as parties of industrial workers.

Educate, agitate, organize

Five. The education of the party. As comrades begin the turn, they learn and relearn our program, learn and relearn Marxism. They are constantly challenged to explain and popularize our ideas to their co-workers. So we are obligated to expand and pay more careful attention to political education.

This is one safeguard against the susceptibility among comrades to move away from being political when this turn is being carried out. All history tells us this is a danger.

Six. Improving our newspapers and turning them more and more into workers papers. It is through our party press that we can speak to the largest number and broadest layers of workers. It's how we explain why the need for the labor movement to begin thinking socially and acting politically is a life-or-death question.

Our own members are the single most important audience for the party press, along with those in our class and among the oppressed who look to us for political analysis and leadership. What we put in our newspapers, and how we explain things, helps us train our cadres as worker-bolsheviks rather than radical trade unionists. It helps steel the party against economist tendencies to reduce the struggles of the allies of our class—women, the oppressed nationalities, and so on—to union struggles or to struggles between employees and employers. It helps combat any false ideas that international or other broad political questions cannot be presented to workers at any given period.

Seven. The turn makes more important, not less important, the building of *campaign parties*—parties that carry out centralized political campaigns dictated by the national and international class struggle. We need parties that speak politically to the workers through our actions and our political campaigns, not primarily through how we relate to issues or struggles on the job. As the turn is made, these party campaigns are vital safeguards against rightist and economist pressures that have historically affected revolutionists in the working class. If there is one thing that the turn does not change, it is our absolute opposition to any spontaneist concepts of how to build the party and attract workers to it.

Eight. We have begun to learn valuable lessons about the relationship of the turn to our participation in building the struggles of women, oppressed nationalities, and around issues such as nuclear power or international solidarity. We've learned not to confuse our trade union or factory fractions with our fractions set up to lead work in various other particular struggles.

Of course, there is an interlink. There is a crossover of membership. But we can't reduce one organizational form to the other to carry out our work. To do so simply reflects internally the wrong tendency to reduce the struggles of women, of oppressed nationalities, and of other mass struggles to battles in the factories or the unions. Our turn is a turn outward, not inward.

Struggles that develop inside and outside the labor movement need to be combined and thereby mutually strengthened. Our turn, and the political factors underlying it, greatly expand the possibilities and openings for industrial workers and their unions to be brought into other struggles. We participate in these struggles not only as activists and leaders in them, but more and more as conscious revolutionary leaders of the labor movement.

Our goal is to hasten the convergence of the working class, its struggles, and its organizations with the battles of all the oppressed. We can say in all truthfulness to the oppressed, "Your struggles must not be subordinated to any other struggle." It's only a revolutionary leadership of the working class that can say this and *act* on that basis. This is crucial to the ability of the working class to forge needed and lasting alliances with all sections of the oppressed in a common battle against the exploiters.

Nine. We have discovered that where the turn has been driven through, women comrades and comrades of the oppressed nationalities have developed more confidence in the party and more confidence in themselves as leaders of their class, their particular struggles, and, above all, as leaders of the party.

The turn brings out the best in comrades.

Our turn toward the industrial working class and unions also points in the direction of helping to solve the crisis of leadership in the movements of women and the oppressed nationalities. Today, these struggles confront a crisis of class perspectives. They need to develop a proletarian composition, orientation, and leadership to move their struggles forward. As partisans and participants in these struggles, we will help accelerate the resolution of the leadership crisis from our base in industry, involving our coworkers in these movements and fighting to bring the power of the labor movement behind them.

I want to end on some questions that have been raised about the turn.

Is it mechanical? Is it a gimmick? Is it a factory obsession?

Well, I guess you could say we have a certain obsession about getting large fractions of comrades into great concentrations of industrial workers. We might quibble over the word. But we plead guilty.

Is it mechanical? Yes, in a certain sense. The mechanics of actually driving through the turn are a precondition for politically carrying it through.

Is it a gimmick? No. It's not a gimmick. Unless our entire political analysis is wrong.

The leadership of the Fourth International, the International Executive Committee [IEC], must lead the turn.

It must lead through political analysis, in order to situate the turn in the unfolding world class struggle.

It must lead by more of its members going into industry.

It must lead through coordination of the turn on a world scale, facilitating the exchange of experiences and information among the national leaderships and comrades in industry in different countries.

This means that the IEC, like all other leadership bodies of our movement, will have to begin organizing its work differently. The agendas of its meetings will have to change. The questions it must consider and deliberate on will broaden.

For example, the next IEC meeting must concretely look at the statistics on the progress of the turn and assess their political and organizational implications.

The only way the success of the turn can be measured is to look honestly and cold-bloodedly at the figures—the number and percentage of comrades in industry in each section, the number of functioning industrial fractions, the number of leadership cadres who are carrying out the turn. Only by reviewing these figures can we assess the progress in carrying out the central decision of this congress. This is what we must do at the next IEC meeting.

The more successful we have been in drawing the lessons and implementing the resolution, the quicker the turn *per se* will be behind us. The turn is a radical *tactical* move necessitated by the historical development of our movement and the current stage of world politics. It is an abnormal response to an abnormal situation—a situation in which the big majority of our members in every section have *not* been industrial workers. Once this historically necessary tactic has been carried out—once the abnormal situation of our current social composition and arena of work has been changed—the turn will be behind us. If it is carried out to the end, the tactic ceases.

Several comrades have told me, "Don't forget to point out that our movement faces a crisis, that we have a great number of problems." There's an important factor to remember in connection with this. The problems we face don't reflect decisive setbacks for the working class such as those in the 1930s—the rise of fascism and world war—or a political retreat such as that in the 1950s.

The crises and problems we face are ultimately rooted in our need to prepare for challenges and opportunities posed by an ascending class struggle and a situation in which the balance of forces on a world scale is shifting to our class. These struggles have not been decided. The biggest ones are still to come. And they are going to bring forward new forces from our class and its allies.

Building a mass world party

Given these revolutionary prospects, the turn is also decisive in putting the Fourth International in the position to accomplish what will be the most important challenge in building a mass world party of socialist revolution.

Everywhere we exist in the world today, we have only small propaganda groups. To accomplish the tasks we've set for ourselves, we must be able to turn to layers of revolutionists that come from other directions and other traditions—*revolutionists of action* such as the layer that came out of the Cuban revolution or the Nicaraguan revolution today, left currents that arise from the crisis in the union movement and the reformist parties. Our capacity to link up with them, to attract them to our program and convince them of its necessity, to merge our forces and theirs into a common political and organizational framework—this is the only way we can build a mass world party. It can't be done simply through recruitment to our sections.

But this historic task can be accomplished only by organizations rooted in industry and composed of industrial workers.

We often point out that even relatively small revolutionary parties can grow tumultuously during mass upheavals, being forged out of the fighters that come forward out of these class battles. This is true. It is what happened to the Bolsheviks in 1917.

But this can *only* be true for parties of industrial workers who have already been tested in action and have experience and respect in the workers movement. It cannot happen from outside the heart of the working class. Those who are on the outside when such developments occur will simply be bypassed; the opportunity will be lost.

This is the goal of the turn. To place our cadres where they must be to build workers parties that are capable of growing out of the big class battles that we know are on the agenda throughout the world. Otherwise, our program, which the world proletariat needs to chart a course to victory, will remain a lifeless document rather than a guide to mass revolutionary action.

We make no guarantees that the turn will bring us correct tactics, timing, or political savvy in meeting opportunities such as this. No promise whatsoever. These matters will be up to the comrades on the spot in each section and each new situation. We simply guarantee that these decisions *cannot* be made correctly without the turn, without parties composed in their overwhelming majority of industrial workers.

Finally, we should dispense with one myth. I was struck by it when reading a document that contains an exchange between leaders of the British Socialist Workers Party and comrades from the International Marxist Group.[4] The British SWP warns that several years ago their American organization tried to place the big majority of its comrades into industry and the experience ended in disaster. Here's what they had to say:

Now, while we completely agree with the *objective,* the solid implantation of revolutionaries in the industrial working class, we believe that the *method* proposed to achieve it can only lead to disaster. "Proletarianisation" or "industrialisation"—i.e., transplanting ex-students into industry—is only a substitute, and a dangerous one at that, for the real task of building workers parties.

"Industrialisation" has certain superficial attractions. It yields quick results—it leads to significant increases in the number of manual workers among the members. These results are however achieved at a high price. The petty-bourgeois comrades sent into industry are forced to adapt to their new environment. Their first priority is to make themselves acceptable to their work-mates. The natural consequence is that they play down, or completely conceal their politics and concentrate upon making themselves effective trade unionists. A gulf opens up between their life as revolutionaries and their life as worker militants. Within the workplace their priority is not to win over other workers to revolutionary politics, to sell the party's paper, to present a programme of struggle against the bosses, but to establish themselves as good militants pure and simple. Within the organisation they often become a conservative force, tending, for example, to take what they believe to be a "super-proletarian" (i.e., reactionary) line on questions of, for instance, sexual oppression, and to adopt generally economistic positions.

At the same time, "industrialisation" tends to create two tiers of membership within the organisation. There are the "worker-Bolshevik cadres" who have made the transition from petty bourgeois to "proletarian" and who therefore tend to regard themselves as an elite, and the rest, who exist, not to build the party and rank-and-file organisations in their own workplaces, but to "service" the "proletarians." Work in the white-collar unions and among students, far from negligible spheres of activity, tends to suffer severely under this sort of regime.

We are not inventing this scenario. It has happened in odd instances within our own organisation. It happened to the International Socialists in the United States, where "industrialisation" created a paper which hardly mentioned politics, a bloated full-time apparatus, a conservative layer of "proletarianised" students and, at the bottom, demoralised white-collar workers and students. The end result is that the organisation has dissolved itself into various rank-and-file union caucuses and a monthly propaganda magazine.

The conclusion the British SWP draws from this experience is: *Don't go into industry. The turn is wrong.*

We say just the opposite. We say the reason the IS [International Socialists] experience led to failure—and it was abysmal—was because of the program and leadership of the organization that carried it out. The reason it failed is that this organization counterposed going into industry and "union work," on the one hand, to the development of a politically rounded workers paper, Marxist education, and systematic political campaigns, on the other. When they made the turn, the leadership consciously *de-*

politicized all party institutions.

If such false counterpositions are made, then the turn will fail. You do lose comrades. And you can't recruit and hold politicizing young workers. When the party is falsely told to *choose* between an effort to get comrades into industry and carrying out organized political campaigns, then, of course, colonization will fail.

But we have a totally different approach. We don't think that comrades who have been recruited from and trained in important protest movements and struggles of the oppressed will become less political, less feminist, less opposed to nuclear power when they become industrial workers and union militants. We believe—and our experience already confirms—that comrades become more confident and more effective in all these struggles.

Ultimately, underlying opposition to the turn—whether consciously or not—is the idea that somehow workers are inherently less revolutionary, less political, and more prejudiced than other sectors of the population. That's absolutely false.

We are convinced that workers are *not* less political than other sectors of the population. To the contrary, we're convinced that as the struggles of all the oppressed deepen, industrial workers will more and more take the lead.

But to carry out the turn, we have to face facts. We have to look cold-bloodedly, honestly, and thoroughly at our current size, composition, and problems. There are no tricks or formally correct definitions that can help us become parties that are proletarian in composition as well as program. We have to start from our *real* composition, so we can judge the real tasks and opportunities before us.

Meeting the opportunities

There is no reason for pessimism. We should look at the crisis we face and the problems we confront as reflections of a period that is opening in which we can *resolve* them. The turn will give us the political perspectives we need to grow and move forward.

On a world scale, we are the only organized revolutionary alternative for the labor movement. Every other international current has failed.

We are convinced that in making the turn to the industrial working class, we must simultaneously build a world party and our national sections. We cannot build revolutionary workers parties anywhere in the world without the simultaneous struggle to build the world party.

And that world party cannot and will not be built unless its components are *workers parties,* rooted in industry, in countries throughout the world.

In driving through the turn, we open the door to the entire next stage in constructing the international party of socialist revolution that is needed by the working class to topple world capitalism.

A new stage of revolutionary working-class politics

I. The focus of the political resolution

As a result of our February 1978 turn, we now have a significant percentage of our party in industry. The draft political resolution registers the richer and more concrete understanding we have gained about the character of labor's resistance to American capital's austerity offensive and the complexities of the changing political consciousness of the working class.

On the basis of this understanding, and our changing class composition, we can *act* more and more as a party of worker-bolsheviks. We can see more of the political and organizational implications for our movement as the class polarization widens. We begin to be a part of the working class in composition, not only in program.

First and foremost, we want to deepen the turn into the indus-

The general line of this report on the resolution "Building a Revolutionary Party of Socialist Workers" was approved by the National Committee of the Socialist Workers Party, April 29, 1979. SEE PAGE 441 FOR NOTES

trial unions. We must drive ahead toward our goal of leading the large majority of American Trotskyists into industry. There is still unevenness among the party branches and locals in achieving this. There is still unevenness in the size, concentration, and functioning of industrial fractions, and—most important—in the political centrality of the fractions to branch and local political activity.

The turn is a vital necessity. A party that doesn't center its political work in the most powerfully organized and strategically located components of its class, when the possibility to do that exists, can only degenerate. Our experience has made us more convinced of the necessity of the turn today than when we adopted it a little more than a year ago.

After discussions with comrades around the world we're convinced of something else, also. A radical, sweeping turn to colonize the large majority of our comrades into the industrial working class and trade unions is a vital necessity if we are to begin solving the problems and meeting the growing opportunities facing the entire world Trotskyist movement. That's why the turn is at the core of the World Political Resolution and is the central focus of the discussions leading up to the 1979 World Congress of the Fourth International.[1]

Getting our forces situated within our class where we will have our fingers on the real political pulse of this country is a necessity. But we shouldn't transform it into a virtue—it's not a moral question or a solution to all political or party-building problems. It simply poses them in a new way—a way in which they *can* be solved. It's a *tactic* to accomplish a decisively important political goal: bringing the composition of our party into harmony with our proletarian program. Becoming a party of worker-bolsheviks.

If we drive ahead implementing the turn, then by the time of our summer conference in 1980 the party will meet the goal of getting the large majority of our members and leaders into industry and centering our political work around our industrial fractions. When that's done, the *turn* will simply be the *permanent* political orientation of our party toward the main organizations of our class, the industrial unions.

That should make us all the more committed to drive through the turn to the end, so that—as a party of socialist industrial workers—we can get on with taking care of business.

The organizing drive and strike at the Newport News shipyard, the nuclear power plant accident at Three Mile Island, Vietnam's aid in overthrowing the Pol Pot regime in Kampuchea and Peking's invasion of Vietnam, the overthrow of the shah of Iran, double-digit inflation again, the new gas crisis, erosion of job conditions, the rollback of abortion rights, the collapse and breakdown of health and pension plans, Black youth unemployment—all these and many more aspects of the worldwide capitalist offensive, and the resistance it is sparking, convince us that we're correct in how we size up the political situation.

We get further confirmation from what we're learning from our co-workers in industry. Things are changing. There's the beginning of a desire and willingness to fight back. Many are looking for answers, and they are willing to think about radical solutions—which is all we ask.

Of course, it's important to understand what we mean when we say that the working class is moving to center stage in American politics. As we've explained, in one sense it is the American ruling class that is at center stage. Because of the misleadership of American labor, the bosses still hold the offensive today. They're on the prod: pushing austerity, chipping away at democratic rights, trying to weaken the unions and deepen divisions in the working class.

When we say that American workers are moving to center stage, we mean two closely intertwined things. First, the industrial workers are the central target of the rulers' offensive. As we explain in the political resolution, that's who the employers are after. To drive up their profits they have to take on the big industrial unions, which are the most powerful institutions of the oppressed and exploited.

Second, we mean that the working class is moving to the center in the *resistance* to the offensive in the fight back. We're pointing to the impact of the 1974-75 depression on the consciousness of millions of young workers. We're talking about the skirmishes with the bosses that continually break out. We're talking about new moods, new attitudes. The growing tendency to turn to the unions seeking power and support in the fight for Black and women's rights, or against nuclear power. And the growing *need* to turn in that direction in order to find the leadership that can move the struggle of the oppressed forward.

This was exemplified by the initiative, the combativity, and the openness to new ideas that we encountered among the striking workers at Newport News. We don't see struggles of that scope breaking out all across the country right now, but those attitudes are not unique. That's what is happening in our class. We're far enough along in the turn to know that for a fact.

All this means that we can begin to build a new kind of party *today*. We're not going into industry solely to prepare for things we expect to happen tomorrow. As we said at our December 1978 plenum, our experience demonstrates that socialist workers can do political work in the class in the here and now. We know that from our experience of the past year.

But to do that effectively, we have to take the *politics* implied by these changes and our industrial turn and put them together. We have to take a new and fresh look at all our party institutions and campaigns. A new and fresh look at what we can do, how we do it, and what we're after. A new and fresh look at the relationship between strategy and tactics—learning to gauge all our tactics in light of our overall proletarian strategy.

II. The roots of revolutionary strategy

It's helpful to step back and ask ourselves the basic questions: What is Marxism? What are we all about?

Two months before Marx and Engels drafted the Communist Manifesto, Engels, working together with Marx, wrote a couple of editorials attacking a petty-bourgeois German theorist named Heinzen (whose sole importance in history is that he served as a foil for Engels).

"Herr Heinzen imagines communism is a certain *doctrine* which proceeds from a definite theoretical principle as its *core* and draws further conclusions from that," Engels wrote. "Herr Heinzen is very much mistaken. Communism is not a doctrine but a *movement;* it proceeds not from principles but from *facts.*"[2] That's where the program comes from, Engels said.

Marx and Engels incorporated this central concept at the heart of the Communist Manifesto:

"The theoretical conclusions of the communists are in no way based on ideas or principles that have been invented, or discovered, by this or that would-be universal reformer," they wrote.

"They merely express, in general terms, *actual* relations springing from an *existing* class struggle, from a historical movement going on under our very eyes."[3]

This might seem obvious, but it sometimes helps to go back and remind ourselves of the obvious, of our fundamental starting points. Historical materialism discovered that history is the history of class struggles. Marxism is simply the generalized interests of one of the two major classes involved in that struggle in the modern world—the working class.

Communists "have no interests separate and apart from those of the proletariat as a whole," Marx and Engels wrote in the Communist Manifesto. "They do not set up any sectarian principles of their own, by which to shape and mould the proletarian movement."

Marx and Engels then went on to pinpoint the internationalism of the communist movement, and its task in overcoming the national and other divisions imposed on the working class by capitalism.

"The communists are distinguished from the other working-class parties," they say, "by this only: (1) In the national struggles of the proletarians of the different countries, they point out and bring to the front the common interests of the entire proletariat, independently of all nationality. (2) In the various stages of development which the struggle of the working class against the bourgeoisie has to pass through, they always and everywhere represent the interests of the movement as a whole."

From here, Marx and Engels conclude: "The communists, therefore, are on the one hand, practically, the most advanced and resolute section of the working-class parties of every country, that section which pushes forward all others; on the other hand, theoretically, they have over the great mass of the proletariat the advantage of clearly understanding the line of march, the conditions, and the ultimate general results of the proletarian movement."[4]

Marxists *are part of* the working class, not something outside of it. The revolutionary Marxist party is not simply the bearer of a program that constitutes the "Marxist wing" of all progressive struggles.

The Marxist party analyzes *all* classes and their conflicts, all politics, from the point of view of the historic goals of *our* class—the class that we are simply the most conscious and organized part of and the most consistent fighter for. The class whose task is to govern, expropriate the exploiters and oppressors, and lead a great social movement to reorganize society to eliminate oppression and construct socialism.

The working class is created by its enemy—the capitalist class, the profit system. Workers don't *choose* to participate in the class struggle, they are *forced to* by their condition. This is what makes Marxism scientific, not utopian. And more and more workers in this country are becoming conscious of this class struggle as the rulers' offensive escalates—every day in the factories, and around the big social and political issues such as unemployment, discrimination, and war.

This working-class perspective and strategy—that's all Marxism is. Of course, that "all" encompasses the future of humanity.

That's what our party is about, too. We're part of the working class. Our program expresses the interests of the working class. We explain the historic goal of our class—political power, a workers government to organize the transformation of all social relations. We explain and analyze current conditions to build bridges toward the achievement of that goal. And we explain labor's "line of march"—the strategy that can organize and mobilize our class to do the job.

Leninist strategy of party building

Before 1917 *exactly* what kind of party was needed to lead the working class to power wasn't clear. But a relatively small number of revolutionists, who under Lenin's leadership became the cadres of the Bolshevik Party, were building the one that was going to do it and settle the question. Between the late 1890s and the 1905 Russian revolution, Lenin wrote a number of important articles explaining the character of this party. His most well-known work on the subject is, of course, *What Is to Be Done?*

In these articles, Lenin started from the simple idea of Marx and Engels that Marxists—who were called social democrats at that time—represent the interests of a class; and that this class, the working class, is the only class capable of being consistently progressive. He explained what this implied about the kind of party that was necessary in the epoch of imperialism to advance the workers' interests and lead society forward.

Lenin pointed out that only the working class can be a consistent fighter for democratic rights and political liberty. (He was talking about the fight against tsarist tyranny, but most of the points he made apply to the fight against political oppression under whatever form of capitalist rule.)

Lenin explained in these articles that the revolutionary proletarian party must champion all the struggles of the oppressed. If it doesn't do that, then it's not a revolutionary party, and it won't be worthy or able to lead the workers to power. We've stressed this idea over and over again, incorporating it at the heart of our resolutions, including the one we're discussing here today.

Lenin explained that the workers as a class have the biggest stake in the "*complete* democratization of the political and social system, since this would place the system in the hands of the workers." [5] The workers sorely need democratic rights to carry out the struggles for their most basic economic and political demands, he pointed out.

By standing out as the vanguard fighters for democratic rights, the working class will strengthen the movements of all the oppressed, strengthen the struggle for political liberty, and spur on every other force in these fights.

Lenin also had some important things to say about the strategy needed to build the revolutionary proletarian party.

In an article he wrote in 1899, Lenin first listed a series of things that pointed *away from* a revolutionary working-class strategy. The task of the party, Lenin said, is "not to draw up plans for refashioning society, not to preach to the capitalists and their hangers-on about improving the lot of the workers, not to hatch conspiracies. . . ." In other words, not to think up schemes like the Socialist Labor Party does. Not to crusade for alternative lifestyles. Not "socialist social work," or ultraleft adventures to "spark" the workers into action.

Instead, Lenin said, the task of the party is "to organize the class struggle of the proletariat and to lead this struggle, the ultimate aim of which is the conquest of political power by the proletariat and the organization of a socialist society." [6]

That's at the heart of the Leninist strategy of party building—making the organization and mobilization of our class and its march toward power the axis of everything we do. In everything the party projects, we must always answer these questions: Does it advance the class consciousness, self-confidence, and class-struggle experience of the workers? Does it do more than some alternative course to change the relationship of class forces to the advantage of the oppressed and exploited? Does it help prepare the working class for the fight to take power and govern? Does it promote the development of the working-class vanguard, the revolutionary party?

That's where the need for revolutionary centralism in the proletarian party comes from. Centralizing the party around a program that advances the interests of the working class, and around the fight to apply that program. It was from this class perspective that Lenin developed his concept of the centralized revolutionary party—the necessity of a proletarian composition, its character as a combat leadership of the mass working-class vanguard, the need for democratic decision-making and conscious leadership selection.

These fundamental concepts of the Leninist strategy of party building can sometimes seem abstract. But as the capitalist crisis deepens, as we become part of the industrial working class and its changing unions, as the party becomes more of a working-class organization in composition as well as program—as these changes unfold, the importance of these basic ideas becomes more and more a part of our day-to-day experience.

Before the October 1917 revolution in Russia, Lenin's party-building strategy was understood by few other revolutionists in the socialist movement, and consciously rejected by many. From April 1917 on, however, when Lenin returned from exile and advanced his perspectives for the proletarian revolution in Russia, his strategy began to be understood by growing numbers of revolutionary-minded workers there and—after its success—abroad.

Following the October revolution, these ideas were discussed and incorporated into the program of the first four congresses of the Communist International and into the program of the Communist Party of the Soviet Union. These resolutions are part of our heritage and of our revolutionary program today. After April, the Bolsheviks, under Lenin's leadership, applied many aspects of what we now call the transitional method.

But the most complete elaboration and systematic development and explanation of the transitional method was done by Trotsky.

The Transitional Program is the application of the Leninist strategy of party building to solve what Trotsky called the "historical crisis of the leadership of the proletariat." It built on the conquests of the Bolsheviks and of the Communist International before its

Stalinization. Trotsky's contributions to the Leninist strategy of party building were incorporated in the Transitional Program adopted by the founding conference of the Fourth International in 1938.[7]

It's worth stepping back to look at the transitional method, where it came from, and how it relates to our tasks as working-class revolutionists today.

Before World War I, the Marxist movement talked only of principles and tactics; it didn't really have a strategy.

Principles are what we've sometimes called "red light" questions—if you start crossing them, a big red stoplight should flash on in your head. You don't support imperialist wars. You don't breach class independence.

These are principles. They are more often things "thou shalt not do" than things "thou shalt do."

Principles are very important. They are not just dreamed up. A high price is paid for them in blood. They are lessons drawn from the experiences of the working class and its struggles. If you begin breaching them, you cannot build a revolutionary working-class party.

The need for a strategy

In 1928, a full decade before he drafted the Transitional Program, Trotsky wrote about the pre–World War I socialist movement's lack of a strategic conception.

"Prior to the war," he wrote, "we spoke only of the tactics of the proletarian party; this conception conformed adequately enough to the then prevailing trade union, parliamentary methods which did not transcend the limits of the day-to-day demands and tasks.

"By the conception of tactics," Trotsky explained, "is understood the system of measures that serves a single current task or a single branch of the class struggle."

But that's not enough, Trotsky said. "Revolutionary strategy on the contrary embraces a combined system of actions which by their association, consistency, and growth must lead the proletariat to the conquest of power."[8]

"Tactics are subordinate to strategy," Trotsky said. And strategy serves as the indispensable link between tactics, on the one hand, and principles and the socialist goal, on the other.

World War I showed that the majority of leaders of the Second International did have a strategy—only it was not an acknowledged one and it led to disaster. Their strategy was to rely on their own bourgeoisie, to rely on a gradual accumulation of reforms under capitalism.

At the end of the war, however, the Bolsheviks showed in practice the kind of strategy needed to lead the working class to power.

By the mid-1920s, the revolutionary wave in Europe had subsided without further victories for the workers. The world capitalist expansion of that decade got under way.

There are some instructive parallels between what happened during the period of relative prosperity of the 1920s and the two and a half decades of economic expansion that followed World War II.

Periods such as these always create the illusion that reform is realistic. Capitalism doesn't seem to be a crisis-ridden system. A lot of workers seem to be doing pretty well. Fewer and fewer workers sense a social crisis; those who do, or who understand that crises are built into the capitalist system, are a small minority.

All these things have a big impact on the working class and the revolutionary workers movement. Whether consciously or not, there develops a tendency to drift back toward the old division between tactics and principles. The need for a strategy for the working class to take power becomes clouded.

The fundamental class-against-class basis of politics becomes disguised in such periods. That is, the struggles that do break out often seem unrelated to class divisions in society. Many social issues don't outwardly appear to have much to do with class oppression and exploitation.

Those issues that are recognized as class-against-class by the general population, including big layers of the working class, come to be viewed very narrowly—what are often called "bread and butter" issues. These are seen as very limited struggles that don't challenge the overall status quo. Political and social issues, on the other hand—including political solutions to economic needs—are not recognized as class questions at all.

The crisis in 1929 shook things up. It was the beginning of the end for illusions about capitalism's reformability, its rosy future, its crisis-free existence. More and more working people began to say, "No! There must be another way."

The Transitional Program

During the Great Depression of the 1930s, "bread and butter" issues became life-or-death questions that took on a direct social and political form. But it also became increasingly clear that social struggles were part of the class struggle, all part of the struggle between the exploiters and the exploited.

Under these conditions, and after extensive discussions with American comrades and comrades from Europe who could make it to Mexico, Trotsky drafted the Transitional Program in 1938. This exemplifies the strategy and method that we must understand more thoroughly than ever today so that we can apply it under new and different conditions to build the revolutionary party.

If it's not understood that the Transitional Program is a strategic document aimed at furthering the construction of proletarian combat parties, then the whole point is missed.

That's exactly what Isaac Deutscher does in his biography of Trotsky. He misses the whole point.

The Transitional Program, Deutscher says, "was not so much a statement of principles as an instruction on tactics, designed for a party up to its ears in trade union struggles and day-to-day politics. . . ."[9]

Exactly wrong! It is neither a "statement of principles" nor—least of all—an "instruction on tactics." It *was* designed to help parties "up to their ears in trade union struggles and day-to-day politics"—to help them step back and judge where they were going. What was their strategy? Was this strategy being advanced by the tactics they were employing in trade union activity and other day-to-day political struggles?

Trotsky put it this way in the Transitional Program: "Naturally it's a tremendous acquisition that we are rooted in the trade unions, but it's very important not to lose our world strategic line. Every local, partial, economic demand must be an approach to a general demand in our transitional program. . . ."[10]

In some talks George Breitman gave five years ago at one of our summer educational conferences, he pointed out that this strategic understanding was precisely the greatest contribution of the Transitional Program to the SWP. It provided the party "with a coherent and viable strategy or set of strategic concepts perhaps for the first time in this country," George explained, "and certainly on a scale we had never known before."

That was the aim of the Transitional Program. And that was the aim of the section we called "Labor's Strategic Line of March" in the resolution, "Prospects for Socialism in America," adopted by our 1975 convention.

Trotsky explained this basic concept again in the introductory section of the Transitional Program. "The strategic task of the Fourth International lies not in reforming capitalism but in its overthrow. Its political aim is the conquest of power by the proletariat for the purpose of expropriating the bourgeoisie."

A few sentences later, Trotsky continued: "The present epoch is distinguished not because it frees the revolutionary party from day-to-day work but because it permits this work to be carried on indissolubly with the actual tasks of the revolution. . . . it carries on this day-to-day work within the framework of the correct actual, that is, revolutionary, perspective." The party becomes capable of imparting this perspective to more and more workers.

"Insofar as the old partial, 'minimal' demands of the masses clash with the destructive and degrading tendencies of decadent capitalism," says Trotsky, "and this occurs at each step—the Fourth International advances a system of *transitional demands.*"

The essence of these transitional demands, Trotsky explains, "is contained in the fact that ever more openly and decisively they will be directed against the very foundations of the bourgeois regime.

"The old 'minimal program' is superseded by the *transitional program*," Trotsky concludes, "the task of which lies in systematic mobilization of the masses for the proletarian revolution."[11]

Labor's strategic line of march

Following these introductory remarks comes the section of the Transitional Program in which Trotsky lays out the "line of march of the proletarian movement" (to use the phrase from the Communist Manifesto). I remember that when I first read this part of the Transitional Program nearly twenty years ago, it seemed interesting but not "relevant." I'm sure many of us had that experience. But read it again today.

In a nutshell, these were some of the main ideas Trotsky laid out for the labor movement and its revolutionary leadership.

First, the defense of the workers against the twin scourges of unemployment and inflation, which are endemic to capitalism. The heart of Trotsky's solution is a sliding scale of wages and hours— what we would call a full cost-of-living escalator and a shorter workweek with no loss of pay. The capitalists, not workers, are responsible for unemployment and inflation, Trotsky pointed out. So they, not the workers, should pay the price. Workers should be guaranteed full protection of their living standards and job security.

Secondly, Trotsky dealt with the trade unions—the class institutions that are central to the fight for such things as the sliding scale of wages and hours. Workers have to strengthen their unions. The illusion exists that the unions are strong, he explained, but they're not strong so long as their strength goes unused.

Socialists have to chart a course to turn them into revolutionary unions, Trotsky said. That's what we're after in projecting our program for a class-struggle left wing in the labor movement. The unions must not be tied to the capitalist class, its government, or its parties, Trotsky said. The class independence of the unions must be fought for and preserved. There must be democracy in the unions, so that the workers themselves can use the unions to fight for their interests. Trotsky talked about the need for solidarity, both within the class and with all the struggles of the masses.

It's clear from Trotsky's discussions about the Transitional Program with American comrades that the slogan of an independent labor party would have come in here. But it was omitted on request of the American comrades so that they could discuss it more fully. There were disagreements on this question among American Trotskyists at that time. We finally adopted the labor party slogan shortly after the Transitional Program was issued by the founding conference of the Fourth International.

Above everything, Trotsky wrote, look to the youth and bring an entire new layer of militant workers into the union leadership. Prepare in this way to sweep aside the old, conservative, class-collaborationist leaders. The Transitional Program, Trotsky said, is such an invaluable weapon for the working class because of both the "confusion and disappointment of the older generation, and the inexperience of the younger generation."

Educate and train the younger generation of workers in class-struggle methods, Trotsky explained. Only along that road can the power of the unions be unleashed. Only along that road will more and more workers begin to say no to the restraints the trade union bureaucracy imposes on their struggles.

Trotsky went on from here to explain the importance of strike committees. We saw this come to life at Newport News at the big meeting where the workers voted to stay out until Tenneco withdrew some of the humiliating back-to-work conditions it had initially insisted on.

Then Trotsky dealt with workers control. There were two sides to this. One was opening the capitalists' books—gaining knowledge for the working class and public at large about everything that big business and the capitalist government hide from us. The workers should shine a spotlight on all the so-called business secrets, the preparations for war, the connections among the war in-

1 MINERS ON STRIKE IN SULLIVAN, INDIANA, MAY 1993, TO FORCE THE BUCK CREEK COAL COMPANY TO NEGOTIATE A CONTRACT. 'THE GUYS WHO OWN THIS MINE RAN THE PYRO MINE IN KENTUCKY WHEN IT EXPLODED AND KILLED TEN MEN. WE DON'T WANT TO BE THEIR NEXT VICTIMS," EXPLAINED ONE STRIKER.

Communists base ourselves among the young workers especially, those who are the most combative and politically conscious. We look toward their mobilization, organization, and heightened class awareness.

Mourn For The Dead-Fight For The Living
IMPERIAL FOODS FIRE VICTIMS

David Michael Albright, 24
Rose Lynnette Wilkins, 30
Jeffrey Antonio Webb, 24
Mary Lillian Wall, 50
Josie M. Coulter, 40
John Robet Gagnon, 39
Brenda Gail Kelly, 31
Janice Marie Wall Lynch, 43

Fred Barrington, Jr. 37
Josephine Barrington, 63
Elizabeth Ann Bellamy, 42
Rosie Ann Chambers, 31
Rose Marie Gibson Peele, 39
Mary Alice Arnold Quick, 38
Martha E. Ratliff, 36
Donald Bruce Rich, 24

Peggy Anderson, 50 - Margaret Banks, 24 - Philip R. Dawkins, 49 - Bertha Jerrell, 40
Michael Morrison 31 - Gail V. Campbell, 33 - Cynthia Ratliff, 20 - Cynthia S. Wall, 41
Minnie May Thompson, 30

Without the fight to transform the industrial unions into revolutionary instruments of class struggle, there is no way for our class to prevent the social breakdowns, catastrophes, the gnawing uncertainties and insecurity, and the threat of imperialist wars.

2 (LEFT) MEMORIAL FOR WORKERS KILLED IN FIRE AT POULTRY PLANT IN HAMLET, NORTH CAROLINA, SEPTEMBER 1991. BOSSES KEPT EXITS PADLOCKED. **3** (TOP) AFTERMATH OF U.S. BOMBING ON ROAD TO BASRA DURING IRAQ WAR, FEBRUARY 1991. ONE MEMBER OF THE AIR FORCE BRASS CALLED THE U.S.-ORGANIZED SLAUGHTER A "TURKEY SHOOT." **4** (BOTTOM) PROTEST AGAINST U.S. WAR IN THE PERSIAN GULF, SALT LAKE CITY, UTAH, DECEMBER 1990.

To drive up their profits the employers have to take on the big industrial unions—the most powerful institutions of the oppressed and exploited.

5 [TOP] STEELWORKERS LOCAL 8888 PICKETERS AT NEWPORT NEWS SHIPBUILDING CO., APRIL 1979. VICTORY OF DRIVE TO ORGANIZE 18,000 WORKERS, WITH BLACK WORKERS IN THE VANGUARD, SHOWED THAT CIVIL RIGHTS BATTLES AGAINST JIM CROW SEGREGATION CREATED MORE FAVORABLE CONDITIONS FOR THE STRUGGLES OF WORKING PEOPLE.

6 (OPPOSITE) THOUSANDS OF MINERS AND SUPPORTERS RALLY IN CARBO, VIRGINIA, TO SUPPORT 98 STRIKERS OCCUPYING A PITTSTON COAL FACILITY, SEPTEMBER 1989. SOME 44,000 UMWA MEMBERS IN 11 STATES WALKED OFF THE JOB FOR 6 WEEKS IN SUPPORT OF THE PITTSTON MINERS DURING THEIR STRIKE.

7 (LEFT) DEMONSTRATION IN PEORIA, ILLINOIS, IN SUPPORT OF UAW STRIKE AGAINST CATERPILLAR COMPANY, MARCH 1992.

The ultimate target of the rulers' austerity drive is the industrial workers, for the very same reason that the industrial workers have been at the center of our strategy since the founding of Marxism—their economic strength; their social weight; the example they set for the whole class.

8 (TOP) STRIKING MEATPACKERS ORGANIZED BY UFCW LOCAL P-9 AND THEIR SUPPORTERS GATHER OUTSIDE THE HORMEL PLANT IN AUSTIN MINNESOTA, APRIL 1986.

9 (BOTTOM) RAIL WORKERS RALLY IN GILLETTE, WYOMING, IN THE DAYS LEADING UP TO APRIL 17, 1991, WHEN 235,000 MEMBERS OF EIGHT RAIL UNIONS WENT ON STRIKE. NINETEEN HOURS INTO THE WALKOUT, CONGRESS DECLARED IT ILLEGAL AND TOP UNION OFFICIALS CALLED IT OFF

A growing number of class battles, combined over time with a deepening social crisis, uprisings in the colonial and semicolonial countries, and imperialist wars, will transform politics and the labor movement in this country.

10 (ABOVE) GARMENT WORKERS DEMAND $15,000 IN UNPAID WAGES. SAN FRANCISCO, OCTOBER 1992.

11 STEELWORKERS FIGHT BACK CHALLENGED THE ENTRENCHED BUREAUCRACY IN THE USWA FROM 1975-1976. ED SADLOWSKI (TOP, AT LEFT), FIGHT BACK'S CANDIDATE FOR UNION PRESIDENT, CAMPAIGNS AT U.S. STEEL SOUTH WORKS. CHICAGO, AUGUST 1976.

12 (ABOVE) EASTERN AIRLINES STRIKERS AND SUPPORTERS MARCH IN LABOR DAY
PARADE, NEW YORK, SEPTEMBER 1989. RANK-AND-FILE MACHINISTS SET
EXAMPLE FOR LABOR MOVEMENT IN FIGHT AGAINST THE EMPLOYING CLASS'S
PREMIER UNION BUSTER, FRANK LORENZO.

13 (TOP LEFT) *MILITANT* AND *PERSPECTIVA MUNDIAL* SALESPEOPLE DISCUSS WORLD POLITICS AND WORKING-CLASS STRUGGLES WITH MEMBERS OF THE UNITED FOOD AND COMMERCIAL WORKERS UNION PICKETING IN HARRISON, NEW JERSEY, MAY 1993;

14 (LOWER LEFT) . . . WITH CONSTRUCTION WORKERS AT THE SITE OF THE EXXON OIL SPILL, VALDEZ, ALASKA, APRIL 1989;

15 (BOTTOM CENTER) . . . WITH FARM WORKERS ON STRIKE IN EASTERN WASHINGTON, OCTOBER 1992;

16 (BOTTOM, RIGHT) . . . AND WITH STEELWORKERS, APRIL 1977. ONE-WEEK EFFORT SOLD OVER 4,000 COPIES OF THE TWO PERIODICALS AT STEEL PLANTS, MAKING THE BASIC STEEL AGREEMENT AVAILABLE TO USWA MEMBERS.

17 (TOP RIGHT) SELLING THE SOCIALIST PRESS AT A MEATPACKING PLANT IN ST. PAUL, MINNESOTA, APRIL 1992. WEEKLY PLANT-GATE SALES ARE ORGANIZED BY SOCIALIST WORKERS IN CITIES ACROSS THE UNITED STATES AND IN OTHER COUNTRIES.

**Workers cannot develop revolutionary
political conclusions by generalizing from
their own struggles and experiences alone.**

The U.S. labor movement must aggressively champion the international solidarity of working people. The ruling class seeks to place the blame for the growing ills of capitalism onto the workers of other countries.

Get your
ID now!
TO
Make your X for
freedom
ANC — X
NOW IS THE TIME!
ANC

18 (LEFT) AFRICAN NATIONAL CONGRESS VOTER EDUCATION RALLY. MADADENI, NATAL MIDLANDS, SOUTH AFRICA, MAY 1993.
19 (RIGHT) GARMENT WORKER IN MEXICALI, MEXICO, NEAR BORDER WITH U.S., DECEMBER 1992.

In presenting a socialist perspective, we point to the achievements of revolutionary Cuba, where the workers and farmers took power into their own hands and used that power to uproot capitalism and begin the construction of a socialist society.

20 (TOP) WORKER TAKES THE FLOOR DURING DISCUSSION AT THE JOSÉ DÍAZ COLINA FACTORY ON THE POLITICAL CHALLENGES CONFRONTING THE CUBAN REVOLUTION, HAVANA, CUBA, JANUARY 1994.
21 (BOTTOM) CUBAN VOLUNTEER WORKERS HARVEST CABBAGE TO MEET FOOD SHORTAGES, HAVANA PROVINCE, JULY 1993.

For working people, solidarity means advancing our common class position against our common class enemy on a world scale, refusing to allow the employers and their government to divide us and set us against each other.

22 (LEFT) STRIKING PEABODY COAL MINER SPEAKS AT SEND-OFF RALLY FOR SHIPMENT OF HUMANITARIAN AID TO CUBA, SEATTLE, WASHINGTON, JULY 1993.

23 (TOP) CUBAN YOUTH LEADER PÁVEL DÍAZ HERNÁNDEZ (AT CENTER) MEETS WITH WORKERS IN DECATUR, ILLINOIS, WHO ARE FIGHTING A LOCKOUT BY OWNERS OF THE A.E.STALEY CORN-PROCESSING PLANT, APRIL 1994.

24 (BOTTOM) NORTH AMERICAN *BRIGADISTA* AND NICARAGUAN FARMWORKER WORK TOGETHER ON HOUSING CONSTRUCTION PROJECT IN MORILLO, A COMMUNITY IN SOUTHERN NICARAGUA, JANUARY 1988.

The unions should take the lead in demanding that health care, decent housing, and adequate pensions be government financed on a nationwide scale. Every gain in this will reinforce the strength and unity of the class as a whole.

25 (TOP) TUITION INCREASES AND BUDGET CUTS AT THE CITY UNIVERSITY OF NEW YORK SYSTEM RUN INTO ORGANIZED STUDENT OPPOSITION, MAY 1989.
26 (BOTTOM) GROCERY STORE WORKERS IN NEW YORK AND NEW JERSEY TAKE STRIKE ACTION IN A DISPUTE OVER HEALTH BENEFITS AND WAGES, NEWARK, NEW JERSEY, MAY 1993.
27 (RIGHT) PUBLIC WORKERS DEMAND GOVERNMENT FUNDED HEALTH CARE, OUTSIDE NEW YORK CITY HALL, OCTOBER 1990.

A new class-conscious political vanguard, with a composition reflecting the changed composition of the work force, will transform the unions into instruments of class struggle—into a powerful movement of workers who think socially and act politically.

28 (TOP) STUDENT CONTINGENT LEADS MARCH OF 12,000 IN BOSTON DEMANDING DESEGREGATION OF SCHOOLS AND AN END TO RACIST ATTACKS ON BLACK STUDENTS, DECEMBER 1974.

29 (BOTTOM, LEFT) STEELWORKERS JOIN WITH MINERS, MACHINISTS, RAIL WORKERS AND OTHERS AT DEMONSTRATION IN HARRISBURG, PENNSYLVANIA, TO MARK THE SECOND ANNIVERSARY OF THE NEAR-MELTDOWN OF THREE MILE ISLAND NUCLEAR REACTOR MARCH 1981.

30 (BOTTOM, RIGHT) EASTERN AIRLINES STRIKERS AND OTHER UNIONISTS TAKE PART IN MASSIVE MARCH FOR ABORTION RIGHTS. WASHINGTON, D.C., APRIL 1989.

As young workers go through experiences in struggle of setbacks and advances, of victories and defeats, a growing number will acquire revolutionary combat experience and their consciousness will be transformed.

31 (TOP) STRIKING DRYWALL WORKERS BLOCK ENTRANCE TO A CONSTRUCTION SITE, ANAHEIM, CALIFORNIA, AUGUST 1992. MASS PICKETING INVOLVING THOUSANDS OF WORKERS IN SOUTHERN CALIFORNIA WON A UNION CONTRACT AFTER 5-MONTH STRIKE.
32 (BOTTOM) DEFENDING AN ABORTION CLINIC FROM RIGHT-WING ATTACK, WASHINGTON, D.C., JANUARY 1993.

33 (RIGHT) FARMERS LAUNCH NATIONAL STRIKE IN RESPONSE TO TIGHTENING COST SQUEEZE. SHOWN, PART OF TRACTORCADE OF MORE THAN 8,000 IN ATLANTA, GEORGIA, DECEMBER 1976. **34** (ABOVE) FARMERS DEMONSTRATION DEMANDS AN END TO FORECLOSURES, PLATTSBURG, MISSOURI, MARCH 1985.

An alliance with the farmers is essential to defend the unions and lead a successful struggle to bring to power a workers and farmers government in the United States.

PHOTO CREDITS: **1** HARVEY McARTHUR **2** JANE ROLAND **3** DENIS BRACK/REUTER **4** DAVE WULP **5** JON HILLSON **6** MARY IMO **7** JIM GARRISON **8** TOM JAAX **9** MIKE GALATI **10** VED DOOKHUN **11** EARL DOTTER/PHOTOJOURNALIST **12** ERNIE MAILHOT **13** PHIL DUZINSKI **14** JANET POST **15** HARVEY McARTHUR **17** JON HILLSON **18** NIGEL DENNIS/ANC DEPARTMENT OF INFORMATION AND PUBLICITY **19** TED SOQUI/IMPACT VISUALS **20** AARON RUBY **21** ARGIRIS MALAPANIS **22** HARVEY McARTHUR **23** LUIS MADRID **24** DAVE WELTERS **25** SELVA NEBBIA **26** PHIL DUZINSKI **27** ROBERT FOX/IMPACT VISUALS **28** FLAX HERMES **29** FRED MURPHY **30** NANCY BROWN **31** ELIZABETH STONE **32** MARGRETHE SIEM **33** RICHARD RATHERS **34** JEFF POWERS ■ ALL PHOTOS ARE COURTESY OF THE *MILITANT* NEWSPAPER UNLESS OTHERWISE NOTED.

dustries, the connections between big business and government regulatory agencies, and so on. The labor movement must be mobilized to expose contrived shortages and hidden stockpiles, to get at the truth behind the disastrous breakdowns inflicted on the population under capitalism.

Connected to this is the fight for actual control on the job— control over the pace of the line, control over safety, control over how the job is organized. This becomes a school for the working class in preparing to manage and plan the entire economy under a workers government. Lenin banged away at this lesson after the October revolution: You can't simply leap into workers management even when the workers hold political power. It takes time and experience. Workers control is a school for the entire reorganization of production, for real planning.

Then Trotsky turned to the expropriation of selected industries; in his discussion with some American comrades he agreed that the term "nationalization" can have the same content if properly explained. The goal of the workers government is to expropriate the entire capitalist class and establish a planned economy, Trotsky said.

But sometimes all hell will break loose under capitalism, posing the need to take a vital industry out of the hands of the capitalist profiteers. A particular industry will become crucially important in meeting people's needs, but criminally incapable of doing so. It may undergo a total breakdown. Something won't work. It will greatly endanger workers and their environment.

We've seen this best around the energy crisis, but it comes up around other particular industries as well. In cases such as these, Trotsky said, we make a demand on the capitalist government that it take over these industries, that it nationalize them and that they should become public utilities rather than remaining privately owned and operated.

There should be full public knowledge about all aspects of the operation of these publicly owned industries; there should be no secret files, secret meetings, or handpicked boards. The whole thing should be out in the open. Tied to this is the fight by the workers in these industries to control all the conditions under which they work and to use their special knowledge and position to make sure that everything is out on the table. These demands point in the direction of expropriating all basic industry and the banks.

Trotsky then turned to the need of the workers to defend themselves and their unions against the bosses' hired goons and fascist gangs. This begins on the most basic level with the strike picket lines and encompasses the entire system of measures that the workers will have to take as the class polarization deepens and the fight for political power is posed more and more sharply. A proper understanding of strategy and tactics here is a life-or-death matter for the workers movement.

From here, the Transitional Program moves on to a broad range of issues facing the labor movement; the need for an alliance with the farmers; war, which is an especially important question for the youth who have to fight and die in imperialist wars; racism and national chauvinism, particularly in countries with large oppressed nationality populations; the fight for democratic rights.

All of this leads up to the fight for a workers government and the organization of councils or soviets—that is, the workers' struggle for political power to reorganize society on a new basis.

Summing up the transitional approach toward the end of the document, Trotsky writes; "All methods are good which raise the class-consciousness of the workers, their trust in their own forces, their readiness for self-sacrifice in the struggle. The impermissible methods are those which implant fear and submissiveness in the oppressed in the face of their oppressors. . . ."[12]

And Trotsky ends up with the slogans: Open the road to the youth! Turn to the woman worker! Those are pretty good slogans for our party today.

This was the line of march Trotsky proposed as a revolutionary proletarian strategy for the workers movement. Its entire purpose was the construction of Leninist parties that could lead the workers to power. "The present crisis in human culture is the crisis in the proletarian leadership," Trotsky wrote at the end of the Transitional Program. "The advanced workers, united in the Fourth International, show their class the way out of the crisis."

From Marx and Engels, through Lenin to Trotsky: these are the roots of our revolutionary working-class strategy.

Strategic offensives and strategic retreats

As I said earlier, Trotsky discussed the major points in the Transitional Program with the American comrades in the months prior to its final drafting and adoption. In one of these discussions, Trotsky said that the document could be called an action program, but that he didn't think that quite hit the nail on the head. It's a "strategic conception," he explained, a "transitional program."

Its aim is to help "the masses in overcoming the inherited ideas, methods, and forms" of the bankrupt labor misleaders. We have to "advance slogans that are not in the vocabulary of the American working class" yet, Trotsky said. We can't be afraid to do that.

"The strategic tasks consist of helping the masses, of adapting their mentality politically and psychologically . . . to the objective situation of the social crisis of the whole system."

Trotsky explained that we will begin to raise many of our ideas in the context of defensive struggles by the workers. The workers won't be ready to take power or to join the revolutionary party in large numbers. "But in the present situation we must be oriented for a strategic offensive," Trotsky said, "not a retreat." Through the transitional approach, the party presents to our class the perspective of this strategic offensive against their exploiters, this strategic line of march toward a workers government.

All our tactics must be adjusted to this task, because as the attacks by the rulers come down, as the system rots, more and more workers begin looking for answers. They begin to fight back. They suffer defeats, standoffs and stalemates, and win some partial victories. As they go through these experiences, the strategic line of march outlined in the Transitional Program makes more and more sense. It's the only way out of the catastrophe that capitalism has in store for them.

But then Trotsky posed a question. "We cannot predict the rhythm and tempo of the development" of things, he said. The bourgeoisie may find a political respite. In that case, he explained, the party and our class can't undertake a strategic offensive; "we will be obliged to realize a strategic retreat." Not a tactical retreat, not a pause, but a strategic retreat.

Of course, that's the opposite of the situation that the party and the workers face today. Capitalism is not about to enter a period of sustained economic expansion and begin granting major concessions to working people. But such a situation *was* forced on the party during the postwar years of Cold War witch-hunting and capitalist expansion.

The post-1947 retreat

The years following 1947 marked a big political retreat of our class. American capitalism had emerged from World War II in a strengthened position. Internationally, Stalinism had throttled revolutionary upsurges in Western Europe. Here in this country, the trade union bureaucracy tightened its hold over the CIO unions, joining in the capitalist witch-hunt by launching an anticommunist "housecleaning" in the labor movement.

The unions were terribly weakened during the retreat. Our class was weakened. Workers have begun to find this out in recent years as they try to use the unions once again to defend their living conditions.

The bureaucracy sought to convince a layer of relatively better-off workers that it was somehow in their interests to accept the class-collaborationist schemes by means of which the unions were being cut apart and the power of the unions sapped. But they didn't explain that the key thing happening to labor during the capitalist expansion was not the real wage increases. The key thing was that the unions—the only institutions American workers have to defend themselves—were being gutted and tangled in red tape.

During those years, a retreat of major historical proportions took place, a large-scale retreat of our class. So we did what Trotsky said a party would have to do in such a situation: we organized a strategic retreat.

Of course, we didn't drop the Leninist strategy of party building or our transitional method. We didn't just preserve it like pickles in a jar either. Some of us first learned Leninism and the transitional method during those years. We applied them and used them to the degree the traffic would bear.

Nonetheless, there were stiff limits on our ability to apply many aspects of our program. We explained, propagandized, and educated—but to fewer and fewer workers.

There seemed to be a rift between our strategy and tactics. Our strategic line of march for the working class became more and more a promise for the future, not something that seemed realistic or relevant in any immediate sense. We never did anything that contradicted or cut across this strategic orientation, but it was less and less immediate. It was less and less often the basis of what candidates could talk about with any hope of being listened to and understood. Less and less the basis of what we could realistically propose to any large layer of thinking militants in the working class.

The day-to-day political openings that the party had the responsibility to respond to seemed further and further removed from the strategic line of march of American labor.

The party itself became more isolated from our class, not by our own choice but because of objective conditions beyond our control. Our class composition changed. Where fruitful political work was possible changed. Many of our proletarian organizational norms were intentionally loosened in practice to deal with the new conditions, to organize an orderly retreat. Where a party member worked, within certain obvious limits, became a private not a party matter.

The detour around the roadblock

In this period the trade union bureaucracy constructed a massive roadblock to the revitalization of the class struggle. They consciously put themselves at the service of American capitalism and held back the workers. They stood in the way of the use of union power to promote workers' interests and to lead the fight against such evils as Jim Crow discrimination.

But after about a decade of this retreat, the revitalization of the class struggle that we have called the "detour" began to occur. The detour was a historical step forward. It was the beginning of a comeback from the retreat of the working class—the revival of the class struggle in a number of forms.

The first evidence of a move forward, the first push around the roadblock came with the civil rights movement in the late 1950s. It was a proletarian movement, a movement of the oppressed Black nationality. But it was dominated by a petty-bourgeois leadership.

The labor bureaucracy distinguished itself at best by lip service to the fight to wipe Jim Crow off the books. Because this petty-bourgeois layer was sitting on the power of American labor, there was minimal union involvement in the civil rights battles. The campuses became more a place to turn for support than organized labor. Many Black unionists participated, though not *through* their unions—but *around* them.

Despite this lack of union support, some significant concessions were won by the civil rights movement. Victories over Jim Crow were won without proletarian leadership and without the mobilization of organized labor. This pattern was largely repeated in the success of the anti–Vietnam War movement and the initial victories of the women's movement.

In light of these victories, it seemed on the surface to many radicals that it wasn't necessary to win the support of the majority of American workers or of the unions in order to advance social struggles. This led to confusion in the radical movement, illusions about how long and under what historical conditions victories could be scored without bringing to bear the power of American labor.

In addition, the union bureaucracy held outright reactionary positions on many issues. They were defenders of the white job trust in the skilled trades. They supported the Vietnam War. They resisted a major influx of women into industry.

To a lot of young radicals the idea of reaching out to the workers movement seemed a futile gesture at best, if not contradictory to the goals they were fighting for. They confused the reactionary labor officialdom with the ranks of the unions, who were being affected by these struggles. There was even a tendency to see the working class as the most reactionary, not the most progressive class in society.

"Ugh, the unions!" you could hear some radicals say. "Ugh, the workers! They don't want Black people to have good jobs, good schools, or equal rights. They don't want Chicanos to have equality. They don't give a damn about Cuba. They're sexist. They don't care about atomic testing or war. They want wages and jobs from the war industry, etc., etc."

This may be a bit of a caricature, but such attitudes were common, if not a majority sentiment in the radical movement not so long ago. It was behind the thinking of those who in the earliest days of the antiwar movement viewed GIs as the enemy—"mercenaries"—rather than as a potentially powerful component of the struggle.

Of course, we always fought against these reactionary pettybourgeois views. The *Militant*, our candidates, and the Young Socialist Alliance did our best to present a class understanding and strategy. But ours were not the views of the majority of activists.

The goals of the civil rights movement and other progressive struggles were not viewed as being in the class interests of the majority of workers. The only way many activists could conceive of going to the labor movement for support was purely on the basis of a moral appeal, not class necessity, class interest, class unity.

When they did appeal for support from the labor movement, they almost always looked to the "progressive" leaders, not to the ranks.

The tactics of these protest movements seemed unrelated to any strategy to radically transform the American labor movement, and through that to transform society. In fact, the tactics themselves began being viewed as a strategy. Protest marches began to be seen as a strategy. Or sit-ins were seen as a strategy. Of course, these are actually tactics. But they seemed to have no relationship to any strategy of a class.

A litany began to develop even in our own party—especially during the antiwar movement. It went like this: "Hold a teach-in. National Conference. Nonexclusion. Action coalition. Single-issue. March on Washington or National Days of Protest." We can all add ten or twenty other things to it. Most of us can remember it.

Of course, for the most part, this litany turned out to be tactically correct for the movements and the conditions in which we were operating. But someone hearing it over and over again could easily forget that we were repeating a litany of tactics, not explaining a strategy.

But we got away with it. In doing so, we were lucky, because there's no such thing as a precedent for tactics—even in the same movement, with the same goals, two weeks later. Every tactic is specific and concrete. Each one is unique. They are nonrepeatable. (That's another reason, by the way, why Deutscher was so off in calling the Transitional Program an "instruction on tactics.")

Of course, having a lot of experience in varied situations makes you a better thinker, a better fighter, a better judge of tactics. But not because you automatically repeat what you did before; that's the kiss of death. You're a better tactician because you're more experienced. Tactics must always be thought out carefully and linked to your overall strategy.

The truth is that despite the outward appearance of just a litany of tactics, we had a carefully thought-out strategy underneath what we did in the antiwar movement—a proletarian strategy, a Leninist strategy.

Our strategy had to do with raising demands and fighting for methods that could appeal to labor; that could appeal to the workers in uniform, the GIs; that could link the antiwar movement to other struggles and more powerful social forces. We were totally conscious of the class composition of the antiwar movement, of its leadership, and of our relative weight in it. We didn't drop our proletarian military policy: we consciously altered it and applied it under new conditions.[13]

Nonetheless, it was sometimes easy to forget that what we were doing was linked to the line of march of our class. It was easy for this underlying strategy to be forgotten in the press of day-to-day activity. The Black, antiwar and feminist movements were having a big impact on the consciousness of workers, especially young workers. But the roadblock thrown up by the bureaucracy was still forcing social struggles to detour around the unions. The fact that these were all aspects of the class struggle was still being camouflaged. And the vague concept that there was no limit to what could be won without the involvement of labor grew.

The revival of the class struggle in new forms, the detour, took place during a prolonged period of capitalist expansion. While the Black population saw much less of the fruits of the economic expansion than did whites, even for Blacks it was the longest stretch of relative prosperity in history. The ideas that developed, the forms of struggle, the social forces that were involved, the confusions that grew up—all were marked by the fact that this was a prosperity radicalization.

This is unlike the period we are entering today.

We took the detour. We jumped into all the struggles. It was the beginning of the bounce back from the strategic retreat and the isolation from our class. Without the right approach to that radicalization, we wouldn't be where we are today.

That's what the fight with the "For a Proletarian Orientation" tendency [FAPO] was all about at our 1971 convention. The question was: Were we right in taking the detour? Or should we have instead stayed on the main road that had become impassable? Were we going to get mired in the mud because we wouldn't accept the need for the detour?

The FAPO did more than just get bogged down in their sectarian rejection of the struggles that were unfolding. For them, rejecting the detour became a road out of the workers movement.

Because the party took the detour, and rejected FAPO's *false* concept of what a proletarian orientation is, we are in a position to move forward today.

In the report on the draft 1971 political resolution that we approved at our May plenum that year, we explained the relationship between the struggles that had developed up to that point, and the working-class radicalization we knew was coming:

> In addition to the growing direct effect of the radicalization on the consciousness of sectors of the working class and the working class as a whole, the resolution analyzes a second factor: the necessity, flowing from the evolution of the world capitalist economy, for the ruling class sooner or later to attack the wages and living standards, the conditions on the job, and eventually the economic organizations of the working class, the trade unions.
>
> It is imperative to note that the workers will not involve themselves in decisive numbers in mass political struggles solely through the steady influence of radical attitudes on them by the political and social struggles that have characterized the deepening radicalization; nor will this occur solely through economic struggles. It is going to come through a combination of the two.
>
> And here we can't give any blueprints or predict the timing of exactly when or how this will occur. But we do know that there will be a combination of resistance to attacks on the workers by the capitalist rulers with changes in the workers' consciousness caused by the struggles of the radicalization as a whole. It will be this combination that will give a historically concrete and unique physiognomy to the radicalization and revolutionization of the mass of workers, as large numbers of workers begin to involve themselves in struggle.[14]

That stands up astoundingly well a full eight years later.

Only a few days after our August 1971 convention, we saw one of the first direct austerity moves by the rulers that laid the groundwork for today's changing consciousness in the working class and the unions: Nixon's wage freeze. That was followed by the meat shortage in 1973, the initial energy crisis in 1973 and 1974, and the worldwide recession of 1974 and 1975.

Impact of 1974-75 U.S. depression

The events of 1974-75 were a watershed. The war in Vietnam ended in a major defeat for U.S. imperialism. There was the first American depression in the lifetime of most young workers, and of most members of the SWP.

The identity of the enemy became clearer. The enemy was less likely to be seen as whites or men, and more often recognized as the government and capitalist employers. The strength and goals of this enemy became clearer. The capitalists' greater inability and unwillingness to grant concessions became clearer.

The rules had changed. The kind of leadership needed to propel the struggles of the oppressed and exploited had changed. What was needed in order to win had changed. The kind of power, program, and strategy needed had changed.

As a result, the class-against-class character of politics is less and less camouflaged today. There is the beginning of a convergence between, on the one hand, our strategic line of march, our strategy as outlined in the Transitional Program; and, on the other hand, our day-to-day tasks and the way we must look at politics to explain what's going on and what the workers can do about it. It's easier to see the one while doing the other.

As new opportunities open up in the ranks of the labor movement, it's easier—and more necessary—today to consciously weigh our tactics against our overall strategy. Does a particular tactic advance us along this road? Does it—even if "principled" in itself—take us off on a tangent given alternative uses of our forces and energies? Does it go in the wrong direction altogether?

It's easier for comrades to see themselves as cadres of a vanguard party of workers that intends to become a mass party of the American working class. It's easier to see ourselves as a party that must win the confidence of American workers, so that we cannot only speak for our class but also lead them in struggle against the employers and the government.

Our strategy and program have become more relevant and realizable in the eyes of thousands, and tomorrow millions, of workers. Our tasks and our perspectives have to be rooted in an understanding of these changes if we are to give honest, realistic, and accurately optimistic answers to the oppressed and exploited about what will be necessary to solve the growing problems they face.

To do this we have to understand more fully the *political* centrality, not merely the organizational centrality, of our party fractions in industrial unions. Unlike the period of the retreat, unlike the period of revival during the detour—*today* we can do fruitful political work in our class and its central mass organizations throughout the country. When it's possible for a revolutionary proletarian party to do that, then that's what it must do or pay the price of political disorientation and organizational decomposition.

Our turn is putting us where we must be today to apply our strategy in light of these changing conditions. That's where we are winning influence for our ideas, educating ourselves and our coworkers, taking on our political opponents. The industrial workplaces and unions are our arena to build support for the fight against nuclear power and weapons, for ratification of the Equal Rights Amendment, against racial discrimination, and around the other major political issues confronting our class. That is the central arena for all our party campaigns.

Social weight

We also have to look more closely at the social weight of various political struggles today. This has a great deal to do with how we set our priorities, and how we allocate our resources.

We define the political importance of all issues by the social weight of the section of the population affected by it. By this, we don't mean the size of some layer of the population. We are not talking simply about numbers. For example, working farmers, as producers of vital food and fiber commodities, have greater social weight than college students. This is true even though there are more college students than farmers.

We're also not talking primarily about conjunctures, about the ups and downs in how much public attention is focused on an issue at any particular time. Social weight cannot be gauged by the relative size of demonstrations around various issues at any given time.

By social weight, we are gauging *the relationship to the working class* of various layers of the population and of the issues that affect them. We're talking about social power and potential political clout. As revolutionists we begin from the understanding that the most powerful, the decisive social force is the working class, which must govern, and that the industrial workers are its most powerful component.

This criterion of social weight holds even in a country where the working class is a minority of the population. What we're interested in is the relationship of the struggles of social layers, nationalities, and oppressed groups to the working class. How these struggles relate to all the things the working class as a whole must fight for and conquer on its way to being able to govern. How they help advance the transformation of the unions.

This class framework provides a way to determine the sections of the American population with the greatest social weight: Blacks, Chicanos, Puerto Ricans, women, farmers, the youth. These sections of the population play a central role in the economic, social, and political structure of capitalism. Their struggles and demands pose a profound challenge to capitalist rule.

Take the fight against racism, for example. The fight for Black and Chicano rights especially. This is central not only because of the size and history of the nonwhite populations. It is also crucial because of the percentage of Blacks and Chicanos in the working class, the proletarian composition of these oppressed nationality populations, and the resulting stake of the working class, as a class, in all the questions confronting Blacks and Chicanos.

Women make up more than half the working class and around 40 percent of the labor force. More than 50 percent of all women between sixteen and fifty-five are in the workforce today, and more are entering.

The superexploitation of these layers drags down the wages and job conditions of all workers and is a source of enormous profits for the capitalists. The employers introduce racist and sexist prejudices into the working class in order to keep the oppressed and exploited weak and divided; this becomes especially crucial to the employers at times of rising class combativity. In addition, the oppression of women is vital to the family, which is an indispensable social and economic unit in capitalist society.

It's for these reasons that the demands raised by the oppressed nationalities and women are in both the immediate and the historic interests of the entire working class. The fight around these demands plays a central role in the mobilization and transformation of the labor movement. They advance the unity and self-confidence of our class and point toward the fight for a workers government to restructure all social relations and wipe out all oppression and exploitation.

All political struggles are aspects of the class struggle. But that is merely the beginning of wisdom. We have to recognize that some issues are central to the line of march of our class, while others are peripheral. Some of the central issues are imperialist war, unemployment, inflation, social breakdowns, atomic radiation, race and sex discrimination, police brutality, restrictions on democratic rights.

Without fighting around these issues, the working class cannot prepare itself to govern, cannot marshal the allies it needs to fight for power, and—more and more—cannot even guarantee its physical survival.

How did we determine that the death penalty is a central political issue, for example? After all, it directly affects only several hundred people right now. But we say that capital punishment is a weighty question, nonetheless, because it has to do with class exploitation and oppression. It's not the capitalists who suffer from the death penalty in the United States today. It's the working class, and within the working class it's the oppressed nationalities who suffer most. The death penalty is a weapon of terror wielded by the ruling class and its courts against the working class, especially the most oppressed sectors, in order to keep them cowed. That's what makes it an important question, not just our sense of moral outrage that this brutal ruling class claims the right to murder human beings.

Social weight is a very important guide to us in deciding how to use our resources most efficiently. What our comrades should be doing. Which organizations or coalitions we should be participating in, to what extent, and to what ends. It helps us determine which issues are more peripheral to the workers' march to power, and the practical conclusions we must draw from that judgment.

It helps us determine that the question of imperialist war is weightier than the death penalty, but that both are central issues for our class.

It tells us that the *Weber* affirmative-action fight[15] should be a central party campaign, while we choose to throw less resources into the just struggle around Indian fishing rights.

It tells us that the fights for ERA ratification, abortion rights, and child care have greater social weight than the struggle for legislation guaranteeing full civil and human rights for gays and lesbians.

It guides us in relating to issues such as the repeal of marijuana laws, the rights of the handicapped, and saving wilderness areas and endangered species. We support these demands, publicize them in the *Militant* when struggles around them arise, solidarize with them. But we do not allocate major forces to intervene in coalitions organized around them.

This relates to another of the litanies that sometimes crops up in our press or in leaflets. We will sometimes, without stopping to think about it, reel off this list of victims of capitalist oppression: "Blacks, Chicanos, women, gays." But this creates an inaccurate impression of our judgment on the social weight of these four groups. The social weight of gays is qualitatively less than that of Blacks, Chicanos, and women.

The social weight criteria also help us understand more fully our class approach to the fight for democratic rights.

Democratic rights are indivisible—that is, the denial or abuse of the rights of any section of the population is a threat to all democratic rights. Any denial of democratic rights is against the interests of the working class and must be fought by the labor movement.

While democratic rights are indivisible in this fundamental sense, however, they are not all politically equal in terms of strategic importance, in social weight. The democratic rights that are most crucial to the proletariat are freedom of speech, the right to assemble, the right to organize, freedom of the press, etc. Without rights such as these, the working class cannot organize as a class economically or politically.

The other category of democratic rights most crucial to the working class includes those that directly affect the most proletarian sections of the population and those of its most decisive allies. The rights of Blacks and Chicanos, for example, from self-determination on down to every aspect of the fight against racism and discrimination. The rights of women. The rights of youth.

Finally, social weight helps us give a clearer definition, a class definition to a term that is sometimes misused—the term *radical*. That word doesn't communicate much unless it's given a class definition. Is a tactic radical if it's wild? Is an issue radical just because it's shocking to bourgeois morality and respectability? Was the brutal, capitalist Pol Pot regime radical? Fascists are radical, aren't they?

We, of course, mean something very precise when we use the word; we're giving it a class definition. Building opposition to the *Weber* suit is radical. Telling the truth about Newport News is radical.

The labor party is a very radical concept, although many petty-bourgeois "radicals" don't think so. It is a historic, radical break by our class from dependence on the Democratic and Republican parties, the parties of the capitalist exploiters.

No separate roads
We often used to say that the winning strategy in the antiwar movement was mass demonstrations. But that wasn't a strategy. That was

a specific tactic that we often advocated, flowing from our overall strategy, which was a working-class strategy. We consistently fought for political demands and methods of struggle that would maximize the opportunities to draw in the working class, the unions, the GIs, Blacks, and Chicanos. That was our aim. It was the best way to defend the Vietnamese revolution and the best way to move forward the consciousness and mobilization of our class.

But properly understood, we do have a mass-action strategy—a strategy of mobilizing our class in action around a program that represents its historic interests. The shah of Iran was brought down by the mass action of the Iranian workers and their allies. Strikes, factory committees, soviets, insurrections, workers militias—all these elements of the organization and mobilization of the workers and our allies outlined in the Transitional Program are forms of mass working-class action.

But we don't have a "mass demonstration" strategy, in the sense of a "march on Washington" strategy. Those are tactics.

We don't have a collection of separate isolated winning strategies for various social struggles. One for the Black struggle. One for the fight for women's rights. One for the antinuclear movement.

We have a strategy for the revolutionary transformation of the labor movement and for the use of that power to transform society. We have a strategy to mobilize our class and its allies to fight for a workers government.

From *that* strategic framework, we can figure out what steps are necessary to advance all progressive struggles. How they can link up with the decisive social power needed to win. What tactics can advance the overall fight against oppression and capitalist misrule.

What do we mean when we say that a social protest movement is "independent"? First, we mean that it must be independent of the ruling class. We also mean that it should fight resolutely for its demands. It shouldn't subordinate its goals, or wait on other social forces, including the unions, to take up its banner before taking up the fight itself.

But these movements *cannot* be independent of the shifts in the relationship of class forces. They *cannot* be independent from the influence and pressures of the two main contending classes. And they *must not* be independent of a working-class strategy to move forward and to transform the labor movement. Otherwise they have no hope of securing any lasting victories, because that's where the power to transform society lies.

More and more, it's hard to make even small gains, or defend past gains, without applying this strategic understanding. That's what we mean in pointing out that there can be no separate strategies for these struggles.

This doesn't in any way mean that struggles that erupt outside the labor movement should wait, or that they are less important today than they were in the past. To the contrary.

With correct leadership and a conscious working-class strategy and program, these struggles can play a decisive role in advancing the transformation of American labor. They can help drive forward the process of getting the unions to think socially and act politically. They can help in the development of a class-struggle left wing necessary to get the bureaucracy off the backs of the working class, so that union power can be used on behalf of all the oppressed and exploited.

But they will be able to do so only to the extent a leadership that is proletarian both in composition and outlook comes forward. A leadership that is conscious of where it's going, what it's doing, and why it must link up with the power of American labor.

Every single social protest movement today badly needs a pamphlet like George Breitman's *How a Minority Can Change Society*.[16] They have the untapped potential to put forces into motion that will deeply affect the working class—the social power that can and must change society from top to bottom.

In saying this, of course, we always recognize that while each of these struggles is an aspect of the class struggle, each has a special character, a different specific political function. It's not their job to directly forge a class-struggle left wing in the unions; they couldn't do that if they wanted to. That will be done by the most class-conscious workers as they run into the necessity to use union power to fight around all aspects of the rulers' offensive.

So our insistence that these movements have no *separate* winning strategy is not a prescription for abstention. It's the opposite—a guide to participation and intervention.

As the revolutionary socialist wing of the American labor movement, we participate in important social struggles to bring a working-class perspective, the only winning perspective, into the fight. We are socialist workers who want to bring the power of our class and our unions into the struggle around these issues. And we want to raise these vital questions in our unions as part of our strategic goal of transforming the unions into instruments of revolutionary social and political change.

III. Resolving the crisis of proletarian leadership

How does this general framework—our understanding of the relationship between revolutionary principles, strategy, and tactics—help us more effectively orient to what's been happening in the American class struggle the past few years? How does it shed light on what's been happening in the labor movement, where the Black movement stands, the current stage of the women's liberation struggle, the significance of the fight for affirmative action, and the developing struggle against nuclear power and weapons?

Bosses bumped into workers' resistance
It is striking how far off the mark the *Wall Street Journal* was on its prediction that the Rubber Workers union would be a pushover in the contract talks this spring. The Rubber Workers were going to be held well inside Carter's wage guidelines. An article in the *Journal* several weeks back gave all the reasons: the shift of plants to the South; the percentage of the rubber industry that's nonunion; etc. They predicted an easy settlement.

What happened? Was the *Journal* wrong about the bureaucracy? No. But the employers once again bumped into the workers behind the bureaucracy. It happened during the coal strike last year, and it's happening more often.

This doesn't mean that we'll see a lot of victories. We'll often see stalemates or setbacks because of the crisis of leadership and political perspectives in the labor movement. But the two big contestants in the class struggle—the workers and the ruling class—are more and more meeting in battle. The bosses have the offensive right now. But as we've seen from the coal strike and Newport News, the battle itself has a powerful impact on class consciousness and combativity.

A plaintive remark a couple of days ago by UAW president Douglas Fraser was revealing. It showed how much the combination of the bosses' growing demands and the workers' changing attitudes is putting the bureaucrats between a rock and a hard place. They're as willing and eager as ever to serve as the transmission belt for the bosses' pressure into the working class, but as the resistance mounts, their ability to straddle these two fundamental classes is more and more tenuous. So the labor fakers begin screeching at the bosses not to make their lives impossible with the workers they collect dues from.

When the *New York Times* interviewed Fraser about the auto negotiations coming up this summer, he had the following to say about Carter's wage guidelines: "We were more supportive of the program than any other union. But if you're going to have a voluntary program," Fraser complained, "workers have to have a perception that it is fair and nondiscriminatory."

Note that Fraser doesn't say that it has to *be* fair and nondiscriminatory; just that workers have to have that *perception*. Many workers, for example, had a perception throughout much of the fifties and sixties that things were getting better for a lot of them and for their unions. That was a *false* perception and a *false* consciousness. It wasn't based on reality, which was that their unions were being weakened by class collaboration and that this would catch up with them with a vengeance.

These changing perceptions among workers are extremely important. For Fraser they're a big problem. For us, they're a growing opportunity. An opportunity to get a hearing for our ideas and strategy.

The heart of this is not the exact stage or depth of the impact of radical ideas on the workers right now. We're still at the beginning. What's important to us—and what has Fraser so worried—is that perceptions are changing. They must and will change more.

It's the changes and the direction that we must understand. The trends. The skirmishes that we are seeing today—while limited—are not holdovers from a period of upsurge that is petering out in a capitalist prosperity and witch-hunt. They're not flukes. They're not dead ends or aberrations.

They are the first stirrings of a process that we know will grow as the rulers intensify their attacks and the working class is pushed to fight back. What is today still the exception will more and more become the rule as the class struggle in this country and internationally heats up. That's what is qualitatively new and different today.

Let's look at what we learned from the Newport News strike, for example.

Newport News

We began to take a look at the Newport News organizing drive at our last plenum back in December [1978]. We didn't know too much about it then, but it looked pretty important. This outfit called USWA Local 8888 had organized a big shipyard of 18,000 workers in right-to-work-for-less Virginia, and now they wanted recognition and a contract. Nobody else in the radical movement seemed to pay much attention to it or care much about it. But we said that it looked like the single most important strike coming. It turned out we were right.

As the strike unfolded, many aspects were similar to the coal strike last year. Of course, there are differences between the composition and character of the UMWA and Local 8888, but that's not so important to us as the similarities.

The union ranks took a measure of democracy at a crucial turning point and altered the outcome of the strike. In making a tactical retreat, and preparing to enter the next battle in the best possible position, they changed for the better what they had to face on the job.

The *Wall Street Journal* hit wide of the mark here, too. Before the union ranks met and voted they already had 8888 laid out on a morgue slab. They were gloating.

But the workers, a little union democracy, and a tactical misjudgment by the cops and Tenneco all came together to change things. And we got a glimpse of the future.

The workers reversed the rout that the USWA bureaucracy had set them up for in accepting Tenneco's back-to-work conditions. The workers staved off going back under conditions that would have cut them apart in the worst possible way, making the next stage of the battle far more difficult. The decision to return to work is not the end of a war, remember. It's just the first battle.

Those 8888 militants learned some big lessons when the cops attacked their picket lines and tried to bust up their headquarters last week. They call it Bloody Monday now.

And seeing those club-swinging cops roaming around smashing the heads of Black and white strikers made a few other workers in the Tidewater area take a new look at the strike, too.

The Newport News battle tells us a lot about the effects of the civil rights movement, the role of the Black struggle. It's a big mistake to look at what happened in the South over the past twenty years in too narrow a framework. It's not just that some important civil rights were won, narrowly construed.

There were elements of a social revolution in the South; Jim Crow was smashed. The South today is more desegregated than many of the big northern industrial states; studies have shown that.

This was a big victory for our entire class, Black *and* white. It means that there has been a sort of leveling-out process in some of the conditions of the class struggle throughout the country. The

South is more like the rest of the country than ever before. The big difference today is not the Jim Crow system and all the social, political, and economic features that flowed from that. That *was* the big difference from the defeat of Reconstruction through the 1960s.

The big difference today is that the southern working class is still much less unionized than in the North. That *is* one of the legacies of Jim Crow, and the class-collaborationist policies of the labor bureaucracy. But, as Newport News showed, the battles that demolished Jim Crow have created much more favorable conditions for solving this important remaining difference as well. It's a big challenge confronting American labor—and the entire union movement will be fighting from a position of weakness until it is met.

A great deal was changed in the South by the civil rights movement. The consciousness of the working class was dramatically changed. Not only Black, but also white workers became more capable of moving in a class-conscious direction; their attitudes were profoundly altered. They became more capable of seeing their common class interests with Black workers—which is absolutely necessary to move forward. There was a rise in the self-confidence of the Black workers. The composition of the workforce changed, as more and more Blacks fought their way into industry. There has also been a rise in the number of women workers, like everywhere else. Finally, there is a lot more industry in the South today. In addition to the textile and other traditional southern industry, there are more auto plants, steel mills, electrical assembly plants, rubber factories, and so on.

The origins of the 8888 organizing drive directly reflected these important changes in the South. The vanguard was made up overwhelmingly of Black workers inside the yard. They sensed what these changes meant. They sized up how they could take advantage of these changes to put together a new struggle, in a new way, and with broader forces—white and Black workers, men and women. They took the initiative to draw the USWA into the fight.

The Newport News workers also learned something about the

importance of solidarity. Although the support they got from unionists around the country fell far short of the potential had the USWA officialdom energetically pursued it, the workers nonetheless got a taste of what solidarity can mean.

They also got a taste of what the bureaucracy will *never* mean by solidarity. They never mean solidarity inside the labor movement or with the oppressed. The bureaucrats' solidarity is with the capitalist government. They try to teach the workers to look to the government, to look to the National Labor Relations Board, to look to some mediator, to look to the courts. That's what USWA president Lloyd McBride and the entire USWA officialdom tried to drum into the heads of the 8888 workers.

But from their own experiences with the cops, the capitalist politicians, the courts, and the NLRB, the Newport News workers began learning something about where they must really look for allies, and why. The process is just beginning. It's still being thought through. It's not all totally understood. There are still hopes that the courts or the Carter administration will come through with some real assistance.

But the question is posed right out in the open. This, too, presents the bureaucracy with difficulties. George Meany personally sent letters to AFL-CIO affiliates telling them to hold no Newport News solidarity activities without an explicit go-ahead from the USWA officialdom. The deliberate intent of this was to put the kibosh on solidarity, including in cities where union support meetings were already in the planning stages.

McBride gave his infamous press conference where he said there had been a "tactical blunder," an unfortunate misunderstanding. Some people, McBride said, were incorrectly portraying the Newport News strike as part of a crusade to organize the South.

"I don't look on this as a crusade," McBride insisted. "We are not interested in broadening the dispute beyond our efforts to get a contract."

But without a crusade to organize the South, it will be much more difficult to get a contract. That's another lesson the Newport

News workers are learning. They have everything to gain, and nothing to lose, from projecting their fight as a struggle for workers throughout the South and throughout the country.

How the SWP participated

Our party was the first and the only group on the left to size up correctly the stakes at Newport News. I couldn't believe my eyes in reading the opponent papers over the past couple of weeks. Papers such as the *Guardian* hardly ever had datelines from Newport News. They didn't send reporters, let alone teams, down there, except for one or two short trips. They didn't understand the importance of going through this experience with the workers there.

The *Militant,* on the other hand, was looked to by literally hundreds of strikers as the only prostrike newspaper—the paper that told the truth, that told their side of the story. A good number of them were quite interested in discussing other ideas in the *Militant* with the party and YSA members who were down there.

We didn't leave our views about solidarity on the level of propaganda and education. We acted on our views. We helped build solidarity not only inside the Steelworkers union throughout the country, but in the UAW, the Machinists, and elsewhere. This was a valuable educational experience, another step forward for our union fractions and for our fraction, branch, and local leaderships.

At each stage of the strike, we sent teams of socialists down to Newport News. We didn't send just reporters and sales teams, but socialist steelworkers as well.

We always acted responsibly. We used our heads. We knew that the ability to shut down production in the shipyard depended on shifting the relationship of forces more and more to the advantage of the strikers, and that was a political question, not a narrow tactical one. We didn't pretend to come in from the outside to dish out tactical proposals to get the strikers out of a jam. We didn't launch into tirades against the USWA leadership, or urge the 8888 workers to do that. We didn't tell them that we had some magical tactic, such as smashing a few scabs, that would solve their problems and bring Tenneco to its knees.

We carefully avoided all these traps. Instead, we concentrated on doing what we could to help shift the relationship of forces in the strikers' direction. We helped get out the truth about the strike both through our industrial fractions and through the *Militant*. We analyzed the strike correctly, and filled the *Militant* with all the other social and political lessons that the workers needed to think out and discuss.

We did this openly as socialists. We were down there as fellow workers who wanted to do what we could to support 8888 and to discuss our views with anyone who was willing to listen.

As a result, there are thousands of people down there who have read the *Militant*. Some of our subscribers pass the paper around a little bit, too. We've met a lot of people who are interested in what we have to say—both about the strike and about many other things.

This kind of receptivity to the *Militant* by workers in the midst of an important strike struggle is something new. We haven't seen it over the past three decades.

What we learned
The Newport News struggle has already had an effect on the party. It had a deep impact on all the comrades who went down there. And we have a lot more to learn.

The things we have had to think through during the Newport News strike are a big help to party branches throughout the South. It's made us think more about the Black struggle. It's made us think more about the question of organizing drives and how we relate to them.

All this will be valuable for socialists throughout the South. It will help us better understand how we can carry out the fight for the Equal Rights Amendment in those states. It will deepen our participation in the Black struggle. It helps us understand the importance in the South, as well as across the nation, of the fight for union democracy, class solidarity, and independent labor political action. It marks another big step toward our goal of being a truly nationwide party of socialist workers.

The Newport News experience can also help us take another step on a question we discussed at our December 1978 plenum. We said then that the term *preparatory period* was misleading. Struggles are going on in the here and now. The new leadership of our class is beginning to be forged in these battles, and we have to be part of that process by driving through our turn. Our industrial fractions can conduct socialist political work in our class *right now.*

Our experience since December shows that we were right in this assessment. But what's true for the party is not necessarily true *in the same way* for the entire working class.

Newport News showed us both sides of the question. It was a dramatic confirmation of the here and now. It represented something *new* in the combativity and consciousness of the working class. New leaders of our class were being forged in that battle. We saw the impact of the civil rights movement and the class solidarity of Black and white workers. The role of women workers. The vanguard role of youth. The lessons about democracy, solidarity, and the obstacles thrown up by the NLRB, the government, the capitalist parties.

On the other hand, Newport News also showed us to what extent the working class *is* still in a preparatory stage. Although the attitudes of the Newport News workers reflected changes among workers throughout the country, strikes and organizing battles such as this are still an exception. As we pointed out last December, there are more and more skirmishes by the workers. But few on the scale of the battle of Newport News.

This can change rapidly, of course. We can't pretend to predict the tempo of developments. And we don't need to.

The working class is still on the defensive against the profit drive of the employers and the government.

This stage of the Newport News battle ended in a stalemate. Other and bigger battles are still ahead.

Last year the coal miners scored a victory against the antilabor offensive of the energy trust and the Carter administration. Yet their contract didn't mark any big advances; and they lost their free health care. Many miners tend to see these aspects more clearly than they see the positive impact of their strike in changing the relationship of forces to the advantage of the working class. Other industrial workers—including socialists—saw that better than they did.

Many Newport News strikers have gotten a deeper understanding of the national significance of their battle by reading the *Militant* and talking to the socialist workers that have gone through the experience with them.

So the here and now that the party sees and experiences is not yet understood in the same way by masses of vanguard workers. They have not yet experienced the power of an upsurge of our class such as occurred during the rise of the CIO in 1936 and 1937. Those kinds of battles are coming. But today, in that sense, our class *is* still in a preparatory period.

Our industrial fractions are not themselves the nuclei of a class-struggle left wing in the labor movement. Right now we don't see a class-struggle left wing taking shape in any of the unions. But we are meeting many of the young workers that will play leading roles in the class-struggle transformation of the labor movement.

What we are building today as we explain and advance the concept of a class-struggle left wing, is a Marxist current in the unions, a current that will be central to the construction of a class-struggle left wing. Everything we do today—around Newport News, *Weber*, the struggles of women, shop floor issues—is aimed at developing the consciousness of militant young workers and building that Marxist current, building the SWP and YSA. That's why we sell the *Militant*. That's what we want to do with our election campaigns. That's the top priority in all our activity through our industrial fractions. We are influencing workers, winning them to our ideas, and winning them to our movement.

Crisis of Black leadership
We've been on the right track the last few years in trying to grapple with what's behind the deepening crisis of leadership in the

Black struggle. But on the basis of our concrete experience in the class struggle and from our understanding of the changes in the working class, we can say a little more.

Both the roots and the solution of the crisis are connected with the working class and the labor movement. The crisis stems from the fact that the labor bureaucracy never gave more than lip service to this struggle. And it opposed any militant nationalist leadership. The solution of the crisis must be found in the new possibilities for the labor movement to be a source of power and a new leadership in the struggle for Black rights.

The civil rights movement from the late 1950s on was a working-class movement in the sense that large numbers of Black workers participated in it. But Black workers or Black unionists were not the leadership of the movement or of its major national organizations. And their fellow white workers were not radicalizing at a comparable pace or in similar numbers. Thus the gap in consciousness between Black and white workers grew. It was this twofold bind—petty-bourgeois leadership and lack of labor support—that the Black movement finally bumped up against, and that kept it from going any further.

In the mid- and late-fifties we saw the beginning of the boycotts, sit-ins, and other developments in the southern civil rights movement. During the mid-sixties new Black organizations came forward, reflecting the growth of nationalist consciousness and the limitations of earlier leaderships. The labor bureaucracy outright opposed the more nationalist organizations and leaders as too "radical" or as "hatemongers."

Then, between 1965 and 1968, there were the urban uprisings. These rebellions were a response to the real and deepening crisis that the Black masses were living through. But it was a response without the social forces, without the allies, without the strategy that was needed to win. From that point until today, there has been a retreat in the organization and mobilization of forces fighting for Black rights.

What was needed to take the struggle forward was: (1) a radical social program that could answer the needs of Blacks; and (2) a working-class leadership consciously striving to mobilize the social forces needed to fight for such a program. But even with this kind of program and leadership, the Black struggle could only go so far without the beginning radicalization of the white workers.

The kind of forces needed to fight successfully even for partial and immediate demands has changed today in comparison with the 1950s and early 1960s. At an earlier stage, concessions had been won despite the total default of the labor officialdom. Because of the worldwide economic crisis of capitalism, however, the ruling class is resisting more and more today; its problems have made it determined to take back, not give more.

This change brought big pressures down on the Black movement. Coalitions were shattered. This was to be expected, since different elements in any coalition represent and are attuned to different class pressures. People who could hang tough or fight things out at an earlier stage became less and less able to. This reflected the changing relationship of class forces, and the growing unwillingness of the ruling class to budge.

In its first decade, the civil rights movement had won some important victories. Congress was forced to pass civil rights legislation in 1964 and 1965. Jim Crow legislation in the South was wiped off the books. Combined with the economic boom of the 1960s, these gains led to an increase in jobs for Blacks. There was an expansion of the employed Black working class.

Despite these gains, however, not a single thing changed the fundamentally segregated character of American society, the socioeconomic second-class citizenship of Black Americans. Blacks and Chicanos are still affected in a qualitatively different and harsher way by unemployment; inflation; the gutting of public education, health care, and social security; the deterioration of housing. They confront inequality and discrimination wherever they turn.

The crisis of leadership today is much deeper than during the sixties. As leaderships hesitated or defaulted at an earlier stage of the struggle, new leaderships would arise. They were far from perfect, and some were quite shortlived. But this renewal of leadership was a continual phenomenon. First there was King's Southern Christian Leadership Conference. Then, in the early 1960s Congress of Racial Equality came to national prominence. The Student Nonviolent Coordinating Committee grew. Malcolm's Organization of Afro-American Unity. The Black Panther Party. There were various important local formations, some of which advocated the right of self-defense against racist terror.

These leaderships would come up and partially fill gaps, raise new ideas, represent new layers.

Today this has stopped. As it has become more difficult to make gains, these types of new leaderships have stopped coming forward. Groups like the NAACP and the Urban League are once again the major national organizations speaking for Black rights.

A new leadership of the Black struggle today must be built around an understanding of the need to mobilize and speak to the interests of Black workers. It must seek to use union power in the fight. It must be composed to a large degree of Black workers. Only this kind of leadership can stand up under today's pressures and put together new organizations to fight for the interests of the Black masses.

A new look at Trotsky

In thinking about discussions I had with comrades in preparing this section of the report, I went back and reread the discussions with Trotsky on Black nationalism.

I realized that when I read them last, big sections didn't have as much meaning to me as they did in the light of all the things we've been discussing the past couple of years. Let me cite just three passages from Trotsky's 1933 discussion with several American comrades.

"The Negroes will, through their awakening, through their demand for autonomy, and through the democratic mobilization of their forces, be pushed on toward a class basis. . . . The Negro proletariat will march over the petty bourgeoisie in the direction toward the proletarian revolution."

Second: "It is very possible that the Negroes will proceed through self-determination to the proletarian dictatorship in a couple of gigantic strides, ahead of the great bloc of white workers. They will then be the vanguard."

Finally: "The Negro can be developed to a class point of view only when the white worker is educated."[17]

When we put these three ideas together, they speak to the current needs of the Black struggle and the prospects opened by the current changes in our class. What's been happening over the past few years is precisely that white workers are being educated. They're changing. They began to be educated by the civil rights battles, the antiwar movement, the struggles of women. Now they're being educated by the blows they're suffering. They're being educated through their own actions—the coal strike, Newport News, and you can think of other examples.

They're thinking about new ideas and rethinking all sorts of old prejudices. That's what comrades in our union fractions are finding out on the job. There's all kinds of unevenness and contradictions, but everything has been shaken up. Millions are starting to get a new kind of education.

This beginning radicalization and rising militancy opens the door to involvement of the unions in the fight for Black equality. Black workers will play a vanguard role in bringing union power into this fight, but this wouldn't be possible without the changes in the working class that are now beginning. Affirmative action, desegregation, police brutality—these affect not only Black rights, they are *class* issues. More and more workers, Black and white, are beginning to recognize this.

Secondly, we should think about Trotsky's comment that Blacks can proceed to the proletarian dictatorship in a couple of strides ahead of the great bloc of white workers. Some comrades in reading that sentence a number of years ago, had the impression that Trotsky was talking about what could happen following the establishment of a separate Black state: given the interlinking of the class and nationalist dynamics, an independent Black state would most likely take the form of the proletarian dictatorship rather than a bourgeois republic.

While that's certainly a legitimate reading of the sentence, the point Trotsky was driving at was much broader. He was pointing to the likelihood that Black workers, through the faster development of their nationalist and class consciousness, would be in the vanguard of the American working class. That they could lead the entire class struggle forward. Not alone, of course. But by playing a vanguard role.

After all, if Black workers can take gigantic strides toward the proletarian dictatorship ahead of big sections of the white workers, what does this say about their propensity to develop class consciousness? To play a leading role in the formation of a class-struggle left wing; in moves toward a labor party? The prospects should be pretty good. (And Trotsky was basing his judgments on a population the big majority of whom still lived in the rural South. How much more true this is today, when the overwhelming majority of Blacks—North and South—are workers. And when a higher percentage than ever before are industrial workers.)

This brings us to Trotsky's third point: that the Black proletariat would march to victory over the Black petty bourgeoisie. This can only become true if the Black proletariat has more powerful allies than the allies of the petty-bourgeois leaders of the Black movement today. The allies of these petty-bourgeois misleaders are the liberal ruling-class politicians, the labor bureaucrats, and other procapitalist forces.

The ally that the Black proletariat needs is a transformed American labor movement.

Looking back at Boston

This is the obstacle we came up against during the Boston desegregation struggle. What actually happened when, after two successful marches in 1974 and 1975, the April 1976 march had to be called off? It was the correct decision as we discussed at the time.

The comrades on the spot up in Boston were on the ball.

Let's look behind the tactics of the struggle in Boston, though. What had really happened?

We bumped into the relationship of class forces. We bumped into the pressures coming down on the Black petty bourgeoisie through the Democratic Party city administration and in other ways. As a result, people who were key elements in the desegregation coalition in Boston crumbled. Some of them had played courageous and decisive roles in the past. Some may do so again in the future. It's not a question of particular individuals.

But the collapse of our allies who were under pressure to scuttle that demonstration simply registered the existing relationship of class forces bearing down on the coalition at that time. The forces representing the consistent interests of Boston's oppressed Black population were not strong enough to neutralize the pressures coming down on the petty-bourgeois leaders. That capsulizes what happened in *class* terms.

It's the same thing that the Black urban uprisings bumped into eight or nine years earlier.

This spotlights the importance of the point in the resolution where we say that the gap between the class consciousness and combativity of the Black workers and that of white workers is narrowing. It's not that Black workers are regressing. The change is in the enormous lag that has existed for decades in the consciousness and militancy of large layers of the white proletariat. That change means that the Black workers' prospects for allies are looking up, and the possibilities to build a proletarian leadership of the Black struggle are growing.

We also drew some wrong conclusions around the time of the Boston struggle. This got us into a little hot water.

We saw many things correctly. We saw the way the class struggle and the struggles of Blacks and women intertwined, combined. We saw that these struggles would strengthen each other. We saw that all the rules were changing, all the things we're discussing at this plenum. We got all that dead right. It's crystal clear and correct in the "Prospects for Socialism" resolution that we passed at our 1975 convention. That part of the resolution reads better today than when it was written.

We also said at the time that there would be "more Bostons," more struggles like that in other cities. As it turned out, with the partial exception of Louisville, there weren't. But that's not where we went off. Wrong projections like that are inevitable. We were right to keep our eyes open for desegregation and bilingual education struggles. We were right to participate in the cutback struggles in New York and elsewhere. We were right in taking initiatives such as the San Antonio antideportation conference. It was correct to jump in where we saw openings for struggle. A party that doesn't do that is dead.

But during this same period we also made an error. It flowed from an inaccurate assessment that our pace of recruitment would be faster than it has been. That was partly because of the "more Bostons" idea, and partly for other reasons. We were recruiting a lot out of our 1976 election campaign around that time. We were expanding rapidly to new cities, new areas of the country.

Where we went wrong was on some of the conclusions we drew from these assessments. We divided up the branches to prepare for more rapid growth and thought that we could start new branches with very few forces. We made some organizational decisions on the basis of what we thought would happen, rather than adjusting our forms to the stage we were really at.

We said, "We better start looking in our own backyards. We better start thinking about branches that are more community oriented."

Given our national analysis, we set up party branches in Roxbury, Boston, and the Lower East Side in New York, etc. We overdivided in the Twin Cities and other places. These were errors. The branches were too small and their political orientation too narrowly conceived.

So we collectively did a number of things we wish we hadn't. We're not geniuses, and we're not perfect. But we were all going in the right direction—toward the working class, toward the Black and Chicano workers, toward the women workers, toward the youth.

It didn't take us too long to see our errors and correct them—but it produced some pain. With the experience of the Steelworkers Fight Back campaign in late 1976 and 1977, we began to get back on the right track.

As far back as 1975 we said we were making the turn. But we were not yet basing it in the unions. We were also going to base it in the communities. We were going to base it on the campus. We weren't ready yet to say the totally correct thing. The base *was* going to be in the unions. *It had to be.*

We would be involved in all sorts of struggles and activities. Struggles would break out in the communities and on campus, and the SWP would be involved. All that was correct.

But the working class has powerful mass institutions—the trade unions. As a revolutionary working-class party, facing the opening of a working-class radicalization, that's where our *base* had to be. When we got that straightened out, we began to make our real turn. And we began bringing our organizational forms more in line with our actual needs.

During this period we just about doubled the number of cities in which there are units of the SWP, and some of our strongest industrial fractions today are in a number of those places.

Proletarian and petty-bourgeois nationalism

We're in a good position today to clarify our understanding of Black nationalism. There's no reason today to revise our view that nationalist consciousness deepens among Blacks as the class struggle deepens.

But we've had a problem in figuring out how to characterize the different currents of nationalism in the Black struggle.

At one time, some comrades tried to draw a distinction between cultural nationalism and political nationalism. Cultural nationalism was no good; it didn't lean toward struggle. Political nationalism was what we were after.

But that didn't quite capture it. Because there's nothing wrong with culture, so long as it's not a substitute for politics. To the contrary. Revolutionary nationalism will always have a cultural expression, an element of revolt against the attempts by the oppressor to impose its own culture on the oppressed. We're for that. It's progressive.

Then we began talking about consistent and inconsistent nationalism. This was closer. Malcolm X was consistent in fighting for the interests of the Black masses we pointed out. That pushed him toward the class struggle, toward anti-imperialism, and toward a bloc with revolutionary socialists. This wasn't a fluke; it was the logic of the consistent pride, self-confidence, and self-assertiveness of an oppressed, overwhelmingly proletarian, nationality.

Unlike the cultural/political distinction, this idea was more useful. But there was something deeper underneath it.

The Black population is not homogeneous. And the pressures on it originate from different classes. It has petty-bourgeois layers, including many at the head of Black organizations. Black nationalism can be an expression of proletarian consciousness, or it can be petty-bourgeois.

What is consistent Black nationalism? Proletarian nationalism.

What is inconsistent Black nationalism? Petty-bourgeois nationalism.

We understand this much better today. It explains why as the class struggle deepens, the vanguard role of Black workers deepens their nationalism, deepens their growing pride and confidence in Black leadership potential and ability. We saw this in the popularity of *Roots*. Malcolm X would be even more popular in the plants and factories today. Far from there being any contradiction, the growing class and nationalist consciousness reinforce and strengthen each other.

We've done some new thinking about the Black party, too. This idea originated in the Black struggle itself; it didn't spring from our heads. It was an expression of the Black movement that we championed, explained, and tried to push as far as we could.

When the Black party idea arose, it wasn't seen primarily as a bridge toward a labor party. It certainly wasn't seen that way by the Black activists who first got the idea. And that wasn't always what we emphasized about it either.

But we didn't equate the idea of independent Black political action with Black control of the Black community, or limit it to that. We always explained that a break from the capitalist parties toward independent Black political action would certainly have had a radical programmatic thrust and a powerful impact on the labor movement.

But if what we say about the tremendous crisis of the Black movement for almost a decade is true, it's obvious that independent Black political action alone could not develop far without it being totally intertwined with changes in the labor movement.

So our decision to focus on explaining the need for a labor party during our 1980 election campaign, and to basically drop the Black party slogan for now, has to do with the changes in and the stage of the class struggle that we've been talking about. It has to do with the changing realities. The same is true of the Chicano party slogan, although the existence of the Raza Unida parties makes this a slightly different question, as we discussed at our last plenum.[18]

As the class struggle intensifies and class consciousness is raised in the process, the concept of a labor party based on the unions can have a powerful impact on thinking Black militants. There's no sleight of hand involved here. We're not pretending that the labor party is a Black party. The labor party is a class party.

But when such a party gets rolling, it's inconceivable that it won't have a very big Black membership and won't champion, and fight around, and be attuned to the big issues of racism, inequality, and the conditions facing the oppressed nationalities.

Related to this is our view of Black caucuses in the unions today. In the late sixties we greeted formations like DRUM and ELRUM [Dodge Revolutionary Union Movement and Eldon Avenue Revolutionary Union Movement], the militant Black caucuses that sprang up in the auto industry in the Detroit area. And we went further. We *advocated* Black caucuses as a step forward for both the Black and union movements.

To advocate them at the current stage of the class struggle in this country, however, would be to sell the Black proletarian vanguard short. Black caucuses may arise here or there. But there's another possibility, more in tune with the way things are actually developing today. We should be explaining the vanguard role that Black workers can play through the unions in the broad transformation of the labor movement—in pushing and organizing it to think socially and act politically through civil rights committees, strike committees, or whatever the form may be. We've already begun to see this around the *Weber* fight and at Newport News. It's not an abstraction.

We believe that Black workers can and will be a decisive part of any steps toward a class-struggle leadership in the unions. They will be in the leadership of the class-struggle left wing, which will put the fight for full equality and class unity at the heart of its program to transform the labor movement.

Independent Black organization
It's important to remember the difference between the Black party concept and our concept of the independent Black organization—an idea that goes all the way back to our discussions with Trotsky forty years ago. Trotsky put the idea quite simply: "that a special organization should be created for a special situation"—the special situation being the national oppression of Blacks.

We stand by that idea. It's inconceivable that the class struggle will heat up without the growth of independent Black organizations fighting directly for Black rights. This is not the same thing as an independent Black political party.

Nor is it in any way counterposed to the idea of a labor party or a class-struggle left wing in which Black workers play a vanguard role. In fact, it is developments in this direction in the labor movement that hold out the greatest hope for a way forward from the total prostration of Black organizations such as the NAACP. The petty-bourgeois national leaderships of these organizations have pushed them into a dead end through their policies of reliance on the capitalist parties. An organization has to earn the right to lead by what it does in practice, and none that exist today have done that. They are increasingly seen as irrelevant or ineffective in the eyes of the masses of Black working people.

The fight for self-determination in all its aspects will remain a permanent part of the class struggle in this country. This is true despite our confidence that Black and white workers will fight together to transform the labor movement and use it as a revolutionary instrument in the struggle for a workers government.

Trotsky once made the point that until Blacks "feel that the domination by the whites is terminated," they won't really know whether or not they want a separate state. That's not going to happen under capitalist rule in this country. The American working class will first have to conquer political power.

To get to that point, Black and white workers are going to be involved in *one* struggle with the *same* strategic goal: a workers government. That's our concept of the combined character of the American revolution. Not a convergence of two separate revolutions, but a single fight for power with combined class and national tasks. Black and Chicano workers will play a vanguard role in that struggle, and in the transformation of the labor movement necessary to get there.

This does not mean, however, that the Black struggle is reducible to the construction of a class-struggle wing in the unions. The revitalization of independent and fighting Black organizations will play an important role in the fight for a workers government that can guarantee Black self-determination.

The growth of united struggles by Black and white workers, such as at Newport News, doesn't mean that there will be fewer desegregation struggles, campaigns against cop brutality, or other forms of the fight for Black rights. To the contrary, as this process accelerates in the unions, there will be more such struggles. More-over, their potential to win will be much greater, since they will have the prospect of bringing the weight of the labor movement into the fight. This is what has been lacking since the very begin-ning of the civil rights movement. This is what is responsible for the current leadership crisis of the Black and Chicano movements. And this is what is changing and holding out the possibility of a revitalization of these struggles.

Our conquests on all these questions are firmer today than ever before. We are the only party on the left that really understands the combined character of the coming American revolution and what that means for the strategy and the day-to-day tasks of revo-lutionists.

That's why we put such stress in the resolution on the fact that our party must be multinational in both composition and leader-ship if it is to lead the American workers to power. Our industrial turn makes possible big strides toward becoming a party that re-flects the young vanguard fighters in the working class. Only a party with such a proletarian composition can be a multinational party. The depth of national oppression in the country and the overwhelmingly proletarian composition of the Black and Chi-cano population dictate that.

We're armed with the only program that can achieve this goal. And we're doing the right thing—throwing our forces into the in-dustrial unions today to meet the growing political opportunities in our class. We have every reason for optimism and confidence.

Women's movement in crisis

We face a similar crisis of leadership in the women's movement. And this crisis is not lessened by the existence of NOW as a na-tional organization.

The political problem is evident when you read the *National NOW Times,* the newspaper of the National Organization for Women. Last month, for example, an award was given by Philadel-phia NOW to the first woman to become a police detective in that city. That's literally true. A cop! The *National NOW Times* also ran a several-column article, with photo, of a meeting organized by NOW to have a "dialogue" and seek "consensus" on the issue of birth control with antiabortion groups.

There is a crisis facing women in this country regarding abortion. The right to abortion—that is, economic, social, and political access—is being brutally cut back. This is not because workers are turning against abortion rights. A Gallup poll released just a few days ago showed there has been no decline whatsoever since 1975 in the percentage of people who support abortion rights. But the economic possibility of having an abortion, and the availability of facilities, have been sharply limited by federal and state legislation. This is one of the "takebacks" the ruling class has implemented since the offensive began in 1974-75.

It will take a social battle to reestablish this right in real life. The "one-sided class war" has come down especially hard on Black and Chicana women, on women of the other oppressed nationalities, and on all working women.

The fight for the Equal Rights Amendment is in crisis, too. The NOW leadership has reduced this struggle fundamentally to organizing political support for Democratic Party politicians, together with attempts to talk people out of taking their vacations in states that have not ratified the ERA.

We give the same answer to the crisis of NOW as we do to that of Black organizations such as the NAACP. There is no "independent strategy" for women that can win. There is no tricky tactic that can circumvent the crisis. There are correct tactics, tactics that can move the struggle ahead, but they must be timely expressions of a strategic vision that places the women's liberation movement in a class perspective. That's the only way to assemble the necessary social forces to win the abortion fight, or win the ERA.

Key to the road forward is the transformation, the revolution, that is taking place as women in the labor force push their way into industry. This transformation began as one of the repercussions of the gains of the Black struggle. When the Civil Rights Act was being debated in Congress in 1964, the southern senators tried to prevent its passage by outlawing discrimination in employment on the basis of sex as well as race. They figured that made Title VII, as that clause of the act is known, so ridiculous, even northern liberals would have to vote against it. But it was passed.

Affirmative-action drive

This provided a legal opening for the affirmative-action drive by women. It gave women a legal club to use to force their way not just into jobs, but into basic industry, with its higher wages and greater unionization. Thousands of suits were filed. One stride forward came with the 1974 consent decree in the basic steel industry which established plant-wide seniority and set hiring goals for women and apprenticeship goals for women, Blacks, and Latinos. From 1975 to 1979, women made a big push into auto, mining, and steel.

Jobs in industry are key to women for several reasons. One is that secretaries, teachers, and social workers simply do not have the raw power that industrial workers have when it comes to winning women's rights or anything else.

But it's more than that. Opening the doors to basic industry has a powerful impact on the consciousness and self-confidence of women, and on the way that men view their female co-workers. Many deeply ingrained attitudes change rapidly. The interconnections between the workers' struggle against class exploitation and women's struggle for economic independence and full equality come to life. Sexist prejudices begin to break down.

The women's movement needs to make the same kind of shift that is necessary for the Black and Chicano movements. To win the ERA, abortion rights, and the other demands of women today will take a stronger, different kind of movement than a decade ago, with a different kind of leadership. But the forces exist to build such a movement.

Working women, and especially women in industry, have to

lead this process, orienting the women's movement toward a strategic axis that can push the movement forward. This includes, of course, the fight against discrimination and harassment on the job. It's not sexual harassment only. The term is too narrow. The fight against sexual harassment is one aspect of the much broader fight of working women—the fight against the harassment of women as a sex, against discrimination, and for the right to get jobs, to hold them, and to have full rights on those jobs.

At the same time that working women need to become involved in the women's movement, they must also take their struggles into the unions, to win support for abortion rights, pregnancy benefits, the ERA, and other needs.

This is the direction the women's liberation movement must go. Not toward the antiabortion forces that support birth control. Not toward women cops or detectives.

This is what we have been raising and arguing in organizations like NOW for nearly two years, ever since we and women we were allied with in NOW drew up the "Defending Women's Rights" resolution in 1977.

What faces the women's movement is a political question and a class question, the same as with the Black movement. The leadership of the women's movement is petty-bourgeois. But the forces coming forward in struggle are working-class women. At the same time there is a growing radicalization among other layers of the working class, including male workers.

The fact that we now have many more comrades in industry allows us to alter the way we do our women's liberation work. Comrades in industry must play an increasing role in the various women's organizations. We need to take another look at what we do in NOW. Instead of shaping our work in the unions to work in NOW, we need to orient our proposals in NOW to meet the changing needs and potential of women in industry. We have to fight in NOW for involving the labor movement in the battle for women's rights.

Our work in the factories and the unions must become the axis of our women's liberation work. We need to pay close attention to the women's caucuses and committees in the unions and in the plants. We should even take a new look at various local units of the Coalition of Labor Union Women (CLUW). No organization of this type should be written off. Because the fighting women's organizations that are going to emerge from the struggles beginning today will not look like anything that exists right now.

The character of NOW as a large national organization gives it a special importance. Its links with the labor movement are also important.

There are two sides to the Smeal-Fraser alliance, for example. On the one hand, it represents an alliance between a section of the labor bureaucracy and the leadership of NOW in an attempt to subordinate the women's movement to the needs of the capitalist class, just as the unions are subordinated. This has political implications. Fraser tells [NOW president Eleanor] Smeal that just electing Democratic Party candidates is insufficient; all progressive forces must work together to reform the Democratic Party.

But there is another side to this collaboration between NOW and a section of organized labor. It reflects pressure coming from below. It reflects the new consciousness that women have of themselves and their fellow male workers, and their search for powerful allies. From this point of view, the mutual interests of Smeal and Fraser provide an important opening.

Against the employers, foremen, politicians

The axis of women's fight is against the employers, their foremen, their courts, and their politicians—not against fellow workers. To the contrary, women should aggressively appeal to all the class-struggle-minded workers on the job, seeking support for women's rights. From our initial experience, we know there is usually a positive response when women fight along these lines. Women in and out of industry can see the attractive power of the labor movement and the potential for support from layers of young, militant workers.

This came through clearly at a District 31 conference of the USWA. An older, Black, male worker got up at this conference and explained:

We have to support the women. The bosses are doing to them just what they did to us when we first came in the mill. They're trying to drive them out. Women still have to fight to establish their right to remain in industry.

This Black steelworker predicted that with the next major downturn, women will face a concerted drive to push them out of industry.

He was absolutely right.

This is one reason we should approach women's committees or caucuses in the unions differently today than Black or Chicano caucuses. We favor and sometimes help initiate women's committees or caucuses, while we don't initiate Black or Chicano caucuses for the reasons I outlined earlier. Of course, we know that working women, like Blacks and Chicanos, will help blaze the trail toward a class-struggle left wing in the unions. They will play a vanguard role in the transformation of the labor movement.

But we have to recognize the different positions of Blacks and women in industry today, the different stage women are at in getting into industry and staying there.

Women face greater obstacles because of their small numbers and their newness in industry. They have to fight the bosses, the foremen, and the whole setup just to prevent themselves from being driven out of the plants. Often the forms don't exist for women to work through these problems and figure out how to use their unions to defend their rights. Special women's committees, as in District 31 of the USWA and in many auto locals, can provide such a form.

Added to this are the special obstacles women face, because of the character of women's oppression in class society, in becoming self-confident leaders of their class and their unions in leading their male co-workers. This is a bigger problem for women than for Blacks, Chicanos, and other oppressed national minorities. It's another reason why women's committees can play a very positive role.

The importance of fighting 'Weber'

The fight by women to get into industry and hang on there also underscores the centrality of the affirmative-action question and the *Weber* case. The importance we have given this fight has been proven correct by one simple thing: the growing number of workers, including male workers and white workers, who are beginning to understand that affirmative action is a *class* question, a question that involves the effectiveness of their unions. The ability to explain this through the *Weber* case is made easier by the fact that the suit also challenges union collective bargaining rights around the issue of job discrimination and upgrading.

Today, Black, Chicano, and women workers as a group comprise a significant percentage of the membership of the major industrial unions. This makes it easier for other unionists to see why, in the interests of solidarity against the bosses' offensive, they must combat discrimination. This mounting pressure from below, in turn, has forced the majority of the labor officialdom to come out in formal opposition to *Weber*. It is responsible for the USWA bureaucracy's decision to fight the case in the courts and to call the recent civil rights conference.

This is an important new development, a promising new trend in the American labor movement.

Of course, it's just a beginning. There is still a big fight ahead to demand that the labor officialdom throw union power behind this struggle, which it has no intention of doing today. There is still a big job in educating workers, especially white workers and male workers, about their stake in the fight and mobilizing them into action around it.

But the opportunities to do this are greater than ever before. More and more workers are willing to listen and agree when opponents of discrimination explain that affirmative action is vitally and directly in the interests of the working class as a class. Affirmative action is not a charity to make up for the past. It's not—as some argue—a morally correct position but materially disadvantageous to males and whites.

Workers are better able today to grasp aspects of the political economy of discrimination—that discrimination does not mean an extra buck for some workers at the expense of women or of Blacks, Chicanos, or Puerto Ricans; instead, it drags the whole class down in terms of real wages and job conditions, and saps the collective ability to fight back against the bosses.

More and more workers are waking up to their class interests, which do not lie in seeking privileges for some. As this happens, they become more capable of seeing the difference between class struggle and class collaboration, between themselves and the union bureaucrats. It becomes clear that it *strengthens* the union to bring in more Blacks, Chicanos, Puerto Ricans, and, yes, women, to make sure that everyone gets the *same treatment.*

There are more and more openings for us to explain and move forward along this axis of struggle.

But we must add the point we made in the March 30, 1979, *Militant* editorial: The kinds of struggles that established the principle of affirmative action will not be sufficient to defend or extend it. More powerful forces and a more conscious leadership are going to be necessary for that.

The *Militant* editorial noted that the civil rights laws were won without the unions really entering the fray. The editorial continued:

This is a new period, in which the capitalist economy is wracked by crisis; in which the employers are driven to harsher and harsher antilabor attacks in order to defend their profits. This is a period of polarization of class forces.

The only class that has an interest in defending affirmative action is the working class. And the fight to defend affirmative action must be taken right to the center of the only mass organizations of the working class—the unions.

Antinuclear work and the turn

We've seen that we cannot do effective work in the Black, Chicano, or women's struggle without building fractions in industry. We understand that the turn is a *political* question and that the fractions must be at the center of our branch, local, and district political life.

But what about our antinuclear work? Isn't this one movement where we can apply the old "antiwar tactics"?

The answer is no.

Of course, it's wonderful to have some big protest marches again around an issue as important as nuclear power and weapons.

But we must begin by looking at the antinuclear movement in relationship to the working class and the unions, not vice versa. The effects and results of nuclear power are a class question. And, as with every other social issue, how to stop nuclear power is connected to the question of how to raise class consciousness and transform the unions.

The *strategy* we were following in the antiwar movement and our *strategy* today remain the same—it is the circumstances and possibilities that have changed. When we say that the antinuclear movement won't be a repeat of the antiwar movement, we're making a very positive statement. We're saying that the potential exists from the outset to bring the power of the labor movement into the fight. And by doing that, at the same time the task of transforming the unions will be advanced.

So we would be making a big mistake and missing a real opportunity if we looked at the antinuclear movement from the point of view of politics ten years ago. The axis of class politics has changed. As we've been explaining in the *Militant*, opponents of nuclear power must have answers to the questions of energy and jobs, that are life-and-death questions to working people.

The antinuke movement must be fit into the strategic line of march of building a class-struggle left wing of the labor movement. That class-struggle left wing will have to take on a broader scope of issues than it did in the 1930s or 1940s. To take just one example, there were no nuclear power plants in those years—although the A-bomb tests were radiating the hell out of American workers and soldiers. Today, nuclear power and weapons is a vital issue for the labor movement and would have to be a central question taken up by a class-struggle left wing and by a labor party.

The nuclear question is at the heart of developing labor's program on the energy crisis. Our proposals there around increasing coal production as an alternative to nuclear power, along with other aspects of our approach to this movement, will be developed through the *Militant* and will be an important component of our socialist election campaign over the coming year.

That's why our job is to take this important question into the unions. We participate in antinuclear coalitions or organizations as socialist workers who want to bring our unions into the fight and who see the antinuclear struggle as a significant aspect of transforming the American labor movement. With that as our strategic guideline, the tactics should fall into place with a little thought and experience.

The petty-bourgeois left

There is a striking difference in outlook today between us and all our opponents on the left. We deal with this toward the end of the political resolution. One of the clearest recent examples has been what some New York radical-pacifists called their "collective sorrow, confusion, and concern" over the events in Indochina this year.[19] They couldn't understand that what was happening there was a *deepening* of the Indochinese revolution.

Of course, it would be easy to explain away every mistake that anyone else makes by saying that they are not in the factories and that we are. Apart from being hollow swaggering, that's simply inaccurate: Some of our opponents are in the factories. Politics is more complicated than that.

But there is a side to this difference between us and the rest of the left that is real. Petty-bourgeois radicals do not have a working-class perspective. They see only one side of the class polarization that is taking place in this country. They do not feel, in the marrow of their bones, that the American working class is the most progressive social power on earth. They do not see any way forward.

Whether they know it or not, these petty-bourgeois radicals have been won over by the propaganda offensive of the ruling class that has accompanied the austerity and prowar offensive. They are awed by the rulers; they see the capitalists at center stage pure and simple. They are profoundly pessimistic and soul sick.

It won't help to argue strategy with them. They could not possibly come up with a winning strategy. They simply repeat old tactics, and any tactic repeated by rote does in fact become a strategy. There is always a strategy underlying whatever you do in politics. Whether you are conscious about it or not, your actions either coincide with the effective strategic line of march of the working class or they do not.

In my opinion the entire left—aside from the SWP and YSA—is to the right of the working class in the basic strategic sense that we are talking about. And this will be true for the leadership of any organization—whether it be NOW, the NAACP, the Clamshell Alliance, or the Raza Unida Party—that does not orient toward the struggles of the working class and mobilizing the power of the working class. This is not a question of intentions or of the merit of individuals; it is a question of being attuned to the political reality of this country and charting a way forward.

Radicalization and polarization

The radicalization and polarization continue—there is no reason to change our view on that. There are a growing number of fighters, a growing number of thinking fighters in the working class.

Contrary to what Brother Fraser says, perceptions *are* changing— they are becoming more accurate.

This opens the door to the possibility of resolving the crisis of leadership of the oppressed battling for their rights. It opens the door to the possibility of an effective fight against war. It opens the door to an effective fight on many issues.

We're just at the beginning of this process. Although we can't predict the tempo, we know that events like the coal strike, Newport News, and Three Mile Island are shaping the consciousness of our class. What we're seeing are still only trends—but trends with a clear direction, and trends that can unexpectedly flare up and accelerate the entire process.

We are not going into a period of economic expansion like the 1960s or reaction like the 1950s. The major conquests of the struggles over the past two decades—the changed attitudes on war, suspicion and distrust of government and big business, greater support for the rights of oppressed nationalities and women—all these are still deeply ingrained in the population.

The American workers are in a preparatory period in this sense: They are gathering forces and gaining class-struggle experience for the battles that are being forced on them by the intensifying assault of the capitalists. The struggles like Newport News, the growing awareness around *Weber* and affirmative action—these are still more the exception than the norm. But there are more and more such exceptions. Class consciousness and combativity are on the rise. This is the trend, not the opposite.

This means that we are in the "here and now" in this sense:

Our party can carry out activity in the labor movement and begin to apply our program there. With that attitude and approach, we will make the maximum possible gains *now* in building our movement and be ready for new openings and opportunities as they arise.

Any branch that is not moving toward having a large majority of comrades in industry is unable to carry out our political campaigns in the most effective arena today. They are missing opportunities. We have to overcome the unevenness among our own party branches in relation to the industrial turn. The industrial fractions, politically led, must become the axis of our work. Industry and the industrial unions must become the arena to which we relate all our campaigns.

This does not mean that the work in industry should become a substitute, or an excuse for abstaining from struggles elsewhere. It means *relating* all struggles, all issues, all movements, to the working class and the unions, not vice versa. It means participating as working-class revolutionists who have our sights firmly fixed on the class-struggle transformation of our unions. It means seeing the industrial unions as the potential source of power, as the focus of our fight to educate and mobilize the forces capable of leading labor and its allies forward.

Of course, there are a lot of rough edges, a lot of problems as we make this turn. Some things get put to the side for a time, or pushed to a back burner. George Breitman once quoted Trotsky as describing the period after the workers have come to power, as they build toward socialism, as a "period of efforts, experiments, errors, crises, reforms, and reorganizations."

George went on to comment that this is also a good description for periods the party goes through in the process of preparing to lead the workers to power.

It's not a bad description of what we're going through now, as we orient ourselves politically, changing the axis of our activity, and the composition of our party, in line with the objective shifts taking place in the American working class.

Finally, we need to continue to deepen the turn. Each time we get a new layer of comrades in, this is often followed by a pause, and then another whole layer gets inspired by the experiences we're having, and they go in. We have to keep this process moving, so that a year from now we can confidently say we've met our goal. Once that's done, there's every reason to believe that, with a little conscious attention, we'll stay there.

Some comrades have asked me why we say we want the *large*

majority of party members in industry. Why don't we say *all*? In places such as Baltimore, we're close to achieving that.

First of all, there are two categories of members who, at any given time, won't be in industry. One group is comrades who are retired or comrades near retirement age who haven't been in industry all along.

Then, there are members who have been asked to take full-time assignments in the branches, locals, districts, or in the center. We're already beginning to see a pattern that will become the norm in the party: Comrades who have experience in industry leaving their jobs for a period to go on full-time, and full-timers who go into industry.

Six months or a year ago, I would have added a third category: comrades who for health or some other special reason "couldn't get hired," or "don't belong" in industry. But our experience tells us that we should look at this category more carefully.

Of course, there are certain physical and health problems that preclude working in most factories. We know that.

But what we're finding out, to our surprise, is that many comrades who we might have ruled out six months ago for reasons of health or age, can and are getting into industry. They're politically convinced and inspired. They want to do it. And they get hired. I personally know of a number of comrades in their forties, comrades who have a back problem, or who have had serious operations—they are getting in and finding that they can do it. Sometimes it means the jobs committee needs to spend some time and effort finding the right job, but it's worth it.

We know now for sure that branches can get a big, big majority of members into industry.

That means we should reaffirm what we said two plenums ago: There is no category of comrades with certain kinds of jobs or union situations who should be exempted from our turn into industry. Over the past year we've gotten the majority of our teachers fraction and government employees into industry. And we want to deepen that process.

Of course, a branch of industrial workers in any big city will attract and recruit workers who are not in industry: public employees, hospital workers, clerks and salespeople and so on. In fact, completing our turn into industry is the best road toward building the kind of party that will be attractive to all strata of the working class.

But as these people become integrated into the party today, they too will want to be part of the turn. They're not in the less powerfully organized, less strategically decisive sections of our class by choice. They will be among the fresh forces that will propel us forward in becoming a party of industrial workers.

And we're already seeing another process. As branches get close to completing the turn, their industrial fractions become one of the party's best sources of footloose rebels to help strengthen another branch or carry out an important project like Newport News.

This perspective opens the door for us to be able to put together a real combat machine—a multinational, proletarian revolutionary party, led by women and men who are worker-bolsheviks.

IV. Summary

There are several broad questions comrades raised that are worth discussing. We don't have to take a vote on them, but we can think them out a little more, and maybe deal with them at the convention.

We have described the radicalization that began in the 1960s, with its unevenness and ups and downs, as the "broadest and deepest" ever. But there's a side of this that deserves more thought.

Is the process developing in the working class today basically a continuation of the radicalization that began in the 1960s?

Of course, there's no use in trying to draw too fine a line. Maybe we should think in terms of different stages of a single process. Protest movements continue—the idea of fighting for your rights. There has been a total change from the quiescence of the McCarthy period. Changes in attitudes on war, government, women, etc., have continued to progress—to penetrate broader layers. All this is part of the continuity of the radicalization.

But there is another side, too. There have been breaks in the continuity as well. New forms of struggle are and will be emerging. They are not and will not simply be a repeat of the struggles of the 1960s or early 1970s. There will be elements of the old forms, but they will occur in new circumstances, new combinations, and with a different social composition.

It seems reasonable to assume the classical forms of class action will play an increasingly significant role. The Transitional Program becomes more and more contemporary. The changes in the working class and in the labor movement indicate this.

I think there has been a real break in continuity of the Black struggle, for example. There were the uprisings between 1965 and 1968, followed by other kinds of struggles such as the emergence of several Black nationalist organizations and the campus open-admissions battles. But since the end of the 1960s, there has been a *retreat*. Not a retreat in the sense of simply being driven back—although the repression and victimizations were a factor.

But there was a *pulling back* in face of the gigantic tasks posed: how to use legal equality to defend and advance the social needs of an entire layer of the working class. A radical social transformation was necessary, but the forces to pull it off were yet to be assembled politically.

Think of what happened between 1965 and 1968. There were virtual semi-insurrections of the Black community in a number of cities. And then . . .

Radical attitudes weren't reversed, nor did struggles end. There were ups and downs, which we analyzed at the time. But in retrospect, I think you can see a break. There was a general upturn of the Black struggle that began with the civil rights movement in the mid-1950s, went through the sit-ins, went through the Malcolm X period, went through the uprisings of the mid-1960s. Jim Crow was swept aside and there was an expansion of jobs for Blacks. But then the struggle came up against a new reality—the limits of past conquests, the lack of new social-economic concessions, the gap in political and social consciousness between the Black and white sections of the working class. Then came the great burst of inflation and wage freeze of 1971, the 1974-75 depression. The escalating Black unemployment rates, the gutting of social services.

Throughout the 1970s the crisis of leadership of the Black movement has deepened, even though there have been ups and downs of the struggle. No leadership has come forward with the answers: Where to go? How to make gains? How to get together the forces necessary to make gains? Who can lead?

The women's liberation struggle is a little different. It arose later and hit the impasse in a different way. But many of the same factors apply.

There is a deep crisis in the women's movement too. It will take a different kind of leadership and more powerful forces to win back the abortion rights that have been stripped away in practice in the last few years, to win the ERA, to fight for child care as part of an expanding public education system, and to begin fighting systematically for the rights of women on the job.

There have been ups and downs on the campuses all along. But we certainly can't speak of an existing student movement today. There has been a great change since the period of roughly 1968-72. In that period if you had taken a survey on almost any campus, you would have found a significant number of students who considered themselves socialists or revolutionaries. But students bumped up against new obstacles, shifts in the relationship of class forces.

The ruling-class offensive, the movement of labor toward center stage in the resistance, and the class character of the polarization (disguised by ruling-class propaganda as a general move to the right in the attitudes and expectations of the "people") have had an ideological effect on campus and academic circles. Liberalism (or "New Deal" liberalism as it is often called) seems to offer no way forward; and the Marxism that millions in these circles at least tipped their hats to, becomes a withered or unrecognizable critter if it's not connected to the working class or linked up with the continuity of the Marxist movement. Marx and Engels's explanation that Marxism is a class movement more than a doctrine takes on its full meaning. Superstition, pseudoscience, and cults of self-indulgence, not socially conscious activity, have become the counter-pole to the job-oriented grind.

This has facilitated an anti-working-class, rightist shift in the liberal intelligentsia—marked especially by reactionary positions on issues such as affirmative action by organizations such as the Anti-Defamation League.

What about the crisis of the Chicano movement? There have been very positive changes in the last decade, like the growth of self-confidence of the Chicano people, and the farmworkers' struggles. Attitudes are quite different from fifteen years ago. But it's hard to find something you can call a movement—significant forces and organizations really fighting, mobilizing to advance Chicano rights.

The crucial thing, the reason for optimism, is that we see the beginnings of radicalization in the working class, and the industrial unions are moving toward the center of this. And big class battles, or the mobilization of labor's power in major social protests, will rapidly reawaken political confidence and activism among allies of all kinds.

Putting together an accurate picture of what has happened in this country over the last decade includes analyzing the *break* in continuity from the 1960s radicalization, as well as the continuity.

That radicalization was a prosperity radicalization. There was not a single official recession in the 1960s after the one in 1961. That kind of radicalization is bound to be different from the one we're entering. The elements driving the sixties radicalization forward were different. The organizations of the working class as such never came in behind these struggles in a significant way. In fact, the labor bureaucracy fought an ideological battle against nationalism, feminism, and socialism, and for a long time against antiwar attitudes, too.

Marches and 'mass actions'

To make this point about the different stages of the radicalization does not imply a negative judgment about either one. Making the distinction is important, though, to help us stop and think. Forms and tactics appropriate to the earlier stage won't necessarily be applicable now.

Not every march, even a big march, is a mass action. Mass actions, in the class sense, are things like sitdown strikes, factory occupations, the mobilization of entire sections of the population, as in some of the civil rights marches. Soviets, general strikes, uprisings, and insurrections are forms of mass action. These are an integral part of our strategy.

We saw some mass marches against the Vietnam War, but I don't think any of them were mass actions in this class sense. Maybe a few of the May 1970 actions began to approach it. But we saw a lot of marches that were not massive, and a number of very big ones that were not mass actions in this fundamental sense. We called them propaganda actions. And they became damned effective.

Why do we get mesmerized to some degree by the march question? I think because it was the most effective thing we did for a number of years. Building the antiwar marches were good times for us. They had an effect on world politics and aided the Vietnamese revolution. They attracted a lot of serious people. The party grew.

We are always looking for action. We're looking for people who are ready to act and not just talk, not just lobby, not just write postcards, not just lick stamps for the Democrats. And we look for every chance to involve our fellow workers in protest actions.

But if what we're saying is accurate, we have to look at the mass-action question in a new way. A different class is becoming dominant in today's struggles. The working class and its organizations were not dominant or even prominent in the whole previous period. Our class has its own way of moving and forms of struggle connected with their unions, their workplace, their source of power.

This is not a negative development. It is part of the positive readjustment we can make coming out of the past two decades. And it also helps us more clearly appreciate the extremely positive, the historic, character of what we've called the "detour."

The detour gets you where you are going. *It's the only way around a dead end or a roadblock.* Thank god we took the detour! If we hadn't, we wouldn't be where we are today.

We do not pretend to be able to offer the various allies of the working class a set of proposals and tactics that can guarantee victory, isolated from involving the workers and their organizations along their line of march. That's not what we need to contribute to those struggles today.

What we face today can seem only *subtly* different from a decade ago. But actually, it is *very* different, and it's positive.

We have to say to NOW members, for example: How did we get to this situation? Why haven't we won the ERA, turned back the attacks on abortion rights? It's not *simply* that we need more demonstrations—as we do. It's more fundamental. Partly the problem is not understanding who the enemy is. Partly the problem is that we don't have powerful enough forces. Partly the problem is the stage of development and thinking of the more powerful forces we need on our side.

We have to explain: What is the nature of the crisis? Why are they so determined to prevent us from having the ERA and abortion rights? What forces will it take to get them?

We have to continue to explain why NOW must orient to working women, especially those who are organized in the most powerful industrial unions. We have to explain why this is important.

We have to think out how to encourage and deepen the collaboration between the unions and the women's movement. Many women do sense the power of such an ally, and more workers are realizing that gains for women will strengthen the unions.

Obviously, we will continue to encourage the women's movement to take realistic initiatives all along the way. We will make proposals for actions, local campaigns, etc.

But we add that actions—even another large, pro-ERA march like the one July 9 last year—are not the whole answer. A question of perspective and class orientation is involved, and I don't think we're quite used to explaining this straight out. The easy way out is simply pushing for actions—without having the basic discussion on orientation that is crucial if we are to really get out of the impasse. That's why we must see the women's movement through the eyes of our class and the openings in the unions, not vice versa.

A minority can't change society

It's worthwhile going back and reading George Breitman's pamphlet *How a Minority Can Change Society*. The title is one of those trick titles, to get you to read the pamphlet. Then you find out that a minority *can't* change U.S. society. Only the working class, in its majority, can change American society today.

But a minority can act in such a way in their own interests, that they play the vanguard role in bringing other, additional forces into motion so they both can obtain their goals in the process of changing society. Serious people involved in different protest organizations are ready for what we have to say. Because they sense that something big is happening. We are literally threatened with a catastrophe in this country. Our living standards are all plummeting. Three Mile Island almost melted down and took Harrisburg and a few other cities with it. Toxic chemicals are seeping out of the ground all over the place. The White House keeps probing the possibility of using American soldiers, trying to push toward war. Speedup and the gutting of job safety threaten the health and lives of millions of workers.

Don't a lot of workers sense the magnitude of these problems? What is the answer to the social catastrophe that Black Americans face? Why is there no progress, why are there no concessions? Why do the bosses and the politicians keep retreating on desegregation? Affirmative action? Why are they so hard against abortion rights?

Why won't they give the ERA? Why do they keep turning the screws on undocumented workers? These battles can only be won by big forces.

But our understanding of what's involved leads to a way out of the pessimism that marks a lot of activists. Because we can clearly *see* the forces capable of doing this. We can see the forces assembling. And this means a shift in the way we function.

We must no longer view the unions and our industrial fractions in relation to various protest movements, campaigns, or political goal—that is, can we simply get the unions to endorse something we're involved in. *Instead, we should view these political campaigns in relation to the unions and our union fractions.* How can these issues and objectives be used to advance the process of educating and transforming American labor?

We have to find ways to take the initial yeast that exists, in terms of motion and struggles, and use it to advance the revitalization of the unions—the force necessary to change American society, and the source of new power and leadership for movements of social protest in this country.

Why do we approach the *Weber* case differently than we did *Bakke,* for example? With the *Weber* case we have put primary stress on work through the unions, not just because *Weber* is a union case but because we saw we could use it to move in the direction we're talking about. We didn't set out to build nonexclusive *Weber* coalitions everywhere, around this or that demand, this or that action.

These are the strategic questions we need to keep in mind in figuring out how we can participate most effectively as socialist workers in the Black struggle, women's organizations, antinuclear organizations, and so forth. And we must do this without exaggerating the initial stage, and major unevenness, in the beginning radicalization of industrial workers.

Axis of our presidential campaign
On the labor party question.

We're not proposing a labor party campaign for our fractions or a general party propaganda campaign on the question. We're proposing to make the explanation of the need for a labor party the generalizing feature of the campaign that our presidential ticket, Andrew Pulley and Matilde Zimmermann, their supporters, and our state candidates will take to the population in opposition to the Democrats and Republicans.

This is not a campaign to agitate trade unionists to form a labor party. It is not a substitute for timely agitation and action around key elements of our program for a class-struggle left wing in the unions: solidarity, democracy, key social and political questions such as affirmative action, etc. It is not a substitute for using our campaigns to give socialist answers to the central political questions facing working people: war, racism, sex discrimination, nuclear power, and all the rest.

The labor party idea is also not something that our presidential campaign only explains to the unions. We have to take our election campaign to workers who are not in unions, to women who are not currently working, to Black and Chicano organizations, to high school students, to farmers, and to all the allies of the working class. We have to find ways of explaining to all of them why a labor party is a good idea. We want to convince them that this— not support of Democrats or Republicans—is a big step out of the impending catastrophe.

This is what we're talking about, not some agitational campaign in the unions. We see no motion there toward formation of a labor party.

It's not like the situation we faced in the 1960s and early 1970s in regard to the Black party and Chicano party, where there *was* some motion. Some Black leaders raised the Black party proposal—I think it was first William Worthy, then Elijah Muhammad and Malcolm X. Then we picked up on it as a real and significant move by a section of the Black community. The same was true of the Chicano party, where we saw the formation of La Raza Unida parties in the Southwest in the early seventies.

What we're proposing at this plenum is also different from the SWP's labor party campaign during the post–World War II upsurge. At that time, the labor party was being widely discussed in the labor movement. There was the Frankensteen campaign for mayor of Detroit, an independent campaign based in the auto locals.[20]

But today we see no moves toward a labor party, and only the first stirrings of discussion around it in the unions. So I stress that what we are proposing is a propaganda axis of our presidential campaign, not a general campaign by the party that begins with propaganda and then maybe moves immediately toward action. This is an important point.

At the same time, we do see the growing need for a labor party, the pressing objective need. And for a small, vanguard election campaign, we must give a positive political answer that generalizes our perspective, that flows from what we will be saying about the way forward and the forces necessary to move forward.

What we say is: Labor must break from the two capitalist parties. It's the working people who can find the answer. Not those who exploit us. Not those who live off war, racism, and sexism. Not those who won't allow us to use our productive capacities to create a decent life, who bring us radiation and catastrophe.

The labor party proposal flows from a growing objective need. It will get a hearing.

We want to take the idea of the labor party into the main organizations of the allies of the working class. We don't want to do this in an artificial way, like mindless sectarians, like pests. We don't want to be seen as people with an obsession. You know the kind. Whatever's on the agenda, up shoots a hand and people groan, "Here comes Labor Party Jones." If you do it that way, no one pays any attention.

Nor do we want to counterpose this idea to other fruitful work we have been doing, other positive proposals. However, the labor party idea will help us explain things to people we are working with, to generalize our political orientation. For example, we have to bring this idea of the labor party into NOW. If for no other reason we would have to do this because of the participation of the NOW leadership in Fraser's Progressive Alliance. Think of the symbolic meaning of the Fraser-Smeal alliance. On the one hand, the UAW—symbolic of the whole industrial-union wing of the organized labor movement. On the other hand, NOW—the most prominent nationwide organization open to all women who want to fight for their rights, whatever its weaknesses and contradictions.

These two forces demonstratively appear together—in a press conference, at an organizing meeting—saying that a coalition is needed linking the labor movement, the women's movement, the Black movement, the Chicano movement, the environmentalists, and others. A coalition fighting for the rights of all.

At the same time, we know that this coalition is on the wrong political course: support to the Democratic Party. We think this is hurting NOW. And it's hurting the UAW. We think it's hurting the Black struggle. We think it's derailing the fight for all the goals the coalition purports to be for.

We say the idea of the coalition is great. The organized labor movement on one hand, and women, Blacks, Chicanos, those fighting to protect the environment on the other, are attracted to each other for correct reasons—because they reinforce and strengthen each other. But we have an alternative political course to supporting the Democrats, one that will take us all forward. The labor party idea has to come in here as part of our explanation.

This is what we will want to do in the *Militant*. This is what Matilde Zimmermann, Andrew Pulley, and all our candidates will want to explain. It's a concept we will be taking to the entire population.

Class-struggle left wing

A couple of comrades made the correct point that progress toward a labor party cannot leap way out ahead of progress toward building a class-struggle left wing in the unions. The labor party idea is one aspect—although an indispensable one—of our more general perspective for assembling the forces to transform the labor movement.

At the same time, we know that motion around some aspect of a class-struggle left-wing program can sometimes spurt ahead, including possibly on the labor party front, and that this can be part of the uneven emergence of a nucleus of a class-struggle left wing. That is, the two developments can't be held hostage to each other, placed in some *a priori* sequence, any more than one can somehow develop in isolation from the other.

By definition a class-struggle left wing in the unions can't develop very far without the fight to organize a labor party. This is precluded. And a labor party could not conceivably be launched in this country without a gigantic shake-up of the unions, without all kinds of discussion, organization, motion, on a whole range of issues and demands. It would change everything.

We also don't hold the proposal for a labor party hostage to democratizing the unions. For a while we used a wrong formulation on this. We would say: "for a labor party based on a democratized, revitalized, fighting labor movement." This is confused tactically.

We have the right and the obligation to demand of the current, elected leadership of our unions that they stop supporting the Democrats *right now*. The elected leadership of the unions, as they are now, should break from the capitalist parties and help launch a labor party. And the 1980 campaign is a very good time to talk about it and explain it.

It's the employers who try to argue that it's not realistic to start a labor party. That's all fakery. It's *easier* to start a labor party than it was to start the various capitalist parties—the Whigs, the Democrats, the Republicans—because a labor party already has a base—the unions.

Twenty-five lessons from the 1970s and perspectives for the 1980s

At our spring 1978 National Committee plenum, we decided to make the turn to lead the party into industry. The heart of that decision was to immediately move toward getting the great majority of members and leaders of the Socialist Workers Party into industry and the industrial unions in order to do political work in, and as part of, the decisive sectors of our class.

Underlying this decision was our estimate of the state of the world economy and changes in world politics following the defeat for U.S. imperialism in Vietnam and the 1974-75 worldwide recession; the economic and political changes in this country—the deepening class polarization and beginning growth of combativity and class consciousness among American workers; and what all this means in preparing the party to lead the struggles of the oppressed and exploited.

The general line of this report on the resolution "Building a Revolutionary Party of Socialist Workers" was approved by the Thirtieth National Convention of the Socialist Workers Party, held August 5-11, 1979.

SEE PAGE 442 FOR NOTES

For the first time in three decades we could do political work in the decisive sectors of our class, and we had to subordinate everything to get ourselves into position to make the most of that opportunity.

Reviewing the progress of our turn and the national and international events of the past year and a half, the Political Committee this spring drafted the political resolution before us here, submitted unanimously to the party by the National Committee from its May 1979 plenum. This resolution pulls together the continuity of the political lessons we drew from the radicalization of the past two decades; the world political situation as it affects U.S. politics and as U.S. politics affects it; and the lessons we've already learned from our turn and the initial experiences of our growing industrial fractions.

A counter–political resolution was submitted by a minority of comrades.[1]

The party has now had several months of discussion in the internal bulletin. Many of the articles have been among the richest we've had for years. They've been based on our party's concrete, practical experience in the industrial working class and unions. Comrades have had to think out how to concretely apply our resolutions and our transitional method. This was especially noticeable in a number of articles by comrades who drew on their experiences in industry.

This report will inevitably pass over important points raised in the discussion, and simplify some others. To obtain the maximum clarity on the central disputed political questions before the delegates, we thought it would be helpful to boil them down to twenty-five points that capture the political heart of the draft resolution.

Vietnam and the decline of U.S. imperialism

One. The Vietnam War changed American politics from top to bottom. What was previously considered impossible—even unthinkable—*happened.* It happened in a prolonged, drawn-out painful way. It happened before the eyes of the entire American population via television. It happened to the sons, nephews, husbands, and neighbors of millions and millions of Americans.

And slowly but surely, the American working class drew some conscious conclusions. "No more Vietnams!" has become perhaps the most popular single slogan in this country. And this suspicion of U.S. foreign policy and unwillingness to fight Washington's wars has been reinforced by Watergate and the events that have occurred in this country since the pullout of American troops in 1973.

Two. The continuing impact of Washington's defeat in Vietnam has a direct bearing on one of the biggest factors in world politics: the growing inability of the U.S. rulers to wield their military power against the workers and toiling masses around the world.

Since the last time we adopted a major political resolution there have been victories and advances for our class in Nicaragua; in Iran; in Vietnam, Kampuchea, and Laos; in Angola and the other former Portuguese colonies; in Ethiopia; in Afghanistan. The capacity of the toiling masses in the colonial world *to snap back* from defeats and the brutal repression of vicious regimes, and to battle and overthrow their oppressors, has been demonstrated again. We could not have asked for a more inspiring or convincing example than the Nicaraguan people, who—in the face of ruthless violence by the National Guard—drove Somoza and Somozaism out of their land.

We've witnessed the growing preponderance of the proletariat and the semiproletarian urban masses in the revolutionary process in these countries. The very advances of the neocolonial bourgeoisies under the tutelage of imperialism creates the proletariat that then bites its creators. To extract surplus value, the dependent national capitalists have to try to build up the economy, thereby building up the proletariat, which then turns on them. That's what the bourgeoisie calls injustice!

The extent of this process of urbanization and proletarianization was dramatically revealed in a 1979 report by the World Bank. According to that study, 51.5 percent of the world's population will be living in urban areas by the year 2000, as against 29 percent in 1950 and 39.3 percent in 1975. The study also predicted that by the year 2000 there will be some forty cities with populations of more than 5 million in the semicolonial countries, compared to twelve in the industrialized countries; and eighteen cities with more than 10 million people in the semicolonial countries.

American imperialism has discovered that the junior partners it counts on—the so-called surrogates, the reactionary leaders such as Somoza and the shah—are less and less able to hold back the class struggle for themselves and their masters.

Ironically, the United States, whose government used to continually intervene in Cuba, now finds Cuba intervening in it! That's the meaning of the Castro leadership's astute initiative toward opening a dialogue with Cubans in this country.[2]

Despite these political problems, however, U.S. imperialism remains world capitalism's only strategic nuclear power. Though its hands are more than ever tied by the antiwar attitudes of the American working class, Washington's military budget and the size and diversity of its strategic weapons and nuclear arsenal continue to grow. Withdrawal of American combat units from South Korea is postponed. New nuclear-armed strike forces are announced. Proposals to reestablish selective service registration and the draft proliferate in Washington. Trial balloons are continually sent up to see how far aggression can go—an aircraft carrier off Indochina, "advisers" and warships to Yemen and the Arab Gulf, talk of the determination to protect "our" oil reserves in Saudi Arabia.

Underneath all this there's the ultimate contradiction facing American imperialism: it must be able to intervene militarily around the world or else capitalism will be overthrown piecemeal. But to do so, the rulers have to take on the American working class, which more and more sees that it has no stake in Washington's military adventures abroad. And this contradiction is the most decisive in world politics.

Economic crisis of capitalism

Three. This political crisis of the use of American military power takes place within the framework of the relative decline of the American economy and the developing world capitalist crisis that began in the early 1970s. The international capitalist system has entered a long period that tends toward basic economic stagnation and explosive inflation, as opposed to the overall economic expansion that characterized most of the quarter century following World War II.

Superimposed on this economic stagnation is a growing tendency for social and political crises to break out even in the most stable capitalist countries, threatening a crisis of the entire social relations of capitalism.

Of course, American capitalism can still make some concessions. It can, it has, and it will make more as the class struggle advances. But there is no possibility of major, stable economic concessions—like a new, gigantic social security plan, for example —that the employers might grant in hopes of reversing the radicalization of the American workers and dampening their growing combativity.

The antilabor offensive launched by U.S. imperialism in 1971— Nixon's wage freeze and other measures to "zap labor"—was followed by the rigged meat and oil shortages of 1973; soaring double-digit inflation; and the 1974-75 depression, setting off the biggest round of layoffs and austerity attacks in three and a half decades.

The ruling-class offensive is aimed at weakening the main class organizations of American workers—their unions. To increase their rate of profit by intensifying the exploitation of industrial workers, the employers must go after the industrial unions. They have no other choice.

This does not mean that the immediate goal of the capitalists is to destroy or wipe out the major industrial unions; when they feel tactically ready to do that, you won't have to be told about it at an SWP convention or read about it in a resolution. But *right now* the bosses are aiming to systematically weaken, undercut, and drive back the industrial unions in any way possible. They are probing to see how much they can take back, how far they can go in attacking the most powerful organized sections of the American working class.

That has been the policy of the American ruling class for nearly a decade, and its implementation has been accelerating since 1975. It has been stepped up further over the last few months.

Therefore, without the fight to transform the industrial unions into revolutionary instruments of class struggle, there is no way for our class to prevent the social breakdowns, catastrophes, the gnawing uncertainties and insecurity, the threat of imperialist wars, that come down more and more heavily on working people.

The ruling class can't simply plan in advance what to do—when to push and when to pull back. They don't exercise control of the economy; capitalism is an anarchic system. The bosses are faced by mounting competition, growing uncertainties, and spiraling problems of their own. They are by necessity pragmatic, driven to weigh the short run over the long run. The economic and social forces referred to in our draft resolution are not only out of *our* control, but often beyond the control of the very capitalists who set those forces in motion to begin with.

Of course, the capitalists sometimes contrive crises, like the oil and gas shortages. They planned those; they secretly rigged them behind the scenes. But then—in the middle of their scheme something else happens that they hadn't planned—like Three Mile Island. This unplanned and undesired near-disaster coincided with the planned energy crisis; and it backfired on them. It set back their plans to use the phony oil shortage as a cover to drive toward expansion of nuclear power production.

Crisis of expectations

Four. There is a growing realization among American workers that they face catastrophic conditions or the mounting possibility of catastrophe. This changing consciousness, this anticipation that good times don't lie ahead, didn't develop overnight. The cumulative impact of the blows over the past decade have shattered the illusion that no matter how bad things are today, at least they'll be a little bit better next year. Now the expectation is that conditions will probably get worse. That's what the average American worker has come to expect.

Over the past ten years we've gone from the steady inflation that began toward the end of the Vietnam War; to the little downturn—the first in ten years—at the turn of the 1970s; through the explosion of double-digit inflation in 1973-74; to the meat and oil shortages those same years; followed by the capitalist takeback offensive, which struck particularly hard at social services and at teachers and other public employees; to the deepening of racial inequality; the driving of millions of Black youth into permanent unemployment; topped off by the first worldwide recession in thirty-five years and the first extensive unemployment faced by the workers in this country since well before World War II.

The recovery from that depression has been an extended one, but it has been shallow and uneven, with continuing high levels of unemployment despite a major expansion of jobs. The official jobless rate during the recovery never dropped below levels that marked the worst points in the recessions of 1948, 1954, and 1970.

On top of that, prices have continued to climb (they will be in double digits again this year); oil and gas shortages have erupted; planes fall out of the air; consciousness of the dangers of nuclear disaster has grown; taxes have shot upward; forced overtime grinds us down; and a new recession has begun.

What is the cumulative effect of all this? It has qualitatively changed the attitudes, expectations, and consciousness of American workers. Initially stunned by the suddenness and ferocity of the assault, they are more and more ready to fight back today.

One of the most striking proofs of this was President Carter's attempt to mollify and reassure the American people when he spoke on television a couple of weeks ago. Carter bemoaned the "crisis of confidence" in this country as a "fundamental threat to American democracy."

"We've always believed in something called progress," Carter said. "We've always had a faith that the days of our children would be better than our own.

"Our people are losing that faith. Not only in government itself but in their ability as citizens to serve as the ultimate rulers and shapers of our democracy. . . .

"For the first time in the history of our country," Carter complained, "a majority of our people believe that the next five years will be worse than the past five years. Two-thirds of our people do not even vote.

"As you know," he continued, "there is a growing disrespect for government and for churches and for schools, the news media, and other institutions. . . . [Americans] were taught that our armies were always invincible and our causes were always just, only to suffer the agony of Vietnam. We remember when the phrase 'sound as a dollar' was an expression of absolute dependability until ten years of inflation began to shrink our dollar and our savings."

Yes, Carter was right in pointing to a "malaise" in the country. There is a terrible malaise that haunts American workers and lays on us like a deadweight. But what Carter couldn't explain is that the source of that malaise is capitalism.

Yet Carter hit the nail on the head in pointing to a loss of faith in the likelihood of progress. American workers no longer believe that steady progress is possible for them.

The public reaction to each new breakdown or crisis that occurs is more skeptical than the reaction to a comparable event a year or two earlier. In regard to the current gas crisis, for example, fewer workers believe the propaganda about the Arabs causing it, while they overwhelmingly hold the oil monopolies to blame. Or contrast the reaction to Three Mile Island to the near-meltdown at the Fermi breeder reactor near Detroit a decade ago—an even more serious accident in terms of its potential damage.

You can think of other examples. The bristling reaction to each new trial balloon by Washington about military intervention abroad or the threat of a new war. The more sympathetic reaction to the recent independent truckers strike—reflected as well in the less openly hostile stance of the Teamster bureaucracy—compared to the owner-operator actions back in 1978.

Rail workers in Minnesota had a brilliant stroke when—as part of the campaign they're waging against the Milwaukee Road bankruptcy fraud—they put out a button and tee-shirt with the simple slogan: "Investigate Milwaukeegate." They didn't have to say another word to any other worker. They just held up the word "Milwaukeegate," and it told the story.

The button is being worn up and down the Milwaukee line as the symbol in defiance of management and contempt for the government, who together can produce nothing but "Milwaukeegates." The rail workers love them. The bosses despise them.

Changing composition of the working class

Five. Why is this happening? Why do we see this dramatic evolution of class consciousness today? What's underneath it, above and beyond the impact of the crisis and its effects?

Here we have to look at the changing structure and composition of the American working class, and at the social and political struggles originating outside the union movement that paved the way for today's battles.

Over the past decade or so, we have seen persistent struggles by the Black and Chicano populations and by women. These struggles preceded and are intertwined with the current process of working-class radicalization. The civil rights and women's rights struggles resulted in major changes in social and political attitudes. They helped improve the relationship of class forces, heightened the self-confidence of oppressed layers of the working class, and advanced the consciousness within the entire working class of its common *class* interests in combating race and sex discrimination. Over and over again, we saw the vanguard role of the

Black population, Black workers, in transforming the American labor movement and advancing the class consciousness and combativity of the entire class.

The composition of the American working class is strikingly different than it was several decades ago. For example, in the last nineteen years alone, the number of women in the workforce has shot up from 33 million to 42 million. In September 1978 there were fewer than 2,000 women coal miners; by spring '79 there are more than 2,500. And figures like these are still rising.

These changes continue as the capitalist crisis deepens. They affect the political character of workers' attitudes and the explosiveness of their reactions to the employers' antilabor offensive.

The first big test for both the employers and the workers came in 1977 and early 1978 when the capitalist class and its government targeted the United Mine Workers, aiming to cripple the power of this major industrial union. The miners, with solidarity throughout the labor movement, rebuffed the coal operators and Carter administration. Workers throughout the country discovered during the coal strike that the weak officialdom was not the union—the fighting miners were the union.

The ruling class can't even take secure refuge in the right-to-work-for-less South any more or in the so-called Sun Belt. It's no longer safe territory for the employers. The impact of the mighty struggles that defeated Jim Crow, combined with the national and world events of the last decade, has provided tremendous impetus to the class struggle in the South, making it one of the key factors in American politics today.

We've noted this in the organizing drive by Steelworkers Local 8888 at the giant shipyard in Newport News, Virginia; the United Auto Workers victory at the new GM assembly plant in Oklahoma City; and the general rise of union consciousness and organizing drives in North Carolina and elsewhere. We see it in the revival of the Black struggle in Decatur and Birmingham, Alabama, and in Tupelo and other northern Mississippi towns.

The class polarization is deepening in the South, the composition of the workforce is changing, and the opportunities for socialist workers are greater there than ever before.

Finally, this ruling-class austerity offensive increasingly targets the industrial workers and the industrial unions and pushes this decisive sector of our class to the center stage of American politics. The attacks themselves make it increasingly clear that underneath all political developments two classes confront each other—us and them, the workers and the capitalists. In order to chart a winning strategy for any oppressed layer in society or for any progressive social goal, it becomes more and more important to understand the social weight of the contestants and the relationship of forces between the two main classes in society.

The main trends in the American working class today—under the combined impact of the worldwide capitalist austerity drive, the social protest movements of the sixties and seventies, and the changes in the composition of the workforce—are not unexpected by our party. We meet these new developments with a cadre prepared both by our political conquests and practical political experience of the past decade and a half. As we foresaw in our 1971 political resolution, "Perspectives and Lessons of the New Radicalization":

> Both our reformist and ultraleft opponents exhibit a tendency toward *economism* in their ultimately pessimistic view of the role of workers in the radicalization process. They see struggle over wage and job issues, *in isolation* from the political issues and motive forces of the radicalization, as the sole way the workers will be brought into struggle. This error is tied to their misconception—and hope—that independent movements like Black nationalism and feminism will somehow fade away when the "real" struggle begins.
>
> The decisive mass of workers will not be politicized until the underlying international economic crises force American imperialism into a showdown with the labor movement. But the issues that have already been raised in the current radicalization are not peripheral to the process of social discontent; they are central to it. And *in com-*

bination with [emphasis added] the workers' struggles over wage and job issues, they will lead to politicalization and radicalization of the working class. The independent and uncompromising demands of the various movements will be an additional aid to the workers' struggles against the efforts of the reformists to channel the burgeoning radicalization into the dead end of class collaboration.[3]

These processes are well under way, opening opportunities to do political work in our class and to begin drawing together the initial forces that can transform the American labor movement into a mighty force for revolutionary change.

We will be participating in the struggles of women, the oppressed national minorities, and other progressive social protest movements as socialist workers, actively working to bring a winning perspective—that is, a proletarian perspective—into the fight.

Deepening polarization

Six. There is a deepening class polarization in the United States. This does not mean that fascism is around the corner, or even just down the road. And history has shown that the workers will have their chance to take political power before the decisive onslaught of fascism.

What is happening right now is that, as the working class and the industrial unions are targeted—even targeted by name—by the spokespeople for the ruling class and by the bourgeois politicians, it becomes increasingly easy to recognize two fundamentally antagonistic sides lining up for the big political battles. Politics is less and less seen as simply the clash of good and bad, differing individual opinions, or even a conflict between a disembodied "right" and "left" detached from real social forces.

This class polarization with its initial glimmers of class politics is becoming one of the fundamental factors in the changing American political scene. It exposes the most basic underpinnings of capitalist society. "The history of all hitherto existing society is

TWENTY-FIVE LESSONS *325*

the history of class struggles," wrote Marx and Engels at the beginning of the Communist Manifesto. That is the starting point of Marxism, historical materialism, and communism. All politics reflects the struggle of class against class.

The growing consciousness of this fundamental fact of politics, brought into sharper focus by the class polarization today, points out the road to resolving the problems of all the oppressed and exploited. It points along the road of mobilizing the workers and their allies to fight for a workers government that can begin to take up the task of constructing a society truly in the interests of humanity.

This is understood by a relatively few workers today, but it will be understood by many more in the days to come. It holds out a perspective of scientifically grounded optimism for our class and its allies.

Each of the social movements, such as the Black and Chicano movements, the women's liberation movement, and all progressive social protest struggles unfold in accord with their own autonomous laws of development. The dynamics of these struggles cannot be reduced to the laws of the struggle between capital and labor, let alone the laws that govern the fight to build a class-struggle left wing in the unions. These social movements march in step to their own pace and rhythms and cannot be regimented to the schemas of the Stalinists, social democrats, and sectarians of all stripes. Understanding their specific laws, participating in these struggles, following their course of development, championing their progressive demands, is decisive in building a revolutionary workers party.

From the recognition that these struggles are relatively autonomous, a conclusion is sometimes drawn that is *not* true. These social movements are *not* independent from the unfolding of the class struggle, from the relationship of class forces established in that struggle, and from the state of confidence, consciousness, and politicalization of the vanguard of the working class.

To the contrary, the class struggle sets the political framework within which all social movements operate. It determines the form of their development and the prospects for their success or failure, while it is itself in part shaped by the course and outcome of these social movements. A dialectical assessment of the current stage of the class struggle and the interplay of class forces is therefore essential for all social and political activists in understanding which way to go, where to look for allies, where to find new leaders, what's the wisest strategy, what's realistic given current conditions, and so on.

The class polarization in this country cannot and does not reduce any social struggle or organization of the oppressed to the laws of other struggles or organizations. What it does do, however, is enable them to join their struggles with those of the most advanced layers of the working class and others among the oppressed and thereby have a progressive impact on the social consciousness of the vanguard fighters of our class. That's why we emphasize the interaction and interdependence of the struggles of the oppressed and the labor movement and the mutual effect on their confidence, leadership, and class consciousness.

Petty-bourgeois political perspectives

Seven. As this class polarization deepens, an ideological polarization follows in its wake. The ruling class must *propagandize* to attempt to reverse the widespread antiwar attitudes among working people. It must *propagandize* to justify its takebacks and attacks on Blacks, women, the handicapped, rebellious youth, and others. It must try to *explain away* its responsibility for catastrophes and breakdowns by putting the blame on the Arabs, "foreign imports," the "unruly" unions, "welfare cheats," and other scapegoats.

This concerted propaganda offensive puts tremendous pressure on the petty-bourgeois intelligentsia, including the radicals among them. Witness the virtually universal condemnation in this milieu of Vietnam's invasion of Kampuchea; their collapse before Washington's "boat people" campaign, à la Joan Baez; the exposé by "socialist" radicals in the *New Republic* that Julius Rosenberg was really a "commie spy" after all; the recent announcement by

Monthly Review editor Paul Sweezy before an audience of 1,000 in New York that he no longer thinks Marxism provides an adequate explanation of existing postcapitalist societies.

These phenomena are symptomatic of the ideological pressures emanating from the ruling class. The petty-bourgeois intelligentsia in unison with the capitalist media refer to this as "a crisis of Marxism." It's actually a crisis facing all those who look for answers to great theoretical and practical political problems elsewhere than from a *working-class point of view,* a Marxist point of view. That's why the draft resolution characterizes this as a "crisis of petty-bourgeois politics."

The political disorientation in this quarter is different from the impact of the capitalist crisis on the petty bourgeoisie as a whole, especially on those exploited sectors that are the weightiest potential allies of the working class, such as working farmers. Intensifying struggles by the working class against big business and its political parties will divide the petty bourgeoisie and attract entire layers to the camp of the workers and oppressed. That will happen as they see the massive battalions of American labor move into action, fighting for the interests of all its allies, providing decisive answers to the capitalist crisis.

But prior to this working-class upsurge, until the American labor movement is able to attract allies in large numbers, this crisis of perspective among the petty-bourgeois intelligentsia and radicals will tend to deepen. The less they're connected with the working class and its basic institutions, the less they will be able to grasp the political situation and respond to its main trends in a progressive fashion. And the more they will be susceptible to self-absorption, reactionary mystical concepts, and pressures to subordinate everything else to "making it."

The party's turn to industry
Eight. These initial seven points lead to one simple and imperative political and organizational conclusion for revolutionary socialists: to get the great majority of our members and leaders into in-

dustry *now*—both here and around the world. That's the only way we can become involved in, get in touch with, and affect and be affected by these important changes in politics.

Regardless of the pace, which will vary from country to country, the changes described in our draft resolution will put their mark on the rest of the twentieth century. Only by turning to the industrial workers can we prepare a leadership that is capable of leading the working class to power. It's the only way to position ourselves to meet the political responsibilities and take advantage of the opportunities we know are coming.

This is how we will be in the strongest position to regroup with revolutionary currents that originate in the mass movement, which we must do if we are to construct proletarian parties and a mass revolutionary international. These currents will initially be drawn to us not because they are conscious of our programmatic continuity with the Bolsheviks, but because of the attractive power of growing parties of socialist industrial workers that have been tested in class combat and have shown the capacity to lead and to score victories.

Attracting the best of the American left, the most combative currents of proletarian fighters among all layers of the oppressed —that's exactly what our turn will enable us to do. And it will happen elsewhere in the world as the parties of the Fourth International become organizations of industrial workers.

Only along this road will our movement earn the confidence of broad sections of the oppressed and exploited necessary for us to attract the most important revolutionary current that has so far arisen outside our own ranks—the Castroist current in Cuba and revolutionists such as those in Nicaragua, most directly influenced by it. As the crisis of capitalism drives the toilers to fight back, other revolutionary currents will arise both in the semicolonial world and in the labor movement and among the oppressed in the advanced capitalist countries. We must be able to reach out to these fighters and link up with them, winning them to the perspectives of Leninism. Only parties of industrial workers can exert that attractive power through their capacity *in action* to advance the interests of the toilers.

Revolutionary unions

What does all this mean for the trade unions themselves? How does our turn to industry relate to our strategic aims of transforming the labor movement into an instrument of class struggle, constructing a revolutionary proletarian party, and leading the workers and oppressed in establishing a workers government?

That's the subject of the next eight points.

Nine. First, what are our goals in the unions? Our goal is quite simple: to do everything possible to transform the American unions, as Trotsky explained, into "instruments of the revolutionary movement of the proletariat." What we do is aimed at advancing toward revolutionary unions as combat organizations of the American working class.

In the process of doing this, we'll build the irreplaceable *political* instrument of our class—a revolutionary party of industrial workers.

As revolutionary socialist workers, our starting point is not confined to the economic functions of the unions, as basic and vital as those functions are. That's how the class-collaborationist misleaders of labor want the workers to see their unions. By promoting that narrow conception, the bureaucrats have steadily weakened the capacity of the unions to defend the economic interests of the members.

In contrast, our starting point is the social character and political life that surrounds and dominates everything the unions do, including the economic gains they can win. We must chart our strategic approach and judge all our tactics in the labor movement by keeping our sights fixed on the class-struggle leadership that is beginning to emerge from the ranks. That is where the future of the unions lies.

We don't begin with the unions as they seem right now, or as they were a few years ago. Instead, we chart our course from the ways the unions are changing, in the light of what they are becoming, and what they *must* become if they are to survive. We give no guarantees to anyone about how many unions will be transformed into revolutionary instruments of struggle. No guarantees at all; we're not prophets but scientific revolutionaries who work to steer developments in the right direction.

One thing we do know. The socialist victory is inconceivable without the *struggle* to transform the unions into revolutionary instruments. And the construction of a revolutionary workers party is impossible without participation in that struggle.

As class battles unfold, there will be far-reaching changes in organizational forms that we can't foresee or imagine. Some organizations will be entirely destroyed; others will be transformed and revolutionized. The fight itself is what is decisive in forging a revolutionary proletarian leadership.

We will see mass revolutionary actions and upheavals of our class and its allies that will upset and spill over any organizational forms that currently exist—whether in the factories, in working-class neighborhoods, wherever.

Through it all, our strategic goal is the fight for revolutionary unions and the construction of a proletarian combat party out of that struggle.

Ten. What, then, do we have to do to move toward this goal of revolutionary unions? What do we counterpose to the class-collaborationist perspective of the encrusted union bureaucracy, which seeks to hold back and sap the power of the American working-class movement? Against this class collaborationism— which is the bible of the current labor officialdom—socialist workers explain the need for, develop the program of, and attract and educate key parts of the initial cadres of *a class-struggle left wing in the unions.*

Our elementary programmatic guidelines for this task are simple. We've often summed them up this way:

• The fight for *union democracy* in all its forms, so that the power of the workers can be brought to bear;

• The fight for *solidarity* with other workers—organized and unorganized—and with the struggles of all oppressed and exploited here and around the world;

• The fight for *political independence* from the capitalist state and all its instruments, including the bourgeoisie's two-party system.

Our industrial fractions are learning how to combine three things in advancing these programmatic goals:

1. Socialist propaganda—sales of the *Militant* and *Perspectiva Mundial*, our election campaigns, talking politics with co-workers, and so on;

2. Organizing around, talking up, and involving our co-workers and our unions in struggles around all sorts of broad social and political issues—from the ERA to nuclear power and crushing the Ku Klux Klan, from solidarity with the Nicaraguan revolution to defense of Iranian revolutionists;

3. Becoming part of all the struggles around wages, job conditions, and speedup that develop continually and will increase as the bosses step up their offensive.

Developing a Marxist current

We would oversimplify matters if we looked at our work in the unions solely as preparing for a class-struggle left wing—which as yet has no organizational form—and in that process directly recruiting workers to the party. Because within this overall framework, something else begins to happen—something that will be an important gauge of the success of the party and the work of our industrial fractions. That's the growth of a Marxist current.

The party will attract around us a layer of workers—tens to begin with, then hundreds, and later on thousands. They may not join the party immediately. But they will follow our press, attend some of our forums, go with us to a conference or demonstration, support our election campaigns, be influenced by our members, and become better acquainted with our ideas. They will lock to the SWP as an identifiable and alternative political pole. They will start picking up the basic concepts of Marxism and reading some of our literature.

Our capacity to draw around us such a layer of workers will be an essential ingredient in the process both of forging a class-struggle left wing and building the party. It's a key conquest of the small but growing number of steady *Militant* readers and subscribers our fractions are developing among their co-workers.

This is nothing new in the revolutionary working-class movement. Ever since the British industrial bourgeoisie tried to crush the spirit of those they forcibly turned into the first proletarians, there has been a layer of workers who resisted, were inclined toward revolutionary action, toward fighting for their own class interests by any means necessary, and toward looking for a program that could help them move forward.

That is what Marxism really is. It expresses the interests of that class—the ideas those vanguard workers are looking for and need in order to win. We want to attract those rebels in the plants, mines, and mills, attract them to our press, win them to our ideas. We want to get them interested in revolutionary socialist ideas and recruit the best of them to the SWP.

Eleven. Do we have a model to go by? What will a class-struggle left wing look like? I've often been asked that. The only honest answer is that we don't know for sure.

We've seen the embryonic development of class-struggle formations in the past—such as the Trade Union Educational League in this country in the 1920s, the Shop Stewards Movement and the Minority Movement in Britain, and so on.[4] None of these, however, really give us a preview of the form and character a class-struggle left wing is likely to take in the American labor movement in the last two decades of the twentieth century.

We know that the prospects are advanced by the emergence of fighters in specific struggles around union democracy, solidarity, and so on. We know that the process will almost certainly be interconnected with winning over the leadership of certain union structures—committees, locals, districts, etc. But we can't predict the precise forms or foresee the exact process, and there's no point in speculating.

Nonetheless, there's one educational example in American labor history of significant motion toward a class-struggle left wing and the development of a revolutionary union leadership. That's the leadership of the Minneapolis Teamsters Local 544 in the 1930s and the Midwest organizing drive spearheaded by it. This experience gives us a great advantage because our party led Local 544 and one of its central leaders—Farrell Dobbs—wrote a detailed record of this experience and its lessons for us to read, study, and absorb.

Those four Pathfinder Press books—*Teamster Rebellion, Teamster Power, Teamster Politics,* and *Teamster Bureaucracy*—are worth reading, rereading, and reviewing every year. The more comrades get into industry, get to know the unions, and begin operating as part of party fractions, the more we'll get every time we go back to those books. We'll find something new and richer than we remembered each time.

Of all the periods of significant trade union work by our party, this one is the most relevant for us today. It's more relevant than the period right before World War II. While the party at that time had made a proletarian turn, we had to operate under severe restraints and with great caution due to the crackdown on the militants as Roosevelt prepared to lead America into the war.

The federal indictment and conviction of our leading comrades, with the cooperation of the top Teamster officialdom, occurred in this period. As a result, our trade union work was marked by a mode of functioning different from what the party now faces in the labor movement.

The Teamster experience is also more directly relevant than the party union activity after the end of the brief postwar labor upsurge. A great deal of valuable work was done during those years by our trade union fractions. But like the prewar period, these years, too, were marked by conditions very different from those we now face. From the middle of 1947 on, the American labor movement was in retreat, despite sporadic struggles and upsurges. As America entered the Cold War and witch-hunt, a great deal of effort had to be put into tactical maneuvers to buy time and hold off attempts to drive class-struggle militants out of the unions. We often supported this or that lesser-evil caucus or candidate for a union post just for the sake of survival. We correctly sought to maintain a small number of cadres in the unions in preparation for any possible upsurge—which, as it turned out, did not come for decades.

The Teamster experience from 1934 through 1938 transpired during years of deep capitalist crisis and growing working-class militancy and radicalization. An entire generation of rank-and-file workers were beginning to look for an alternative. By 1934 a mass labor upsurge was in the offing—whether it would come a year later, or three, or five was not important. There was a growing desire to fight back and growing capacity to do so.

This is the period—its rise and fall—that Farrell recounts in the Teamster books.

The Minneapolis branch consciously colonized the trucking industry. Farrell's first book explains that party leaders carefully thought out this question. Given the agriculture and milling in the area, they considered trucking the central and decisive industry in Minneapolis. Fortunately, our members could also get into this sector and build a party fraction. So that's what we did.

The branch leaders in Minneapolis were looking for the young workers who were beginning to radicalize, who were willing to fight. They were open to the possibility that even a younger worker who voted for Herbert Hoover in November 1932 might be leading militant working-class struggles only a year or so later. That's what happened with Farrell Dobbs. He voted Republican a little more than a year before he helped head up some of the greatest battles in the history of the American working class.

The Minneapolis socialists understood and valued aspects of such situations that were seen by many others as obstacles—for example, the inexperience and rawness of the young workers. As

Farrell points out, this meant the ranks didn't have to unlearn so many things. They hadn't been brainwashed to believe that a layer of labor bureaucrats was to their left.

Once these young workers went into action, they learned fast. True, it took a series of blows from the employers before they looked to their union, and some further blows before they looked beyond their initial union leaders.

None of our party cadres in Minneapolis began as elected leaders of Local 544. Not a single one held an official post—not only before the strikes, but throughout the coal yard strike in the winter of 1934 and the big strike battles later that year.

With the sanction of the union officials, we began by working with other rank-and-file militants to set up the unofficial strike committee. Only after the second strike did the rank and file demand that the tested leaders of that battle be elected to the top union posts. The workers ran up against a lot of former officials who got in their way, but they also found a couple who were changed by these experiences, came over, and were very helpful. As Farrell explains, we did not find—and never would have found—Bill Brown by looking for *him*. Instead, by organizing and mobilizing the ranks, we bumped into Bill Brown along the way.

Once this new Teamster leadership got rolling, it practiced the kind of class-struggle politics we've been discussing. Local 544 was a democratic union, controlled by the ranks. It practiced solidarity with the unemployed, the unorganized, other unions in Minneapolis, working farmers, and others. The Teamsters acted on the knowledge that solidarity was not only part and parcel of advancing the overall struggle, but also the only way of defending and building their own union.

From the very beginning, these revolutionary union leaders waged a fight for a labor party and mapped an orientation toward winning the ranks of the Minnesota Farmer-Labor Party to the class-struggle program. They didn't wait until a class-struggle left wing was formed in the labor movement before advancing this perspective. In fact, from 1934 on they were out ahead of the rest of American Trotskyism on this question, because the existence of the FLP in Minnesota posed it more sharply and immediately than in the country as a whole.

The leaders of Local 544 mobilized the ranks to use union power. It was the most democratic union in U.S. history. Its members used every sort of flanking tactic and tactical nuance that comrades are beginning to get some acquaintance with today. These Teamster leaders fought politically against the coming imperialist war and against government frame-ups of union militants.

In doing all this, these revolutionary union leaders developed not only the nucleus of a class-struggle left wing and a growing layer of union cadres around it. They also brought around them a Marxist current inspired by Trotskyism who read their press more or less regularly, knew their basic program, and absorbed more and more of their ideas.

The Trotskyists in the over-the-road organizing campaign also recruited a nucleus of party members all the way from Louisville to Cincinnati, from Dallas to Detroit—nuclei of truck drivers and other workers who were members of our party.

We discovered that thinking workers appreciated the real meaning of a revolutionary party in combat situations—revolutionary centralism, political homogeneity, internal democracy, and a solid proletarian composition.

So, although there's no model of a fully developed nationwide class-struggle left wing in the labor movement, at least we're fortunate to have had an experience where leaders of the Trotskyist movement consistently applied our program and methods in a period of rising labor struggles.

Even here, as Farrell cautions in the Teamsters series, we'll find no tactical guide. The books project a broad strategic framework and give a concrete account of rich class-struggle experiences that may have a lot of similarities to situations we'll confront. But we won't derive a single specific tactical formula out of these books— or out of *any* book. Such moves will be worked out by the comrades involved in the particular situation on the basis of the circumstance they confront.

We should keep another caution in mind. The class struggles of the 1980s will be marked not only by the trends we presently see developing in the working class, but by the radicalization that came before and by the events that lie ahead.

The method of the Transitional Program

Twelve. The deepening crisis of capitalism more and more drives home the importance of the method of the Transitional Program.

The Transitional Program itself generalizes the line of march of our class to power. It explains the fundamental class conflicts that dominate the death agony of capitalism. And it pinpoints the key obstacle to the progress of socialist revolution—the crisis of leadership of the world working class.

It's certainly not a tactical handbook for trade unionists in the 1930s, as Isaac Deutscher disparagingly dismissed it in the third volume of his biography of Trotsky. Instead, it formulates our basic program and provides the strategic framework for all our political work.

It is not enough to learn the specifics of that program. We must also absorb and be able to use its *method* in responding to fresh events that continually come up, the new combinations of circumstances that no one—including Trotsky—could have foreseen.

That method is simple. Its essence can be boiled down to three items.

First, Trotsky explained, revolutionists act in ways that give workers and the oppressed more confidence in themselves and in their capacity to struggle, that inspire them not to give in, that convince them they *can* affect politics and change the world. That's an antidote to what they've been taught by all the institutions of capitalist society.

We seek to convince our class that it can affect society by fighting together and fighting uncompromisingly. We seek to convince them in the course of day-to-day battles that there is a general solution that they alone can bring about to emancipate themselves and all their allies.

This is the combative spirit we seek to inculcate in our explanations of union democracy, class solidarity, and labor political independence as central axes of a transformed labor movement.

As Trotsky put it toward the end of the Transitional Program, "All methods are good which raise the class consciousness of the workers, their trust in their own forces, their readiness for self-sacrifice in the struggle.

"The impermissible methods," he said, "are those which implant fear and submissiveness in the oppressed in the face of their oppressors, which crush the spirit of protest and indignation or substitute for the will of the masses—the will of the leaders; for conviction—compulsion; for an analysis of reality—demagogy and frame-up."[5]

This spirit of combative class independence will be crowned by the formation and federation of soviets—mass, workers organizations or councils that will wage the fight for power and also be the organizational bedrock on which to begin the socialist reconstruction of society.

Second, our method is to operate as worker-revolutionaries. As Trotsky explained in *In Defense of Marxism*, workers know in their bones that they live in an imperfect world—one they want to improve and change. They treasure every advance and fight to preserve every inch of conquered territory. They don't begin with schemas, checking to see whether or not reality measures up to abstract norms—and if it doesn't, criticizing whatever leadership exists, retreating to the trenches to await a better day.

Workers are subject to the coercion of real conditions of life. They start from their current points of support and try to move forward from there, using whatever weapon they have at hand.

The Transitional Program is designed to build bridges from the problems the workers face, and their understanding of them, to broader socialist solutions.

This brings us to the third crucial aspect of the method of the Transitional Program—its starting point. The decisive goal is to change the consciousness of the workers through struggle, experience, and the correct political projections.

But the foundation of the program is not the state of mind of the workers at any given moment. It starts not from the subjective side but from the *objective* economic and political situation—the needs of the class and the developing contradictions of the capitalist system.

In both his March and May 1938 discussions with the American comrades on the Transitional Program—available in the Pathfinder book *The Transitional Program for Socialist Revolution*—Trotsky emphasized and reemphasized this point. Not understanding this, Trotsky believed, could skew political judgments about what the party should be doing and saying.

The Transitional Program, Trotsky said, "is a help to the masses in overcoming the inherited ideas, methods, and forms and adapting themselves to the exigencies of the objective situation."

"This transitional program," he said, "must include the most simple demands. We cannot foresee and prescribe local and trade union demands adapted to the local situation of a factory, the development from this demand to the slogan for the creation of a workers soviet.

"These are both extreme points," Trotsky explained. The job "of our transitional program [is] to find the connecting links and lead the masses to the idea of the revolutionary conquest of power. That is why some demands appear very opportunistic—because they are adapted to the actual mentality of the workers. That is why other demands appear too revolutionary—because they reflect more the objective situation than the actual mentality of the workers.

"It is our duty to make this gap between objective and subjective factors as short as possible," said Trotsky. "That is why I cannot overestimate the importance of the transitional program."[6]

In a later discussion, Trotsky continued:

"Some comrades say that this program draft in some parts is not adequate to the state of mentality, the mood of the American workers. Here we must ask ourselves if the program should be adapted to the mentality of the workers or the present objective economic and social conditions of the country. This is the most important question.

"We know that the mentality of every class of society is determined by the objective conditions, by the productive forces, by the economic state of the country," Trotsky told the American comrades, "but this determination is not immediately reflected. The mentality is in general backward, delayed, in relation to the economic development. This delay can be short or long. . . .

"The program must express the objective tasks of the working class rather than the backwardness of the workers," he said. "It must reflect society as it is, and not the backwardness of the working class. It is an instrument to overcome and vanquish the backwardness. That is why we must express in our program the whole acuteness of the social crisis of the capitalist society"—what our political resolution calls the catastrophes and calamities facing the American workers.

"We cannot postpone or modify objective conditions which don't depend on us," Trotsky said. "We cannot guarantee that the masses will solve the crisis; but we must express the situation as it is, and that is the task of the program."

With this crucial starting point in mind, he says, "It is a pedagogical task, a question of terminology in presenting the actual situation to the workers."[7]

In other words, we have to state the truth but in a manner that makes our ideas most accessible and understandable to the workers. That's a task we encounter every day on the job, that our candidates grapple with, and that we constantly try to improve on in the *Militant* and *Perspectiva Mundial.*

Finally, Trotsky comments, "Naturally, if I close my eyes I can write a good rosy program that everybody will accept. But it will not correspond to the situation; and the program must correspond to the situation. I believe that this elementary argument is of the utmost importance."

But Trotsky assures us that the decay of capitalism itself is the paramount factor in bridging the gap between objective reality and the current consciousness of the workers.

"The class consciousness of the proletariat is backward, but consciousness is not such a [rigid] substance as the factories, the mines, the railroads," he explains. "It is more mobile, and under the blows of the objective crisis, the millions of unemployed, it can change rapidly."

That's what we're beginning to see today under the blows of the past five years.

This, then, brings us back to the problem of how to present our demands, how to explain our slogans so we can do our utmost to close the gap.

The socialist alternative in 1980

Thirteen. Nineteen eighty is a presidential election year. This provides us with a special platform for explaining our ideas. As long as the capitalists keep holding national elections every four years, we'll keep on using them to present a socialist alternative on all the big issues facing the American workers.

What will be the central issues of the 1980 campaign? We don't know all of them for sure. But many are already clear: solidarity with the Nicaraguan revolution; opposition to Washington's war drive; explaining and concretizing the sliding scale of hours and wages as an answer to capitalism's double whammy of unemployment and rocketing prices; the need to nationalize the energy trust, the Milwaukee Road, Chrysler, and other industries that are raising such havoc with the lives of millions of working people; struggles around union democracy and class solidarity in the labor movement; projecting a way forward for the Black struggles from Detroit to Decatur; the fight to beat the ERA deadline and preserve abortion rights; shutting down nuclear power.

The presidential campaign also offers the broadest opportunity to explain the need for American labor to break with the capitalist two-party system—with the Democrats and Republicans—and launch a labor party based on the unions.

The objective need for a labor party—for a break by the labor movement from the two big-business parties—is more pressing than at any time since we began running presidential election campaigns in 1948. This is reflected not only in the more frequent use of the capitalist government against workers' struggles, but also in the growing disposition of the bureaucratic misleaders of labor to get themselves off the hook, to complain publicly about problems with the Democratic Party, and to warn the rulers that the ranks may turn away from it in disgust.

Trotsky thought the *objective need* for labor political independence should be the starting point for revolutionists in figuring out when to advance this slogan. He saw it as a specific application of the method of the Transitional Program, which we discussed earlier.

In a May 1938 discussion with American comrades, Trotsky stressed:

> I say here [about the labor party] what I said about the whole program of transitional demands. The problem is not the mood of the masses but the objective situation, and our job is to confront the backward material of the masses with the tasks which are determined by objective facts and not by psychology.
>
> The same is absolutely correct for this specific question on the labor party. If the class struggle is not to be crushed, replaced by demoralization, then the movement must find a new channel, and this channel is political. That is the fundamental argument in favor of this slogan.
>
> We claim to have Marxism or scientific socialism. What does "scientific socialism" signify in reality? It signifies that the party which represents this social science departs, as every science, not from subjective wishes, tendencies, or moods but from objective facts, from the material situation of the different classes and their relationships.

Only by this method can we establish demands adequate to the objective situation, and only after this can we adapt these demands and slogans to the given mentality of the masses.[8]

That's where we must start from today. Objectively, there's no question that the need for and timeliness of the labor party is greater now than in any previous presidential campaign we've run. Moreover, there's an increasing ability to get a hearing on this among working people. Comrades in our industrial fractions confirm this assessment, and we put it to a successful test in the Chicago mayoralty campaign of Andrew Pulley.

We must adjust *how* we present this slogan to the current mentality of the workers and the stage of development in the overall class struggle. That's why we project the slogan right now, *not* as an agitational campaign but as an important general axis of our election propaganda. That s the way we explain to fellow workers our alternative to the bankruptcy of the two-party system and the labor bureaucracy's dead-end reliance on the Democratic Party.

We also have to be alert to sharpening our agitation around Nicaragua, the energy crisis, attacks on the Black community, the ERA ratification drive, moves to establish wage controls, and so on. These put both the capitalist politicians and the labor fakers on the spot, raising the need for a labor party. There's no solid wall between so-called shop floor issues and broader social and political questions; the two will push forward the class struggle in rich combination.

Whether, how, and under what conditions the labor party will emerge as a slogan of agitation and action will depend on big changes and advances in the class struggle that we can't foresee. They've not yet ripened.

But whatever specific issue our campaign is concentrating on—whether it be a war threat, the energy crisis, layoffs and double-digit inflation, organizing the open-shop states, or the fight for Black, Chicano, and women's rights—it gives us an occasion to explain in this election year the need for a labor party to carry these struggles onto the political level.

We explain this to our co-workers and to as many other workers as we can reach through our campaign. We explain it to the oppressed. We explain it to everyone we talk to during the election campaign. Since people are thinking more about parties and politics at such times, we can get a better hearing. We are expressing our working-class viewpoint on a topic that is being considered and debated in society at large.

Regardless of our central agitational issue and action campaigns at any given time, labor party propaganda will remain central to our election campaigns. The Democratic Party will be a prominent actor in any conflict or controversy where the need for a political solution and a political alternative is posed.

That's the way we want to utilize the labor party idea in 1980, relating it to the big issues facing our class and its allies, and to the fight to implement our solutions to these problems.

Presented in this way, the labor party idea can appeal to a broad spectrum of the oppressed in this country. It helps us project our conception of a labor movement that actively champions the struggles of the unorganized and the unemployed, Blacks and Latinos, women, farmers, and youth. It can begin to make sense to feminists in the National Organization for Women who are fed up with the Democrats and, through experiences such as the upcoming Labor for Equal Rights Now conference in Virginia, are beginning to look to the labor movement as a crucial ally. Our candidates can win a serious hearing for the idea before Black, Chicano, and Puerto Rican audiences, in NAACP chapters, and in organizations of working farmers. The kind of labor party we're fighting for would attract serious fighters in all these struggles into its ranks.

Our call for a labor party is an invaluable aid in building our own party, the revolutionary proletarian party. As our resolution points out, those workers most favorably inclined to the labor party idea today will be attracted to the SWP; we are the most consistent advocates of labor political independence. And our proposals on the program that a labor party should fight for appeal to young workers, Black and Latino workers, women workers, farmers, and all those shafted by the bosses and their twin parties.

The actual formation of a labor party would dramatically shift the relationship of class forces, opening the way to the more rapid construction of a mass SWP.

Trotsky explained it this way to the American comrades:

"Should we use both slogans or one? I say both. The first, independent labor party, prepares the arena for our party. [It] prepares and helps the workers to advance and prepares the path for our party."

Over the next eighteen months, Andrew Pulley and Matilde Zimmermann, our presidential and vice-presidential candidates, will be talking to working people about all the pressing national and international political issues, including the need for a labor party based on the unions. And they'll be urging workers who agree with them to support the SWP campaign, to subscribe to the *Militant* and *Perspectiva Mundial,* and to join the SWP and YSA.

The two ideas go hand in hand.

Labor's strategic line of march

Fourteen. The end point of what we call labor's strategic line of march—the goal of all our work and all the struggles of our class —is a workers government. We view all our political work within this framework. From Marx through Lenin and Trotsky, this has been the goal sought after through the mass revolutionary action of the working class and its allies. Our aim is to lead the American workers toward governing the country on their own account.

This underlines the importance of the interplay between the unions and the various social protest movements. It helps drive home the need for proletarian leadership in these struggles, and their deepening impact on the unions and on the social and political consciousness of millions of workers.

We make no predictions that the unions will lead the struggles of Blacks, Chicanos, and women. We certainly don't believe that the independent struggles and organizations of the oppressed can or should be dissolved into the unions nor will they wait on the unions before they spring up—they never have. Of course, the more unions that move toward becoming revolutionary organizations of class combat, the more union power will be used to fight around social and political issues on behalf of all labor's allies. The mass mobilizations of the workers will grow more powerful and proletarian leaders will come to the fore in all the major social struggles. That's what we fight for.

From this standpoint, the changes going on among young workers hold out encouraging prospects for the revolutionary movement. What is happening in the mines, mills, and plants points to a significant continuity with the radicalization that came before. It confirms what we said in our 1971 resolution:

> Our opponents do not think that the young, militant workers who will revolt are capable of ever becoming antiwar, feminist or pro-feminist, nationalist or pronationalist, and self-reliant. If that were true, the American workers would also be incapable either of mobilizing the oppressed masses to overturn American capitalism or shouldering the immense task of constructing socialism.
>
> Thus at bottom our opponents are utopians. They really do not believe that the ranks of the American workers can do the job. And, in practice, for reliance on the workers they substitute reliance and dependence on other forces—the sectarians, their mechanical political fantasies; and the reformists, the liberals and progressive bureaucrats.[9]

Social weight and political centrality

Fifteen. We have also begun to develop a better understanding of the strategic importance of correctly gauging the social weight and political centrality of various struggles and issues. This is essential to the allocation of our forces and the establishment of political priorities. We champion *all* progressive struggles. But in deciding where we should concentrate our energies, we should always begin by stepping back and assessing how a particular struggle fits into advancing the working class to greater self-confidence and organization along the road to political power.

Key to our ability to help transform and lead American labor is our understanding that the oppressed national minorities, women, and working farmers are the central strategic allies in the movement for a workers government. Only by correctly judging the social weight of its various allies, and acting in accordance with that judgment, can the working class exert the maximum leverage in changing the relationship of class forces to its advantage and to the advantage of *all* its allies.

Class consciousness

Sixteen. We talk a lot about class consciousness but it is often quite an elusive concept.

What do we mean by class consciousness? It means beginning to look at society in collective terms rather than personal terms. To see things primarily not as *me* but as *we*—as part of a class. There's no way of turning a worker or anyone else who thinks only in petty individual terms into a proletarian revolutionist. Thinking of yourself and what you can accomplish *as part of a class* and *what your class can accomplish*—that is the jumping off point of class consciousness.

It may begin in all kinds of ways—the pressures that make personal solutions look more difficult and less realistic; the discovery that other people face the same difficulties you do and are asking for help, offering to help, and showing a way to fight together.

Something else happens when you begin to think as *we* rather than *me:* you begin to understand that there is another *we* who are a *they*—that's the ruling class. *They* are the enemy. There's another class that's the enemy of our class. And any policy based on collaboration with that enemy weakens *us* because it strengthens *them.*

Racism, sexism, protectionism, pro-imperialism, warmongering, you name it—all of them weaken our common fight as a class because they strengthen the enemy and shift the relationship of class forces further to our detriment. Any concession to these reactionary ideas weakens our class, weakens our unions, lowers our wages, worsens our working conditions, and threatens our posterity and ultimately even our own lives.

With this understanding, we wage a battle against any of those in our class—usually the relatively better off—who are the most susceptible to the class-collaborationist misleaders of the labor movement and their reformist notions.

As class consciousness deepens, it takes on an added dimension: the responsibility of our class to lead not just the unions but all progressive struggles and movements. If we workers are to defeat the enemy—if we're to be worthy of support in taking on the enemy—we must throw our power behind the struggles of the oppressed for their rights. In providing such leadership, we will improve the chances of strengthening and transforming the unions themselves.

This spotlights the important impact of movements outside the unions in changing and advancing class consciousness in the labor movement. This is essential to our class-struggle perspective.

We say that Black and Chicano nationalism will increase as class combat intensifies and the working-class radicalization advances. The nationalism of the oppressed is an ideological reflection of a specific form of the class struggle. It marks an advance in class consciousness. It increases the self-confidence and fighting capacity of decisive layers of the working class. It provides a sounder basis for unity against the common class enemy, not the opposite, as sectarians and class-collaborationists alike contend.

What we've written about this question over the past two decades is being proven more and more true. Our party learned a big lesson in this regard from Malcolm X in the short time we worked with him. We never met anyone who was more of a Black nationalist than Malcolm X. But we also never knew anyone more capable of working with fellow revolutionists—regardless of color—for a common goal.

That is why solidarity is more than merely a question of proletarian morality, although that is important. Beyond that, however, solidarity is a sign of increased *class consciousness.* It enhances the possibility of unity in combat—unity in the unions, unity in the class as a whole, unity among the most oppressed layers of the class, unity with workers and farmers around the world. Solidarity is a gauge of class hatred of the exploiters and determination to join with all other victims of capitalism in a common fight for a better world.

The 'Weber' victory

The civil rights battles and nationalist upsurge of the sixties played a crucial role in the evolution of class consciousness in this country. The same was demonstrated once again in the recent victory in the *Weber* case.

The battle to overturn the *Weber* decision was a big victory not only for Blacks, Latinos, and women, but for the whole of American labor. The changes in consciousness in the working class brought about by the accomplishments of the Black struggle played a decisive role in making a successful fight against *Weber* possible.

In March 1979 well over 1,000 people attended a civil rights conference called by the United Steelworkers of America. Most of those participating were rank-and-file workers, as well as many local, district, and international officers; Black, white, and Chicano; male and female; young and older.

It was an interesting conference, as the *Militant* article indicated. Comrades who were there can give you an even better feel of the event. Speaker after speaker explained the importance of the fight for affirmative action and the meaning of the fight against *Weber* for working people, for the rights of everyone, and for the union itself. Speakers explained how this fight strengthened the USWA. It was clearly seen as linked with the Newport News strike and organizing drive.

To top it off, USWA president Lloyd McBride gave a speech that dramatically confirmed what's been happening in the American working class over the past several years. McBride's role and character have not changed, but he's had to adjust to the changed attitudes in the ranks of the USWA. McBride explained that "our union is committed" to defending the affirmative-action plan negotiated by the USWA at the Kaiser plant in Gramercy, Louisiana. He called for a defeat to the *Weber* challenge and explained that the establishment of plant-wide seniority by the court-ordered consent decree several years ago has strengthened the union. "Seniority is ours, not the employers," he told the conference. "The employer was using it when it belonged to us."

This is a very important point. Opponents of equality for Blacks and women have often tried to argue that seniority must not be tampered with to correct inequalities in regard to discriminatory layoffs or job upgrading. McBride's comments help give legitimacy to the need for labor to advocate changes in seniority plans to help ensure real equality and class solidarity.

Of course, McBride is not really committed to affirmative action. McBride is committed to only one thing—affirmative inaction on the part of the USWA membership. But that McBride felt under pressure to make such a speech to more than 1,000 steelworkers is proof of a qualitative change in working-class consciousness over the last eight years.

Conferences such as these show that something new is happening in the labor movement. And there are many other examples, as comrades in industry confirm day in and day out.

Along with the big USWA organizing drive in Newport News— the biggest southern organizing effort in nearly a quarter century— there was an important victory for workers at the big new GM plant in Oklahoma City. I was sitting with a cup of tea at about 7 a.m., watching CBS television news the morning after those workers had voted 2-1 for the UAW.

The reporters first interviewed GM management, who said they had honestly thought there had been no chance of the union winning. They said they were very surprised. After all, many workers had told them they didn't want a union. So obviously something had gone seriously wrong.

Then CBS interviewed a few workers—all of them white—who represented GM's company union. They just mumbled and tried to get off camera.

Finally, there was a film of the celebration by the majority of the workers who had won—white and Black, young and old. It was a broad, militant, and proud rally.

These changes among American workers open up new vistas for the social struggles ahead.

Building our industrial fractions

We've learned quite a bit this past year. We've made significant progress in carrying out the turn. We now have the largest industrial fractions in the history of the party.

What, then, are our next steps? How do we proceed both on the political and organizational level in completing the turn, building strong industrial fractions, and conducting more and more of our activity through those fractions? The concluding nine points will address these important questions.

Seventeen. Since the February 1978 plenum, we've said that our goal is to get a large majority of the party into industry and the industrial unions. Comrades sometimes ask me what a large majority is. Let's start with the fact that, according to our current figures, 11 percent of party comrades are asked to be on full time. Another 4 percent are retired or close to retirement. Another 4 or 5 percent are students on campus. That totals about 20 percent.

So I guess a large majority is about 30 percent.

At the beginning of the turn a year and a half ago, the National Committee underestimated the party and its cadres. Consciously or unconsciously, we assumed there was a layer of comrades who—for some vague and unstated reason—should not go into industry. Secondly, we assumed there would be a layer that wouldn't go in—some sizable layer who would personally not want to do what we've all been waiting for.

This has turned out to be false. The lesson we have learned, that the party has taught us in less than eighteen months, is a lesson for the entire Fourth International. We've learned that when the membership and leadership are politically convinced of the opportunities for work in our class, layer after layer of comrades become inspired to go into industry. They get themselves in a personal position to do so and are helped out through the collective effort of their branch committees and local leadership bodies. All kinds of seeming obstacles—this or that health problem, this or that time for adjustment—are eventually overcome both through personal commitment and collective political organization.

Of course, there are extreme individual cases where such a step is not possible. But there are no broad categories of exceptions. Our turn is a general policy, and it *has* to be in order to be carried out to the end. We have former lawyers, doctors, dentists, professors, members of the building trades, teachers, and all varieties of public employees who are either already in industry or looking. Members of the National Committee, the Political Committee, staff writers, and editors have all been released to be part of the turn. Increasingly, there will be a turnover, as comrades in industry are asked to take on full-time party assignments and vice versa.

The turn is universal. Everyone who is not in industry, and who can be inspired and finds it possible to go into industry, is welcome. We'll help get them in.

There's no "balance" whatsoever to our turn. We are putting all our eggs in one basket. Because that is the only way to build the nucleus of a proletarian party, the biggest industrial fractions, the most effective participation in the mass movements and in struggles of all kinds. It is the way to ensure the party the greatest political influence in the 1980s.

This is a deliberately and thoroughly unbalanced tactic—and it must be carried out that way. Or it won't work.

This is not because we think we know the exact spot where the next big social and political explosions will take place, or how many, or at what exact tempo, or in which order. We don't. All we know is that such explosions *will* take place, and that when they do, industrial workers will respond to them. In doing so, they will strengthen the fight to transform their unions and to advance every struggle of the oppressed and exploited.

Our turn is the best way to ensure that we will be part of these battles, that we will be in a position to advance our program and provide class-struggle leadership, and that a revolutionary party will be constructed and strengthened all along the way.

Eighteen. No individual comrade can be expected to accomplish these goals by herself or himself. We are building strong industrial fractions that function as a disciplined team. We carry out our work in industry as we do everywhere else—collectively.

As we succeed in doing this, we're discovering that the self-confidence of comrades gets a boost, as does their overall interest in politics and understanding of Marxism. As a socialist industrial worker, it's easier to grasp Marxism as the generalized interests of a class. Comrades discover a new way of reading everything, fresh angles we probably missed the first time around. Comrades who didn't think they would ever write for the *Militant* are becoming worker-correspondents.

A nationwide party

Nineteen. Our goal is to get into the big plants, the big mines, the big mills, the big rail yards. We want to be in position to work with and influence the largest possible numbers of industrial workers in sizable workplaces and union locals.

But we should also remember that we're building a nationwide party. This country has no Petrograd. The American workers are not going to win by taking power just in Baltimore or Chicago or Pittsburgh. Our class is spread throughout this country, in cities of many sizes and different specific political and social characteristics. The Miamis, the Albuquerques, the Winston-Salems, the Schenectadys, the Salt Lakes—not the Baltimores, Chicagos, and Pittsburghs—are more representative in size and character of the cities where the majority of the American working class lives and works.

Only a nationwide party can be involved in, keep in touch with, and help generalize the experiences of the American working class.

There are hundreds of places in this country such as the Tidewater region of Virginia and the Piedmont region of the Carolinas: areas with no gigantic single cities but with large proletarian concentrations in basic industry—sometimes unorganized, sometimes highly unionized.

Cities such as Miami, Albuquerque, Salt Lake, San Antonio, and Washington, D.C., are all important political centers of this country, despite their *relatively* smaller concentrations of industrial workers. There is a large and important working-class Cuban community in Miami, and sizable Central American communities in both Miami and Washington, D.C. Given the changing attitudes toward the Cuban revolution among Cubans in this country and the developing struggles in Central America, it is important to have branches in these cities for these reasons if no other—and there are plenty of others.

San Antonio, Phoenix, and Albuquerque are important centers of the Chicano population, as is Salt Lake City. Chicanos make up an important section of the industrial workforce in these cities, and there are many undocumented Mexican immigrant workers, as well.

Our party cannot afford to ignore the politics of these cities, or to lapse into illusions that we can "wait until later" to begin participating in the political life of all but the ten or twenty major U.S. industrial centers.

There is another misconception I've sometimes heard—that New York or San Francisco are petty-bourgeois cities, not very important for a proletarian party. This is nonsense. These are major political centers of this country.

We're an activist party, an interventionist party, but we can never afford to forget that we're still a small propaganda party. It is crucial that we maintain and expand a nationwide public presence for socialism in this country through our election campaigns, through regular forum series, through bookstores, through sales of our press, through being out on the street corners talking socialism, through carrying attractive political banners in demonstrations.

If we can't have a functioning unit with a well-stocked bookstore and attractive public headquarters in cities such as New York and San Francisco, then we're doing something wrong. Some comrades may have to drive a way to work to begin with, but that doesn't make us any different from many of our co-workers. Like the rest of the working class, we're mobile.

Unlike the rest of our class, however, we're also willing to turn away from nine- and ten-dollar per hour jobs to move to the unorganized Sun Belt, to go to the Piedmont, to go where the more poorly paid and less unionized workers live in this country. With somewhat less than a quarter of the workforce in unions right now, the conditions in places such as these are representative of those facing a majority of the American working class.

Two guidelines

Twenty. Trotsky and Jim Cannon laid down two basic guidelines that our fractions are finding to be good starting points:

• Trotsky explained the need for workers to think socially and act politically;

• Cannon urged us to talk socialism.

The more progress we make in our turn, the more we've found that these are the best guides for our fractions in industry. We're making the turn precisely because of the burgeoning politicalization and radicalization of sections of the working class. The combination of what is happening to workers on the job and what they see happening to them in capitalist society as a whole causes them to be more and more interested in politics, and more and more to turn to their unions for answers. These are the factors that transform their consciousness and that we must relate to.

We want to be known on the job by our paper; we're the *Militant* people, the *Perspectiva Mundial* people. We've made progress on this. Socialist workers are selling the paper on the job during their own shift and at the gates during other shifts.

We also like to be known as the supporters of the *Militant,* because in that way our co-workers know who we are when fights spring up around one thing or another. This avoids confusion. We're the advocates of the fight against nuclear power. We're the supporters of Black rights and women's equality. We're the people who are defending the Nicaraguan revolution and think the energy monopolies should be nationalized.

Comrades are discovering that being an SWP candidate is one of the very best ways of introducing yourself and your ideas on the job. We want to urge our co-workers to become supporters of socialist candidates. Our comrades can take part in the contest of stickers and tee shirts that goes on in the plants nowadays. We can plaster Pulley and Zimmermann slogans all over ourselves. We can pin a Pulley button next to our Milwaukeegate button.

At the steel fraction meeting a few days ago, a comrade working at Sparrows Point said he has one co-worker whose hard hat says "Vote Socialist Workers" on the right and "Jesus Saves" on the left! That's OK. We can get a friendly competition going to see whether we can get a workers government before the Second Coming.

Another glimpse into the growing spirit of defiance among young workers came up at the Machinists fraction meeting. A comrade said that after the recent DC-10 crash, McDonnell Douglas went on a big propaganda blitz to whitewash the plane. They put out tee shirts with a picture of the DC-10 and gave them away to their workers. One of them took a pair of scissors, cut out one of the engines, and wore the shirt to work.

Young workers are both imaginative and defiant. Our danger is not in becoming too much like them, but being afraid to become too much like them.

Next year this whole country is going to discuss which of the rotten gangs—those of Carter, Kennedy, or some Republican—is going to run the White House. We have a working-class alternative, a socialist alternative. This is how socialist workers are going to be operating in the factories.

Becoming leaders of our unions

Twenty-one. There was some give-and-take in the internal bulletin around the question of whether or not the comrades should seek out or accept union office. Two concepts were sometime incorrectly equated.

Socialists in the unions, of course, seek to be leaders and to take *leadership responsibility.* But this is *not* identical with taking union posts.

There are no hard-and-fast rules on tactical matters like this. But we see no reason to change what we've said over the past few years. Each specific case is a tactical question, but in general we *lean away* from union officeholding today.

But we lean *toward* finding ways of being responsible union militants, union builders, and union leaders. Our aim is to use union strength—and, whenever possible, union structures—to fight for workers' interests. In the process, the ranks will be mobilized and the unions will begin to change.

Sometimes this will take the form of helping to revive moribund committees in the locals—civil rights committees, environmental or educational committees, participating in social committees, whatever. Sometimes we'll help initiate committees, as we've done around the question of women's rights in many areas, or around solidarity.

The bureaucrats want to nip everything in the bud, to keep social thinking and politics outside the plants and outside the union. *We want them inside.*

Our experience is that the industrial fractions that operate most politically and most audaciously are also becoming the best at union work, at participating with their co-workers in job-related struggles, at drawing militants around them.

For example, the Milwaukee Road campaign is being organized through some extremely capable work within the official union structure—an ad hoc committee called together with official sanction. As it turned out, however, the five workers who formed the initial core of the committee were all *Militant* subscribers. We're working with them on the Milwaukee Road drive and they're reading our press—that's a good combination.

This is also happening at places like the Sparrows Point steel mill in Baltimore. Comrades operate openly as socialist workers and are at the same time helping to invigorate the internal political situation in two of the biggest steel locals in this country. They've gotten official union solidarity activities with the coal and Newport News strikes; helped initiate active women's rights committees in both locals; held a union-backed forum on *Weber* at the union hall; got discussion going on plant safety; and helped transform some union meetings into political events that have an impact on the workers who attend them.

The same is true in USWA District 31 in Chicago, where we've been involved in antinuclear and Africa solidarity work, as well. It's true in Toledo, where comrades helped establish an official Solidarity Committee in their UAW local. It's true of many of our fractions.

We do compare these experiences with what the Minneapolis Trotskyists set out to do in the 1930s. That is what we're trying to do today. That's who we're trying to emulate. Like them, our eyes are on the ranks, not on "progressive" union officials. We want to influence the young workers. That's where we'll build our Marxist tendency. That's where we'll find the initial cadres of the class-struggle left wing. That's where we'll win working-class fighters to the revolutionary program and the revolutionary party.

Twenty-two. Comrades have made spectacular progress implementing the turn projected at the February 1978 plenum, before the discussion and vote at this convention. Why? Because the party was politically prepared for this step.

Looking back, the party leadership began preparations for this new stage of party building fifteen years ago. Farrell Dobbs was pulled out of the National Office and onto the *Militant* to help follow the union movement, to write about it, to aid the necessary transition in leadership. Farrell's articles laid the basis for our first major pamphlet on the unions in many years—*Recent Trends in the Labor Movement*, which we published in 1967.[10] It's still available. Comrades should go back and read it.

We made a big decision at the end of the sixties to ask Frank Lovell to come back to New York to help organize our trade union leadership, and we gradually built up a national steering committee of knowledgeable comrades.

Farrell wrote a number of memoranda for the Political Committee on several key questions developing in the labor movement. The whole party benefited from his memorandum adopted by the Political Committee in 1969 on Black caucuses in the unions, their meaning, the interpenetration of the Black radicalization with the labor movement. He also drew up a memorandum, adopted at our 1969 convention, applying our proletarian military policy to the fight against the Vietnam War and the growing opposition to the draft.

The party went through the experience of the Right to Vote Committee in the United Transportation Union at the very beginning of the 1970s.[11] We responded quickly as a national party to the 1969 General Electric and 1970 postal strikes. We were prepared for Nixon's 1971 wage freeze, and the 1973 meat and energy shortages. We recognized the meaning of the explosive inflation at the opening of the seventies and of the 1974-75 depression that followed. We correctly sized up the Coalition of Labor Union Women when it appeared in 1974, recognizing it as a sign of what was coming.

We began working more systematically with comrades in union situations. We developed sizable fractions of teachers and public workers, collaborating with them on a local and national level. These fractions aggressively took up the questions of racism, social service cutbacks, and labor political action that face teachers and public employee unions today. Comrades in the building trades, especially in the Bay Area, did important work, using their union base to build solidarity with labor battles and other progressive struggles. Our entire national cadre gained invaluable experience from these initial battles in the labor movement, and our comrades won respect from their co-workers. Many of them are now leading the party's turn into the major industrial unions.

By the time of our 1973 convention, we wrote in our political resolution:

> While there is no discernible motion toward the formation of a class-struggle left wing in the unions, there are new openings for party activity. Our primary job is explaining the program which can become the basis for forming a class-struggle left wing. . . .
>
> The most important tools for our propaganda efforts aimed at the unions and workers generally are the press and the election campaigns. We should seek ways to utilize these tools in reaching workers, paying special attention to industries where there are contract negotiations, strikes, or where we have comrades working or in contact in some way. Should there be major showdowns in any of this year's contract negotiations, coverage of them in our press will be a key opportunity to explain our program.
>
> Comrades on the job should seek to find ways to present our ideas to fellow workers. In general, our working comrades should be known as socialists, as supporters of Socialist Workers Party election campaigns, and as workers who are uncompromising supporters of the struggles of the oppressed nationalities, of women, and of the protests that have characterized the radicalization in general. They should also be experts on the conditions of their industry and workplace, and be able to discuss these questions in light of the major issues of the economy and class struggle as a whole. Comrades in unions should keep well-informed on the politics of their unions.
>
> There are no general openings in the labor movement at this time that would justify a policy of colonization of our members into the unions. Our best method of reaching radicalizing workers in the unions at this time is through our general propaganda efforts.
>
> At the same time, branches should strive to maintain comrades in

industries that are important to the political life of the city where the branch is located.

Two years later, at the May 1975 plenum where the National Committee adopted the "Prospects for Socialism" resolution, Barry [Sheppard] proposed another step in the organization report:

"The branch organizers and executive committees should consider how they can help guide comrades seeking jobs into important unions and important industries in their cities," Barry said. "They have to think through the industries and union structures in their areas, and decide where we can do political work in the coming period. We have to pay close attention to this job. Where we have comrades in workplaces or unions, we want to form fractions so they can meet and discuss what they can do, even if all they can do at first is sell the press. . . .

"Now taking these organizational steps will not be of any value if the branch leaderships don't make an adjustment in their thinking and organization so that they pay political attention to the functioning of the fractions," sounding a note we've all become acquainted with since that time.

"We don't project any great, spectacular leaps forward immediately in this kind of work," Barry said. "We'll make contacts, begin to recruit, and begin to develop our work.

"We're talking about the beginning of a turn that will develop further in the future. . . . We don't rule out sudden explosions or new opportunities where we may be able to do more work in the unions. But it will take hard work and it will take time to build up these fractions and get them functioning more and more as party political fractions in the mass movement."[12]

All these experiences and discussions found us ready to meet the opportunities of the Sadlowski campaign in 1976 and 1977, and for what some comrades at that time dubbed "the turn within the turn" early in 1978.

So there was nothing sudden, nothing un-thought-out, nothing unprepared. Comrades were never kept in the dark. There were no surprises. Just a steady accumulation of experience and timely responses to changing situations in the class struggle itself.

Of course, we made mistakes. But we never made the mistake of missing where we were going. Some of our mistakes were painful. We misorganized certain things. We didn't see quickly and clearly enough after 1975 that the industrial unions would have to be the axis of our turn. We experimented with different organizational forms on the local level—and paid a price. We're finally getting that cleared up, as we learn what kind of branches, locals, districts, and fractions are needed by a party of industrial workers, a nationwide party, a party that responds to all the big national and world events of the day.

Boston busing struggle

The party's national orientation toward the Boston desegregation struggle in 1974 and 1975 was a crucial part of our preparation for the turn to industry. We met with flying colors the test of a proletarian party—its ability to intervene effectively and decisively to advance the interests of the oppressed. We helped the Boston Black community fight the racists to a standoff and preserve the busing plan in that city. Because of the relationship of class forces in Boston and in the Black movement, the struggle ran its course before a decisive victory could be scored. But a great deal was accomplished nonetheless, as Jon Hillson recounts in *The Battle of Boston.*[13]

The Boston desegregation battle was the single most decisive political combat experience for an entire layer of the party leadership, including a big Black component of our leadership. We won many militant fighters for Black liberation to the socialist movement out of our solidarity work with that struggle—in Boston and around the country. Many of them are now helping to lead the party into industry and prepare the way for a revitalization of the Black struggle under proletarian leadership.

Our ability to respond as we did to the Boston events was part of the proof that we are building the only kind of party that can lead a turn into industry—the kind of party we have today.

Twenty-three. What were the party's conquests of the 1960s and 1970s? Recognition of the combined character of the coming American revolution—the permanent revolution as applied to the United States; the character and permanency of the independent struggles and organizations of the oppressed the multinational character of our party, its composition as a party of male and female fighters. All these are permanent acquisitions.

But our biggest conquest is that we built the kind of party that could size up the changes in its class and *make this turn.* We gathered the initial cadres capable of doing revolutionary political work in our class, taking the lead in fighting to transform the labor movement, and building a revolutionary party of industrial workers.

We're not going through this experience in the SWP alone. This is an international experience, and that's what should be registered here at our convention. We are now making this turn as part of a world party, as part of the experience of the entire Fourth International.

America and the world revolution

Twenty-four. Every major question of *world* politics is also an *American* question. We inherit the final legacy of the imperialist epoch. We are building a party in the great strategic bastion, the stronghold of the vicious world capitalist system. What we do—or don't do—will have a decisive effect on everything that happens in the world and *to* the world.

If we believed that U.S. capitalism and its labor lieutenants were capable of keeping capitalism on an even keel for an extended period, then the tasks the political resolution lays out would be wrong. The kind of turn we are proposing would make no sense.

But we don't believe that. We think capitalism and the ruling class are incapable of heading off the crisis it has now entered. The rulers can deal heavy blows to the workers. But they cannot prevent the battles or stop the crisis.

What about the union bureaucrats? Can they keep the lid on American labor? The truth is that, while the unions can suffer defeat after defeat because of their grip, the bureaucrats are ultimately an extremely weak layer. When our class moves into high gear, we will shove them aside and make way for the militants.

So, the only basis for hesitation about carrying out the turn to the end, at least the only one that makes any sense, is if you believe that, compared to other classes, workers are naturally more economist and workers parties congenitally more conservative. Or if you believe that when you pick up a welding tool or go into a plant, you somehow cease being Black, Latino, female, lesbian, young, or whatever.

That's not an uncommon view among petty-bourgeois radicals and liberals. But it's nonsense. You don't cease being anything you are when you go into a factory—except unemployed. But both as an individual and as part of a proletarian party, you do *add* tremendously to your strength and capacity to think, experience, analyze, and affect what's going on with your class and its allies.

We don't promise a socialist revolution tomorrow or at any definite date. Our turn has nothing to do with prophecies or impatience.

But we *can* promise some things about the 1980s. Trotsky sketched a strikingly similar perspective back in 1921 in an address to the Third World Congress of the Comintern. We plagiarized bits and pieces of this speech in the section of the draft resolution on "The Catastrophe Facing American Working People."

"The question, which is raised by many comrades abstractly, of what will lead to revolution: impoverishment or prosperity, is completely false when so formulated," Trotsky explained. "Neither impoverishment nor prosperity as such can lead to revolution. But the alternation of prosperity and impoverishment"—the good times and the bad—"the crises, the uncertainty, the absence of stability—these are the motor factors of revolution."

The "tranquil mode of existence [of the labor bureaucracy] has also exerted its influence upon the psychology of a broad layer of workers who are better off," Trotsky pointed out. "But today this blessed state, this stability of living conditions, has receded into the past"—as is beginning to happen today. "In place of artificial prosperity has come impoverishment.

"Prices are steeply rising, wages keep changing in or out of consonance with currency fluctuations. Currency leaps, prices leap, wages leap and then come the ups and downs of feverish fictitious conjunctures and of profound crises.

"This lack of stability," says Trotsky, "the uncertainty of what tomorrow will bring in the personal life of every worker, is the most revolutionary factor of the epoch in which we live. . . .

"This absence of stability drives the most imperturbable worker out of equilibrium. It is a revolutionary motor power."[14]

That's what we promise. Nothing less, nothing more. Not the victory of the socialist revolution—that will depend on many factors, including ourselves and what we do. But the battles are coming and the revolutionizing will occur. The 1980s and the 1990s will be marked by mighty battles that will decide a great deal about the future of the human race.

We're also convinced, as Trotsky predicted, that revolutionists of action are going to come out of the American working class by thousands and thousands. They're going to learn Marxism in giant leaps and bounds. So that brings us to our last point:

Twenty-five. Our task is to do just one thing—to build an American party with our co-thinkers of the Fourth International that can lead these working-class fighters in wiping this bastion of imperialism off the face of the earth and open the road to the socialist future of humankind.

Summary

Andrew Pulley and Matilde Zimmermann will be out on the road for the next fourteen months campaigning in the name of the Socialist Workers Party and presenting socialist answers to millions of American working people. They will be campaigning around the issues in the world and domestic class struggle comprising the most pressing questions facing American working people. We'll be finding new ways of popularizing our basic ideas and responding clearly and decisively to whatever emergency questions arise during the campaign—whether they pertain to wars, revolutions, catastrophes, or crises.

At the same time, our answer to the question: "What mass alternative do working people have to the Democrats and Republicans?" will be what it has been since our first presidential campaign in 1948—"The unions must build a labor party." Only this time, we're going to have more ammunition. The need for a break from the Democrats—the need for a labor party—is going to be clearer to more people.

We don't think there has yet been any qualitative change in consciousness of American workers around this question. But we do think events during our election campaign will enable the socialist candidates and their supporters to advance our labor party slogan more popularly.

How should comrades in industry raise the labor party? Unless we run into special opportunities in the labor movement, they will use it as a major aspect of their socialist campaigning with co-workers on the job. It's Pulley and Zimmermann's direct answer to the bureaucracy's proposal to throw resources of the labor movement behind the Democratic Party and all the pernicious effects of that class-collaborationist policy from the shop floor to the threats of war, discrimination, and social catastrophe.

It's something our campaign will educate on wherever we're active. In the unions. In NOW. At speaking engagements. On television, when we get the chance.

The two-party system has served the capitalists well. Once it goes, they have nothing in reserve. The two-party system doesn't have the flexibility of the parliamentary system with multiparties all within a capitalist political framework. This is an important political and historical factor built into the particular mode of bourgeois rule that has evolved in this country.

That's one reason why the stakes are so high in the fight to form a labor party. It's certainly not something that the employers' obsequious labor lieutenants are going to arch off into lightmindedly, especially given the advancing capitalist crisis and growing potential for an explosion of working-class radicalism. That's the *least* likely variant of how a labor party could get rolling in this country.

A break by a significant section of the labor movement from the Democratic Party would shatter that party and disrupt the entire capitalist political equilibrium. The seriousness with which the rulers would respond to such an occurrence was indicated by their reaction to a crisis that posed much less of a direct challenge to their current political set-up: Watergate. A glimpse into their behind-the-scenes maneuvering was revealed July 15 when Gen. Alexander M. Haig—former NATO commander who is now seeking the Republican presidential nomination—appeared on NBC's "Meet the Press." Haig was Nixon's chief of staff during the unraveling of the Watergate cover-up. From that vantage point, he explained to the "Meet the Press" panel, he personally knew that "the prospects for some extra-constitutional solution to that grave crisis were very strong in the evolution of the give-and-take of events of the time."

The escalation of workers' struggles and changes in the relationship of class forces underlying the formation of a labor party would certainly propel wings of the ruling class to give serious consideration to "extra-constitutional" measures.

Despite such fears among the rulers, and the consequent resistance by their agents in the labor movement, the pressures are building toward a crisis of the two-party system. Our capacity to explain the labor party as a realistic perspective is growing.

Given the existence of the industrial unions, we can explain that workers have a more powerful base to build on than did the Republican Party in 1854, when it was launched in Ripon, Wisconsin, at a meeting of antislavery Whigs, Free-Soilers, and a few renegade Democrats.

We'll get a serious hearing for the idea. We'll be able to generalize our socialist solutions on a political plane. The idea of a labor party will become identified with the Pulley-Zimmermann campaign in the plants. Most important, it will help win workers to the SWP.

We should present it in the same light as was done in Pulley's mayoral campaign in Chicago earlier this year. It can make sense in the Black community. It can make sense to women's rights activists in NOW. It can make sense to people we work with in the antinuclear or Nicaraguan solidarity movements. Keeping this in mind will help us project the kind of labor party we're fighting for: one that involves and fights for all the oppressed and mobilizes the power of labor in their behalf.

Our labor party propaganda is not a substitute for any activity, orientation, or program of action for any organization—including the unions. We're not interested in mouthing slogans, but in getting a hearing for our ideas from serious-minded people.

The turn
We had a rich discussion on the turn—what we're trying to do and why. There's another angle that wasn't touched on in the discussion. What we are doing now—driving to get the big majority of this party into industry and into the industrial unions—would be the correct political course today no matter what else was happening in American politics. We're not making the turn because of what is not occurring somewhere else. It's not because we're pessimistic about the possibilities of struggles by students or other sectors of society. It has nothing to do with what we think may or may not happen outside the unions.

Our turn has to do with what is changing in the American working class. When our kind of party has the opportunity to go to the weightiest and most powerfully organized sections of our class and do political work, we have to do it. That's ABC for a proletarian Marxist party that strives to lead the workers to a socialist revolution.

Doing so *strengthens* everything we do. It strengthens the party. It strengthens every member of the party. It strengthens our participation in every struggle of the oppressed.

The turn can only improve the situation of revolutionists and class-struggle-minded workers inside the labor movement. It can only heighten the self-confidence of Blacks and those who want to fight for Black rights; of Chicanos and those who want to fight for Chicano rights; of women and those who want to fight for women's rights. It can only give new vitality to antinuclear coalitions and action coalitions around Nicaragua. When we participate in these struggles, we now have the best opportunity in more than a quarter-century to begin involving the unions and interest their members in our ideas and activities.

The only way we can do effective work in these struggles is by carrying out the turn to the end. We'll see mass actions like we never dreamed of in the coming years! And as members of this party, we'll be part of them. We'll help lead them. We'll help provide them with a class-struggle program and an anticapitalist direction.

As the report emphasized, there are no tactical prescriptions that can be laid down to guide the work of our industrial fractions. But we bend the stick away from union posts and away from involvement in opposition caucuses. There may be exceptions, but as a rule they're premature and not the correct next steps along our strategic line of march. This is one of the points being reaffirmed in this report.

The fractions doing the best union work are also those doing the best general political work. The comrades leading the turn don't see any opposition between the two.

Every time I hear that such-and-such a fraction is doing a fantastic job around some union question, it turns out it's also been selling the *Militant* like crazy and that the branch and district leadership has been helping them carry out rounded political work in an organized way. Every time I hear, "Those comrades have really got a hot thing going around some antinuclear action," it turns out they're also becoming better and better in functioning in the plant and in the union.

We make mistakes. We have some false starts. We get halfway up a blind alley, have to back up, and then head down the road.

But that's just life as opposed to death. That's intervening instead of preaching. That's learning while we act. We actually had no right to expect we would do this well. Remember, the turn just began at the end of February 1978—a year and a half ago.

We'll build our Marxist current in the American labor movement with the young workers. This will do more than anything to strengthen the collective political intervention of our party in every political or social struggle, to the extent our numbers allow. A workers party will do it better than a nonworkers party. Otherwise, all Marxism goes out the window.

This should give us a scientific basis for revolutionary optimism. When we note the growing opportunities for proletarian leadership of the Black struggle, for example, we're talking about a new stage of upsurge of the oppressed Black nationality. That's bound to come, and it's bound to be strengthened by the changes in American labor. These struggles will invigorate every other sector of the struggle, including the unions. They will further affect the consciousness of the entire working class.

The most important message to the 1,500 or so comrades who are carrying out this turn is: *This is your party.* You can and should get your hands on good histories of past experiences in the labor movement and talk to veterans of earlier periods. You'll learn crucial things about our strategy.

But no matter where you look or how much you read, you'll find no advisers who know as well as you what's going on among young workers in the factories, mines, and mills. No one can tell you how our political ideas are faring or what tactics can implement them.

We will build this party through working together to develop fractions that function as a team, building up our national fractions, electing our national committees, and strengthening our local, district, and branch leaderships. This party will be built and led by the industrial workers who are leading the turn and by those who will be attracted in growing numbers to Marxist ideas and join our ranks.

Educating the leadership of
a proletarian party

Toward the end of the second world imperialist slaughter much of the Socialist Workers Party leadership found themselves guests of Sandstone federal penitentiary. In the tried and true tradition of the revolutionary movement, they took advantage of this time to do some serious studying.

The comrades at Sandstone pointed out that among the many lessons we learned from the Russians is that one of the few times revolutionary leaders get to study is when they are in prison.

This neglect is not because of irresponsibility or disorganization. It's because revolutionary leaders always face the responsibility to lead. Whatever might be any individual's intentions, it's usually impossible to take major segments of time away from dealing with responsibilities toward the class struggle. Most of us in this room can testify to this from our own experience.

But if this situation is understandable, and in fact a sign of

The general line of this report was approved by the National Committee of the Socialist Workers Party, January 6, 1980.

SEE PAGE 443 FOR NOTES

leadership on a personal level, it's not a sign of leadership on the collective level.

Remember that among the comrades who found themselves at Sandstone were Ray Dunne, Carl Skoglund, Farrell Dobbs, and Jim Cannon. They discussed this question at some length. This was the period after the split with the petty-bourgeois opposition,[1] when the upturn in the class struggle had begun toward the end of the war, and the comrades were thinking ahead. Just as they saw the need to reorganize other aspects of party life, one of the products of Sandstone was the idea of organizing and planning education in a new way.

They discussed the need to motivate, organize, and take greater collective responsibility for the education of the thinking workers who are the cadre of our party. To organize it as consciously as we organize other day-to-day party work. A special aspect of this plan was to organize the training of the leadership.

Out of these discussions came Jim's letters from prison on education, which reflected the thinking of the comrades there. It was in these letters that the first party leadership training school was proposed.[2]

Revolutionists of action

Leninists are revolutionists of action. And we have the obligation to make sure that we are as well equipped as possible to lead correctly in action—that is, guide our class as surely as we can along its strategic line of march.

For this reason the comrades at Sandstone proposed that the party should systematically take sections of the elected leadership of the party and, for a period of about six months, assign them to cease being leaders and revolutionists of action in the normal sense of the term. The party would take responsibility for assigning them to change the form of their day-to-day activity and to work on sharpening their tools of political understanding and ability to use the Marxist method.

There was another consideration involved in this proposal, a consideration that these comrades knew and understood very well and that was dealt with in some of the letters. Our party, its cadres, its leadership must be able to stand up to the pressures of the long haul.

Most of us in this room have been in the party for ten to twenty years. But this is just the start. Like other equipment, the wear and tear starts to show. If we don't begin to organize the regular retooling of the leadership as part of our education, we will lose some comrades unnecessarily. On an individual level there's no way to force the leadership to develop a pace and mode of functioning that will sustain comrades for the long haul. We tend to strain to the limit and push ourselves. We should shoulder *general* responsibility, as well as carry out concrete assignments. That's why the party asks us to participate in a leading body—and then we push ourselves even more.

This question of pace is very important over the long haul. We have to think not only about how we train ourselves, develop, and work together as leaders, but about how we can make sure it's not just for twenty years, but for forty or fifty years.

The party has a tremendous investment in each comrade. It is hard to measure this investment. But the loss of any cadre means taking a piece out of the party, not simply a part out of a machine, but more like a hunk out of an organic thing. We not only lose an individual, we lose all that comrade's connections with other individuals. There is a break in the common experience and responsibility, a tear in the muscle of the organism.

So the comrades at Sandstone were convinced that this kind of educational plan was essential to sustain us over the long haul.

They raised several connected ideas that I think we should incorporate in our plans. They insisted that education is not the road to leadership. Leaders are those who lead in whatever needs to be done, those who are willing to shoulder more responsibility than others. Over time the party sorts out who it looks to for leadership, who is leading in practice, and this is formalized in elected leadership bodies.

You don't become a leader by educating yourself. No one asks you how many years you have spent in what school, or how many volumes of what books you have read before you're elected to an executive committee or asked to accept leadership responsibility. You can read everything in print by Marx, Engels, Lenin, and Trotsky and that won't make you a leader.

But the comrades at Sandstone pointed out that the party has the responsibility to take those who have come forward as leaders and organize to deepen their education. It must be done in order to strengthen the leadership, to make it better able to serve its function, to shoulder its responsibilities.

Politics and theory

The second point is that the purpose of this school is not to train theoreticians. It's to train revolutionary politicians. The development of theory is necessary in the revolutionary movement. But this is not something we can accomplish in four, five, or six months of the leadership school.

Marxist theory is not developed by self-styled theoreticians sitting down and thinking up ideas. It is developed by revolutionary politicians confronting class-struggle experiences and generalizing the lessons from those experiences and from the past lessons of the workers movement.

How did Joe Hansen, for example, add to our thinking on the workers and farmers government? It wasn't just a bright idea, or even something he derived from a close reading of our Marxist forebears. And it wasn't by sitting down one day and working on it because it was what he was "interested in." It was the Cuban revolution, which presented some new questions as well as opportunities. These forced us to draw on our past theory, and on the experiences of the Bolsheviks and the Comintern, to deepen our theoretical and political understanding of the workers and farmers government. That's the way it always happens. It always begins with confronting immediate political questions.

What the school can do is to help increase the capacities, and sharpen the intellectual tools, of flexible, principled, revolutionary politicians who have given their lives to the movement and who intend to continue to do whatever is necessary to advance the movement. These comrades can come out of the school stronger, more self-confident, and better equipped to carry these responsibilities.

Of course, you don't gain self-confidence by sitting and reading about dialectics, but as you gain in political capacity and self-confidence, you *are* better able to understand dialectics and consciously use the method of Marxism.

The thinking machine

Another good way of looking at this question was developed by Comrade John G. Wright. I first learned about it several years ago when Farrell gave me copies of some letters John G. Wright wrote in 1945 to George Breitman. I don't know how much else he wrote on this concept, but the letters I read are wonderful.

Usick—as he was generally known in the party—pointed out that comrades are used to thinking of the party as functioning collectively in many different ways—as a combat instrument, as a political instrument, and so on. But they don't tend to think of the party as a collective, organic, thinking machine.

But surely this is one of the party's biggest responsibilities. The collective thinking capacity of the party as a whole is more powerful than any individual lines of thought, and more powerful than simply a summation of thoughts. Of course, individuals each think individually. But as the party grows, it must develop not only in numerical strength and political capacity, but also as a thinking machine, as a party that can regularly come together and think out the political questions that it faces. Gearing individual thinking into this process is a proletarian trait.

In addition to being a thinking machine, the party is also a collective memory bank for the working class. It stores up the lessons learned by our class in struggle, generalizes them, gives them a coherency, and draws on them in new class-struggle situations to help advance along the line of march to power. That is part and parcel of being the *vanguard* of a class.

We are told that implementation and administration are often *collective* efforts, but the creation of ideas is always and only an *individual* effort. This is a counterposition often made in bourgeois society, a counterposition that pervades the way we are taught to think. But it is not true. Without the collective thought and views of our cadres, the party could not develop, move forward, and meet new challenges in the class struggle.

In fact, it is only when we see the party functioning in this way that individual contributions can be understood. We all know George Novack's pamphlet on the role of the individual in history, using examples such as Lenin and Castro. But as George also explains, Lenin's individual role—in April 1917, for example—was totally conditioned by his being part of a machine, of a collectivity. Without the Bolshevik Party, his individual role would not have been very important, historically speaking.[3]

One of the things we want to do through the school is to understand this better, and strengthen ourselves as a thinking machine.

Mining the legacy

Another point that should be made is that the school will not be aimed at "criticism." That is, our job will not be to read Marx and Engels to seek out and discover their mistakes. This is quite popular these days in petty-bourgeois circles that call themselves Marxist. Of course, Marx and Engels did make errors, but they can't do much about them now.

The truth is it doesn't really take much study or intelligence or class-struggle experience a hundred years later to spot a few places where Marx or Engels were wrong. The much bigger test of wisdom is to recognize how profoundly correct the fundamental writings of Marx and Engels have been proven to be by the development of capitalism and the class struggle over the past century.

So what we want to do at the school is to dig into, to discover and rediscover, the ideas that guide our movement, to understand where they came from; and to see how, in some ways, we are reliving the same experiences that made Marx and Engels become Marxists in the first place. Of course, we will do this as critical-minded individuals; there is no other way to study and advance.

It's along this line that we will proceed. We intend to mine this legacy to help us in what we have to do—to mine it even more efficiently and more intensely than our comrades are now doing in the coal mines.

Finally, we need to get rid of the petty-bourgeois mystique of "the student." No matter how hard we try or how long we've been in the movement, I think there remains a kind of mystery and fetishism about students that is inculcated by our whole society. If there ever was a class institution, it's education. And attitudes toward education are shaped by this fact.

Most of this conception of "the student" is a myth. Anyone capable of accepting and carrying responsibility in our movement is by definition also a student. As Jim Cannon explained, much of what this involves is unlearning what you thought you learned in the past. The job before us is to organize ourselves collectively to strengthen ourselves along these lines. We agree that all educational institutions are class institutions. And ours will be no exception. It will serve the interests of our class.

The school and the turn

The proposal to launch the school at this particular time runs parallel with taking a significant step forward in the education of the party in general. Comrades remember the decision we made at our last convention to carry out the fall educational program. I think we made progress in this.

And, our steps forward in systematic education in the party are connected with the turn to industry and rooted in what's happening in the class struggle nationally and internationally. Comrades will remember that the proposal to relaunch the school was first made at the same plenum where we decided to make the turn.

We explicitly related the school to three tasks:

First was the process of transition in leadership, which had already occurred on a certain level but is also a continuing process. This related to the series of discussions we had about the expanding leadership experiences of Black, Latino, and women comrades who are leaders of the party and what this means for the strengthening of the party and the turn itself.

Second, we related the school directly to the opportunities and obligations posed by the turn. That is, we saw we had to deepen our understanding of many basic ideas because we had to explain them to other workers, and explain them clearly.

And third, we were convinced that, as our cadres became more thoroughly involved in the day-to-day battles of our class, it would be possible to really learn Marxism, absorb it in a way that was not possible in previous periods, no matter how carefully we studied or organized ourselves. This is true because Marxism is a unique thing. It is the totally self-conscious expression of the interests of a class. The more we are part of that class, the more Marxism is understandable, useable, and indispensable.

So, when we decided to make the turn, part of that decision was to prepare for and launch the school as part of the process of deepening our education. We raised this at our last convention, and now we are setting the date and choosing the first student body.

The role of ideas

I think the political discussion we've had over the past couple of days drives home one of the things we have talked about at our two previous plenums. The role of ideas is increasingly important in the class struggle in this country.

We are at a stage in which the radicalization of the working class does not express itself through any mass organized forms. There is no class-struggle left wing, not even the nucleus of one in any meaningful sense. There is no large political party that is part of the workers movement. There are no radicalized mass organizations of the oppressed with a proletarian line. The working class has no voice, no mass vehicle either for expressing its historical political interests or for representing thinking workers who begin to develop class-conscious ideas.

But we know that this situation cannot stop the large-scale increase in thinking and debate that is going on in the working class. The depth of this process has been confirmed over the past several years since we began the turn.

We know that the great majority of American workers are not socialist. But we do not have to go up against an antagonistic, hostile, or indivisible wall. Whatever name we put on it, what we are doing is pulling together a Marxist current in the American working class. We're doing this through the actions of party members in the plants, the mines, the mills, and the unions. We are pulling this current together by drawing a limited number of people toward us and around us, people who look to us. Another larger layer doesn't necessarily look to us for leadership, but more and more recognizes us as representing a distinct point of view. We attract their attention, and often their interest and respect.

This process of discussion continues to grow and develop, regardless of the contradictory lag in organizational forms. We have no way to predict how long it will take before this contradiction begins to be resolved.

This all takes place in an explosive framework on a world scale. The working class is confronted more and more directly with the question of war and problems posed by the epoch of imperialist decline. These affect every worker in terms of his or her economic life, political life, and personal future.

We have discussed previously the class polarization that is taking place, and we've polemicized against the various half-baked views that lump white workers together with their exploiters as part of the problem. But we also know that this question is complicated. The class polarization is reflected within our class. All workers don't think as we do about an issue or automatically take a class-struggle position. What is important for us is the openness to debate and the possibility to change minds. I think comrades got an accurate sounding of how we can take part in this debate through what we did with fellow workers in discussions and through the *Militant* forums around the events in Iran.

Two sides of one offensive

The key thing for us is to absorb the two sides of what is happening in this country—the side that we have been discussing today and yesterday under the reports on the world political situation, Iran, and Nicaragua; and the side we have discussed over the past six months at plenums and conventions—that is, that the offensive of the American rulers to politically reestablish their capacity to fight a major imperialist war is identical with their offensive against the living standards, working conditions, and rights of the American workers.

The austerity offensive and the militarization offensive are fundamentally one. There are not two separate ruling classes, one that is out organizing right-wingers to wave flags, and another that is trying to ram a disastrous contract down the throats of the Chrysler workers, force the steelworkers to accept being killed in the mills, and so forth.

What has marked this past period, especially since our 1979 convention, is the utter inadequacy, if not treachery, of the entire official leadership of the American labor movement in face of these two aspects of the rulers' offensive. And this includes the secondary leadership who consider themselves "progressives." When it comes to supporting the struggle of the Iranian people, for example, this "progressive" layer of unionists is blind to the *class* issues involved—that is, going along with the employers' foreign policy is a disaster for the working class.

Because of this default in leadership, the working class has been dealt further blows over the last four months. The Fraser leadership refused to fight the demands of Chrysler; the labor bureaucracy has gone along with the various aspects of the offensive against Blacks and workers in the cities, along with the offensive against the allies of the American workers both here and around the world. These blows have weakened the unions. One of the symbols of this, for example, is the employers getting their man, Sam Church, in as head of the United Mine Workers.

At the same time, however, there have been shifts in attitudes, debates, and progressive changes on other issues. Discussions are taking place in the ranks of labor not only on the questions of war and the economic offensive, but on issues like nuclear power, nationalization, and women's rights.

Reactionary probes, such as those by the religious hierarchies, or the evangelical reactionaries, give rise to resistance and debates. One thing that's fascinating, for example, is all the trouble that the clerical hierarchy keeps having with women in this country. The Mormons just had to expel one for supporting the Equal Rights Amendment. The Jewish elders are trying to stop them from becoming rabbis. And the only Catholic clergy who had the guts to stand up to the pope on his visit face to face, were nuns. These are all reflections of the changes that are continuing to occur in attitudes on broad social questions.

But the gap is a serious one—the gap between the need for a response, and the lack of any organized resistance. The gap between the desire for some kind of resistance, and the lack of any vehicles to even give expression to this desire and need. One of the ways in which we can hasten the closing of this gap is by introducing the correct ideas. This will help move our class toward resistance and political consciousness being expressed in an organized form.

The great debate

A great debate is taking place in the American working class—expressed in all sorts of indirect forms. And all the big questions facing the world centrally involve the question of U.S. imperialism. As Trotsky pointed out, its tentacles reach into every powder keg around the world, so that when something happens anywhere in the world U.S. imperialism is shaken.

This truth seems to be confirmed more and more rapidly today. Every big event in the world becomes an immediate issue for the

American workers. It's not only the U.S. ruling class that must have a foreign policy and a world view, the American working class needs its own foreign policy based on its own world view and interests.

This pressure from world events is more and more rapidly expressed in political changes in this country. For example, at the same time that the rulers are trying mightily to move political attitudes to the right and shouting about patriotism, the intransigence of the Iranian people in fighting for their just demands keeps undermining the U.S. government's credibility and authority. Yesterday, there was an article in the newspaper about the second group of preachers who went over to Tehran for Christmas and stayed until January 3. Unlike the first group, which included William Sloane Coffin and Bishop Gumbleton, most of this second group of church figures urged on their return that the shah be sent back to Iran.

One of the spokespeople for this group was Dr. Jimmy Allen, former president of the Southern Baptist Convention and a close personal friend of President Carter. Dr. Jimmy Allen called Ayatollah Khomeini "a man of great principle," and warned that it would be a terrible mistake for the people of this country to accept the caricature of him as an inept religious fanatic. These religious figures reported that they had been shown the wounds of person after person who had been tortured under the shah, and that this has to be the starting point for the American people in assessing what is happening in Iran today.

One of them, Reverend Kirby of Princeton, said, "The Iranian people are angry at the American government, not at the American people." He said the American people must be told the truth. We can only say, Amen!

Three generations of rights

This gap and the contradictory pressures we've been talking about were reflected in another article in yesterday's newspaper, an article titled "Protecting Workers' Rights" by Victor S. Kamber, who is the assistant to the president of the AFL-CIO's building and construction trades department—no flaming bolshevik. His article is a revealing indication of the pressures of the times.

We have discussed previously the changes in the way people in this country conceive of their rights. One way to look at this is that the American working-class movement has gone through three "generations" on the question of its rights.

First came the bourgeois democratic rights, with various limits, which were championed by the working masses more than anyone else during the rising tide of bourgeois revolutions. These include historic conquests such as the right to assembly, freedom of speech, freedom of worship, and so forth.

Then a second generation of rights were conquered to one degree or another during the 1930s. These were economic and social rights such as the right to unemployment insurance and the right to social security.

Victor Kamber says we now need a new national "Workers Bill of Rights"—which would guarantee a third generation of rights. A bill of rights "that would protect the worker who finds dangerous negligence in the manufacture of an airplane or automobile, or an apartment building and wants to do something about it." A bill of rights "that protects the women on the job from sexual harassment and embarrassment." A workers bill of rights that protects the right of private citizens "to speak out on political issues without fear of reprisals from employers or supervisors." Kamber says no worker should be discriminated against for expressing political beliefs, on or off the job, on any issue—whether it's gun control, company management, or abortion.

He says this workers bill of rights should "make it perfectly clear that a man's or woman's private life is just that—private." This means employers should not be allowed to use lie detectors in preemployment interviews, to compile information about employees not related to their job performance, or to use surveillance or private investigative agencies.

He says this is the kind of bill of rights that is needed to extend the rights we have and to make sure working people get the full benefit from them.

Now I don't think Victor Kamber intends to fight for these rights. But this is an example of the contradiction that exists. A part of the union officialdom that has totally defaulted in face of the deepening crisis feels the pressure to come out with this proposal in a nationally syndicated newspaper article. One with which we agree.

This is the framework in which we see the role of educating our cadre and the importance of improving our ability to explain ideas, to relate our ideas to the line of march of the working class—to explain the most basic questions clearly and to the end.

Workers are thinking people. They will be won to a revolutionary party through conviction that that party knows what's happening and has answers to the big questions. That is especially true in the kind of period we are going through today.

Relive the making of Marxism

What do we propose to study at the school?

We propose that we study the basic political works of Marx and Engels, relive the making of Marxism. We should come to Marxism like Marx and Engels came to it. Obviously we can't experience the condition of the working class in England, or the revolt of the Silesian weavers, in the same way they did. But I think as we read and study all the writings and correspondence, we will discover that Marx and Engels were much more like us than we thought—like us and like the people we're going to be recruiting.

We want to discover Marxism as they did: from the proletariat. We want to follow how the working class led them from being radical democrats to being the first Marxists, scientific socialists.

We want to concentrate on the basic political works of Marxism. We want to see how Marxism was systematized, continually enriched, and made a more accurate expression of the interests of this new class.

In proposing that we go back to Marx and Engels to better prepare for this new stage in U.S. and world politics, we are taking our cue from Lenin. In the first edition of Krupskaya's *Reminiscences of Lenin* [originally titled *Memories of Lenin*] she points out:

"Lenin carefully studied the experiences of revolutionary struggles of the world proletariat. These experiences are brought out very clearly in the works of Marx and Engels. Lenin read and reread these works over and over again. He re-read them at every new stage of our Revolution."[4]

Krupskaya's account also contains some good pointers for the school about, as she put it, "how Lenin worked, how he studied Marx and Engels, what guidance he derived from them in estimating our struggle."

All politics was changed

I think a case could be made that Marx and Engels's greatest contributions were political as opposed to philosophical or economic. The role of Marx and Engels as the founders of our politics is often lost sight of because the other breakthroughs they made were so important—discovering the laws of motion of capital and developing their critique of all existing philosophy. We're used to thinking of these as their greatest contributions.

But there was no deeper contribution by Marx and Engels than in the realm of politics. All politics was transformed by Marxism, by the recognition that the class struggle has been the driving force of recorded history, and its logic in our epoch leads inevitably to the dictatorship of the proletariat. Terms like *class, government, party,* and *program* all took new meanings after Marx and Engels. *Politics* came to have a new meaning.

This change in meaning coincided with the beginning of struggle for what has developed into the third generation of rights now being fought for on a world scale. And only with this third generation was the idea even born that *everyone* has the right to be a political person. This idea did not exist in the bourgeois revolutions of the late eighteenth century, such as the French and American revolutions. In even the most radical of these revolutions, political rights were limited according to property ownership, occupational status, sex, or other conditions—not to speak of the status of slaves.

In studying the birth of Marxism we will also be studying history, but in a special way. We want to discover where we—our class, the working class—came from. The modern industrial working class has existed for a very short time in the total history of humanity. It was created at the same time that industrial capital came into being and grew along with it.

It is important for us to see how wage labor and capital had to develop together, and had an interrelated evolution. We will explore the revolutionary impact of the realization that neither capital nor wage labor is eternal. They didn't always exist, they were created by specific forces, and they will be gotten rid of by specific forces. And these forces are created by the existing economic conditions. As Marx put it, capitalism "creates its own gravediggers" —the proletariat.

Secondly, we will see how all wealth comes from us. The exploiters never created a thing, never in the history of humanity. Everything comes from the working people, and it is simply an elementary human responsibility to take it back and use it for the good of humanity.

A third thing we will discover is that no matter how progressive capitalism was in revolutionizing the instruments of production and creating a worldwide productive system, it was a horrendous, brutal, and violent system from the start. We won't read all of *Capital* at this school, but we will read the sections that explain where the working class and capital came from and how machines were born. And when we read these sections, anyone who has worked on machines will recognize a lot of things. Every advance for humanity was paid for in the death, blood, torture, and toil not only of workers but of the whole producing population. This was true from the very beginning.

IV. THE REVOLUTIONARY PERSPECTIVE AND COMMUNIST CONTINUITY IN THE UNITED STATES

INTRODUCTORY NOTE

After the deep 1980-81 recession in the United States and its accompanying sharp rise in layoffs, the bosses opened up a sustained offensive against the rights and living standards of the working class. The top union officials hid behind the results of the 1980 presidential election in order to argue that, with Ronald Reagan now in the White House, little could be done to combat the employers' mounting takeback demands. In making this claim, the bureaucrats covered up the growing bipartisan character and the rightward course of U.S. government domestic policy, a central theme of the documents in this book.

The bosses took advantage of the prostrate labor officialdom to accelerate antilabor attacks and union busting. Contracts containing lower wages for new hires ("multi-tier agreements") and other concessions became the order of the day, not only as a way for the employers to boost profits but even more importantly to reinforce divisions in the working class. Not only did real wages (that is, not simply what the boss pays a worker but what that paycheck can purchase in the face of inflation) steadily decline from the early 1970s on, but outright cuts in hourly wage rates became a feature of more and more union agreements.

During the opening years of the 1980s, the bosses pressed the unions—with the notable exception of the United Mine Workers—into an open rout. Sensing no leadership in the unions willing to fight to win, workers in most cases simply chose not to fight. They voted for union contracts under which the bosses made significant inroads into workers' living standards and safety and other job conditions. The bosses' offensive against the working class in the United States coincided with an escalation of Washington's war drive in Central America and the Caribbean, aimed at blocking the extension of the socialist revolution in the Americas that had opened in Cuba over two decades earlier.

By 1985, the Socialist Workers Party had established fractions of party members in nine major industrial unions: the Amalgamated Clothing and Textile Workers Union (ACTWU), the International Association of Machinists (IAM), the International Ladies' Garment Workers' Union (ILGWU), the International Union of Electronics Workers (IUE), the Oil, Chemical and Atomic Workers (OCAW), the United Auto Workers (UAW), the United Mine Workers (UMWA), the United Steelworkers (USWA), and the United Transportation Union (UTU).

In 1986 the party opened new branches in three Midwest cities—Des Moines, Iowa; Omaha, Nebraska; and Austin, Minnesota—that are located in the center of the meatpacking industry in the United States. The party soon established a tenth industrial union fraction in the United Food and Commercial Workers union (UFCW). These steps were taken in response to a round of struggles by packinghouse workers in the Midwest in the mid-1980s, as well as to strengthen the party's political contact with working farmers and their organizations.

In the early 1980s the meatpacking bosses had launched a major restructuring of the industry. In several rounds of contract negotiations, they succeeded in driving down wages and in brutally speeding up production lines, leading to an epidemic of carpal tunnel syndrome and other repetitive-motion injuries. In face of this all-out assault on their conditions and on their unions, packinghouse workers began to fight back in the mid-1980s.

The struggle of UFCW Local P-9 against the giant Hormel company in Austin, Minnesota, in 1985-86 became an example and inspiration to workers around the country. The Hormel workers faced the combined power of the company, the cops, the courts, the governor, the Minnesota National Guard, and the big-business-owned media. To meet this formidable challenge, workers reached out for support from other working people across North America and even increasingly around the world.

With the connivance and open treachery of the UFCW officialdom, Hormel finally succeeded in getting its concession contract, refusing to rehire 850 of the original 1,500 workers who went out on strike. But the example of the P-9 strikers had opened the way for other packinghouse workers throughout the Midwest to take on the bosses and to fight against the onerous conditions being foisted on them. Although most of these strikes were lost or stalemated, they demonstrated that union power could be used to mobilize the ranks and win active solidarity from other workers and unionists. The pattern of the rout that had marked the early 1980s was broken. Other fights soon followed among paperworkers, airline workers, coal miners, and others.

Among the young SWP members who joined the effort to establish party branches in the centers of meatpacking was Mark Curtis, who moved to Des Moines, Iowa, in 1986. Curtis got a job at the Swift packinghouse there and became involved in protests against racist discrimination, for women's rights, against U.S. military intervention in Central America, against farm foreclosures, and in other political activity. At Swift he was known on the job as a defender of immigrant workers, many of whom were being victimized by the company and the government.

In March 1988 Curtis was framed up on rape and burglary charges. He was arrested and brutally beaten by Des Moines cops only a few hours after he had left a meeting to defend sixteen Mexican workers and one Salvadoran worker at Swift who had been pulled off the line, thrown in jail, and threatened with deportation. No physical evidence linked Curtis to the crime. Nonetheless, he was convicted, largely on the testimony of a cop who had a prior record of falsifying reports. Curtis began serving a twenty-five-year sentence in September 1988. From behind bars, he has joined with his supporters around the world to get out the truth about the frame-up and fight for his freedom. He continues to discuss and practice working-class politics among his fellow workers in prison. In spite of the international campaign to win his release, Curtis remains in prison nearly six years later. An account of the facts in the case are presented in the pamphlet *The Frame-Up of Mark Curtis* by Margaret Jayko, published by Pathfinder.

The final chapter of this book examines the political continuity of the Socialist Workers Party's turn to industry since the late 1970s with the party's earlier efforts during the labor radicalization of the 1930s and the second imperialist world war to build a proletarian vanguard rooted in the industrial unions.

The turn to the
industrial unions

RESOLUTION OF THE SOCIALIST WORKERS PARTY

The capitalist class in the United States is driving to alter fundamentally the relationship between labor and capital that was established following the end of the post–World War II strike wave. That labor upsurge held off the attempts by the U.S. imperialist victors in the war to deal the kind of blows to the union movement that they had dealt at the end of World War I.

The current offensive of the employing class began a decade ago, with the 1974-75 world recession, and has been building since that time. It is taking place under the lash of intensifying international capitalist competition and in the framework of the stagnation of the world capitalist economy and the imposition of a crushing debt burden on the semicolonial countries.

This onslaught, its effects, and the emerging resistance to it by the ranks have moved the industrial working class and its unions

This is the first section of the resolution adopted by the January 1985 special convention of the Socialist Workers Party. The full text of this resolution can be found in *New International* no. 4.

SEE PAGE 444 FOR NOTES

393

to the center of politics in the United States for the first time in almost four decades.

A growing number of class battles, combined over time with a deepening social crisis, uprisings in the colonial and semicolonial countries, and imperialist wars, will transform politics and the labor movement in this country. We have entered the initial stages of a preparatory period, which will lead in coming decades to a prerevolutionary upheaval marked by revolutionary struggles of a kind that workers and farmers in the United States have not waged in more than a century.

There is today a gap between the current experiences and consciousness of the working class, and the radically transformed conditions and methods of struggle that will emerge as social, economic, and war crises tear apart the current framework of relative social stability and bourgeois democracy.

Combative workers today see no political perspective that bridges the gap between today's conditions and the qualitatively changed situation in which the revolutionary battles will be fought that will culminate in the establishment of a workers and farmers government in the United States.

Nonetheless, as young workers go through experiences in struggle of setbacks and advances, of victories and defeats under those radically altered conditions, a growing number will acquire revolutionary combat experience and their consciousness will be transformed. A new class-conscious political vanguard will emerge, whose composition will reflect the changed composition of the workforce, and the weight of Blacks, Latinos, and women within it. These workers will carve out a class-struggle left wing within the labor movement. They will chart a course toward transforming the unions from instruments of class collaboration with the employers and their government into instruments of revolutionary struggle for the interests of working people of city and countryside, and of all the oppressed. They will *think socially* and *act politically,* and they will use *union power.* Under these conditions, and only under these conditions, will the *mass* revolutionary working-class party be built that is needed to lead the struggle for a workers and farmers government.

Today, a worker who understands that the course of the current labor officialdom is gutting union power and leading to a dead end still must make an individual leap in consciousness in order to see the strategic line of march of the proletariat toward power. But even under the impact of today's initial experiences, these leaps can and are being made. Opportunities are being created for the Socialist Workers Party to influence a still small but important layer of the working class and the labor movement, and to recruit to the party the most politically conscious workers. This deepening proletarianization and political education of the party is decisive not only in rising to today's challenges and meeting its pressures, but in preparing for what is coming.

1. Ruling-class offensive

For twenty-five years, beginning in the second half of the 1940s, prolonged capitalist economic expansion made it possible for broad layers of U.S. working people to wrest significant concessions from the exploiters. That quarter century, however, was also marked by the institutionalization of the class-collaborationist methods of the union bureaucracy, and a political retreat of the labor movement. The result was a terrible weakening of the unions. But this fact was hidden, since workers were able to continue wresting gains from the employers despite the obstacle of the class-collaborationist policies followed by the union misleaders.

The officialdom focused attention on the slow but steady improvement in real wages of those sections of the working class already in the strongest unions. The bureaucracy sought to convince layers of relatively better-off workers that it was in their interests to support the class-collaborationist policies through which the unions were being tangled in red tape and their fighting power was being sapped. It did not talk about the trade-offs it made, which further weakened union power. There was no sustained effort to organize the unorganized, including workers in the South. Control over job conditions, line speed, and safety was increasingly relinquished. The bureaucracy turned its back on any fight for nationwide government health care and improved retirement and unemployment benefits for the working population as a whole. Instead, it sought to negotiate industry-by-industry "fringe benefits," more and more tied to the profits of individual industries and companies. The ties that were being forged between the rising union movement in the 1930s and fighting farmers were ruptured, and replaced by efforts by the union bureaucracy to line up farm organizations in the Democratic Party camp. There was no support by the labor official-dom to efforts to organize farmworkers until the late 1960s, when the struggle led by the United Farm Workers in the California fields forced a measure of backing from the AFL-CIO tops.

The misleaders of the industrial unions collaborated with the bosses in helping to keep Blacks, Latinos, women, and other discriminated-against sections of the working class restricted to the lowest-paid and dirtiest jobs, with the fewest opportunities for training and upgrading. When the struggle for Black rights burst forward with renewed force in the late 1950s and early 1960s, the union bureaucracy refused to use the enormous potential power of the unions to aid this growing fight. Instead, the class-collaborationist course of the officialdom all too often led to its denunciation of the most combative and uncompromising vanguard in the struggle for civil rights. All the while, the ranks of the labor movement were becoming more heavily Black, Latino, and then, female.

The bureaucratic misleaders of the Congress of Industrial Organizations drew support for their procapitalist and class-collaborationist policies from the better-paid and highest-seniority layers of the CIO industrial unions. This new labor aristocracy, which had developed within the CIO unions themselves, became the base on which the bureaucracy rested, following the pattern that had previously been established in the craft-divided unions of the American Federation of Labor (AFL).

The labor bureaucracy's class-collaborationist course also found expression in its support for the bipartisan foreign policy of U.S. imperialism and the growing attacks on democratic rights at home. The bureaucracy backed the capitalists' anticommunist witch-hunt, including going along with measures that were aimed directly at restricting the rights of the unions, such as those contained in the Taft-Hartley Act. It backed the U.S. war against Korea. The labor officialdom became a mainstay of support for Washington's massive military budgets. It backed the growing protectionism of sections of the capitalist class as the competitive advantage of U.S. industry slipped in the face of stiffening competition from other imperialist powers.

The big majority of the AFL-CIO bureaucracy supported Washington's war against Vietnam. It condemned revolutionary Cuba and supported the efforts by the U.S. government to bring the workers and farmers of Cuba to their knees. It backed the policies of the imperialist government of the United States in seeking to crush the struggles for national liberation by the oppressed throughout Africa, Asia, and Latin America.

The 1974-75 international recession signaled that the capitalist class no longer had the margin for the kind of economic concessions to working people that had established the framework for U.S. politics for the previous two and a half decades. The years since have seen a bipartisan shift to the right in capitalist politics, accompanying the escalating assault against labor and its allies. There have been more and more takeback contracts. A growing number of these include provisions that for the first time introduce permanent divisions within the union by establishing lower wages and less protection for new hires than for those already working. These "two-tier" contracts mark a significant step toward institutionalization of new divisions that undermine the unifying character of the industrial union structures—a major advance over craft union structures—that were won in many industries through the battles that gave rise to the CIO in the 1930s.

There has also been an increase in open union busting and in foreclosures and brutal dispossessions of farm families. We have seen cutbacks in government social programs; escalating attacks on past gains of Blacks, Latinos, and women; and a sustained chipping away at democratic rights.

These have gone hand in hand with an escalation of the imperialist war in Central America and the Caribbean, and other threats and preparations for the use of U.S. military power against workers and farmers abroad.

CLASS POLARIZATION

During the quarter century of relative economic expansion and stability following the post–World War II labor upsurge, social conflicts were widely viewed solely in terms of conflicts between the "haves" and "have nots," or between Blacks and whites.

Today these social conflicts can more easily be seen as expressions of the fundamental class struggle between capital and labor—between the exploited producers and those who exploit them. Social and political struggles have a more direct and rapid reflection within the labor movement. A broader layer of workers understand that solidarity with farmers' struggles, Black rights, women's rights, and fights against U.S. military intervention abroad are labor issues. These issues should be raised in the unions for action, not just talk.

The ruling-class offensive—carried out both by the employers directly and by their government—will result in a growing tendency for the irreconcilable conflict between the capitalists and working people to find expression more openly in political life and for the unions to be drawn into involvement in these struggles.

Class polarization gives an impulse to the radicalization of the most combative workers. At the same time, it emboldens rightists to make probes, to become more "radical" themselves. Wind is put in the sails of proponents of right-wing views on such issues as Black rights, women's equality, the rights of unions, the rights of immigrants, government social programs, and military intervention by imperialism abroad. Their reactionary propaganda falls on particularly receptive ears among the tens of millions in the middle-class and professional layers who directly benefit from the current policies of the government and big business. For these layers, which have been substantially increased by the recent evolution of the structure of the economy, 1975-85 has not been a bad decade; their economic position has significantly improved.

There is also a growing ideological differentiation among working people—workers and farmers alike. More rank-and-file workers become combative and more politically class conscious, in spite of the trade union officialdom's failure to chart any class-struggle way forward.

But a minority, especially among the relatively privileged layers, the aristocracy of labor, are misled into thinking that various rightist solutions offer a way out for themselves and the section of the working class with which they identify. They look toward collaboration with the capitalist class as it pursues its goals at home and abroad, rather than toward class struggle as the way forward. Those workers who respond to the pressures of the capitalist offensive in this way identify more firmly with the interests of "their" country, "their" industry, "their" company. They become even more susceptible to the ideological weapons that the rulers use, especially all the varieties of national-chauvinist, racist, anti-woman prejudices, and other reactionary ideas that cover up opposing class interests. A similar political differentiation has begun to grow among working farmers.

2. The turn to the industrial unions and proletarianization of the party

An essential part of the strategic line of march toward the establishment of a workers and farmers government in the United States is the fight for the transformation of the industrial unions—the most powerful existing organizations of the working class—into revolutionary instruments of class struggle for the interests of the exploited and oppressed.

During the long postwar period of capitalist expansion, political conditions in the United States stood in the way of effective revolutionary work by socialists in the industrial unions. The political and economic situation that opened in the mid-1970s made it possible once again for communists to advance this fight from within the industrial unions. This dictated a sharp turn. The SWP decided to get a large and stable majority of its members into the industrial unions and to build national fractions of its members in these unions.

Without such a turn to the industrial unions a retreat from the struggle for a proletarian party would have been unavoidable. The party's internationalism, its political homogeneity and centralization, and its revolutionary centralist character would have been eroded. The working-class composition of its milieu, its membership, and its leadership would have been diluted instead of strengthened. It would have become more white and anglo. There would have been even greater pressure on party members who are female to retreat from the demands of political leadership and lose their political self-confidence. The party would have been more susceptible to the pressures of a growing economic and social crisis and war preparations—pressures originating in the bourgeoisie and transmitted through various petty-bourgeois layers and organizations. It would have been more vulnerable to cliquism and permanent factionalism, and therefore less democratic. If a revolutionary proletarian party does not base its membership in the industrial working class and industrial unions when it is politically possible to do so, this inevitably results in the erosion of its program.

The Socialist Workers Party's proletarian orientation and perspective of the development of a class-struggle left wing in the labor movement constitute a permanent strategic axis, which we seek to advance whatever the political situation may be. Under the present conditions in the United States, as in the rest of the capitalist world, the sharp turn to the industrial unions is necessary to advance this perspective.

Structure and organization of the party's turn

The goal of the turn is a large majority of party members and leaders in industrial union jobs and effectively functioning national industrial union fractions.

Over the last six years the party has succeeded in establishing nine national fractions: United Auto Workers; United Steelworkers; United Mine Workers; International Association of Machinists; International Union of Electronics Workers; Oil, Chemical and Atomic Workers; United Transportation Union; and, most recently, the International Ladies' Garment Workers' Union and the Amalgamated Clothing and Textile Workers Union. In those cases where union structures encompass workers in both the United States and Canada, we are building joint fractions with our comrades of the Revolutionary Workers League, the Canadian section of the Fourth International.

These nine national industrial union fractions have become a basic part of the structure of the SWP. National fractions strengthen the party as a nationwide, politically centralized force. Party members who belong to each of these industrial unions meet together regularly as a fraction in the local area, and hold frequent meetings of the national fraction. Local industrial union fractions elect a fraction leadership. The party's goal is for all of the national industrial union fractions to be able to develop sufficient size, stability, and common experience to elect their own national leaderships. This process requires direct attention to the work of the fractions by the central leadership of the party, as well as continuing steps to advance the integration of the comrades in the industrial union fractions into the leadership of the party's work as a whole.

Members of the industrial union fractions help lead not only the party's work in the labor movement, but its political work in general. They lead the party's participation in broader social protest struggles and take responsibility for the committees that organize the party's propaganda work, finances, education, and other tasks. The party's collective experience in industry and the leadership of the work of our national industrial union fractions are increasingly reflected in the composition of the elected leadership bodies from the branch level to the National Committee.

From the beginning, building national fractions in the industrial unions has been linked to efforts to deepen the education of the party in our political continuity with the modern communist workers movement—from its founding in the middle of the last century to its most recent qualitative strengthening with the emergence of the Cuban Marxist leadership, and its further reinforcement by the leaders of the Nicaraguan revolution and the team that was led by Maurice Bishop in Grenada.

Simultaneously with the turn, the party relaunched its leadership school, which focuses on studying the birth and development of the working-class political program and the efforts by Marx and Engels to build proletarian parties and a proletarian International. The party also projected the publication of a political magazine, *New International,* in collaboration with the Revolutionary Workers League of Canada. In 1981 the branches began organizing classes on the political works of Lenin as the central axis of our branch educational activities.

The increasingly multinational character of the working class in the United States, which is reflected in our own recruitment of more members whose first language is Spanish, has posed more sharply the need for the party as a whole to be able to function politically in Spanish as well as English. Circulation of *Perspectiva Mundial,* the biweekly Spanish-language voice of revolutionary Marxism in the United States, has become a regular aspect of sales on the job and at plant gates, as well as at political events and elsewhere. Learning Spanish is a daily part of the leadership school. Many branches have found ways to help us study and improve our ability to speak Spanish. Bilingual leaflets and translation of forums and election campaign meetings into Spanish have become regular features of party functioning in a number of branches.

3. Political axis of party work in the industrial unions

The party's political work in the industrial unions takes as its starting point the world class struggle, the crisis of the international capitalist economy and imperialist world order, and their manifestations in this country. It is these forces that establish the conditions under which the struggle to defend, strengthen, and transform the unions takes place. It is only with this broader perspective—not the narrow framework of union politics—that the road can be charted toward constructing a class-struggle left wing in the labor movement, whose goal will be the transformation of the unions into instruments of revolutionary struggle against the employers and their government.

Members of the SWP in the industrial unions function on three different levels.

First, they are members of the revolutionary party. Like all party members, whether in unions or not, they are constantly seeking ways to promote knowledge about the party and its activities, to involve others in its work, and recruit them to membership. This includes everything from selling subscriptions to *Perspectiva Mundial* and the *Militant,* to strengthening the internal party committees and branch institutions, publicizing an election campaign rally or forum, and explaining the party's views on political events to those who are interested.

Second, as workers, they seek to involve other workers in political activities. They encourage their co-workers to come down to the party headquarters to attend a forum, to join a demonstration that the party is helping to organize against the war in Central America, to get involved in protests against police brutality or other racist attacks, or to read the program contained in the charter of the National Black Independent Political Party.[1]

Third, they are union activists with a revolutionary perspective for the unions. The union fractions of the SWP strive to develop the ability to function as effective units that are integrated into the labor movement. In this sense, our fractions function collectively as union politicians. Their goal, as part of nationwide fractions, is to help forge a new union leadership, which will come forward from the ranks and will fight to unleash union power to defend the workers' interests. They operate within the union structures and realities of today, with a clear view of the revolutionary transformation that will occur tomorrow.

Our union fractions have begun to accumulate important practical experiences in functioning on all of these levels, each of which is essential to carrying out communist work in the unions. We have confronted a wide variety of tactical questions on the shop floor, in skirmishes with bosses and right-wingers in the unions over our fight to freely express our views, in union strike situations, and in dealing with the bureaucracy on the local and national levels. We defend our right, and develop our ability, to function on the job and within the unions as political activists with a world view and a program for our class to defend its interests against the rulers' offensive at home and abroad.

The political axis of our work in the industrial unions centers on the fight for solidarity, union democracy, and independent working-class political action.

WORKING-CLASS SOLIDARITY

Competition among individual workers is the basic condition inherent in the existence of the proletarian class under capitalism. Counteracting this by collectively organizing the workers to defend their common interests against the employers is the fundamental historical role of the unions. This is why unions arose and why this form of working-class organization will never disappear as long as capitalism exists.

Thus, solidarity is a life-or-death question for the labor movement. Solidarity of workers with other members of their own class is the opposite of collaboration with the exploiting class—whose interests lie always in dividing the working class, as well as dividing workers from their allies.

The employers' offensive adds even greater importance to solidarity among the workers within each industry and each union, as well as to active solidarity by the entire labor movement with the struggles forced on individual unions. The need for classwide solidarity as the struggle sharpens reinforces the responsibility of the unions to take the lead in organizing the growing nonunion sector of the working class and fighting for jobs for the unemployed.

The unions should also take the lead in organizing working-class solidarity with other producers exploited by the capitalist class. Labor should mobilize support for working farmers in their struggle for a living income against the tightening squeeze by capitalist landlords and owners of the banks, grain monopolies, and big farm equipment and supply companies. The unions also have a stake in backing the struggles by owner-operator truck drivers against the capitalist owners of the giant trucking companies, oil monopolies, and the banks.

Solidarity includes mobilizing the broadest possible layer of the labor movement and the farmers organizations to support the struggles, and champion the demands, of the superexploited layers of the working class—Blacks, Chicanos, Puerto Ricans, immigrant workers, women workers, and young workers.

This means supporting demands for affirmative action in hiring, training, and upgrading; for parallel seniority lists to combat discriminatory layoffs; against deportations and threats against foreign-born workers; and other demands of the oppressed both on the job and within the unions themselves.

Solidarity also means active participation and leadership by the labor movement in struggles for school desegregation and busing, against police brutality and capital punishment, for women's right to abortion, for adequate child-care facilities, against rape and other acts of violence against women, for the right of political asylum for refugees from U.S.-backed dictatorships, and for bilingualism in education and public affairs.

The need for the U.S. labor movement to aggressively champion the international solidarity of working people is becoming more urgent as the ruling class seeks to place the blame for the growing ills of capitalism onto other countries and the workers of those countries, and as it increasingly drags U.S. working people into a war in Central America and the Caribbean.

The unions are endangered by the increasingly open racist and chauvinist propaganda against Japanese and other peoples of color, which is central to the boss-inspired "Buy American" campaign. The labor movement needs to take the lead in combating the violence and abuse against Asians in this country that is reinforced by these reactionary appeals.

Solidarity means advancing our common class position against our common class enemy on a world scale, refusing to allow them to divide us and set us against each other. The unions should organize support for the struggles by union workers in other countries—miners in Britain and South Africa; garment and textile workers in Hong Kong and South Korea; trade unionists in El Salvador, Grenada, Honduras, and Guatemala; auto workers in Mexico, Germany, Canada, and Japan. U.S. labor should back demands for a living income by working farmers and struggles for land and against unbearable conditions by agricultural laborers and farmers worldwide.

The labor movement must place itself in the forefront of the struggle against the escalating U.S. military intervention in Central America and the Caribbean. The labor movement needs to stand in solidarity with working people in all nations oppressed by U.S. imperialism, and oppose every move by Washington to use its economic power and military might to crush their struggles for national liberation, democratic rights, economic development, and socialism.

Only along these lines can the common interests of workers here and abroad be effectively advanced, and the ability of the labor movement to fight for its interests and those of its allies be strengthened.

THE FIGHT FOR UNION DEMOCRACY

The capacity of the unions to function as instruments of class solidarity and struggle is sapped by the bureaucratic stranglehold of the class-collaborationist officialdom. The fight for rank-and-file control of all union affairs and policies is necessary in order to mobilize union power to combat the employers and the capitalist government. There must be democracy in the unions so that the workers themselves can use the unions to fight for their interests. In the course of their resistance to mounting attacks by the employers, the militant workers will learn that in order to be able *to act* effectively as a fighting unit, they must have democratic control over their organization. They must have the right *to know* all information relevant to deciding on union policy; they must have the right *to vote* on union contracts; they must have the right *to elect* union officers.

Only with this kind of democratic control by the membership over the unions can common experience in struggle against the employers lead to strengthening the unions by forging a more solidly united combat formation, a more homogeneous fighting machine. This was a cardinal lesson of the rich experiences of the Teamsters union in Minneapolis in the 1930s, and of the organizing drive in the Midwest it spearheaded, guided by a revolutionary union leadership.

The fight for union democracy is inseparable from the fight for affirmative action to upgrade jobs and skills; to improve opportunities for Blacks, Latinos, and women; and to end discrimination within the unions. Union democracy cannot be won when members are treated as second-class citizens on the job or in the union. And to the extent that union democracy is lacking, those democratic rights that have been won by Blacks, Chicanos, Puerto Ricans, and women are less secure and more vulnerable to reversal, since the labor bureaucracy's class-collaborationist policy in-

evitably leads to sacrificing union solidarity with the most oppressed, and to allowing the employers to deepen divisions within
the working class.

INDEPENDENT WORKING-CLASS POLITICAL ACTION

The unions must chart a course that advances the interests of the
working class and the oppressed regardless of the profits and prerogatives of the propertied class. That is, they must break from
bourgeois politics. Independent working-class political action is
the class-struggle alternative to the union officialdom's current
class-collaborationist course of subordinating labor's interests to
the framework imposed by acceptance of the profit system.

The labor movement can pursue a consistent class-struggle
course only by breaking through the illusion that the problems
confronting working people can be resolved within the bourgeois
electoral setup. This electoralist illusion is promoted by the bourgeoisie and its labor lieutenants, who argue that "real" politics is
synonymous with election campaigns for public office.

Real politics is the opposite, however; it is concentrated and
generalized economics. It is reflected in all the institutions of capitalist society. But it originates in what goes on every day in the
clash of class forces in the factories, in the fields, in the streets, and
on the battlefields of war. That is where the basic relationship of
class forces is decided. Only by recognizing and acting on this reality can a union leadership unleash labor's political power, and
alter the political course of the United States.

Such a union leadership will think socially and act politically. It
will give a revolutionary direction to working people of city and
countryside, confident that out of the determined struggle to defend our own class interests a new society will emerge.

Independent working-class political action points above all toward the workers and our allies establishing a government that
acts to advance our interests, not those of our exploiters—a workers and farmers government. Taking political power out of the
hands of the exploiters is the only way to halt once and for all the

escalating attacks against the unions and against every struggle by working people and the oppressed. It is the only way to end the use of government power to advance the class interests of the exploiters at the expense of working people. It is the only way to end imperialist war, racial oppression, and discrimination against women.

The struggle to meet the most elementary needs of the working class and to defend the unions' right to exist as fighting workers organizations requires a political instrument independent of the capitalist parties that administer the state for the exploiters. The unions must break from the capitalist two-party system and forge an independent labor party that can mobilize the producers to fight for a workers and farmers government. And they must support every initiative by the exploited and oppressed that is an advance along this road.

4. Strategic perspectives in the labor movement

How does the Socialist Workers Party advance these strategic perspectives, this program, in the labor movement?

We start from the recognition that an understanding of this class-struggle strategy among broad layers of workers can be advanced only in the course of battles against the employers and the government to defend their conditions of work, their livelihood, and their unions, and through participation in political struggles around such fundamental issues as imperialist war, national oppression, the oppression of women, and attacks on democratic rights. We actively participate in struggles on the job where we work, in battles waged by workers in other cities and industries, and in progressive protest actions initiated inside or outside the unions. We participate in and champion all working-class fights for demands for immediate relief from the effects of the capitalist crisis and for better conditions of work and life. We take these struggles to our unions in the most effective ways we can—be it raising them in our union committees with our elected officials, or at our union membership meetings. We seek to mobilize union support and broaden the discussion on what is at stake for the labor movement in each of these battles.

As participants in these struggles, we advance broader social and class demands, explaining them through our socialist election campaigns, through the *Militant* and *Perspectiva Mundial,* through weekly public Militant Labor Forums in every city where SWP branches exist, and through discussions with other activists in these battles.

We pose the need to fight for greater workers control, exercised through the unions, over working conditions and decisions that affect workers on the job.

We explain the need for the labor movement to fight for social rights such as health care and adequate pensions for all working people. These should be government-financed on a nationwide scale, not tied to the bosses' profits on an industry-by-industry basis. The unions should take the lead in resisting the continual drive by the government and employers to make meeting these life-or-death needs the responsibility of individuals and their families.

We advance immediate, democratic, and transitional demands in different ways and combinations, depending on the concrete political situation. At all times, we seek to explain them in such a way as to increase understanding of the need for a change in which classes govern. Without the axis of our fight being to advance toward the establishment of a workers and farmers government, no series of demands, no program—no matter how far-reaching and radical—can be in fact a revolutionary program.

As we go through battles side by side with other workers, we take advantage of every experience in the international and national class struggle to explain that the capitalist system is the source of the crisis facing our class and its allies. We present a socialist perspective to those in the working class who are thinking about how to organize and lead an effective fight to advance the interests of the exploited.

In presenting this perspective, we can be very concrete, pointing to the achievements of revolutionary Cuba, where the workers and farmers took power into their own hands and used that power to uproot capitalism and begin the construction of a socialist society. We can also point to what is being accomplished by the workers and farmers government in Nicaragua today. These examples show what is possible when a government of the exploiters, which defends the interests of the capitalists and landowners, is replaced by a government of the exploited. How much more will be possible in the United States, given its great wealth and industrial and agricultural capacity, not only to benefit U.S. workers and farmers, but to help feed and raise the living standards of working people around the world!

THE COMING CLASS BATTLES

Workers will come to these conclusions in large numbers only through experiences in major class battles. These will include pre-revolutionary and revolutionary confrontations with the employers and their government in which the question of which classes shall rule will be placed on the agenda. As its combativity grows, the working class will test in action, and strip through layers of, liberal, reformist, and centrist political alternatives before coming to the conclusion that revolutionary political action is both possible and necessary. In the course of doing this, millions of workers will reject the class-collaborationism (including bourgeois electoralism) that is promoted by the union bureaucracy and other misleaders of the oppressed and exploited.

There is a qualitative difference between today's conditions—marked by relatively broad bourgeois-democratic rights—and the conditions under which class conflict in this country will be resolved through a successful revolutionary struggle for power.

Every modern social revolution has resulted from rebellion against some combination of war, social crisis, economic breakdown, and political tyranny. Masses of working people will not start a battle of revolutionary proportions so long as there appears to be another, less demanding road to basic solutions. So long as such an alternative appears realistic, electoral illusions will retain their hold on the working class. This will change qualitatively only as gigantic political and economic crises undercut the capacity of the U.S. capitalist class to maintain its rule with its current methods of bourgeois democracy.

As the social and political situation heads toward such a showdown, life under capitalism will become more and more intolerable. Working people will wage mighty class battles, which will be met by the rise of mass fascist movements and a drive toward dictatorial solutions by the rulers. Under such conditions, tens of millions among the oppressed and exploited will turn for leadership to a proletarian party with a strategy to lead the workers and farmers to conquer power by whatever means necessary.

Between now and then, many other alternatives will be tested and exhausted as workers radicalize, suffer setbacks, regroup, and fight again. Illusions will be shed—including exaggerated expectations about what individual socialists can achieve, whether as leaders of a trade union, some other mass organization, or as elected public officials. These illusions will be replaced by an understanding that only the mobilization of the ranks themselves, with proper leadership, can accomplish what the given relationship of class forces makes possible.

To further this process, our industrial union fractions are growing more experienced in keeping the main line of fire on the bosses. We press for official adoption, or at least toleration, of policies that will strengthen the unions and enable the workers to fend off more effectively the capitalist assault on their living standards and rights. We take advantage of opportunities presented by the officialdom, or of any divisions within it, to bring a layer of rank-and-file workers into discussions and into action against the bosses. We refuse to be drawn prematurely into confrontations with the labor bureaucracy. Under current conditions, such clashes between our small forces—whose ideas and proposals are only beginning to get a hearing and to be understood by broader layers—and the labor bureaucracy would make it easier for the officialdom to isolate our current from the ranks.

Our fractions in the unions respond to proposed union contracts and other questions put to the ranks for a vote by the union officialdom from the standpoint of advancing the interests of the union. We urge a vote for those union contracts that would put the union in a stronger position in relation to the employers than would be the case if the contract were voted down—given the existing conditions in the union, the caliber of its current leadership, and the relationship of class forces it must contend with. Revolutionary workers judge such questions from the point of view of advancing the objective interests of the union, not of passing judgment on the subjective intentions, or the propaganda campaigns and other actions, of the bureaucracy. Workers vote on a contract, not on the overall policy of those officials who negotiated it.

It is also from this vantage point that we approach the question of union elections and posts. We view the election of a revolutionary worker to a union position as a by-product of important strides toward transforming some section of the labor movement along class-struggle lines, not as a lever to initiate this transformation. It can be one result of deepening struggles and combat experiences during which revolutionary workers have demonstrated their leadership capacities. Participation in various union committees can, under certain conditions even today, help advance the work of guiding the ranks of the union to a class-struggle point of view through their own experiences.

Election of a revolutionary worker to a position of general leadership or administrative responsibility in a union, however, does not in itself advance the fight to transform the labor movement.

Such an advance requires a union membership with a certain common experience in struggle and level of consciousness. In and of itself, taking a post has no power to advance the working class in this direction. Acting as though it does is an obstacle to accomplishing what can and must be done today to help bring to bear the power of the ranks in deciding the course of the unions and acting collectively on that basis. Such an approach inevitably leads to prettying up the political character of the "team" a revolutionary worker who takes a post is part of, and condemning the ranks for their lack of appreciation for the efforts of these officials.

We base ourselves among the young workers especially, those who are most combative and politically conscious. We look toward the mobilization, organization, and heightened class awareness of these workers.

TASKS OF THE PARTY

Workers cannot develop revolutionary political conclusions by generalizing from their own struggle and experiences alone. That is why the party has an indispensable role to play. As we go through struggles along with other workers, we present an outlook that generalizes from experiences in different industries, regions, countries, and periods in the history of the modern international class struggle.

Our strategy starts with the actually unfolding line of march of the working class in the leadership of its exploited allies. We do not start with utopian blueprints, electoral schemes, or any other nostrums. We have no unique "identity" that sets us apart from this line of march. We present a course that leads toward the transformation of the unions, and we seek to advance the development of a class-struggle left wing in the unions to fight for this goal. Today we are building our tendency in the industrial unions among those workers who can be won to this course and to the revolutionary party.

Today there is already a layer of workers around the country who have gotten to know and respect party members and the SWP. They are attracted to our press and other activities, and agree with many of our views. Most initially see no road, however, connecting what we do and say today with a winnable fight for a workers and farmers government. Seeking to win those politicized workers to see that road, and to act on those convictions by joining our movement, is a task of the party as a whole, not just the industrial union fractions.

It is the branches that have the responsibility to recruit workers, integrate them into the party, and educate them as worker-bolsheviks. This underlines the importance of branches as politically rounded units in a party increasingly composed of industrial workers organized in national union fractions.

It is the task of the party as a whole, not just the union fractions, to implement our perspectives and organize our participation in political struggles against imperialist war, for Black rights, for women's emancipation, and around the broad range of other social and political questions facing working people. Without this our national union fractions could not function as *political* units. Our fractions in each area could not have a prioritized set of political campaigns to implement, as local units of national fractions. Party campaigns would become narrowed to what the fractions alone could do, and unbearable strains on the fractions would develop.

The party carries out this political task on four fronts.

First, through participation in propaganda actions. This includes not only participation in demonstrations, protest rallies, and action coalitions, but also in national and local gatherings of organizations such as the National Black Independent Political Party, National Organization for Women, Coalition of Black Trade Unionists, and the Coalition of Labor Union Women. Party members join these organizations, and branches and leadership bodies participate in carrying out our political work with these organizations.

Second, the party organizes and sustains a variety of propaganda institutions to help bring socialist views to the widest possible layers of working people. These include the weekly Militant Labor Forums sponsored by the branches, as well as our branch bookstores. Our national, state, and local socialist election campaigns provide an important way to reach larger numbers of working people.

Third, the party organizes weekly circulation of the *Militant* and *Perspectiva Mundial*, which tell the truth about major national and international developments, and advance our class proposals to working people about how to move forward.

Fourth, the party aids the union fractions in implementing this perspective and carrying out these activities in the plants and in the unions.

5. Deepening the turn to the industrial unions

Based on the initial experiences of our industrial union fractions since 1978, the party has taken several new steps over the past few years to deepen the turn.

One of these new steps was adopting the goal of organizing weekly plant-gate sales of *Perspectiva Mundial* and the *Militant* as a norm of membership.

Our goal is to achieve regular weekly contact by every party member with industrial workers, especially those in unions where we are building national fractions. This is another step toward integrating the entire party into the turn—those who are part of industrial union fractions and those who are not, those employed and those laid off—and thus deepening our proletarian orientation. The weekly plant-gate sales are an important way to influence and recruit industrial workers, which is the only way to establish the party as a tendency in the labor movement over the long run.

These plant-gate sales are carried out by teams of branch members. They are part of the weekly rhythm of party activity in every branch. Regular sales at the plant gates help the branches to become familiar with industrial worksites other than those where we currently have members working, as well as to find out about possible job openings. They can help inspire and convince new layers of the membership to join the jobs committees and become part of our industrial union fractions. They enable the party to keep in touch with workers in factories where all or many of our members have been laid off for the time being, or where we have not yet been able to get members hired. And they make it easier to learn of plans for hiring in these plants, facilitating the work of branch jobs committees.

Weekly sales at plants where we already have members employed are an important complement to the political work of the fractions. The regular circulation of our press to the workers at these workplaces is the collective responsibility of the party, not just the industrial union fractions. Only fraction members sell on the job, carry out day-to-day political work there, and participate in union discussions and activities. They are not the only party members, however, who sell the *Militant* and *Perspectiva Mundial* at the factory gate, talk to workers about politics, and bring them to party events and other activities that we are participating in and supporting. In addition, it is valuable for party members in one industrial fraction to get to know workers in other industries by selling at another factory.

A second aspect of deepening the turn has been the establishment of two new industrial union fractions, in the International Ladies' Garment Workers' Union and the Amalgamated Clothing and Textile Workers Union. These new fractions advance the proletarianization of the party. The ILGWU and ACTWU are two of the largest industrial unions in the United States, and they play an important role in the labor movement in both the United States and Canada. Through our orientation to these unions, we are becoming part of a section of the working class that is composed of many recent immigrants and members of oppressed nationalities, and is generally paid wages lower than workers in other industrial unions.

A third product of the turn to industry has been the party's growing knowledge about and orientation toward the struggles and organizations of working farmers. We have begun to meet farmers who hold industrial jobs in order to make a living income and try to keep their land. Over the past few years, we have developed ties with farmers through our election campaigns and other propaganda vehicles, through participation as party members in their struggles, and also as members of industrial unions seeking ways to strengthen links of solidarity and united action between the labor movement and farmers organizations. We have expanded our contact with, and knowledge about, organizations of working farmers. And we have recruited to the party the first of a new generation of farmers who are revolutionaries.

Most recently, we have broadened our political contact with agricultural wage laborers, especially in California, Texas, and throughout the Southwest. We are increasing our political attention to farmworkers' struggles there today. The big majority of these workers are Spanish-speaking, many are immigrants, and all work for low wages and under arduous conditions.

6. For a workers and farmers government

The geographical expansion of the party parallel with the turn to the industrial unions expanded our knowledge about the class structure of the United States. This has encouraged us to learn more about the important place that independent commodity producers occupy in the production of food and fiber in this country. As a result, we have begun to reconquer what previous generations of Marxist revolutionists had explained about the ways in which working farmers are exploited by capital, and the foundation this lays for a fighting worker-farmer alliance against the exploiters.

These experiences led to the decision by the SWP National Committee to propose that the August 1984 convention change the party's transitional governmental slogan from "For a workers government," to "For a workers and farmers government." This change had been adopted by the National Committee in 1982, when it approved the general line of the report, "For a Workers and Farmers Government in the United States." This report was then adopted by the August 1984 party convention.[2]

Our discussion of this proposed change helped us to better understand the need to make the alliance between the workers and the farmers central to our governmental perspective, and to see more clearly how this governmental perspective is integrally tied to our political response to the capitalist offensive against working people at home and abroad.

A second decision, related to the first, is the change in the SWP's statement of purpose. Article II of the Constitution of the Socialist Workers Party has up to now read: "The purpose of the party shall be to educate and organize the working class for the abolition of capitalism and the establishment of a workers government to achieve socialism." In adopting the document, "For a Workers and Farmers Government in the United States," the National Committee approved changing this wording in the party's constitution.

The amended statement of purpose, adopted by the August 1984 convention, reads: "The purpose of the party shall be to educate and organize the working class in order to establish a workers and farmers government, which will abolish capitalism in the United States and join in the worldwide struggle for socialism."

This change accomplishes two things. First, it brings the sequence of events into an order that cannot be misread as projecting the abolition of capitalism before the establishment of a workers and farmers government. The amendment makes it clear that the abolition of capitalism is a task of the new workers and farmers government. We need to establish a revolutionary government before the abolition of capitalism can be carried out.

Second, the new version places the proper emphasis on the fact that the workers and farmers government in the United States will advance toward socialism *along with* the workers and farmers of the whole planet, not ahead of them. The revolutionary government in the United States will place the vast productive power of the U.S. economy at the service of the peoples of the world, especially those in Africa, Asia, and Latin America. By emphasizing that the construction of socialism in this country will be part of this worldwide battle, the amendment underlines the internationalist perspective that guides our party.

Communist continuity
in the United States

RESOLUTION OF THE SOCIALIST WORKERS PARTY

The implementation of the turn to the industrial unions has resulted in some of the biggest changes in the Socialist Workers Party in its history. These changes are made possible by the new opportunities to take strides along the course our party set out on at its beginning.

The aim of the SWP at its founding in 1938 was to construct a proletarian communist party in this country, based in the unions of the industrial working class, which were then on the rise. The party sought to continue the course our founding leaders charted in 1928 when they were expelled by the Stalinist leadership of the Communist Party.

The founding of the SWP was seen as part of building a proletarian leadership of the world revolution, part of advancing the process in each country of constructing revolutionary workers parties committed to implementing the course begun by the

This is section 4 of the resolution adopted by the January 1985 special convention of the Socialist Workers Party. The full text of this resolution can be found in *New International* no. 4. *SEE PAGE 444 FOR NOTES*

Communist International in its first five years, led by the Bolshevik team around Lenin.[-]

In line with that perspective, the SWP played a leading role in 1938 in the founding conference of the Fourth International. The program of this new world organization, James P. Cannon explained, was not based on any "new revelation." It proposed not "a new doctrine, but the restoration, the revival, of genuine Marxism as it was expounded and practiced in the Russian revolution and in the early days of the Communist International."[2]

In 1933 we became convinced by the course of the world class struggle and the role of the Comintern in it that these revolutionary perspectives could no longer be advanced in this country or on a world scale by centering efforts on seeking ways to argue within the Comintern or its parties with the aim of winning a majority committed to reforming these organizations and returning them to a consistent internationalist course of aiding and advancing the fight against imperialism. The establishment of the SWP, and our party's participation in founding the Fourth International, reaffirmed this assessment that the next step forward in the development of genuine communist leadership in this country and internationally would be taken by forces emerging outside the Stalinized Comintern. It would be taken by vanguard workers and farmers generalizing their experiences in revolutionary struggles against exploitation, imperialist domination, and the tyrannical oppression of regimes upholding the rule of the propertied classes.

The correctness of this assessment, and of the political course and organizational conclusions flowing from it, was confirmed by the Cuban revolution in 1959. Throughout the previous two decades, even where parties with origins in the Stalinized Comintern stood at the head of victorious workers and farmers revolutions in Europe and Asia, their leaderships remained primarily within a nationalist framework and did not chart an internationalist course in action.

The emergence of the leadership of the Cuban revolution, however, marked a break from this pattern of "national Communism." It signaled the revival of internationalism not only in political line but in deeds. This leadership did not have its origins as a political current in Stalin's Comintern. It was forged in a political battle against the line of the Stalinist party in Cuba. In the twenty-five years since the conquest of power, it has built a proletarian Communist party.

The development of revolutionary leadership in the Americas has been reinforced since 1979 by the Sandinista National Liberation Front in Nicaragua, which waged a political battle against Stalinist policies in the fight to overthrow Somoza and in the subsequent six years as the leadership of a workers and farmers government.[3] The leadership team around Maurice Bishop also brought fresh forces into this process prior to the overthrow of Grenada's workers and farmers government by the Stalinist Coard faction.[4]

Although so far there have been no parallel advances toward the construction of mass internationalist revolutionary leaderships outside the Americas, the course followed by the Cuban CP and initiated by the FSLN demonstrates the correctness of the decision forty-seven years ago to launch the Fourth International with the goal of advancing the fight to build a new mass revolutionary International.

1. Political foundations of the SWP

The SWP at its founding continued along the line of march charted by the Bolshevik leadership of the Comintern and by the communists in the United States who had tried to learn from, apply, and organize a proletarian party around that perspective in the 1920s. The course on which we started out can be summed up as follows:

1. The SWP's founding convention set the goal of proletarianizing the party. It decided on a turn to industry and the industrial unions as the foundation on which all other accomplishments would be built:

The delegates decided that a "complete reorientation of our party, from the membership up to the leadership and back again, is absolutely imperative and unpostponable. . . . The energies of the party must be devoted mainly to rooting itself in the trade unions, becoming an inseparable part of the trade unions and their struggles."[5] No exception was made for teachers, white collar workers, or college graduates.

"We will not succeed in rooting the party in the working class," the political resolution adopted by that convention said, "much less to defend the revolutionary proletarian principles of the party from being undermined, unless the party is an overwhelmingly proletarian party, composed in its decisive majority of workers in the factories, mines, and mills."

2. This turn was essential to prepare the party to stand up against intensifying bourgeois pressure as the imperialist ruling classes headed toward war.

The coming imperialist war "will be the severest test of all organizations and policies," the 1938 political resolution said. The party "can meet this test only by the rigid safeguarding of the Marxian principles of revolutionary internationalism upon which it is founded."[6]

In contrast to the social democrats and Stalinists, the SWP refused to subordinate the interests of the working people and the oppressed nationalities, in the United States and on a world scale, to the war aims of the "democratic" imperialists. The SWP advanced the Leninist strategy of revolutionary struggle against all the imperialist regimes, whether "democratic" or fascist, first and foremost against one's own.

"Above all it should be borne in mind," the convention declared, "that if the party is to survive the coming war, with its certain persecution and hounding of the revolutionary movement, if the party is to fulfill its great tasks during the war . . . the party membership must be solidly and inseparably connected with the working class." Stressing the point that party fractions in the industrial unions would not be limited to carrying out socialist and antiwar propaganda, but would be part of the organized labor movement seeking to hasten the revolutionary transformation of the unions, the convention added: "There is no better way of accomplishing this connection than by every member becoming an active, responsible, and influential trade unionist."[7]

With the approach of the war, this line was put to the sharpest possible test. The SWP stood firm, though a petty-bourgeois minority buckled and then cracked, splitting away from the party and the Fourth International. The SWP adopted a proletarian military policy to fit the conditions it faced as a minority within the working class and the labor movement in its opposition to the war. Party members served when drafted into the army, along with the rest of their generation. Those conscripted sought all opportunities to explain their antiwar, antiracist, and prolabor views within the armed forces, and defended their democratic rights, and the rights of all citizen-soldiers, to express themselves.

For their opposition to the imperialist war, eighteen leaders of the SWP and the Teamsters union were sent to prison, convicted on charges—under the newly adopted Smith Act—of conspiring to advocate the overthrow of the government by force and violence. Throughout the defense campaign for the party and its class-war prisoners, the SWP sought to popularize the Marxist views for which it was being persecuted, while at the same time mobilizing the broadest possible united action of the labor movement, the Black community, and other supporters of democratic rights to defend the fundamental liberties that were at stake.

3. Central to the SWP's revolutionary internationalist principles was its defense of the Soviet workers state. The convention reaffirmed the communist position that the nationalized industry and land that form the economic foundation of the Soviet Union are a mighty conquest of the world proletariat. Although usurped politically and oppressed by a petty-bourgeois bureaucratic caste, the proletariat remains the ruling class in the Soviet Union. The workers of the world have an enormous stake in defending this proletarian bastion against imperialism.

This position, adopted by the founding convention of the SWP, was challenged there by a small minority of delegates, and in the following eighteen months a full-fledged battle erupted in the party over this question. A petty-bourgeois opposition in growing panic sought to free itself from this proletarian internationalist framework, capitulating to mounting social-imperialist and anti-Soviet moods then sweeping radical middle-class circles. The proletarian cadre of the party defeated this revisionist attack, and the petty-bourgeois opposition split from the party. This political battle could not have been won had the SWP not been uncompromisingly pursuing its orientation toward basing itself in the industrial working class and advancing the application of proletarian organizational norms. The lessons of this chapter from party history are collected in *In Defense of Marxism* by Leon Trotsky and *The Struggle for a Proletarian Party* by James P. Cannon.

The SWP's understanding of what was at stake for workers and farmers in defending the Soviet Union better armed us to draw correct conclusions from the course of events during and after World War II. We have learned that state property, economic planning, and the other historic gains established through the expropriation of the capitalist class by the workers and farmers are even more durable than we had anticipated.

The course of the international class struggle since the opening of World War II has convinced us that we can rule out the possibility, which Trotsky had left open throughout the 1930s, that a section of the petty-bourgeois bureaucratic caste can restore capitalist property relations and become a new exploiting ruling class. Despite the parasitism of the caste and its aping of bourgeois consumption habits, it is too weak to try to overthrow state property—too weak both in relation to the workers and farmers, who are committed to preserving their social and economic conquests, and in relation to the imperialist powers, who are committed to crushing the workers states when history presents an opportunity.

In the face of the permanently aggressive stance of world imperialism, these bureaucratic castes must defend the workers states, although they do so with counterrevolutionary and anti-internationalist methods that are self-defeating in the long run. The conquests of the workers and farmers, however, have proven strong enough to withstand the corrosive effects of the Stalinist policies of the bureaucratic castes. The imperialists have not been able to overthrow any workers state and reimpose capitalism on the workers and farmers of those countries.

The continued existence of the dictatorship of the proletariat in the Soviet Union, and the establishment of workers states in a dozen other countries since World War II, has fundamentally altered the relationship of class forces on a world scale. It is a weighty factor on the side of all those fighting imperialist domination and capitalist exploitation. Each new blow against the world imperialist order weakens the pressure of imperialism on the workers states and strengthens the hand of the workers and farmers against the privileged bureaucratic castes in the countries where they have usurped political power from the producers.

4. The SWP refused to subordinate the fight for the independence and national liberation of India, Indochina, and other African, Asian, and American colonial possessions to the class-collaborationist bloc with "democratic" imperialist governments advocated by the social democrats and Stalinists. It supported China's war of national liberation against Japan, in contrast to the ultraleft "neutral" position taken by those who split from the party. The party called for the immediate and unconditional independence of Puerto Rico. It championed the struggle of the colonial peoples on a world scale against imperialist oppression regardless of whether their imperialist overlord wore a bourgeois-democratic or a fascist uniform.

The Transitional Program, our basic programmatic document adopted in 1938, explained that the battle against imperialist domination and landlord-capitalist oppression in the colonial world would be waged "under the slogans of revolutionary democracy." Only governments based on the workers and peasants "are capable of bringing the democratic revolution to a conclusion and likewise opening an era of socialist revolution.

"The relative weight of the individual democratic and transitional demands in the proletariat's struggle, their mutual ties and their order of presentation, is determined by the peculiarities and specific conditions of each backward country and, to a considerable extent, by the *degree of* its backwardness."[8]

The SWP rejected what the Comintern in Lenin's time had precisely summed up as "the traditions of the Second International, which in reality recognized the existence only of people with white skin."[9] We embraced and acted on Trotsky's view that our world movement "can and must find a way to the consciousness of the Negro workers, the Chinese workers, the Indian workers, and all the oppressed in the human ocean of the colored races to whom belongs the decisive word in the development of humanity."[10]

5. In line with this position, the SWP fought unconditionally for the right of self-determination for the oppressed Black nationality in the United States. The party recognized the vanguard role that Black workers and the Black struggle would play in the transformation of the labor movement and the revolutionary transformation of this country. As Trotsky expressed it, Afro-Americans, because of their position as an oppressed nationality and the most oppressed section of the working class, "will proceed through self-determination to the proletarian dictatorship in a couple of gigantic strides, ahead of the great bloc of white workers."[11]

Throughout World War II, the SWP joined in the fight against every aspect of racism in the armed forces—from the daily indignities Black GIs faced to the institutionalized segregation of the military. In the first years of the war Blacks were kept in Jim Crow units assigned the filthiest and often most dangerous duties. In contrast to the course of the SWP, the Stalinists and the social democrats urged that struggles against racial oppression be subordinated to the war effort, arguing that equal rights for Blacks at home would have to wait until the "war for democracy" abroad was won.

6. The SWP recognized the need for a fighting alliance between

the working class and the exploited farmers, and adopted as our governmental perspective the call for a workers and farmers government in the United States.

Initially in 1938, the SWP had adopted the slogan, "For a workers government." That same year, however, Trotsky informed SWP leaders that he considered this slogan to be a serious mistake, and urged the party to change it to "For a workers and farmers government." Trotsky stressed the importance of the alliance with working farmers in overthrowing the rule of "America's sixty families." Following a discussion, the party adopted this proposal.

After a debate in the National Committee, the SWP also adopted the call for a labor party based on the trade unions, as a way to advance the revolutionary fight for independent working-class political action. We presented the labor party as the next giant step forward in the big class battles that were forging the CIO. We explained the labor party as a political instrument of the working class to struggle for a revolutionary program in the interests of the exploited, leading to the establishment of a workers and farmers government.

Our movement's experiences in the mid- and late-1930s as part of the leadership team of the Minneapolis Teamsters strikes and subsequent Midwest Teamster organizing drives provided valuable lessons for the party in developing our understanding of a proletarian military policy in the internationalist fight against imperialist war, the fight against rightist and fascist reaction, the alliance with exploited farmers, a revolutionary approach to advancing independent labor political action, and the fight for a workers and farmers government.

Grounded in these experiences from the SWP's founding years, we have learned that an understanding of the irreplaceable character of an alliance with the farmers is also essential to developing a strategy to combat divisions within the working class, build alliances with the oppressed nationalities and women, and on that basis construct a party that is proletarian both in program and in the composition of its membership and its leadership.

Armed with this understanding, our members today can understand more completely Fidel Castro's explanation following the 1980 congress of the Cuban Communist Party that the growing percentage of the party made up of workers "means that our Party has become more proletarian and, therefore, more Marxist-Leninist and more revolutionary."[12] An important part of this advance, he explained, was the incorporation into the party and into the party leadership of more women, more farmers, and more leaders of the neighborhood-based Committees for the Defense of the Revolution. A notable step was the inclusion of the president of the National Association of Small Farmers as an alternate member of the Political Bureau, registering a further step forward in solidifying the alliance between the workers and the farmers. This registered the understanding of the Cuban leadership that the worker-farmer alliance is necessary to maintain the strength and unity of both the proletarian vanguard party and the workers state.

7. The SWP learned from Trotsky the Bolshevik lesson about the need to explain to the working class why the labor movement has to think socially and act politically. We acted on this, seeking to carry out the imperative of the Transitional Program, in the 1938 founding document of the Fourth International, that its parties "should seek bases of support among the most exploited layers of the working class," and should, "Open the road to the youth! Turn to the woman worker!"

Our aim was to build a workers party that—in the composition of its membership and leadership, its priorities, and its daily work—oriented to the most exploited and oppressed working people in city and countryside. We combated all expressions of national chauvinism, hidebound craft-union consciousness, and social patriotism—bourgeois attitudes promoted by the petty-bourgeois labor bureaucracy within the working class, especially among its most privileged layers, the labor aristocracy.

8. The SWP saw the turn to industry and the industrial unions as the road to becoming more political, more proletarian, and

thus a more politically homogeneous and centralized campaign party. This turn would lessen the influence inside the party of the traits dominating organizations with a petty-bourgeois composition—cynicism, criticism for the sake of criticism, individualistic resistance to collective effort, disdain for collective accomplishments, preoccupation with personal "roles" in the party, and moods of hysteria and despair under pressure. Proletarianization of the party would strengthen its firmness, seriousness, and democratic character as a revolutionary centralist combat organization of its class. It would lessen tendencies toward cliquism and permanent factionalism, which always diminish workers democracy. Members of the party leading the turn and active in the industrial fractions would be responsible for and take leadership in all aspects of party work, strengthening its professionalism and safeguarding its proletarian norms of functioning.

2. Impact of the 1978 turn to the industrial unions

This proletarian program and Leninist strategy has remained the bedrock of the SWP since its origin, in spite of the unfavorable conditions under which the party has often had to function, and despite whatever tactical adjustments and detours were necessary to continue to advance this strategy.

Beginning with the end of the post–World War II strike wave, the labor movement entered a period of political retreat. During this retreat, SWP members in the industrial unions continued to participate in union struggles and to talk socialism to fellow workers. But we were talking to fewer and fewer recruitable workers. The party's political activity and campaigns became, of necessity, more and more removed from the labor movement. The unions took fewer initiatives around broad social and political questions. There was less opportunity for carrying out party political work in collaboration with fellow workers or through the organized labor movement. This was not by choice but because of objective conditions. We were increasingly forced into a semisectarian existence.

Under these conditions, the party's permanent goal of proletarianization could not be advanced by centering our work around fractions in the major industrial unions. By the late 1950s we no longer had any national industrial fractions. Most local fractions had been dissolved as well. The basis did not exist for ongoing work in the unions by party members. Talking socialism in most sections of the labor movement found less and less response.

Beginning with the upsurge of the civil rights movement at the opening of the 1960s, which eventually mobilized hundreds of thousands, the more than decade-long generalized political retreat of the working class as a whole came to an end. But the political retreat of the organized labor movement continued.

The SWP turned toward the rise in proletarian struggle in this country, which took the form of the upsurge in the Black movement, and to the emergence of a revolutionary working-class leadership internationally through the victory and consolidation of the Cuban revolution. Our movement gained recruits as a result of the radicalization of a layer of young people who were attracted to these struggles, some of whom could be won to revolutionary perspectives. We threw ourselves into the opportunity of joining with others in founding and building the Young Socialist Alliance.

Over the next decade the party oriented toward the rise of Black nationalism and the Malcolm X leadership, and the explosive struggles of the Black nationality. In the process, the party reaffirmed the fundamental positions adopted at our founding on the character and vanguard role of the Black nationality in the United States, and further strengthened these positions as we did so.

We turned toward and became an integral part of the movement against the war in Vietnam.

The party embraced the rise of the new women's movement and the fight for women's rights, throwing ourselves into these battles. In doing so, we incorporated into our program an important addition: our appreciation of the growing weight and role of the fight for women's liberation in the revolutionary struggle for workers and farmers power. We based ourselves on the groundwork laid in the resolutions adopted by the Communist International during its first five years, and we took the lead in drafting the first resolution of the Fourth International on this question, which was adopted by the 1979 world congress.[13]

Since the new radicalization did not primarily come out of the labor movement, the new recruits to the SWP did not primarily come out of the labor movement either. Most new members during this time were students. Thus, during the period from the early 1960s through 1975, the party did not organize to achieve the goal of having a decisive majority of its members in the industrial unions organized through fractions.

Under the political conditions of that period, we rejected colonization of the industrial unions as the main way to advance the proletarianization of the party. As the 1965 resolution on the SWP's organizational principles explained:

> To transform the SWP into a proletarian party of action, particularly in the present period of reaction, it is not enough to continue propagandistic activities in the hope that by an automatic process workers will flock to the banner of the party. It is necessary, on the contrary, to make a concerted, determined and systematic effort, consciously directed by the leading committees of the party, to spread out into all sectors of the mass movement—civil rights organizations which are becoming radicalized and in which workers predominate; labor organizations within industry and among the unemployed; campuses where an increasing number of students are turning toward socialist ideas.[14]

THE INDUSTRIAL UNION FRACTIONS

Our political course enabled the SWP to meet the challenges posed by the next major turning point in U.S. politics. When the new situation marked by the 1974-75 world recession reopened the main road of building a revolutionary workers party based in the industrial working class, the SWP was in position to advance along it. The leadership through the necessary detour had been successful. The continuity of our proletarian orientation remained intact.

Had the SWP not responded to this new situation by making a sharp turn toward building fractions in the industrial unions, we could not have built on the political and recruitment gains of the 1960s and 1970s to advance the proletarianization of the party. The party's membership and leadership would increasingly have become composed of aging cadres based largely among relatively highly paid white collar workers and public employees.

As a result of the turn to the industrial unions in 1978, however, the majority of the party membership is today in industry and industrial unions. Including those laid off and looking for work, and those currently on full-time party assignment, the percentage of members with experience in the industrial unions is more than 80 percent.

The industrial union fractions are an integral component of the party's local and national structure. Branch activity and institutions, and their weekly rhythm, more and more reflect the needs of a party whose members in their majority are industrial workers. The entire membership, those who are in industrial union fractions and those who are not, has become more politically homogeneous in collectively organizing our work to deepen the party's contact with and political influence among young workers in industry.

The composition of participants at party forums, campaign meetings, and other public events is more proletarian today. Our fractions are beginning to bring co-workers to these events. An even greater number of workers, however, come to these activities from workplaces where we do not have fractions—a sign of progress in shifting our general political orientation toward working-class organizations and milieus. The Mel Mason–Andrea González SWP presidential election campaign in 1984 demonstrated our greater capacity to attract workers, especially young workers, and to recruit them to the Young Socialist Alliance and Socialist Workers Party.

As we become more established in industry and in the industrial unions, we also increase our effectiveness as a political party that champions the demands of all the oppressed. We participate in activity around social and political questions—ranging from actions against U.S. intervention in Central America and rallies against racist attacks, to protests to stop farm foreclosures and demonstrations against assaults on women's rights.

As a party increasingly based in the industrial working class, we have developed a more concrete understanding in practice of the vanguard role of Black workers and the Black liberation struggle in the fight to transform the unions into revolutionary instruments of class struggle. Building our industrial union fractions has strengthened the party's ability to recruit Black, Chicano, Puerto Rican, and immigrant workers. It has enabled the party to take steps toward the development of a leadership that is more proletarian, and thus more multinational, in composition.

The fight for the emancipation of women—part of the strategic line of march of the modern working-class movement from its founding—has taken on additional social weight with the influx of women into the labor force over the past three decades, including into the factories, mines, and mills. Our industrial union fractions and their leaderships have many female members, and have collaborated on the job and in the unions with the vanguard of working-class women who have fought their way into industry. We have participated in the fight for affirmative action for women, against sexual harassment on the job, and for the unions to champion the broader social and political struggle for women's rights.

The party has established contacts with militant farmers and farm organizations. We are learning about their struggles, expanding our knowledge of the farm movement and its connections with the labor movement.

As a party with a growing majority of our members in industry, we also understand better the impact of today's deepening class polarization inside the working class and the unions. By going through common experiences with other workers we have learned how these pressures affect different layers within the class, and how they respond.

We have seen close up how the class-collaborationism of the labor officialdom deepens divisions among workers, creates obstacles to an alliance with working farmers, and blocks the unions from championing the demands and aiding the struggles of oppressed nationalities and women. This course above all weakens the unions' capacity to fight the employers.

We have gotten a small preview of the kind of class combat that will more and more be on the agenda in this country. We can see more clearly and concretely the nature of the strategic and tactical tasks that confront the labor movement in forging the solidarity and alliances necessary to defend the unions and lead a successful struggle to bring to power a workers and farmers government in the United States.

NOTES

Capitalism's march toward war and depression

1. For an account of the strike by packinghouse workers against Hormel, see Fred Halstead, *The 1985-86 Hormel Meat-Packers Strike in Austin, Minnesota* (New York: Pathfinder, 1986).

2. Following an eleven-month strike that began in April 1989, the Pittston Coal Group signed a new contract with the United Mine Workers union covering more than 1,900 miners in Virginia, West Virginia, and Kentucky in February 1990. Over the course of the strike some 40,000 UMWA members throughout the Eastern coalfields walked out in support of the action. More than 50,000 supporters from across the United States and around the world visited the union's strike center, Camp Solidarity, in southwest Virginia.

3. For an account of the 22-month strike that defeated Frank Lorenzo's attempt to turn Eastern into a profitable nonunion airline, see Ernie Mailhot and others, *The Eastern Airlines Strike* (New York: Pathfinder, 1991).

4. For an account of the fight by U.S. communists against government spying and disruption, see Larry Seigle, "Washington's Fifty Year Domestic Contra Operation," in *New International* no. 6; Margaret Jayko, *FBI on Trial* (New York: Pathfinder, 1988); and Nelson Blackstock, *Cointelpro: The FBI's Secret War on Political Freedom* (New York: Pathfinder, 1988).

Prospects for socialism in America

RESOLUTION OF THE SOCIALIST WORKERS PARTY

1. On August 2, 1964, two U.S. destroyers patrolling near the coast of North Vietnam were allegedly fired upon by North Vietnamese torpedo boats. President Lyndon Johnson used this staged incident as the pretext to launch the first U.S. bombing raids on North Vietnam and to press through Congress the infamous Gulf of Tonkin resolution, later used as

437

the authority for massive escalation of the war. It was subsequently revealed that the draft of the resolution had been prepared nearly two months before the incident.

2. The Watergate crisis erupted in 1973 with the public exposure of the fact that the White House under President Richard Nixon had utilized burglaries and wiretaps and authorized FBI operations against even Democratic Party political competitors. Such methods had long been used against working-class organizations and the Black movement. The ensuing political crisis, rooted in deep divisions within the ruling class over Washington's defeat in Vietnam, led to the forced resignation of Nixon in 1974. Widely publicized congressional hearings in 1975-76—during which many more facts became known about the murderous operations of the FBI, CIA, and other political police agencies, both in the United States and abroad—further undermined public confidence in the truthfulness of those who spoke for U.S. government institutions.

3. Leon Trotsky was a central leader and, second to V.I. Lenin, the most prominent public figure of the October 1917 revolution in Russia. During the Soviet republic's first ten years, he served as foreign minister, head of the Red Army during the civil war of 1918-20, convenor of economic planning bodies, and a founder and leader of the Communist International. Following Lenin's death in 1924 Trotsky was the principal leader of the fight to defend the revolution's internationalist course against the counterrevolutionary policies of growing petty-bourgeois social layers headed by Joseph Stalin. Expelled from the Soviet Union in 1929, Trotsky was assassinated in Mexico by Stalin's secret police in 1940.

The full text of *The Death Agony of Capitalism and the Tasks of the Fourth International* is published in Leon Trotsky, *The Transitional Program* (New York: Pathfinder, 1977).

4. "The Manifesto of the Fourth International on the Imperialist War and the Proletarian World Revolution," in *Writings of Leon Trotsky (1939-40),* (New York: Pathfinder, 1973), p. 217.

Leading the party into industry

1. In the longest nationwide coal strike in U.S. history, more than 180,000 miners in twenty-two states went out on strike for 110 days beginning December 6, 1977. The UMWA was able to block a major employer ef-

fort, backed by the federal government, to cripple the union.

2. A traveling organizer for the Industrial Workers of the World before and during World War I, James P. Cannon was a leader of the communist movement in the United States following the Russian revolution of October 1917. He was expelled from the Communist Party in 1928 for supporting Leon Trotsky's fight to continue V.I. Lenin's course for building a communist movement. A founding leader of the Socialist Workers Party, Cannon served as its national secretary and then national chairman until his death in 1974.

3. See pp. 53-126 of this volume.

4. Steelworkers Fight Back was the movement, launched in the Steelworkers union in 1975 under the leadership of USWA District 31 president Ed Sadlowski, to oust the entrenched bureaucracy of President I.W. Abel. A central issue in the campaign was the fight to extend union democracy, including the right to vote on contracts.

5. The 1971 resolution is reprinted in Socialist Workers Party, *A Revolutionary Strategy for the 1970s* (New York: Pathfinder, 1972), pp. 38-75.

6. Soviets, meaning "councils" in Russian, arose in the Russian revolutions of 1905 and 1917 as elected representative bodies of workers, soldiers, and peasants that provided coordination and leadership for their revolutionary struggle. In 1917 the soviets, with a Bolshevik majority, overthrew the capitalist Provisional Government and established a workers and peasants government.

7. James P. Cannon, *The Socialist Workers Party in World War II* (New York: Pathfinder, 1975), p. 195.

8. The Experimental Negotiating Agreement was a no-strike pact signed by the USWA officialdom and the basic steel corporations in 1973.

9. *Teamster Rebellion, Teamster Power, Teamster Politics,* and *Teamster Bureaucracy* make up a four-volume series on the 1930s strikes and organizing drive that transformed the Teamsters union in Minneapolis and the Midwest into a fighting industrial union movement. These Pathfinder books were written by Farrell Dobbs, a leader of these battles and later national secretary of the Socialist Workers Party.

10. Fred Halstead, a longtime leader of the Socialist Workers Party and a leader of the movement against the Vietnam War, tells the story of that movement in *Out Now: A Participant's Account of the Movement in the U.S. against the Vietnam War* (New York: Pathfinder, 1991).

11. Cannon, *The Socialist Workers Party in World War II,* p. 195.

12. The Trotsky School was an intensive educational program run by the SWP from 1946 to 1963. Twelve six-month sessions, each attended by approximately eight party leaders and cadres, were held.

13. Cannon, *The Struggle for a Proletarian Party* (New York: Pathfinder, 1972).

14. Leon Trotsky, *In Defense of Marxism* (New York: Pathfinder, 1973).
15. See *The Organizational Character of the Socialist Workers Party* (New York: Pathfinder, 1970).
16. *Organizational Character of the Socialist Workers Party,* pp. 22-23.
17. Cannon, *Letters from Prison* (New York: Pathfinder, 1973), pp. 70-77.
18. After twice failing to qualify for entrance to the University of California at Davis Medical School, Allan Bakke, a civil engineer, filed suit against that school's quota system for minority student enrollment. In June 1978, the U.S. Supreme Court upheld Bakke's challenge, striking down the school's special admissions program and legitimizing Bakke's argument of "reverse discrimination" against whites.

Forging the leadership of a proletarian party

MARY-ALICE WATERS

1. John G. Wright was the principal translator of Leon Trotsky's works into English until his death in 1956.
2. The Cochranites were an opposition current that under the blows of the witch-hunt retreated from the effort to build a revolutionary workers party. They split from the Socialist Workers Party in 1953.
3. In Newport News, Virginia, steelworkers at the giant Tenneco shipyard fought a lengthy battle for recognition of their union, United Steelworkers Local 8888. They struck Tenneco for eighteen weeks in early 1979 and won union recognition later that year.
4. Evelyn Reed, a leading member of the Socialist Workers Party from 1940 until her death in 1979, was the author of *Sexism and Science, Woman's Evolution,* and several other works on the origins of the oppression of women and the fight for their emancipation.

The turn and building a world communist movement

1. See "The World Political Situation and the Tasks of the Fourth International," in *1979 World Congress of the Fourth International* (New York:

Intercontinental Press, 1980).

2. Testifying to the trend toward social crisis within the capitalist powers in Europe, in May 1968 a student uprising in France detonated a pre-revolutionary upsurge, including a nationwide general strike that at its peak involved 10 million workers. Italy witnessed a "creeping May" in 1969, and revolutionary ferment exploded in Portugal in 1974.

3. James P. Cannon et al., *Background to 'The Struggle for a Proletarian Party'* (New York: Pathfinder, 1979), pp. 10, 13.

4. The British Socialist Workers Party, an ultraleft sectarian group, was affiliated with the International Socialists in the United States. The International Marxist Group was the British section of the Fourth International.

A new stage of revolutionary working-class politics

1. See "The World Political Situation and the Tasks of the Fourth International," in *1979 World Congress of the Fourth International* (New York: Intercontinental Press, 1980).

2. Karl Marx and Frederick Engels, *Collected Works* (New York: International Publishers, 1976), vol. 6, p. 303.

3. Marx and Engels, *Communist Manifesto* (New York: Pathfinder, 1970), pp. 27-28. Emphasis added.

4. Marx and Engels, *Communist Manifesto,* p. 27.

5. V.I. Lenin, "The Tasks of the Russian Social-Democrats," in *Collected Works* (Moscow: Progress Publishers, 1972), vol. 2, p. 336.

6. Lenin, "Our Programme," in *Collected Works,* vol. 4, pp. 210-11.

7. Trotsky, *The Transitional Program for Socialist Revolution.*

8. Trotsky, *The Third International after Lenin* (New York: Pathfinder, 1970), p. 75.

9. Isaac Deutscher, *The Prophet Outcast* (New York: Vintage Press, 1965), pp. 425-26.

10. Trotsky, *The Transitional Program,* p. 102.

11. Trotsky, *The Transitional Program,* pp. 114-15.

12. Trotsky, *The Transitional Program,* p. 148.

13. For a description of the proletarian military policy and the SWP's strategy during the 1960s, see *Revolutionary Strategy against the Vietnam War*

(New York: Pathfinder, 1975) and Fred Halstead, *Out Now!* (New York: Pathfinder, 1978).

14. Socialist Workers Party, *A Revolutionary Strategy for the 70s* (New York: Pathfinder, 1972), p. 88.

15. Brian Weber, a lab technician at Kaiser Aluminum in Gramercy, Louisiana, filed suit against the affirmative-action provisions of the USWA's 1974 contract with Kaiser charging "reverse discrimination" against whites. The Steelworkers, other major unions, and the AFL-CIO defended the affirmative-action provisions and, in June 1979, the U.S. Supreme Court rejected Weber's challenge.

16. George Breitman, *How a Minority Can Change Society* (New York: Pathfinder, 1965).

17. *Leon Trotsky on Black Nationalism and Self-Determination* (New York: Pathfinder, 1978), pp. 25-30.

18. The Raza Unida Party was an independent Chicano political party that emerged in Texas in 1970 out of a rise in struggles by the oppressed Chicano nationality. It ran a number of independent election campaigns in southwestern states independent of the Democratic and Republican parties.

19. In late December 1978 and early January 1979, Vietnamese troops aided Kampuchean insurgents in overthrowing the reactionary Pol Pot regime. In response, and following consultation with Washington, Peking's troops invaded Vietnam.

20. Richard T. Frankensteen was elected a UAW vice-president in 1937. He ran for mayor of Detroit in a nonpartisan election in 1945. The SWP called for a vote for Frankensteen. While he won the highest vote in the primary, he was defeated in the general election.

Twenty-five lessons from the 1970s and perspectives for the 1980s

1. A counter–political resolution entitled "Against the Workerist Turn: A Critique and Some Proposals" was rejected by the convention by a vote of 121 to 1.

2. In 1978 the Cuban government initiated a dialogue with Cubans in the United States, inviting representatives of the Cuban-American community to travel to Havana to discuss matters of mutual concern. The fol-

lowing year more than 1)0,000 Cubans living in the United States traveled to Cuba.

3. Socialist Workers Party, *A Revolutionary Strategy for the 1970s*, pp. 68-69.

4. The Trade Union Educatio nal League, formed in November 1920 by William Z. Foster prior to his joining the Communist Party, organized a left-wing current inside the American Federation of Labor. The Shop Stewards and Workers Committee originated among metalworkers in the Clyde valley strike in Scotland in 1915. The Minority Movement was formed in the British Trades Union Congress in 1924, under the leadership of the Communist Party.

5. Trotsky, *The Transitional Program*, p. 148.

6. Trotsky, *The Transitional Program*, p. 101.

7. Trotsky, *The Transitional Program*, pp. 155-56.

8. Trotsky, *The Transitional Program*, pp. 163-64.

9. Socialist Workers Party, *A Revolutionary Strategy for the 1970s*, p. 69.

10. Reprinted as Farrell Dobbs, *Selected Articles on the Labor Movement* (New York: Pathfinder, 1983).

11. The Right to Vote Committee was a rank-and-file organization of United Trasportation Union members demanding membership ratification of contracts, initiated in the Chicago railroad yards in 1969.

12. Jack Barnes et al., *Prospects for Socialism in America* (New York: Pathfinder, 1976), pp. 225-26.

13. Jon Hillson, *The Battle of Boston* (New York: Pathfinder, 1977).

14. Trotsky, *The First Five Years of the Communist International* (New York: Pathfinder, 1972), vol. 1, pp. 233-34.

Educating the leadership of a proletarian party

1. See Cannon, *The Struggle for a Proletarian Party*.

2. See Cannon, *Letters from Prison*.

3. See "From Lenin to Castro: The Role of the Individual in History Making," in George Novack, *Understanding History* (New York: Pathfinder, 1980).

4. N.K. Krupskaya, *Memories of Lenin* (New York: International Publishers, 1930), pp. 186-87.

The turn to the industrial unions

RESOLUTION OF THE SOCIALIST WORKERS PARTY

1. The National Black Independent Political Party was launched in Philadelphia in 1980. Its charter, issued the following year, is reprinted in Nan Bailey and others, *The National Black Independent Political Party* (New York: Pathfinder, 1981), pp. 15-32.
2. See Jack Barnes, *For a Workers and Farmers Government in the United States* (New York: Pathfinder, 1985).

Communist continuity in the United States

RESOLUTION OF THE SOCIALIST WORKERS PARTY

1. The full proceedings of the Communist International's first four congresses, along with documents from the period leading to its foundation, are being published by Pathfinder. The five installments available are:
   - *Lenin's Struggle for a Revolutionary International: Documents 1907-1916;*
   - *The German Revolution and the Debate on Soviet Power: Documents 1918-1919;*
   - *Founding the Communist International: Proceedings and Documents of the First Congress, March 1919;*
   - *Workers of the World and Oppressed Peoples, Unite! Proceedings and Documents of the Second Congress, 1920;*
   - *To See the Dawn: Baku 1920—First Congress of the Peoples of the East.*
2. Cannon, *The History of American Trotskyism* (New York: Pathfinder, 1972), p. 1.
3. For an account of the achievements and worldwide impact of the workers and farmers government that came to power following the Nicaraguan revolution in 1979, and the political retreat of the Sandinista National Liberation Front that led to the collapse of that government in the closing years of the 1980s, see *New International* no. 9, *The Rise and Fall of the Nicaraguan Revolution.*
4. For an account of the accomplishments and lessons of the Grenada revolution and how it was overthrown from within by the Stalinist gang that murdered Maurice Bishop, see "The Second Assassination of Maurice Bishop" in *New International* no. 6.
5. "The Trade Union Movement and the Socialist Workers Party" in James P.

Cannon and others, *The Founding of the Socialist Workers Party* (New York: Pathfinder, 1982), p. 123.

6. "The Political Situation and the Tasks of the Party" in Cannon and others, *The Founding of the Socialist Workers Party,* pp. 109, 106.

7. "The Trade Union Movement and the Socialist Workers Party" in Cannon and others, *The Founding of the Socialist Workers Party,* p. 123.

8. Trotsky, *The Transitional Program,* pp. 137-38.

9. John Riddell, ed., *Workers of the World and Oppressed Peoples, Unite!* vol. 2, p. 696.

10. *Leon Trotsky on Black Nationalism,* pp. 84-85.

11. *Leon Trotsky on Black Nationalism,* p. 30.

12. Fidel Castro, December 20, 1980, speech in *Main Report: Second Congress of the Communist Party of Cuba* (New York: Center for Cuban Studies, 1981), p. 46

13. The resolution adopted by the third Comintern congress, "Methods and Forms of Work among Communist Women: Theses," is contained in *Theses, Resolutions and Manifestos of the First Four Congresses of the Third International* (London: Ink Links, 1980), pp. 121-29.

14. *The Organizational Character of the Socialist Workers Party* (New York: Pathfinder, 1970), p. 21.

INDEX

For further reading

The Communist Manifesto

KARL MARX AND FREDERICK ENGELS

Founding document of the modern working-class movement, published in 1848. Explains why communists act on the basis not of preconceived principles but of *facts* springing from the actual class struggle, and why communism, to the degree it is a theory, is the generalization of the historical line of march of the working class and of the political conditions for its liberation. $3.95

The Transitional Program for Socialist Revolution

LEON TROTSKY

Contains discussions between leaders of the U.S. Socialist Workers Party and exiled revolutionary Leon Trotsky in 1938. The product of these discussions, a program of immediate, democratic, and transitional demands, was adopted by the SWP later that year. This program for socialist revolution remains an important tool for communist workers today. $20.95

In Defense of Marxism:

The Social and Political Contradictions of the Soviet Union
LEON TROTSKY

Writing in 1939–40, Leon Trotsky replies to those in the revolutionary workers movement who were beating a retreat from defense of the degenerated Soviet workers state in face of looming imperialist assault. He describes how the rising pressures of bourgeois patriotism in the middle classes during the buildup toward U.S. entry into World War II were finding an echo even inside the communist movement. And he explains why only a party that fights to bring growing numbers of workers into its ranks and leadership can steer a steady revolutionary course. $24.95

The Struggle for a Proletarian Party

JAMES P. CANNON

In this companion to Trotsky's *In Defense of Marxism,* Cannon and other leaders of the Socialist Workers Party defend the political and organizational principles of Marxism against a petty-bourgeois current in the party. $19.95

Background to 'The Struggle for a Proletarian Party'

LEON TROTSKY AND JAMES P. CANNON

Articles, letters, and reports recounting challenges faced by the Social st Workers Party in deepening its involvement in the organizations and struggles of the industrial working class and unions in the years prior to U.S. impericlisms's entry into World War II. 8½ x 11 format. $6.00

Working-class politics and the trade unions

The Eastern Airlines Strike

Accomplishments of the Rank-and-File Machinists and Gains for the Labor Movement
ERNIE MAILHOT AND OTHERS

Tells the story of the 686-day strike and how a rank-and-file resistance by Machinists prevented Eastern's union-busting onslaught from becoming the road to a profitable nonunion airline. $9.95

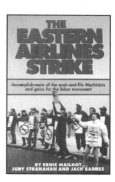

Trade Unions in the Epoch of Imperialist Decay

LEON TROTSKY

Featuring "Trade Unions: Their Past, Present, and Future"
by Karl Marx

"Apart from their original purposes, the trades unions must now learn to act deliberately as organizing centers of the working class in the broad interest of its complete emancipation. . . . They must convince the world at large that their efforts, far from being narrow and selfish, aim at the emancipation of the down-rodden millions."

—Karl Marx, 1866.

In this book, two central leaders of the modern communist workers movement outline the fight for this revolutionary perspective. $14.95

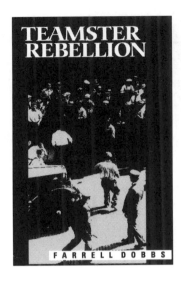

Books by Farrell Dobbs

Writings by a leader of the communist movement in the U.S. and organizer of the Teamsters union during the rise of the CIO

THE TEAMSTER SERIES

Four books on the 1930s strikes and organizing drives, led by a class-struggle leadership, that transformed the Teamsters union in Minneapolis and much of the Midwest into a fighting industrial union movement. Manuals of revolutionary politics, organization, and trade union strategy.

■ TEAMSTER REBELLION
The 1934 strikes that built a fighting union movement in Minneapolis and helped pave the way for the CIO. 195 pp., $15.95

■ TEAMSTER POWER
The 11-state Midwest over-the-road organizing drive. 255 pp., $17.95

■ TEAMSTER POLITICS
Rank-and-file Teamsters lead the fight against antiunion frame- ups and assaults by fascist goons; the battle for jobs for all; and efforts to advance independent labor political action. 256 pp., $17.95

■ TEAMSTER BUREAUCRACY
The rank-and-file Teamsters leadership organizes to oppose World War II, racism, and government efforts—backed by the top union officialdom—to gag class-struggle-minded workers. 304 pp., $18.95

REVOLUTIONARY CONTINUITY

Marxist Leadership in the United States

Dobbs explains how successive generations of fighters took part in struggles
of the U.S. labor movement, seeking
to build a revolutionary leadership to
advance the class interests of workers
and small farmers.

THE EARLY YEARS, 1848-1917
221 pp., $16.95

**BIRTH OF THE COMMUNIST
MOVEMENT, 1918-1922**
240 pp., $16.95

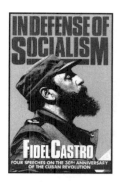

In Defense of Socialism

*Four Speeches on the 30th Anniversary
of the Cuban Revolution*

FIDEL CASTRO

Not only is economic and social progress possible
without the dog-eat-dog competition of capitalism,
Castro argues, but socialism remains the only way
forward for humanity. Also discusses Cuba's role in
the struggle against the apartheid regime in
southern Africa. $13.95

Cosmetics, Fashions, and the Exploitation of Women

JOSEPH HANSEN, EVELYN REED, AND
MARY-ALICE WATERS

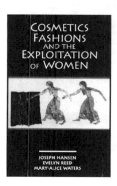

How big business promotes cosmetics to generate
profits and perpetuate the oppression of women.
In her introduction, Mary-Alice Waters explains
how the entry of millions of women into the
workforce during and after World War II
irreversibly changed U.S. society and laid the
basis for a renewed rise of struggles for women's
equality. $12.95

SEE FRONT OF BOOK FOR ADDRESSES

Also from PATHFINDER

Lenin's Final Fight
Speeches and Writings, 1922–23
V.I. LENIN

In the early 1920s Lenin waged a political battle in the leadership of the Communist Party of the USSR to maintain the course that had enabled the workers and peasants to overthrow the old tsarist empire, carry out the first successful socialist revolution, and begin building a world communist movement. The issues posed in his political fight remain at the heart of world politics today. Several items appear in English for the first time. $19.95

The Politics of Chicano Liberation
BY OLGA RODRIGUEZ AND OTHERS

Lessons from the rise of the Chicano movement in the United States in the 1960s and 1970s, which dealt lasting blows against the oppression of the Chicano people. Presents a fighting program for those determined to combat divisions within the working class based on language and national origin and build a revolutionary movement capable of leading humanity out of the wars, racist assaults, and social crisis of capitalism in its decline. $15.95

February 1965:
The Final Speeches
MALCOLM X

Speeches from the last three weeks of the life of this outstanding leader of the oppressed Black nationality and working class in the United States. A large part is material previously unavailable, with some in print for the first time. $17.95

The History of American Trotskyism
JAMES P. CANNON

"Trotskyism is not a new movement, a new doctrine," Cannon says, "but the restoration, the revival of genuine Marxism as it was expounded and practiced in the Russian revolution and in the early days of the Communist International." In this series of twelve talks given in 1942, James P. Cannon recounts an important chapter in the efforts to build a proletarian party in the United States. $18.95

Episodes of the Cuban Revolutionary War, 1956–58

ERNESTO CHE GUEVARA

A firsthand account of the military campa gns and political events that culminated in the January 1959 popular insurrection that overthrew the U.S.-backed dictatorsh p in Cuba. Guevara describes how the struggle transformed the men and women of the Rebel Army and July 26 Movement led by Fidel Castro. And how these combatants forged a political leadership capable of guiding millions of workers and peasants to open the socialist revolution in the Americas. Complete for the first time in English. Introduction by Mary-Alice Waters. $23.95

The Mark Curtis Story: A Packinghouse Worker's Fight for Justice

NAOMI CRAINE

The story of the victorious eight-year battle to defeat the political frame-up of Mark Curtis, a union activist and socialist sentenced in 1988 to twenty-five years in prison on trumped-up charges of attempted rape and burglary. The pamphlet describes what happened to Curtis on the day of his arrest, the fight to defend immigrant rights he was a part of, and the international campaign that finally won his freedom in 1996. $6.00

The Jewish Question

A Marxist Interpretation

ABRAM LEON

Traces the historical rationalizations of anti-Semitism to the fact that Jews—in the centuries preceding the domination of industrial capitalism— were forced to become a "people-class" of merchants and moneylenders. Leon explains how in times of social crisis renewed Jew-hatred is incited by the capitalists to mobilize reactionary forces against the labor movement and disorient the middle classes and layers of working people about the true source of their impoverishment. $17.95

Write for a catalog

The History of the Russian Revolution

LEON TROTSKY

The social, economic, and political dynamics of the first socialist revolution. The story is told by one of the principal leaders of this victorious struggle for workers' power headed by the Bolshevik party. $35.95

The Truth about Yugoslavia

Why Working People Should Oppose Intervention

GEORGE FYSON, ARGIRIS MALAPANIS, AND JONATHAN SILBERMAN

Examines the roots of the carnage in the Yugoslav workers state where the U.S. and European powers are intervening militarily to advance their competing interests. Explains how groups of would-be capitalists—fragments of the former Stalinist regime—are fighting a war for territory and resources. $8.95

Fascism: What It Is and How to Fight It

LEON TROTSKY

Why fascism was able to conquer only in those countries where social democratic or Stalinist parties blocked the workers and their allies from utilizing a revolutionary situation to remove the capitalists from power. $3.00

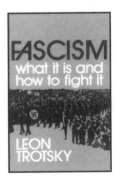

Understanding History

Marxist Essays

GEORGE NOVACK

How did capitalism arise? Why has this exploitative system exhausted its potential? Why is revolutionary change fundamental to human progress. $15.95

New International

A MAGAZINE OF MARXIST POLITICS AND THEORY

New International no. 10

Imperialism's March toward Fascism and War *by Jack Barnes* • What the 1987 Stock Market Crash Foretold • Defending Cuba, Defending Cuba's Socialist Revolution *by Mary-Alice Waters* • The Curve of Capitalist Development *by Leon Trotsky* $14.00

New International no. 9

The Triumph of the Nicaraguan Revolution • Washington's Contra War and the Challenge of Forging Proletarian Leadership • The Political Degeneration of the FSLN and the Demise of the Workers and Farmers Government $14.00

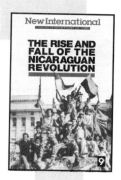

New International no. 8

The Politics of Economics: Che Guevara and Marxist Continuity *by Steve Clark and Jack Barnes* • Che's Contribution to the Cuban Economy *by Carlos Rafael Rodríguez* • On the Concept of Value *and* The Meaning of Socialist Planning *two articles by Ernesto Che Guevara* $10.00

New International no. 7

Opening Guns of World War III:
Washington's Assault on Iraq *by Jack Barnes*
• Communist Policy in Wartime as well as in
Peacetime *by Mary-Alice Waters* • Lessons
from the Iran-Iraq War *by Samad Sharif*
$12.00

New International no. 6

The Second Assassination of Maurice Bishop
by Steve Clark • Washington's 50-year
Domestic Contra Operation *by Larry Seigle*
• Land, Labor, and the Canadian Revolution
by Michel Dugré • Renewal or Death: Cuba's
Rectification Process *two speeches*
by Fidel Castro $10.00

New International no. 5

The Coming Revolution in South Africa *by Jack
Barnes* • The Future Belongs to the Majority *by
Oliver Tambo* • Why Cuban Volunteers Are in
Angola *two speeches by Fidel Castro* $9.00

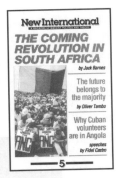

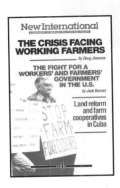

New International no. 4

The Fight for a Workers and Farmers
Government in the United States *by Jack
Barnes* • The Crisis Facing Working
Farmers *by Doug Jenness* • Land Reform
and Farm Cooperatives in Cuba *two
speeches by Fidel Castro* $9.00